Accounting for Business

Second Edition

Accounting
for Business

Second Edition

Tony Blackwood ACMA, ACIS, PGCED

Senior Lecturer in Accounting and Finance,
Newcastle Business School, University of Northumbria

Business Education Publishers Limited

1998

© TONY BLACKWOOD 1998

ISBN 1 901888 04 5

First Published 1995
    Reprinted 1996
    Second Edition 1998

Published by Business Education Publishers Limited
Leighton House
10 Grange Crescent
Sunderland
Tyne and Wear SR2 7BN

Tel. 0191 567 4963
Fax. 0191 514 3277

British Cataloguing-in-Publications Data
A catalogue record for this book is available from the British Library.

Printed in Great Britain by Athenaeum Press, Gateshead

To Fiona, Ashleigh and Ryan

Preface

The aim of this book is to provide a comprehensive introduction to accounting in a readable and accessible style. It is suitable for students following a wide variety of courses including Higher National, degree, postgraduate and professional programmes in non-accounting disciplines as well as managers wishing to improve their knowledge of accounting.

It assumes no previous knowledge of the subject and explains accounting principles and techniques clearly and logically using many worked examples.

After an introductory chapter explaining the nature and purpose of accounting, the remaining fifteen chapters are divided into two further sections:

Financial accounting. The purpose of this section is to enable the reader to understand financial statements, appreciate their limitations and use the information contained within them to assess the performance and financial position of an enterprise. The principles underlying their preparation and the way in which the figures reported are derived are explained clearly and various methods of interpretation illustrated.

Management accounting. This section considers the information requirements of managers and the ways in which these may be satisfied. Techniques which can be used to generate information for planning, control and decision making are explained and demonstrated and the limitations of such information considered.

Each chapter contains a list of learning objectives which should be achieved after studying the chapter, a summary of the main points covered and a set of self assessment questions with worked solutions.

The second edition has been revised and updated to include more end of chapter questions and additional coverage of areas such as the regulatory framework of accounting, partnership accounting and activity based costing as well as updated material on the revised requirements of FRS1 in respect of Cash Flow Statements.

A *lecturer's supplement* containing solution guides for additional end of chapter questions and the eight assignments included in the text is available from the publishers to lecturers adopting the book as a course text.

I would like to thank those who have provided valuable feedback on the first edition of the book and would welcome any further suggestions from both lecturers and students which may be useful in the production of further editions.

Acknowledgements

I would like to thank the following people for their help in the production of this book:

- Caroline, Moira, Paul, Gerard and Chris at Business Education Publishers for all their assistance;

- Gary Walton for his valuable comments and corrections on draft chapters and questions;

- Rosemary Walton and Jeff Wren for their most appreciated comments and advice on draft chapters;

- Tony Gough for permission to adapt and reproduce material used in Assignment No.1 and questions in Chapters 5, 7 and 8;

- David Symons and Andrew Adams for permission to reproduce Assignment No. 5 from their publication *Business Studies* (published by Business Education Publishers);

- Finally and most importantly, I would like to thank my wife Fiona and children Ashleigh and Ryan for their continued support and patience.

Tony Blackwood

The author and publishers would like to thank the following professional bodies for permission to reproduce past examination questions and extracts (and suggested answers in the case of ACCA) for which they have copyright.

- The Chartered Association of Certified Accountants (ACCA)

- The Chartered Institute of Management Accountants (CIMA)

- The Institute of Chartered Accountants in England and Wales (ICAEW)

- The Association of Accounting Technicians (AAT)

All questions (and any suggested answers reproduced by kind permission of ACCA) are referenced in the text to the appropriate body. In all other cases, the solution supplied is that of the author and not the approved solution of the relevant professional body.

All examination questions reproduced by kind permission of the AAT are from old membership examinations and are pre NVQ papers.

Table of Contents

Part 1 Introduction

Chapter 1   An Introduction to Accounting

Part 2 Financial Accounting

Chapter 2   Accounting Principles and Regulations

Chapter 3   Recording Transactions

Part 3 Management Accounting

Chapter 10 Costing

Chapter 11 Cost Behaviour

Chapter 12 Marginal Costing and Decision Making

Chapter 13 Cost Volume Profit Analysis

Chapter 14 Investment Appraisal

Chapter 15 Budgetary Control

Chapter 16 Standard Costing

Part 1

Introduction

Chapter 1

An Introduction to Accounting

Learning Objectives

After studying this chapter you should be able to:

- Explain the purposes of accounting information.

- Identify potential users of such information and describe their needs.

- Distinguish between financial and management accounting.

- Explain the features of effective management information.

- Appreciate the limitations of accounting information.

Introduction

This chapter gives an overview of accounting which provides a useful foundation for the rest of the book in which we will examine accounting principles, methods and techniques in some detail. The purpose of accounting information is explained and its potential users and their particular requirements identified. The chapter concludes by briefly examining the structure of the accountancy profession and the type of work performed by accountants.

Why Study Accounting?

This text is primarily intended for business and management students studying accounting and its purpose is to introduce readers to accounting principles, practices and techniques. Many readers will have no intention of following a career in accountancy and may be wondering why it is necessary to examine the subject in any detail. We will therefore begin by considering some of the benefits of studying accounting principles and practices.

Firstly the primary objective in most business ventures is to increase the value of the business and hence the wealth of its owner(s), through earning profits. For other organisations such as local authorities or charities, the main objective will relate to the effective provision of services rather than profit. However the activities of such organisations and services provided will inevitably be constrained by a limited supply of finance. Consequently employees at all levels are affected by financial considerations and may from time to time be confronted with accounting information. Studying accounting should help you to appreciate the purposes of such information and the procedures associated with its compilation.

As your career progresses you may assume increasing responsibility for managing activities and the planning and decision making which this entails. A knowledge of the accounting information which can be made available, the basis of its compilation and its relevance can help to ensure that such decisions are adequately supported by relevant information.

Finally, published accounting statements can provide external parties with much useful information about a business. Familiarity with the contents of these reports and the ability to interpret them will therefore enable you to assess the performance and financial standing of organisations of which you have no detailed inside knowledge.

The Nature and Purpose of Accounting Information

Accounting can be described as:

Recording, summarising and analysing the transactions and activities of an organisation in such a way as to provide useful information for its owners and managers.

As the prime objective in most businesses is to increase the wealth of the owner(s), the following information will be required to assess business performance.

- How much profit the business has earned in a given time period (or for non-profit making organisations how does income compare with expenditure)?

- What does it own.

- What does it owe to others.

As well as historical information showing the consequences of previous activities, more detailed information will be required for management activities such as:

1. Planning

In the planning process managers must determine what should be done in a forthcoming period to further the aims of the business. As profitability or cost effectiveness is likely to be a priority, they may be guided by accounting information showing the expected financial consequences of alternative courses of action.

2. Control

To achieve business objectives, planned activities must be properly managed and closely controlled. This requires regular information identifying any activities not proceeding as planned, in order that the cause can be investigated and any necessary remedial action taken. Much of this is likely to be accounting information highlighting differences between expected outcomes from planned activities and the actual results achieved.

3. Decision Making

Decision making entails choosing from alternative courses of action, the option which best satisfies an aim or objective. As objectives are often financial, accounting information assessing the financial consequences of alternative courses of action is widely used to guide those responsible for decision making at all levels. Take for example a situation where a business is considering changing a particular operating method. In assessing such a proposal current costs can be compared with those anticipated from the alternative method to determine the financial implications of making the change. A lower operating cost may help to justify adopting the new method, although non-financial issues such as the reaction of employees should also be considered.

External Users of Accounting Information

As organisations grow in size and complexity they become increasingly difficult for owners to manage effectively and professional managers are often appointed to act on their behalf.

As well as the owners there are many other parties operating outside a business who may be interested in its activities. These include:

- potential investors;
- lenders;
- suppliers;
- customers;
- government;
- employees;
- the general public.

To protect the interests of these groups many organisations, including all limited companies, are legally obliged to prepare and publish regular accounting information which may be used to assess their performance and financial position.

The particular interests and information requirements of each group are outlined below.

Owners/Shareholders

As explained earlier, responsibility for the management of larger businesses may not rest entirely with the owners. A large company for example may be owned by thousands of shareholders very few of whom actually work in the business. They will therefore require information which enables them to judge how well the business has been managed on their behalf and accounting reports are an important source of such information.

Potential Investors

As well as the current owners/shareholders those with an interest in buying a business (or a share in it) may use accounting information to help in the assessment of its past performance and current financial position.

Lenders

Lending money to a business involves a certain degree of risk. Subsequent financial problems may mean it is unable repay the debt and lenders may suffer considerable losses as a result. Consequently, before agreeing to provide finance, lenders such as banks will evaluate the financial position and future prospects of the borrower and will be particularly interested in its ability to generate sufficient cash to repay the loan and the value of marketable assets which could be used as security for the loan. To assist in this assessment additional, more detailed information is often requested to supplement that which may be available from accounting statements.

Suppliers

A business represents a potential source of future revenue to those supplying goods or services. Consequently suppliers are likely to be interested not only in the business's survival but also its prospects for growth. Where they offer credit terms suppliers also assume the risks associated with lending and will therefore have a greater interest in the financial stability of customers.

Customers

Customers will be interested in a business's ability to continue providing goods or services at an acceptable price and may use accounting information to help assess its financial position and profitability.

Employees

Employees' main interests are likely to be the prospect of continued employment and the opportunity to share in the success of their employer should the business perform particularly well. In addition to published accounts they may also have access to more detailed internal financial information which may be used in discussions on issues such as pay awards, bonuses and conditions of employment.

Government

The government requires information on company profits in order to assess the amount of corporation tax payable. For unincorporated businesses such as sole traders and partnerships, tax is paid not by the business itself but by the owners based on their income from the business and again accounting information will be required for an assessment of tax due. Value added tax (VAT) is also payable by all but very small businesses and information is required on purchases and sales in order to assess the amount due for a period. Accounting information may also be used by government to compile statistics which may be used in managing the economy.

The General Public

The general public may be interested in the performance of nationalised industries and in the social impact of business organisations. Narrative information contained within accounting reports may give some indication of a business's attitude towards environmental and social issues and its profitability may indicate its ability to meet the cost of implementing adequate controls in these areas.

Financial and Management Accounting

The preparation of accounting information for external parties is known as Financial Accounting and will be examined in Part Two of this book. The compilation of internal management information is referred to as Management Accounting and we will study this in Part Three.

The main differences between these two branches of accountancy are explained below.

Financial Accounting

Financial Accounting has been defined by The Chartered Institute of Management Accountants (CIMA) as:

"The analysis, classification and recording of financial transactions and the ascertainment of how such transactions affect the performance and financial position of an undertaking."

Although management may use financial accounting reports to a limited extent, the main purpose of this information is to inform the external parties described earlier about the past performance of a business and its financial position at a particular point in time.

To protect the interests of these parties the information disclosed and the basis of its preparation is determined by various legal and professional requirements. These have evolved in an attempt to ensure that the requirements of potential users are met and that the information is compiled on a consistent basis which assists in its interpretation.

Management Accounting

Management Accounting has been described by CIMA as:

"The preparation and presentation of accounting information in such a way as to assist management in the formulation of policies and in the planning and control of the activities of the undertaking."

The aim in management accounting is to influence the performance of the organisation rather than merely report the consequences of past events. To satisfy the requirements of managers at all levels, information must be provided in greater detail than that found in financial accounting reports and Figure 1.1 shows how it may typically be broken down.

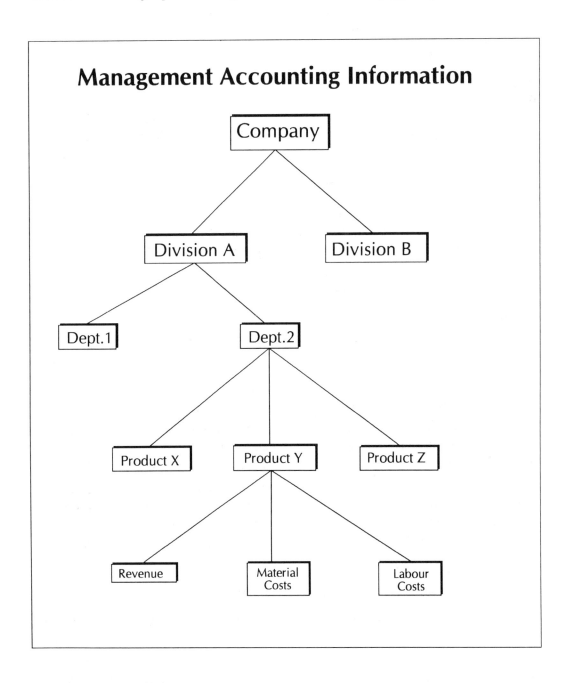

Figure 1.1 Management Accounting Information

Management accounting is unconstrained by legal and regulatory requirements and there is complete discretion over the information which is produced and the manner in which it is compiled and presented. Although we shall examine some commonly used techniques and methods in Part Three of this book, none are obligatory and the information prepared in any particular circumstances should reflect the specific requirements of those for whom it is compiled. Consequently an important part of any management accountant's job is to develop an awareness of the responsibilities and objectives of managers working within the business and to consult with them regularly to ascertain their information requirements.

Effective Information

To ensure that managers benefit fully from information supplied, the following factors should be considered in its compilation:

Relevance

The information should meet the particular requirements of those for whom it is intended. For example a department manager in a large organisation will require detailed information relating to the particular activities for which he is responsible. The chief executive however with far wider responsibilities would become overwhelmed with such detail and will be more interested in a brief overview of each functional area. Where this indicates issues requiring further attention the relevant detail can be provided on an exceptional basis.

Comprehensibility

To derive maximum benefit from the information at their disposal, managers must be fully aware of its message and implications. It should therefore be reported in a manner which is understood by its users and specialised technical terms should be avoided. Assistance should also be available when required to help in its interpretation.

Accuracy

As managers rely on information for guidance in tasks such as planning and decision making, accuracy is an important consideration. Decisions taken on the basis of wildly inaccurate information may be inappropriate and potentially very damaging.

In many situations, such as the evaluation of a proposed course of action, *projected* figures based on future expectations may be required and complete accuracy in these circumstances will be impossible. However provided forecasts are based on reasonable assumptions and decision makers are made aware of the scope for error, the resulting information may still provide useful guidance.

Timeliness

To enable managers to react to information promptly it should be supplied as soon as possible. A two week delay in providing a report which indicates excessive overtime working will delay any corrective action and increase the cost of the problem accordingly.

This desire for timeliness may conflict with the need for accuracy in that completely accurate information may take some time to obtain. In these circumstances it may be necessary to sacrifice a little precision by estimating unknown figures. Provided these estimates are reasonable, the message conveyed should not be materially distorted and any action prompted by the information can be taken more quickly.

Cost Effectiveness

The provision of any information has a cost in terms of staff engaged in its preparation, the use of equipment such as computers and any materials such as paper, files etc. To justify this expenditure the value of benefits derived from using the information should exceed its cost. In practice, determining the precise cost of a particular piece of information may not be easy and the measurement of attributable benefits is likely to be even more difficult. Nevertheless the principle should not be ignored. The use of information within an organisation should be monitored continually and any becoming redundant should be discontinued.

Having now examined the nature of both financial and management accounting, their differences are summarised in Figure 1.2 below.

Financial and Management Accounting		
	Financial Accounting	**Management Accounting**
USERS	External parties	Internal parties
AIM	To report results	To influence performance
TIME FOCUS	The past	The future
LEVEL OF DETAIL	Aggregate information	Detailed information
REGULATIONS	Legal and professional	Discretionary requirements

Figure 1.2 Financial and Management Accounting

Limitations of Accounting Information

Although accounting reports are an important source of information which can help in assessing an organisation's activities and performance they do have limitations. Factors which are likely to have an important bearing on the long term success of a business such as the skills of the management team and employees and relationships with customers, are not reflected in accounting statements. In addition, as we shall see later, items which are included can be difficult to quantify in some cases, relying on judgement and estimations by those compiling the information.

Consequently accounting information cannot provide a full and completely objective picture of a business and its activities and is best used with any other available information.

The Accountancy Profession

To become a qualified accountant it is necessary to gain membership of a recognised professional body. The major accounting bodies are:

- The Institute of Chartered Accountants in England and Wales (ICAEW)

- The Institute of Chartered Accountants in Scotland (ICAS)

- The Institute of Chartered Accountants in Ireland (ICAI)

- The Chartered Institute of Management Accountants (CIMA)

- The Chartered Association of Certified Accountants (CACA)

- The Chartered Institute of Public Finance and Accountancy (CIPFA)

To become a member of one of the institutions listed above, aspiring accountants must pass a series of examinations and may be required to satisfy other requirements such as attaining a satisfactory level of practical experience.

The members of each may do their initial training in different ways and tend to perform different types of work. In the case of the first three bodies listed, training takes place with professional accounting firms providing services such as the preparation of financial accounts, auditing and advice on tax matters. On qualifying although not obliged to do so, many members continue working with such firms. Members of the Chartered Institute of Management Accountants, as the name suggests, specialise in management accounting and the majority train and work in industry and commerce. Membership of the Chartered Association of Certified Accountants can be gained through training and working in either accounting firms or industry whilst members of the Chartered Institute of Public Finance and Accountancy train and work predominantly in public bodies such as local authorities.

Summary

- Accounting is concerned with the provision of information on the activities of an organisation for its owners and/or managers.

- A knowledge of accounting should help you to:

    - Appreciate the value of accounting information.

    - Ensure that business decisions are supported by relevant financial information.

    - Interpret published accounting reports.

- Shareholders in business who are not directly engaged in its management require information which can be used to assess how well it has been managed on their behalf. Many organisations including limited companies, are legally obliged to publish information which may be used for this purpose.

- Other parties interested in the activities of a business may also use published accounting statements to help satisfy their information requirements. These include:

    - potential investors;

    - lenders;

    - suppliers;

    - customers;

    - government;

    - employees;

    - the general public.

- To protect the interests of these groups the compilation of published accounting information is governed by legal and professional accounting requirements.

- 'Management accounting' information is used for guidance in tasks such as planning, control and decision making and is unconstrained by legal and regulatory requirements.

- Effective management information should be relevant to the user's needs, understandable, accurate, timely and cost effective.

- Supplementing accounting information with that available from other sources will produce a more complete picture of an organisation's performance and prospects.

Questions (See Appendix C for Answers)

1.1

(a) Briefly explain four differences between Financial Accounting and Management Accounting.

(b) Describe four characteristics of effective management information and explain the implications of providing information without these features.

1.2

'The increasing use of spreadsheets will make accounting out of date.'

Required

Briefly explain the usefulness of spreadsheets to accountants and comment on the above statement.

(ACCA)

1.3

In any business undertaking or environment with which you are familiar describe the role, or potential role, of the management accountant.

Consider how this role has been, or may be, influenced by the use of the computer.

(ACCA)

Questions Without Answers

1.4

It has been suggested that, apart from owners/investors, there are six separate user groups of published accounting statements: the loan creditor group, the employee group, the analyst-advisor group, the business contact group, the government and the public.

Required

(a) Taking any FOUR of these six user groups, explain the information they are likely to want from published accounting statements.

(b) Are there any difficulties in satisfying the requirements of all four of your chosen groups, given the requirements of other users?

(ACCA)

1.5

Consider the following Operating Statement relating to the activities of Worldwide Tours Limited and:

(a)   Comment on its effectiveness as management information;

(b)   Re-draft the statement in a format which;

    (i)   addresses any deficiencies identified in part (a);

    (ii)   is suitable for the Managing Director of Worldwide Tours and the Operating Manager of each geographical area.

WORLDWIDE TOURS LIMITED
OPERATING STATEMENT JANUARY – JUNE 19X8

Sales	**£**
Europe	605,000
Far East	140,000
North America	325,000
Australasia	90,000
Total Sales	1,185,000
Less Costs	
Wages Europe	185,000
" Far East	25,000
" North America	90,000
" Australasia	15,000
Travel/Accommodation Europe	310,000
" " Far East	65,000
" " North America	170,000
" " Australasia	45,000
Other costs Europe	50,000
" " Far East	10,000
" " North America	15,000
" " Australasia	5,000
Profit	180,000
Profit Margin	15%

I. Blewett
Accountant
27 September 19X8

Part 2

Financial Accounting

Chapter 2

Accounting Principles and Regulations

Learning Objectives

After completing this chapter you should be able to:

- Appreciate the need for principles guiding the preparation of accounting information.

- Explain the following principles:

  - Money measurement
  - Historical cost
  - Separate entity
  - Going concern
  - Realisation
  - Matching
  - Consistency
  - Disclosure
  - Materiality
  - Objectivity
  - Prudency

- Describe the efforts made by the accountancy profession and government legislation to improve the quality of accounting information.

Introduction

The value of any information will be enhanced with some knowledge of the basis on which it has been compiled. For example, when planning a foreign holiday, an indication of expected temperatures may be helpful in choosing the destination. A brochure stating that the temperature in New Zealand will be approximately 35 degrees in January provides incomplete information as it still leaves a number of questions unanswered. Is this early morning or mid-day? In the shade or the sun? Fahrenheit or Celsius? The knowledge that measurements are based on the average maximum daily temperatures in degrees Celsius would reduce this uncertainty and increase the value of the information.

Accounting statements provide information such as the profit earned by a business in a particular period of time and the value of its assets at a given date. However, as with temperatures in New Zealand, there are various ways in which these can be measured and without knowing which has been adopted, the information is likely to be difficult to interpret.

In an attempt to reduce this uncertainty and promote a degree of consistency, accountants apply a number of accepted principles when preparing accounting information. This should make accounting statements easier to interpret and facilitate comparison with:

(a)   Previous results for the business (in order to identify any trends).

(b)   Other businesses (e.g. prospective investors considering a number of companies may wish to use accounting information to compare the performance of each).

A grasp of these basic principles should provide a useful foundation for subsequent chapters where we will examine the recording of business transactions and preparation of accounting statements. You will find it useful to read this chapter again after completing Chapter 5 in order to reinforce the topics covered to that point.

Accounting Principles

Money Measurement

Accounting statements only report those items which can be measured in monetary terms. There are of course many aspects of a business which cannot be measured in this way. For example, future prospects are likely to be influenced by the strength of the management team and skills of the workforce but as these cannot be expressed in monetary terms they are not reflected in the accounts. Consequently, although providing useful information on a business, accounting statements do not show the complete picture.

Historical Cost

This principle requires that the assets of a business are valued at their original purchase price or the purchase price less depreciation for long term assets (we will deal with this issue in detail in Chapter 5).

In times of inflation, prices will of course rise and an asset bought some time ago may now be worth more than the purchase price recorded in the accounts. As a result, the assets of the enterprise may be reported at out of date values with their total worth possibly understated and identical items bought at different times (and at different prices) may be valued differently. Consider a retailer who buys a number of items for resale for £10 each and before selling these, buys another batch for £11 each. He now has a number of identical assets which are recorded at different values in the accounts.

The accounting profession has in the past attempted to address this issue, publishing guide-lines for the preparation of inflation adjusted accounts. However, they provoked much controversy and disagreement and have not been widely adopted.

As we shall see in later sections, there are instances where this historical cost principle may be overridden (e.g. valuing stocks on an average rather than historical cost basis – we will cover this in Chapter 6). However, the general principle is that the purchase price should be used.

Separate Entity

In order that the performance of a business may be properly assessed, its accounting records should be kept separate from those of the owner(s). In the case of limited companies this principle is in accordance with the legal position where the company is deemed to be a separate legal entity to its shareholders. For sole traders and partners, this is not the case and the owner(s) are legally responsible for the actions and liabilities of the business. Nevertheless, the accounting information for such enterprises, should exclude the personal affairs of the owner(s).

In practice this means that sums invested in a business by its owner are recorded as a liability (the business owes the owner this amount). Similarly, any profits made by the business are also shown as liabilities. This often causes confusion – how can profits be a liability? Remember that the accounts reflect the financial affairs of the business as a separate entity and it owes the owner not only the original capital but also any profits arising from that investment.

Going Concern

The going concern concept assumes that the business will continue to operate in the foreseeable future. This is significant in terms of the valuation of assets. Although they may have been acquired at great cost, the 'break up' value of assets in the event of the business ceasing to operate may be relatively low. For example production equipment designed to meet the specific requirements of a manufacturing company may be of no use outside the business and worth only scrap value if the company was to cease trading. However under the going concern concept it is assumed that the business will continue to operate and the equipment is therefore valued at its historical cost less an amount to reflect depreciation.

Realisation

This principle requires that purchases and sales are recorded when legal title to the goods passes between the parties, irrespective of whether or not payment has been made.

The following examples illustrate this requirement:

Example 2.1

Paul runs a furniture shop and in January purchases goods for £2,000 from a supplier offering credit terms of one month. He intends to sell the goods for £3,000.

Although no payment is made until February, the purchase transaction is recorded in January, evidencing that the value of goods held in stock has risen by £2,000. In February a second transaction is recorded (i.e. payment to the supplier).

As the goods are to be sold for £3,000 a profit of £1,000 is expected. However, although the goods have a value of £3,000 at some future date, they are valued at their cost of £2,000 until the sale is made.

Example 2.2

Paul eventually sells the goods in April on credit terms of one month.

At this point the profit has been realised and the sale of £3,000 and a profit of £1,000 are recorded (even though the credit terms mean that payment is not received until May).

Thus the purchase and sale of goods were recorded on the date they were made and the payments recorded separately as follow:

January	- Purchase goods for £2,000.
February	- Payment for purchases £2,000.
April	- Sale of goods for £3,000.
	- Profit of £1,000.
May	- Receipt from customer £3,000.

This approach can create a problem if the customer does not pay the £3,000 as promised. A profitable transaction has been recorded in April and we now know that no profit was actually made (giving a customer goods worth £2,000 without receiving payment does not generate profits!). In these circumstances it would be necessary to adjust the profits reported to reflect the fact that a 'bad debt' had been incurred.

Accounting for bad debts will be examined in detail in Chapter 5.

Matching

The matching (or accruals) principle, states that the profits in a period are measured by comparing sales revenue with the costs incurred in generating that revenue.

Thus in the example used above, the £2,000 worth of goods purchased for resale would not be included as costs in the profit calculation until they were sold. At that point the £3,000 sales income and the £2,000 cost of the goods sold would be 'matched' to give a profit figure of £1,000. Until the sale took place the goods would be recorded as an asset (i.e. stocks) with a value of £2,000.

Of course the business will incur other expenses in addition to the cost of goods for resale and these must also be matched with the income for a period. For example, the costs of office rental for April should be recorded as an expense for that month (to be matched with sales for the month) even if payment has not yet been made. This is known as accruing for the cost and will be dealt with in more detail in Chapter 5.

Consistency

As we shall see later in this book, there is often more than one method of dealing with certain items. Accounting for depreciation is a good example of this and various acceptable methods will be examined in Chapter 5.

One of the most common uses of accounting information is to make comparisons between periods to identify trends for the business. If principles were applied inconsistently, differences in results reported for two periods may be due to calculating the figures on a different basis rather than the performance of the business. Such uncertainty would make accounts difficult to interpret and principles should therefore be consistently applied in each period.

Accounting information is also used to make comparisons between different organisations. However, one problem in doing this is that although each may apply principles consistently from one period to the next there may be inconsistency between organisations and meaningful comparison of their accounting statements can be difficult.

Disclosure

This principle states that the accounting methods adopted should be disclosed in the accounts and in particular any changes in those methods. The conclusion to be drawn is that methods should be consistently applied and disclosed but if for any reason a change is deemed to be appropriate then attention should be drawn to that fact. Given the range of options available for certain items, this should assist in the interpretation of accounting reports by making users of the information aware of the methods used in their compilation.

Materiality

The accounting treatment of a transaction can depend on the extent to which it influences the overall financial results of the business.

For example where assets are to be used over a number of years, their cost should be spread over those years rather than reported in the year of purchase. However, a business may decide that this treatment is unnecessary for low value assets as its effect would be so small that the view of the business presented by the accounts would not be altered.

A decision as to the significance of a transaction will, depend on the size of the organisation. Assets costing under £5,000 may be insignificant for a large company but not for a small business which may impose a ceiling of perhaps £1,000.

Objectivity

Accounting information should be presented without any personal bias. Accountants have a duty to be objective and under the Companies Act 1985/89, to present a 'true and fair view' of the performance of the enterprise and its financial position.

Prudency

If there is any doubt as to the figures which should be reported, then a conservative view should be taken. If in doubt, profits should be under rather than overstated. For example, if there is some doubt as to whether a customer will pay an outstanding debt, this principle suggests that it should be assumed that the money will not be received and profits should be reduced accordingly.

Similarly, if there is uncertainty as to the level of costs incurred in a period (perhaps the business is contesting a sum claimed by a supplier) then a prudent view should be taken and the cost should be over rather than understated.

Where there is conflict between this concept and one of the aforementioned principles, prudence is the overriding requirement. For example it could be argued that in compliance with the matching principle, advertising expenditure should be included in the period in which the resulting sales income is reported. However as there is no guarantee that additional sales will result from the advertising, a prudent view should be taken and the cost reported in the period in which the advertising occurred.

The aim of this principle is to ensure that users of accounting statements are not given an over-optimistic indication of the performance and financial position of a business. This is not to say that a misleading negative view should be presented of course. Although adopting a cautious outlook, an accountant should at all times attempt to present a true and fair view.

The Regulatory Framework of Accounting

Before 1970 the only mandatory requirements in the UK in respect of the presentation of company accounts arose out of Company Law and these were much less strict than current legal requirements. Accounting practices were inconsistent and companies were able to alter them in order to show a favourable picture, creating difficulties in the assessment of a company's performance over time and comparisons between the financial performance of different companies. During the 1960's there were a number of instances where accounting practices produced misleading information and the accountancy profession was widely criticised. Consequently, in 1970 the Accounting Standards Steering Committee (ASSC), later renamed the Accounting Standards Committee (ASC) was established with the objective of seeking to narrow the areas of difference in accounting practice.

Accounting Standards

The ASC sought to achieve its aim by publishing statements on best accounting practice. Having identified an issue which required clarification it firstly issued a discussion document known as a Discussion Draft (DD). After a discussion period and the incorporation of any amendments deemed necessary, a Statement of Standard Accounting Practice (SSAP) was issued. These were approved by the Consultative Committee of Accounting Bodies (CCAB) and authority for them stemmed from the fact that the professional accountancy bodies expected their members to comply with them. The ASC issued 25 SSAP's of which three were subsequently withdrawn. Examples include SSAP 2 which is concerned with the disclosure of accounting policies and requires that the following are adopted as the four fundamental concepts of financial accounting:

- Going concern

- Matching

- Consistency

- Prudency.

Other SSAP's issued cover issues such as accounting for stocks and long term contracts (SSAP 9), accounting for depreciation (SSAP 12) and accounting for goodwill (SSAP 22).

In 1987 the CCAB established a committee chaired by Sir Ron Dearing to review the process by which standards were set and the issues considered included:

- the form standards should take

- their legal status

- the means of ensuring compliance with standards

- the composition of the body responsible for setting standards.

Some of the proposals, such as the requirement for large companies to state that their accounts have been compiled in accordance with acceptable accounting standards, were implemented in the Companies Act 1989. The current procedures for setting accounting standards came into force in August 1990 with the establishment of the Financial Reporting Council (FRC) and incorporate many of the recommendations made by the Dearing Committee.

The Financial Reporting Council (FRC)

The Financial Reporting Council is responsible for standard setting in the UK through its two subsidiaries, the Accounting Standards Board (ASB) and the Review Panel. It is funded by the accountancy profession, the Government, the Bank of England and the stock exchange. It has about 20 members and with representatives from not only the accountancy profession but also other parties concerned with the use, preparation or audit of accounting information, has a wider representation than the CCAB.

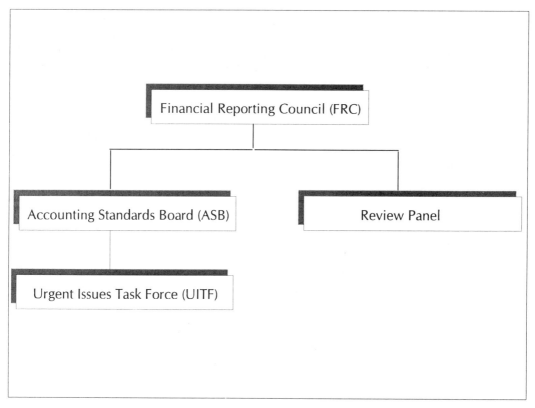

Figure 2.1 The Accounting Standard Regulatory Structure

The ASB has replaced the ASC and can issue new standards, which are now known as Financial Reporting Standards (FRS's), without the approval of the professional accountancy bodies. As well as being more independent, it also has greater power to enforce accounting standards. It has a full time chairman and a technical director as well as part time members who are paid for their services.

The ASB initially adopted the 22 SSAP's issued by the ASC but made clear its intention to review them and has subsequently replaced a number of them, issuing FRS's covering areas such as cash flow statements (FRS1 - which will be considered in Chapter 8), accounting for subsidiary undertakings (FRS2) and acquisitions and mergers (FRS6). The standard setting process entails the initial issue of a Discussion Draft (DD) with proposals for a planned FRS, to a restricted audience. This is followed by a Financial Reporting Exposure Draft (FRED) which is made generally available and provides the opportunity for further discussion before the eventual issue of the FRS.

The Urgent Issues Task Force (UITF) is a sub-committee of the ASB which considers urgent matters not provided for in current standards. Its aim is to assist the ASB in the development of best practice and it acts where the normal standard setting procedure is impractical.

The Review Panel, consisting of about 15 members, has been established to investigate instances drawn to its attention where large companies have not complied with accounting standards. In cases of material departures the panel can request the company to prepare revised accounts and should they refuse to do so, has the authority to refer the matter the court which can order the preparation of revised accounts.

International Accounting Standards

In 1973 after consultation between the accountancy bodies of several countries, the International Accounting Standards Committee (IASC) was established with the aim of harmonising accounting standards worldwide. The ASB has confirmed its support for the IASC and when issuing FRS's explains how they relate to the IAS on the same issue. Compliance with an FRS will usually also guarantee compliance with the relevant IAS.

Compliance with Standards

In setting out the authority for accounting standards, the ASB has stated that SSAP's and FRS's are accounting standards for the purpose of the Companies Act, which requires that large companies must comply with applicable accounting standards and give details of any departures from them. Additionally members of professional accountancy bodies are expected to comply with accounting standards in the preparation and audit of accounting information or else justify significant departures from them. Failure to do so can result in disciplinary action by the relevant body including a fine or even expulsion.

Although accounting standards have been developed for company accounts, it is widely accepted that as they constitute good practice and the same rules are also generally applied when preparing accounts for businesses operating as sole traders or partnerships.

The Impact of Standardisation Initiatives

Although, the initiatives described have resulted in greater standardisation and reduced inconsistency in accounting practice, the problems have not been eliminated. Differences in practice persist and companies continue to attempt to present as favourable a picture of the business as possible. Consequently, some accountants have argued against increasing standardisation, claiming that attempts to do so have not achieved their objectives and that the appropriate accounting treatment is a matter for judgement to suit a particular set of circumstances. It has also been argued that some standards may result in business decisions being taken because of their affect on the disclosure of information rather than on commercial grounds. However whilst it may pose occasional problems for those preparing accounting information, standardisation should be of assistance to those using such information.

The Companies Act 1985/89

The Companies Act lays down statutory requirements in respect of accounting information published by companies including:

- the adoption of the four fundamental concepts outlined in SSAP 2 for the preparation of published accounts;

- the minimum amount of information which must be publicly disclosed by companies. The Act distinguishes between companies in terms of their size with small and medium sized companies being permitted to publish modified accounting reports;

- prescribed formats for published accounting reports;

- the overriding requirement that published accounts should give a 'true and fair view' of the financial position of the company in question. They should therefore be compiled in accordance with the concepts and standards set by the accounting profession which we have considered in this chapter.

The disclosure requirements of the Act will be examined more closely in Chapter 7 where we look at company accounts in some detail.

Summary

- Accounting principles have been established in order to promote consistency in the preparation of accounting information and thus assist in its interpretation.

- The following have been examined in this chapter:

  Money Measurement – Only those items which can be expressed in monetary terms are recorded.

  Historical Cost – Assets are generally valued at their cost (less depreciation for long term assets).

  Separate Entity – The accounting records of a business are maintained separately from those of its owner(s).

  Going Concern – Assets are valued on the assumption that the business will continue to operate in the foreseeable future.

  Realisation – Purchases and sales are recorded when goods are passed (or services rendered) from one party to another regardless of when payment is made. Profits are recorded when a sale is made and until then, goods are valued at their historical cost.

  Matching (Accruals) – Profit for a period is determined by comparing sales revenue with the costs incurred in generating that revenue.

  Consistency – Certain items can be accounted for in a number of ways. Having adopted a particular method it should be consistently applied unless there are good reasons for changing.

  Disclosure – The accounts should disclose the accounting methods adopted and draw particular attention to any changes in the methods used.

  Materiality – The accounting treatment of a transaction can depend on the extent to which it alters the view of the business presented by the accounts.

  Objectivity – Accounting reports should present a true and fair view of the performance and financial position of a business.

  Prudency – A conservative view should be adopted when compiling financial statements and if in doubt, profits should be under rather than overstated.

- The Accounting Standards Board (ASB) provides guidance on specific issues through the publication of standards which accountants are expected to comply with when compiling accounting statements.

- The Companies Act 1985/89 lays down statutory requirements for companies in respect of the preparation and publication of accounting information.

Questions   (See Appendix C for Answers)

2.1

(a)   State and describe the four fundamental accounting concepts as set out in SSAP 2 and the Companies Act 1985.

(b)   Define the terms 'accounting bases' and 'accounting policies'.

(c)   Give two examples of an accounting base and an example of an accounting policy for each accounting base.

(d)   Describe the relationship between fundamental accounting concepts and the statutory audit report.

(ACCA)

2.2

In respect of each of the following situations relating to a small business state which accounting principle should be followed and briefly explain its meaning:

(a)   The owner of the business has taken goods for his own personal use.

(b)   The personnel manager wishes to reflect the good industrial relations record of the business in the accounts.

(c)   At the end of the financial year an invoice for £500 in respect of goods received during the year had not yet been received. The goods had not been sold at that point.

(d)   A customer owing £1,000 is in financial difficulty and there is considerable doubt as to whether it will be able to pay.

(e)   The owner wishes to purchase a vehicle for personal use with cash drawn from the business.

(f)   Existing customers have placed orders which are likely to prove highly profitable.

(g)   The stock of unused stationery at the end of the financial year has been valued at approximately £40. This cost has been included in the running expenses of the business.

2.3

Explain clearly FOUR of the following terms as an accountant would understand them:

(i)   Financial accounting.

(ii)   Realisation.

(iii)   Matching.

(iv)   Materiality.

(v)   Inflation.

(ACCA)

Questions Without Answers

2.4

A scout troop collects subscriptions from its members, and also has to pay 60% of them to central scouting funds. In the year to 31 December 19X8 the troop receives:

For 19X7	£20
For 19X8	£60
For 19X9	£10

It pays to central funds in that year:

For 19X7	£12
For 19X8	£30
For 19X9	nil

Required:

(a)   Produce a summary of the subscription position for the troop for the year 19X8, on

  (i)   a receipts and payments basis,

  (ii)   a revenue and expenses basis.

(b)   Outline the advantages and disadvantage of each basis with reference to appropriate accounting conventions. Give the scout troop leader your recommended method, with reasons. Discuss also any difficult decisions you have to make in deciding your answer to (a) above.

(ACCA)

2.5

    (a)   What is the purpose of issuing accounting standards?

    (b)   What controls are in place to help ensure that they are followed?

Chapter 3

Recording Transactions

Learning Objectives

After completing this chapter you should be able to:

- Explain the concept of the accounting equation.

- Understand the 'double entry' principle used in recording transactions.

- Record business transactions.

- Prepare a trial balance.

- Explain methods of detecting recording errors.

- Appreciate the need to sub-divide accounting records into various ledgers to maintain detailed information.

- Make brief comments on the financial position of a business based on accounting information.

- Understand the traditional method of recording transactions using debit and credit entries in 'T' accounts.

Introduction

In this chapter we will look at the way in which everyday business transactions are documented in the accounting records. In practice this is usually done using computerised systems which guide the user by indicating the data required in respect of each transaction. In addition such systems usually incorporate control mechanisms which regulate the recording process by preventing incorrect data input or producing information highlighting possible errors.

Consequently those engaged in recording transactions on a day to day basis do not necessarily require a detailed knowledge of accounting principles. However in order to make any necessary adjustment to the accounting records and to appreciate how data recorded can be used to produce meaningful financial information, it is necessary to understand the basic principles underlying the recording of business transactions. These will be explained in this chapter using a simple tabular approach to illustrate the effect of transactions on the financial position of the business. This method should provide a sound understanding of principles and a foundation for the subsequent study of techniques used in the preparation and interpretation of accounting statements.

For readers who perhaps work with accountants and who may wish to examine bookkeeping methods and terminology used in practice in a little more detail the chapter concludes by looking at the way in which accountants have traditionally maintained records.

The Accounting Equation

The recording process will be easier to grasp with an understanding of the relationship between various categories of financial items.

As we saw in Chapter 2, when looking at the 'separate entity' principle, the owners' interest in a business is shown as a liability in the accounts of the business. (If you find this is a little confusing, remember that this principle stated that the business accounting records should be maintained separately from those of the owners. As the owners are 'owed' an amount representing their initial capital outlay and any subsequent profits, their interest, known as *the* owners' funds*, is recorded as a liability in the accounts of the business.)*

As all the assets of a business ultimately belong to its owners, the business owes them to those owners and the following relationship must exist:

ASSETS = LIABILITIES

This is known as the accounting equation and can be clarified with definitions of its two elements:

Assets

Assets are measurable resources which are expected to have some future benefit for the business. Examples include premises, vehicles and stocks of goods, all of which may be used in the future in the pursuit of business objectives.

Liabilities

Liabilities are claims on the assets of a business by various parties and may be either:

(a)   Amounts owed to outside parties such as lenders and suppliers of goods on credit. (The term 'liabilities' is commonly used to describe only these external claims.)

(b)   The owners' claim on the assets remaining after external debts have been satisfied. (Known as the 'owners' funds'.)

Distinguishing between these two categories the accounting equation can be expressed as:

$$ASSETS = LIABILITIES + OWNERS' FUNDS$$

or, as the owners' funds consist of the capital originally invested plus any profits generated:

$$ASSETS = LIABILITIES + CAPITAL + PROFIT$$

Recording Transactions

As the relationship between the items shown in the equation must always be maintained, the effect of business transactions must be two-fold.

If, for example, the value of assets is increased by £500, then either:

(a)   Another asset must decrease by £500;

$$ASSETS = LIABILITIES + CAPITAL + PROFIT$$

\+   £500   =

\-   £500   or,

(b)   An element on the liability side of the equation must also increase by £500.

$$ASSETS = LIABILITIES + CAPITAL + PROFIT$$

\+   £500   =   + £500

As each transaction requires two 'balancing' entries, this recording system is known as double entry bookkeeping.

It is widely used in practice and will be demonstrated using the following example.

Example 3.1

Judith started a business selling computer equipment and during the first two days the following transactions occurred:

1.   Judith invested £4,000 of her savings in the business, depositing it into a business bank account.

2.   A further £2,000 was borrowed from a building society and deposited in the business bank account.

3.   A van was bought for £1,500.

4.   Computer equipment for re-sale was purchased for £2,000 and payment made by cheque.

5.   Further equipment was acquired for£3,500 from Middlemas Limited on credit terms.

The transactions can be recorded in a table (sometimes referred to as a worksheet) as follows:

		ASSETS		LIABILITIES		OWNER'S FUNDS	
Item	Bank	Van	Stock	Building Society	Creditors	Capital	Profit
1.	4,000					4,000	
2.	2,000			2,000			
3.	-1,500	1,500					
4.	-2,000		2,000				
5.			3,500		3,500		
Total as at end of day 2	2,500	1,500	5,500	2,000	3,500	4,000	0

$$
\begin{array}{rcccccc}
\text{ASSETS} & = & \text{LIABILITIES} & + & \text{CAPITAL} & + & \text{PROFIT} \\
£9,500 & = & £5,500 & + & £4,000 & + & \text{NIL}
\end{array}
$$

Notes on Each Transaction

1.   In this case the value of both an asset (the bank balance) and the owner's funds (capital) each rose by £4,000 thus maintaining the balance of the accounting equation.

2.   Again an asset (bank) and a liability (a debt of £2,000 outstanding to the building society) increased.

3.   One asset (the van) rose and another (bank) fell by the same amount.

(Note that the cost of the van is not included in the profit column. In compliance with the matching principle explained in Chapter 2, costs are included in the calculation of profit only when the benefit arising from the expenditure has been consumed. As the van has a future benefit it is an asset and the purchase price does not affect profit at this point. We will examine the treatment of this type of asset in more detail when we consider depreciation in Chapter 5).

4.   As with transaction 3 above the bank balance fell and another asset, this time the stock of equipment, rose.

(Note that again, the £2,000 is not at this stage recorded as a cost in the profit column. Under the matching principle costs are not included in the profit calculation until the goods are actually sold. At that time, the sales proceeds will be compared (i.e. 'matched') with the original cost in order to calculate the profit on the sale. Until the sale is made, the stock is recorded as an asset (i.e. it has a future benefit).

5.   Stocks have increased further but this time, as no payment has yet been made, the bank balance is unaltered. Instead, liabilities (£3,500 now owed to Middlemas Limited) have risen, and the balance of the equation has again been preserved.

As each transaction has been recorded with two balancing entries the totals shown in the table as at the end of the second day balance in accordance with the accounting equation. Assets are valued at £9,500 and liabilities and capital also amount to £9,500. As far as profit is concerned remember that in accordance with the matching principle sales revenue is compared with the costs incurred in generating that revenue in determining profit for a period. As no goods were sold during the first two days no profit has yet been earned. To demonstrate this principle we will now consider further transactions in respect of Judith's business.

Example 3.2

During the remainder of the first week the following additional trans-actions occurred.

6.   A school purchased a printer for £500 and paid by cheque (The original cost of the printer was £300).

7.   Equipment was sold on credit to Bill, a local architect, for £2,500 (The equipment had originally cost Judith £1,500).

8.   Wages of £200 were paid to an admin /sales assistant.

9.   Premises rental of £100 for the week was paid.

A revised table showing all transactions in week 1 is shown below:

Item	Bank	Van	Stock	Debtors	Building Society	Creditors	Capital	Profit
	ASSETS				**LIABILITIES**		**OWNER'S FUNDS**	
1.	4,000						4,000	
2.	2,000				2,000			
3.	-1,500	1,500						
4.	-2,000		2,000					
5.			3,500			3,500		
	2,500	1,500	5,500		2,000	3,500	4,000	
6(a).	500							500
6(b).			-300					-300
7(a).				2,500				2,500
7(b)			-1,500					-1,500
8.	-200							-200
9.	-100							-100
Total as at end Wk.1	2,700	1,500	3,700	2,500	2,000	3,500	4,000	900

ASSETS   =   LIABILITIES + CAPITAL + PROFIT
£10,400   =   £5,500   +   £4,000   + £900

Notes on Each Transaction

6a.   A sale has been made and the bank balance increased accordingly. As the business has now earned sales revenue, profit is also increased as a result of this transaction. In terms of the accounting equation we have therefore increased both an asset (bank) and a liability (profit) by £500.

6b.   As the printer has now been sold, the original cost of £300 is transferred from stock and matched with the sales proceeds in the profit column. Thus in this second part of the transaction we have decreased both an asset (stock) and the owner's funds (profit) by £300. A stock account in which purchases are added and the cost of items sold subtracted in this way is known as a continuous stock account. It enables the total cost of goods sold in each period to be easily determined although as we shall see later in the chapter, it is not the only means of doing so.

In terms of profit we have now included income of £500 and costs of £300, and therefore a profit of £200 on the sale.

7a. This transaction is also for the sale of goods. However in this case, as credit terms were offered no cash has yet been received. Therefore rather than increasing the bank balance another asset known as 'debtors' has risen. Debtors are those owing money to the business (hence there is a future benefit) and in this case Bill now owes £2,500 for the goods supplied. Again profits have increased on the liability side of the equation.

7b. As in 6b) above, the cost of the goods sold is removed from stock (where it was held until sale of the goods) and transferred to the profit column. The net effect of the sale on profit is therefore an increase of £1,000. Note that the overall effect on assets was also an increase of £1,000 with stocks falling by £1,500 and debtors rising by £2,500.

8. The bank balance has fallen by £200 and as the benefit arising from this expenditure (i.e. the services of the employee) has fully expired, it is recorded as a cost in the profit column. Thus both an asset and the owner's funds (profit) have fallen by the same amount.

9. Again as the benefit (from using the premises for the week) has been consumed, the £100 is subtracted in the profit column and the bank balance is also decreased.

To test your understanding of the principles covered to this point you should now attempt the following example and check your solution with the answer given.

Example 3.3

During Judith's second week of trading, the following transactions occurred:

10. Computer equipment for re-sale was bought on credit from Kingsmere for £7,300.

11. During the week equipment was sold for £6,300. Customers paid by cheque and the original cost of the equipment was £4,100.

12. Middlemas Limited were paid £2,000 on account.

13. Credit sales to the value of £4,500 were made to Chester Limited. These goods had cost Judith £2,600.

14. Bill paid his outstanding debt of £2,500.

15. Wages of £250 were paid to the admin / sales assistant.

16.   Premises rental of £100 was paid.

Required

(a)   Extend the table used in Example 3.2 by recording each transaction.

(b)   Calculate the new total for each type of asset and liability as at the end of week 2, proving that they balance in accordance with the accounting equation.

Solution

	Bank	Van	Stock	Debtors	Building Society	Creditors	Capital	Profit
Balance From Wk.1	2,700	1,500	3,700	2,500	2,000	3,500	4,000	900
Transaction								
10.			7,300			7,300		
11(a)	6,300							6,300
11(b)			-4,100					-4,100
12.	-2,000					-2,000		
13(a)				4,500				4,500
13(b)			-2,600					-2,600
14.	2,500			-2,500				
15.	-250							-250
16.	-100							-100
Total as at end Wk.2	9,150	1,500	4,300	4,500	2,000	8,800	4,000	4,650

| | ASSETS £19,450 | | = | LIABILITIES + £10,800 + | CAPITAL + PROFIT £4,000 + £4,650 |

Notes to Solution

The transaction types in this example were explained in Examples 3.1 and 3.2 with the exception of the following.

12. Payment to Middlemas Limited reduces both an asset (bank) and a liability (amount owing to creditors).

14. Payment received from Bill increases one asset (bank) and reduces another (amount receivable from debtors).

The Trial Balance

A bookkeeping system in which accounting records are maintained is known as a ledger and each record within the ledger is called an account. The totals (or balances) on each account at the end of a period, can be listed to create a 'trial balance'. The trial balance for Judith's business at the end of week two is shown below.

JUDITH'S COMPUTER SUPPLIES

TRIAL BALANCE AS AT 14.1.X6

	ASSETS	LIABILITIES*
	£	£
Bank	9,150	
Motor Vehicles	1,500	
Stock	4,300	
Debtors	4,500	
Loan		2,000
Creditors		8,800
Capital		4,000
Profit		4,650
	19,450	19,450

* i.e. including the owner's funds

The preparation of a trial balance is the first step in the compilation of accounting reports. However before preparing these reports, various accounting adjustments will be necessary in order to arrive at a final trial balance for a period. These adjustments may include items such as prepayments, accruals and depreciation and will be considered in Chapter 5.

Error Detection

The entries recorded in the accounts will be processed to produce accounting reports on the financial position and performance of the enterprise. Consequently, it is important that adequate controls are established to maintain the reliability of this information.

One such control stems from the need for two balancing entries in respect of each transaction. This should result in a trial balance which confirms that the total value of assets is equal to that of total liabilities. If the trial balance does not balance in this way, a recording error has been made which must be investigated and corrected.

To demonstrate this facility for error detection we will look again at transaction no.5 in Example 3.1, the purchase of goods on credit for £3,500. The correct treatment of this transaction was:

(a)   Increase stocks (an asset) by £3,500.

(b)   Increase creditors (a liability) by £3,500.

Any of the following errors in recording this transaction would be indicated by a trial balance showing unequal assets and liabilities:

(a)   The transaction was recorded with only a single entry

For example although stocks were increased by £3,500, creditors were not. The trial balance would then show the value of assets exceeding liabilities by £3,500 indicating that an error had occurred.

(b)   Although two entries were made, the values did not correspond

For instance stocks were increased by £3,500 but creditors by only £2,500. The value of assets would again exceed that of liabilities, this time by £1,000.

(c)   An account was incorrectly altered

For example £3,500 was subtracted from the stock account rather than added. In this case liabilities would exceed assets by £7,000 (check this by substituting this entry for the correct treatment used in Example 3.1).

(d)   Addition errors

If for instance the correct entry was made for this particular transaction but when the stock column was added at the end of the period, a total of £4,000 was obtained rather than £3,700. Asset values would then exceed liabilities by £300.

The imbalance in the trial balance resulting from any of these errors would draw attention to the problem and once the error had been traced the necessary correction(s) could be made.

Computerised systems can assist in this respect by building controls into the program such as refusing to accept entries which do not balance.

Less Detectable Errors

Not all bookkeeping errors will produce an imbalance and those which do not, may be more difficult to detect. Examples include:

(a)   *Using the same, incorrect figure for each part of the double entry*

For instance increasing both stocks and creditors by only £500. As assets and liabilities would increase by the same amount, a balance would be maintained. However the error may be detected either:

- At the next stock-taking exercise, when the value of stocks actually held would exceed the value shown in the accounts by £3,000;   or,

- When the supplier claimed the £3,500 outstanding and the value of the debt recorded under creditors was only £500.

(b)   *Increasing the wrong asset or liability*

For instance increasing the value of the van account by £3,500 rather than stocks. Again asset and liability values would be equal and the discrepancy may not be detected until the next stock-take.

(c)   *Omitting the transaction*

If a transaction is completely overlooked accounting records will be unaffected and the trial balance will therefore still balance.

Division of the Ledger

The number of accounts used in any bookkeeping system will depend on the level of detail required in the information produced from the accounting records. Consider for example, a business which records details of all vehicles in one asset account named 'Motor Vehicles'. This would make extraction of information on the values of various types of vehicle difficult and time consuming. An analysis of all entries made to the 'Motor Vehicles' account would be necessary, separating those made in respect of each category. This could be avoided by using separate accounts for cars, vans, lorries etc. Information on the value of each category could be obtained very quickly by looking at the balance on each individual account. The total value of all motor vehicles for disclosure in final accounting statements could still be easily ascertained by simply adding the balances on the individual accounts together. Consequently, using many detailed accounts is usually preferable to relatively few from which information extracted may be too general. Computers can help considerably with the administration of extra accounts and the extraction of information from these records.

This principle can be illustrated further by examining the way in which income and expenditure is recorded.

Accounting for Income and Expenditure

Earlier in the chapter, in order to explain the accounting equation, profit was recorded in one account containing income and various types of expenditure (i.e. the cost of the goods sold, wages and rent). Although the total profit for a period could be obtained easily using this approach, a breakdown of its component parts could not. Obtaining the total value of sales for a period for example would require the identification and addition of all of sales entries made to the account. Similarly, it would be necessary to add each wages transaction to obtain the total wages cost.

In practice, a business may have many sources of income is likely to incur many types of cost. In order to analyse profitability, detailed information on these will be required and to assist in this analysis, separate accounts are maintained for each type of income generated and cost incurred. Thus in the earlier examples, separate accounts would be used for sales, the cost of goods sold, wages and rent.

A financial accounting system will therefore contain the following types of account:

- Assets

- Liabilities   *'External' liabilities and* owner's funds (capital and profit)

- Income

- Expenditure

The balances on income and expenditure accounts are used to calculate the profit for the period as shown below:

JUDITH'S COMPUTER SUPPLIES

TRIAL BALANCE AS AT 14.1.X6

	£	ASSETS	LIABILITIES £
ASSETS			
Bank		9,150	
Motor Vehicles		1,500	
Stock		4,300	
Debtors		4,500	
LIABILITIES			
Loan			2,000
Creditors			8,800
Capital			4,000
INCOME			
Sales	13,800		
Profit			4,650
EXPENDITURE			
Cost Goods Sold	−8,500		
Wages	−450		
Rent	−200		
		19,450	19,450

Accounting for Purchases and Stock

As we saw in earlier examples, the cost of goods sold in a period may be ascertained by recording the original cost of every item as it is sold and adding the values recorded at the end of the period. For businesses with high sales volumes, recording the original cost for each sales transaction could be an enormous and time consuming task and computer systems are often employed to do this.

However many businesses such as small retailers may not operate such systems and recording the cost of each item sold is therefore impractical. In these circumstances the cost of goods sold in each period can be ascertained using an alternative method in which total purchases are recorded in a separate purchases account and the stock on hand at the end of each period valued. The total cost of goods sold can then be ascertained as demonstrated in the following example.

Example 3.4

A business wishes to ascertain the cost of goods sold during a period, but has not recorded the cost associated with each individual sales transaction.

However, the following information has been recorded:

Opening stock value	£3,000
Purchases in the year	£87,000
Closing stock value	£6,000

Think for a moment about how the cost of goods sold can be determined from this information before looking at the calculation below:

COST OF GOODS SOLD CALCULATION

	£
Opening stock	3,000
Add purchases	87,000
Goods available	90,000
Less closing stock	(6,000)
Cost of goods sold	84,000

The business started the year with goods worth £3,000 and purchased an additional £87,000 worth during the year. It therefore had goods available to sell with a value of £90,000. At the end of the year, it had only £6,000 worth left in stock, therefore the other £84,000 worth of items must have been sold during the year.

The Debtors (Sales) Ledger

In earlier examples an account called 'Debtors' was used to record:

(a) Amounts owed by customers in respect of goods sold on credit.

(b) Payments received in respect of those debts.

The balance on this account at any time represents the total amount outstanding from customers. However, to help ensure that all outstanding amounts are collected it is also important to know the amounts due from each customer and the date on which they become due.

The account would therefore be sub-divided into separate records for each customer. The document containing these records is known as the debtors (or sales) ledger, an extract from which might appear as follows:

DEBTORS LEDGER

Customer Name:	Craig Ltd.
Ref. No.:	C 14
Address:	85, St. John's Drive Preston,Lancs.
Telephone:	264586

Invoice No.	Dated	£	Due Date
153	3.10.X6	650.00	30.11.X6
194	15.10.X6	325.00	30.11.X6
216	19.10.X6	450.00	30.11.X6
245	25.10.X6	720.00	30.11.X6
267	4.11.X6	425.00	31.12.X6
312	12.11.X6	800.00	31.12.X6
TOTAL DUE		3,370.00	

Aged Analysis
Due – Within 30 Days £2,145.00
 – Within 60 Days £1,225.00

Figure 3.1 Debtors Ledger

As well as the amount due from each customer, the due dates and invoice references are included. This detail is necessary to help ensure that outstanding amounts are collected when due. The 'Aged Analysis' gives an indication of the amounts due in different time periods and can help in cash planning by forecasting anticipated receipts at various future points in time.

Entries to the Debtors Ledger

The double entry required to record a credit sale is:

(a) Increase the customer's account balance in the debtors ledger (an asset).

(b) Increase the sales account, therefore increasing profit (a liability).

In many businesses the volume of individual sales transactions would require a huge number of bookkeeping entries. Consequently a 'batching' system is often used in which the sales invoices issued during a period of time are 'batched' and processed together rather than individually. The total value of the invoices is entered to the sales account and the double entry completed by adjusting individual customer records within the debtors ledger as shown below:

SALES INVOICE BATCH NO. 385

Debtors Ledger (Seven Entries)	£	Sales Account (One Entry)	£
Bannon Ltd.	1,400	Sales 12th Nov.	12,400
Craig Ltd.	800		
Cockburn Ltd.	3,100		
Dowdall Ltd.	2,000		
Oxley Ltd.	2,400		
Webster Ltd.	1,700		
Winstanley Ltd.	1,000		
Total	12,400		

Using one entry to record a number of transactions in this way will reduce the time spent in processing sales invoices.

The Creditors (Purchase) Ledger

Amounts due to trade creditors can be maintained in a similar manner in a creditors ledger containing due dates, invoice references etc. in respect of each supplier. Entries may be posted to the ledger in the same manner as outlined for sales, by batching purchase invoices.

The Cash Book

The cash book is used to record any transactions affecting the bank account. A separate 'petty cash book' may be used to record cash transactions.

The General (Nominal) Ledger

All remaining accounts for assets, capital, expenses etc. are maintained in the general (or 'nominal') ledger from which information may be extracted on the value of assets and liabilities at any point in time, sales income for a period and expenditure incurred on any particular type of cost.

Figure 3.2 illustrates the use of various ledgers in a typical accounting system.

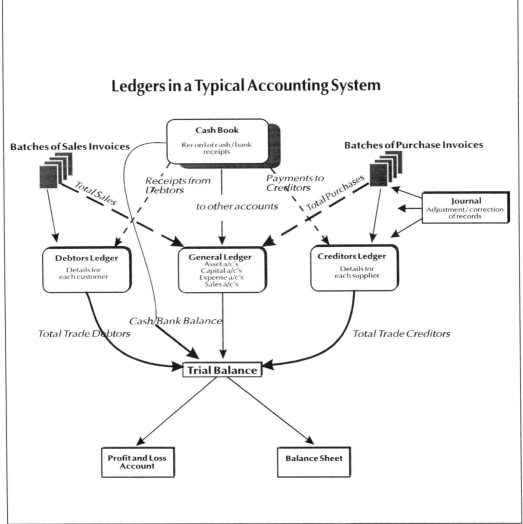

Figure 3.2 Ledgers in a Typical Accounting System

Journals

In many cases an entry in the accounting records is evidenced by a source document such as a purchase invoice, sales invoice or payroll documentation. However, there will be no such document in respect of entries for the correction of errors or period end adjustments needed for the compilation of accounting statements. In these circumstances a journal is used as the source document containing details of the entry. A typical example, correcting an entry made to a van account rather than stock is shown in Figure 3.3.

JOURNAL		
Reference No.: X6/43		
Date: 27.1.X6		
	ASSETS	LIABILITIES
	£	£
Stock account	3,500	
Van account	-3,500	
Narrative		
Correction of purchase transaction posted to van account in error.		

Figure 3.3 An Example of a Journal

Interpretation of the Accounts

As we shall see in later chapters accounting records can be used to prepare statements giving a view of the performance and financial position of a business. We will consider the interpretation of such information in some detail in Chapter 9. However, even at this relatively early stage in our studies it is possible to draw conclusions about the following aspects of Judith's business from the information we now have:

The Financial Position

The balance on each account in Judith's business at the end of week two in Example 3.3 can tell us something about the financial position of the business at that point in time:

Assets

The bank balance stood at £9,150, the business had a van worth £1,500 and stocks of computer equipment valued at £4,300. In addition it was owed £4,500 in respect of goods sold to customers (i.e. Chester Limited).

Liabilities

The building society was owed £2,000 and there were debts of £8,800 outstanding to suppliers (£1,500 to Middlemass Limited and £7,300 to Kingsmere Limited). In terms of the owner's funds, the capital invested amounted to £4,000 and the business had made profits of £4,650.

Profitability

The profit column indicates that the profit for the two week period was £4,650. If we look at the figures for the two weeks in Examples 3.2 and 3.3 more closely we can see that this was earned as follows:

	£	
Sales Income	13,800	*(500 + 2,500 + 6,300 + 4,500)*
Less the original cost of the goods sold	–8,500	*(300 + 1,500 + 4,100 + 2,600)*
Gross Profit	5,300	
Less Expenses – Wages	– 450	*(200 + 250)*
– Rent	– 200	*(100 + 100)*
Net Profit	4,650	

The profit arising from buying and selling goods (i.e. the gross profit) was £5,300 and after meeting the running expenses a net profit of £4,650 remained.

This is a simplified version of an important accounting statement known as the Profit and Loss Account which will be examined in detail in Chapter 4.

The Traditional Method of Recording

The tabular approach to recording transactions has been used to this point to help readers to understand:

(a) The operation of the accounting equation.

(b) The effect of business activities on the financial position of the business.

This should provide a good understanding of bookkeeping principles which will be useful in later chapters in which techniques for the preparation and interpretation of accounting statements are considered.

However, for readers who wish to acquaint themselves with accounting terminology and methods in more detail, the next section examines the methods traditionally used by accountants in bookkeeping systems.

We will begin by taking another look at the accounting equation.

$$ASSETS = LIABILITIES + CAPITAL + PROFIT$$

As we have seen, profits are calculated by subtracting various expenses from income. The equation can therefore be expressed in the following terms:

$$ASSETS = LIABILITIES + CAPITAL + (INCOME - EXPENSES)$$

or, by re-arranging the equation,

$$ASSETS + EXPENSES = LIABILITIES + CAPITAL + INCOME$$

Thus the value of all the asset and expense items should equal that of the liability, capital and income items.

Accounting entries which increase the value of assets or expenses are known as 'debit' entries and those increasing liabilities, capital or income are called 'credit' entries.

$$ASSETS + EXPENSES = LIABILITIES + CAPITAL + INCOME$$

$$DEBIT \qquad = \qquad CREDIT$$

Decreasing the value of an item is achieved using the opposite type of entry as summarised below:

	Assets/Expenses	Liabilities/Capital/Income
To Increase	DEBIT	CREDIT
To Decrease	CREDIT	DEBIT

Following the double entry principle, every transaction must be recorded with both a debit and credit entry of equal value.

This principle can be illustrated using transaction no. 3 from Example 3.1, the purchase of a van for £1,500.

The debit and credit entries would be recorded as follows:

- Increase an asset (the van account)   *Debit £1,500*
- Decrease another asset (bank)   *Credit £1,500*

The debit represents the item on which money has been spent (a van in this case) and the credit indicates what has been given up by the business (i.e. £1,500 from the bank account).

Had the van been bought on credit, the transaction would have been recorded as follows:

• Increase an asset (the van account)	*Debit £1,500*
• Increase a liability (creditors)	*Credit £1,500*

In each case there has been a corresponding debit and credit entry maintaining the balance of the accounting equation.

The traditional way to record the debit and credit entries is in 'T' accounts as shown below:

Debit				VAN ACCOUNT				Credit
Date	**Ref.**		**£**					
2.1.X6	3	Bank A/C	1,500					

Debit				BANK ACCOUNT				Credit
				Date	**Ref.**			**£**
				2.1.X6	3	Van A/C		1,500

Notes

- The debits are shown on the left side of the account and credits on the right. There is no logical reason for this, it is merely the customary method of presentation.

- Each account shows the date of each transaction and a unique reference number. Further details relating to the transaction (E.g. the actual invoice document) are usually filed under this reference to permit detailed investigation of the entry should this be required.

- The account contains a cross reference showing the account in which the other half of the double entry has been made.

Look again at Examples 3.1 and 3.2 and determine the accounts in which debit and credit entries would be recorded in respect of each of the nine transactions in week one. (Assume that a purchases account is used rather than a continuous stock account.) Compare your conclusions with the solution given below.

	Amount £	Debit	Credit
1.	4,000	Bank	Capital
2.	2,000	Bank	Building Society
3.	1,500	Van	Bank
4.	2,000	Purchases	Bank
5	3,500	Purchases	Creditors
6.	500	Bank	Sales
7.	2,500	Debtors	Sales
8.	200	Wages	Bank
9.	100	Rent	Bank

The 'T' account for the bank after having recorded all nine transactions is shown below:

Debit				BANK ACCOUNT			Credit
Date	Ref.		£	Date	Ref.		£
1.1.X6	1	Capital A/c	4,000	2.1.X6	3	Van A/c	1,500
1.1.X6	2	Building Society	2,000	2.1.X6	4	Purchases A/c	2,000
3.1.X6	6	Sales A/c	500	5.1.X6	8	Wages A/c	200
				6.1.X6	9	Rent A/c	100
Total Debits			6,500	Total Credits			3,800

The total debits entered (or 'posted') to the account exceed the credits by £2,700, hence the balance on the account at the end of the week is £2,700 debit.

As we saw earlier, assets are increased by debit entries therefore a debit balance represents a positive bank balance (a credit balance would indicate a liability meaning that Judith was overdrawn at the bank).

You may find this a little confusing when on looking at a bank statement you see that an account with a positive balance is referred to as being in credit. This is because the bank is providing information from their records and a positive balance is a liability (i.e. a credit balance) from their point of view as they owe the relevant sum to the account holder.

The closing balance on the bank account at the end of one accounting period is carried forward to become the opening balance in the following period. Assuming for the purpose of illustration that the accounting period for Judith's business is one week (it will usually be longer in practice) the £2,700 closing balance on the bank account will be carried forward to week two as shown below:

Debit				BANK ACCOUNT			Credit
Date	**Ref.**		**£**	**Date**	**Ref.**		**£**
1.1.X6	1	Capital A/c	4,000	2.1.X6	3	Van A/c	1,500
1.1.X6	2	Building Society	2,000	2.1.X6	4	Purchases A/c	2,000
3.1.X6	6	Sales A/c	500	5.1.X6	8	Wages A/c	200
				6.1.X6	9	Rent A/c	100
				7.1.X6		Balance carried forward	2,700
			6,500				6,500
8.1.X6 Balance brought forward			2,700				

The other 'T' accounts would appear as follows at the end of the first week:

Debit			CAPITAL ACCOUNT			Credit
Date	**Ref.**		**£**	**Date**	**Ref.**		**£**
				1.1.X6	1	Bank A/c	4,000
7.1.X6		Balance c/f	4,000				
			4,000				4,000
				8.1.X6		Balance b/f	4,000

Debit			LOAN A/C (B. Society)			Credit
Date	**Ref.**		**£**	**Date**	**Ref.**		**£**
				1.1.X6	2	Bank A/c	2,000
7.1.X6		Balance c/f	2,000				
			2,000				2,000
				8.1.X6		Balance b/f	2,000

Debit				VAN A/C			Credit
Date	**Ref.**		**£**	**Date**	**Ref.**		**£**
2.1.X6	3	Bank A/c	1,500				
				7.1.X6		Balance c/f	1,500
			1,500				1,500
8.1.X6		Balance b/f	1,500				

Debit				PURCHASES A/C			Credit
Date	**Ref.**		**£**	**Date**	**Ref.**		**£**
2.1.X6	4	Bank A/c	2,000				
2.1.X6	5	Creditors A/c	3,500				
		Closing balance*	5,500				

Debit				CREDITORS A/C			Credit
Date	**Ref.**		**£**	**Date**	**Ref.**		**£**
				2.1.X6	5	Purchases A/c	3,500
7.1.X6		Balance c/f	3,500				
			3,500				3,500
				8.1.X6		Balance b/f	3,500

Debit				DEBTORS A/C			Credit
Date	**Ref.**		**£**	**Date**	**Ref.**		**£**
4.1.X6	7	Sales A/c	2,500				
				7.1.X6		Balance c/f	2,500
			2,500				2,500
8.1.X6		Balance b/f	2,500				

Debit				SALES A/C			Credit
Date	**Ref.**		**£**	**Date**	**Ref.**		**£**
				3.1.X6	6	Bank A/c	500
				4.1.X6	7	Debtors A/c	2,500
						Closing Balance*	3,000

Debit				WAGES A/C			Credit
Date	**Ref.**		**£**	**Date**	**Ref.**		**£**
3.1.X6	8	Bank A/c	200				
		Closing balance*	200				

Debit				RENT A/C			Credit
Date	**Ref.**		**£**	**Date**	**Ref.**		**£**
3.1.X6	9	Bank A/c	100				
		Closing balance*	100				

N.B. Closing balances on income and expenditure accounts are used to calculate the profit for the period and are cleared from each account at the end of each accounting period rather than carried forward to the following period (this procedure will be examined more closely in Chapter 4).

The balances at the end of the period can be extracted from each account and a trial balance compiled as follows:

JUDITH'S COMPUTER SUPPLIES
TRIAL BALANCE AS AT 7.1.X6

	Debit £	Credit £
ASSETS		
Bank	2,700	
Motor Vehicles (Van)	1,500	
Debtors	2,500	
LIABILITIES		
Capital		4,000
Loan		2,000
Creditors		3,500
INCOME		
Sales		3,000
EXPENDITURE		
Purchases	5,500	
Wages	200	
Rent	100	
	12,500	12,500

The trial balance can now be used to prepare accounting statements for the period. We will examine this process in detail in Chapter 5.

Summary

- A business owes its owner(s) the sum originally invested and any profits subsequently generated.

- The owner's interest is therefore recorded as a liability in the accounts of the business.

- The assets of the business ultimately belong to its owner(s), therefore

    ASSETS = LIABILITIES.

- External parties such as lenders may also have a claim on assets. Therefore, distinguishing between claims by external parties and the owners, the accounting equation states that:

    ASSETS = LIABILITIES + CAPITAL + PROFIT

- Transactions must be recorded with a two-fold entry in order to maintain the balance of this equation. This recording system is known as double entry bookkeeping.

- At the end of a period a list of balances can be obtained from individual accounts to produce a trial balance.

- A trial balance which does not conform with the accounting equation indicates an error in the recording process.

- Individual accounts are maintained in ledgers and fall into one of the following categories:

    Assets
    Liabilities (including owner's funds)
    Income
    Expenditure

- Details of amounts due from credit customers are held in a debtors (sales) ledger.

- The creditors (purchase) ledger contains details of amounts owed to credit suppliers.

- Cash and bank transactions are recorded in a cash book.

- Journals are used to make adjustments to accounts such as the correction of errors.

- Accountants traditionally record each transaction with debit and credit entries of equal value.

- Debit balances indicate assets or expenses whilst credit balances indicate liabilities or income.

- A trial balance is used for the compilation of accounting statements.

Questions   (See Appendix C for Answers)

3.1

If profits are good and liabilities are bad, why are they on the same side of the balance sheet?

(ACCA)

3.2

Arnold started a business selling books to local schools. The following transactions took place during the first month:

March 1   Deposited £10,000 of his savings in a business bank account.

2   Withdrew a cash float of £400.

3   Purchased a delivery van for £6,000 paying by cheque.

4   Purchased stock for £6,000 on credit from Scholars Limited

7   Sold books which had originally cost £800 for £1,600. The customer paid by cheque.

12   Rented a warehouse for £250 per month and paid one month's rent by cheque.

13   Filled the van with petrol and paid £30 cash.

14   Purchased office stationery for £120 cash.

16   Sold goods which had cost £1,800 to Newtown High School for £2,800. 10% was paid by cheque immediately with the balance to follow within two months.

18   A local printer produced advertising leaflets for £200. These were paid for by cheque and distributed on the same day.

20   Paid £350 by cheque for repairs to the van.

24   Purchased stock for £2,000 and paid by cheque.

26   Sold books which had been purchased at a cost of £1,400 for £2,700. A cheque was received in full settlement.

28   Newtown High School returned unwanted books which they had previously purchased for £250. Arnold had originally bought the books from Scholars Limited for £200.

31   Arnold withdrew a monthly salary of £1,300 from the business bank account.

Required

Prepare a table showing how each transaction affects the financial position of the business.

3.3

Lynn has recently opened a shop selling gloves. Her transactions in the first week were as follows:

1. £5,000 was invested in the venture and paid into the business bank account.

2. Shop fittings were purchased for £1,200 and payment made by cheque.

3. 100 pairs of gloves were bought for £5 each and again a cheque was used for payment.

4. 50 pairs of gloves were sold for £10 each.

5. Wages of £150 were paid.

6. A further 30 pairs of gloves were bought for £5 per pair on credit terms from J. Bloggs.

7. J. Bloggs was paid £50 on account.

8. A department store bought 40 pairs of gloves on credit for £9 per pair.

9. Rent of £100 for the week was paid.

Required

(a) Prepare a table showing how these transactions would affect the financial position of the business.

(b) Record the transactions in 'T' accounts (using a purchases account to record stock acquired for re-sale).

(c) Prepare a trial balance as at the end of the week.

3.4

Dean Adams operates a small retail business and on preparing a trial balance as at 30th June 19X8 he found that it did not balance. Subsequent investigation uncovered the following bookkeeping errors:

(i) Cash sales of £2,300 were recorded as expenses. The correct entry was made in respect of the cash receipts.

(ii)   The purchase of a vehicle for £5,400 was recorded in the bank account as £4,500.

(iii)   A monthly standing order in the sum of £350 for electricity charges was paid in June but not recorded.

(iv)   A payment of £820 to a credit supplier was recorded as a receipt from a customer. The entry to the bank account was however correct.

(v)   A payment of £800 for rent had been recorded in the cash book but the double entry was not completed.

(vi)   Credit sales of £4,000 were recorded as cash sales.

Required

(a)   Assess the effect of each error on the trial balance.

(b)   Determine the amount by which the trial balance did not balance.

Questions Without Answers

3.5

Catherine started a business selling audio equipment on 1st October 19X0 and in the first month the following transactions occurred:

1 Oct.	Catherine invested £10,000 cash in the business.
2 Oct.	£9,800 was deposited in the business bank account.
4 Oct.	Purchased office furniture and fittings for £3,200 paying by cheque.
6 Oct.	Goods were bought for £2,800 and paid for by cheque.
9 Oct.	Sold goods for £240 cash.
10 Oct.	Sold goods on credit for £1,600.
11 Oct.	Purchased further goods on credit for £1,650.
12 Oct.	Sold goods on credit for £880.
13 Oct.	Paid rent for the month by cheque £500.
14 Oct.	Paid wages to staff by cheque £320.
15 Oct.	Paid sundry expenses £110 cash.
17 Oct.	Sold goods for £600 cash.

18 Oct.   Paid £500 into bank.

21 Oct.   Bought goods on credit for £1,700.

22 Oct.   Sold goods on credit for £740.

23 Oct.   Paid credit suppliers by cheque £1,920.

26 Oct.   Received cheques to the value of £1,250 from credit customers

27 Oct.   Bought a second hand delivery van for £2,500 and paid by cheque.

28 Oct.   Paid wages by cheque £380.

31 Oct.   Sold goods for £670, receiving a cheque in full payment.

Required

(a)   Enter the transactions for the month in Catherine's accounts.

(b)   Determine the balance on each account as at 31st October and prepare a trial balance as at that date.

3.6

The effect of successive transactions on the financial position of a business is shown in the following table:

Transaction		a	b	c	d	e	f	g
Assets	£	£	£	£	£	£	£	£
Motor vehicles	8,500	8,500	8,500	8,500	8,500	8,500	8,500	8,500
Fixtures and fittings	6,100	6,100	6,100	6,100	6,100	4,500	4,500	4,500
Stock	4,200	4,200	4,550	4,030	4,030	4,030	4,030	4,030
Trade debtors	3,600	3,100	3,100	3,940	3,940	3,940	3,940	3,940
Bank	4,900	5,400	5,400	5,400	3,400	3,400	2,600	4,100
Cash	620	620	620	620	620	2,220	2,220	720
	27,920	27,920	28,270	28,590	26,590	26,590	25,790	25,790
Liabilities								
Capital	8,000	8,000	8,000	8,000	8,000	8,000	8,000	8,000
Profit	8,620	8,620	8,620	8,940	8,940	8,940	8,940	8,940
Loan	5,000	5,000	5,000	5,000	3,000	3,000	3,000	3,000
Trade creditors	6,300	6,300	6,650	6,650	6,650	6,650	5,850	5,850
	27,920	27,920	28,270	28,590	26,590	26,590	25,790	25,790

Required

Explain the transaction which has occurred in each case.

3.7

Ashleigh opened a small fashion store on 1/1/X7 and at the end of the first year of trading asked an inexperienced bookkeeper to draw up a trial balance. The resulting figures are shown below:

Trial Balance as at 31.12.X7		
	Dr	Cr
	£	£
Capital		8,000
Bank overdraft	2,350	
Shop fittings	6,500	
General expenses	12,750	
Purchases	66,200	
Rent		6,800
Sales		105,300
Salaries	26,700	
Debtors		4,750
Creditors	7,000	
	121,500	124,850

The following bookkeeping errors have been detected in respect of the year's transactions:

(a)   Additional capital of £2,000 provided by Ashleigh during the year was entered in the sales account.

(b)   Shop fittings costing £4,500 were recorded as general expenses.

(c)   Credit sales of £1,500 had been posted to the debtors ledger but not to the sales account.

(d)   Bank interest of £150 was recorded in the bank account but not in the general expenses account.

(e)   Cash sales of £250 had been accounted for as credit sales.

(f)   A payment of £2,600 to a supplier was incorrectly recorded in the creditors ledger as £2,300.

Required

Re-draft the trial balance in the light of the errors identified, ensuring that items are correctly classified as debit or credit balances.

3.8

James opens a shop on 1st July 19X2, and during his first month of business, the following transactions occurred:

19X2

1 July	James contributes £20,000 in cash to the business out of his private bank account.
2 July	He opens a business bank account by transferring £18,000 of his cash in hand.
5 July	Some premises are rented, the rent being £500 per quarter payable in advance in cash.
6 July	James buys some second-hand shop equipment for £300 paying by cheque.
9 July	He purchases some goods for resale for £1,000 paying for them in cash.
10 July	Seddon supplies him with £2,000 of goods on credit.
20 July	James returns £200 of the goods to Seddon.
23 July	Cash sales for the week amount to £1,500.
26 July	James sells goods on credit for £1,000 to Frodsham.
28 July	Frodsham returns £500 of the goods to James.
31 July	James settles his account with Seddon by cheque, and is able to claim a cash discount of 10%.
31 July	Frodsham sends James a cheque for £450 in settlement of his account, any balance remaining on his account being treated as a cash discount.
31 July	During his initial trading, James has discovered that some of his shop equipment is not suitable, but he is fortunate in being able to dispose of it for £50 cash. There was no profit or loss on disposal.
31 July	He withdraws £150 in cash as part payment towards a holiday for his wife.

Required:

(a) Enter the above transactions in James' ledger accounts, balance off the accounts and bring down the balances as at 1st August 19X2.

(b) Extract a trial balance as at 31st July 19X2.

(AAT)

Chapter 4

An Introduction to Accounting Statements

Learning Objectives

After studying this chapter you should be able to:

- Explain the purposes of the balance sheet and profit and loss account.

- Describe the various categories of items shown in a balance sheet.

- Appreciate some of the limitations of information contained in a balance sheet.

- Explain the principles underlying periodic profit measurement.

- Distinguish between capital and revenue expenditure.

- Describe the accounting treatment of owners' drawings.

Introduction

Accounting records detailing business transactions contain useful information for those interested in the financial affairs of a business. These include owners, suppliers, customers and lenders who will be interested in factors such as:

- The total value of assets owned by the business.

- The claims on those assets by outside parties (and hence the balance which is due to the owners).

- The ability of the business to meet liabilities as they fall due.

- The profitability of the business.

To satisfy these requirements the detailed records, which may contain hundreds of separate accounts, must be classified and summarised in a meaningful way. This is achieved through the preparation of accounting statements and in this chapter we will look at two of the most important statements, the Balance Sheet and the Profit and Loss Account. The information content of each will be examined and typical formats illustrated.

This should provide a foundation for the following chapter, which considers in some detail, the preparation of these statements from a trial balance.

Accounting Periods

Although financial statements can be prepared from accounting records at any time, it is usual to do so at pre-determined intervals. The date at which they are compiled is called the accounting date and the time elapsing between each date, the accounting period.

Many organisations are required to prepare accounting information on an annual basis. Companies for example, are legally required to publish information annually under the provisions of the Companies Act 1985/89 and many other businesses must do so for tax purposes. Consequently an accounting period of one year is very common. The accounting date is self determined and 31st. December or 31st. March (coinciding with the end of the tax year) are popular choices.

As well as external purposes, such as compliance with the requirements of the Companies Act or the Inland Revenue, organisations will also require accounting information for internal purposes such as planning, control and decision making. It is therefore common practice to also establish shorter accounting periods, perhaps monthly or weekly, for the production of internal management information. The nature of this internal information will be examined in Part 3 of the book, which covers management accounting.

The Balance Sheet

The balance sheet provides a view of the financial position of a business at a given point in time. It has been described as a 'snapshot', presenting a picture of the business as at the accounting date.

The statement shows:

(a)   *What the business owns* – its assets.

(b)   *What it owes* – its liabilities.

An example is given in Figure 4.1.

BERNIAN FASHIONS

BALANCE SHEET AS AT 31.12.X6

ASSETS		£
FIXED ASSETS		
Shop fittings		10,000
Vehicles		7,000
		17,000
CURRENT ASSETS		
Stock	4,500	
Debtors	1,500	
Cash/bank	3,000	9,000
TOTAL ASSETS		**26,000**
LIABILITIES		
OWNER'S FUNDS		
Capital		5,000
Retained profits		10,000
		15,000
LONG TERM LIABILITIES		
Building society		7,000
CURRENT LIABILITIES		
Trade creditors		4,000
TOTAL LIABILITIES		**26,000**

Figure 4.1 The Balance Sheet

This information may be used to answer questions such as:

What assets does the business own?

We can see in Figure 4.1 that the business has various assets which have been collectively valued at £26,000. These have been classified and listed separately and we will consider each type later in this chapter.

Who is entitled to those assets?

The business has debts outstanding to the building society and trade creditors who are entitled to £11,000 worth of the assets. The remaining £15,000 is therefore attributable to the owner.

This has been funded from two sources:

(a)   An initial capital investment of £5,000.

(b)   Profits of £10,000, which could have been withdrawn by the owner, were instead left in the business and therefore effectively reinvested.

Can the business meet liabilities as they fall due?

Assessing the ability of the business to meet debts as they become due requires information on a number of factors. As liabilities represent claims on the assets of the business, we could consider its ability to meet external liabilities (i.e. the building society and trade creditors) from the assets on hand. The balance sheet shows that it can do so comfortably with assets valued at £26,000 and liabilities of only £11,000.

However, not all assets can be used to settle liabilities. Ultimately cash will be required and an important consideration is therefore the ease with which assets can be converted into cash. This is known as liquidity and the balance sheet, in which assets are classified and valued, can help in its assessment. The balance sheet in figure 4.1 shows that of the total asset value of £26,000, shop fittings and vehicles represent £17,000. These are longer term assets which are unlikely to be converted into cash in the near future. The value of the more liquid assets is of greater relevance and in this case these are stock, cash and debtors which with a collective value of £9,000 are insufficient to meet total liabilities. However although long term liabilities such as loans, must be settled at some stage, the business has some time to generate cash for this purpose and it is the short term debts for which cash is required most urgently. The balance sheet, in which long and short term liabilities are separated, shows that of the £11,000 outstanding, only the £4,000 owed to trade creditors is due for repayment in the short term and this can be more than covered by liquid assets valued at £9,000.

The assessment of liquidity will be addressed more fully in Chapter 9 when we look at the interpretation of accounting statements in some detail. At this stage however, you should at least be aware of some of the potential uses of the information contained in the balance sheet.

The Balance Sheet Format

Various formats may be used when preparing balance sheets and a more popular method, using the information from Figure 4.1, is shown below:

BERNIAN FASHIONS

BALANCE SHEET AS AT 31.12.X6

		£
FIXED ASSETS		
Shop fittings		10,000
Vehicles		7,000
		17,000
CURRENT ASSETS		
Stock	4,500	
Debtors	1,500	
Cash/bank	3,000	
TOTAL ASSETS	9,000	
LESS CURRENT LIABILITIES		
Creditors	(4,000)	
NET CURRENT ASSETS (*i.e. Current assets – current liabilities*)		5,000
LESS LONG TERM LIABILITIES		
Building society		(7,000)
NET ASSETS		**15,000**
Financed by,		
OWNER'S FUNDS		
Capital		5,000
Retained profit		10,000
		15,000

Figure 4.2 The Balance Sheet Format

In the first section of the statement, liabilities are subtracted from the assets to show assets valued at £15,000 attributable to the owner of the business. The second section shows how these assets have been funded.

We will now consider each item in the statement in turn:

Fixed Assets

Fixed assets are long term assets, from which benefit is expected for a number of accounting periods. In Figure 4.2 these assets comprise shop fittings and vehicles, both of which we would expect to be used for a number of years. Other possible examples include land, buildings, office equipment and production machinery.

Although their revaluation to reflect changing prices over time is permitted, they are generally valued in accordance with the historical cost concept. That is to say on the basis of their original cost, less an amount representing depreciation in value over time.

Intangible Fixed Assets

As well as "tangible" assets such as fittings and vehicles a business may also have "intangible" fixed assets (i.e. assets with no physical form). An example is purchased goodwill where a business is bought from its owner for an amount exceeding the value of its net assets. The excess payment may be in recognition of factors such as the reputation of the business or its good relationships with customers and suppliers, each of which may produce future benefits. The valuation of goodwill and its accounting treatment will be dealt with in the next chapter.

Current Assets

These are short term assets arising in the course of everyday activities which are expected to be converted into cash relatively quickly as illustrated in Figure 4.3:

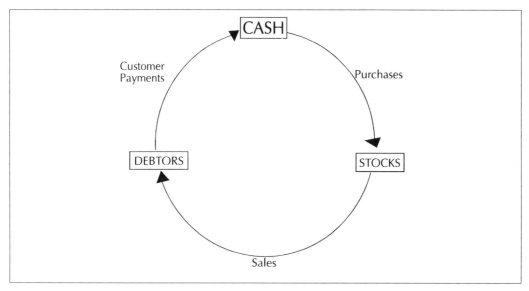

Figure 4.3 The Cash Cycle

The cash cycle commences when cash is released to pay for goods purchased for resale. Unless bought to satisfy a specific customer order, the goods may be held in stock for some time awaiting sale. When the sale occurs, there may still be no cash receipt. If credit terms are offered to customers, there will be a further delay until the debt is settled. In the meantime, the outstanding amount will be recorded as a debtor.

Thus stocks and debtors are short term assets reflecting intermediate steps in the conversion of cash outflows into cash returns from customers. As well as fixed assets, most businesses must invest in these current assets in order to function effectively on a day to day basis.

Current Liabilities

Current liabilities are short term debts due for repayment within one year. They represent finance provided by parties such as banks and suppliers offering credit, which will help to fund the investment in current assets.

In Figure 4.2, the balance sheet shows an investment of £9,000 in current assets. However suppliers have provided credit of £4,000, leaving the balance of £5,000 to be funded by the business. This figure is referred to as 'net current assets' or 'working capital'.

Long Term Liabilities

As we saw earlier, it will be useful to provide some indication of the settlement dates for liabilities. Those which are not due for repayment in the short term (and for which cash is consequently not required in the near future) are therefore listed separately under the heading Long Term Liabilities. Long term in this context usually means due after more than one year.

The Owner's Funds

The funds provided by the owner of the business have arisen from two sources :

- The £5,000 *capital originally invested.*

- Retained *profit of £10,000.*
  The owner is entitled to any profits generated and may either withdraw them for personal use or leave them in the business. The amount left in the business (known as retained profit) effectively represents additional investment by the owner which may be necessary to ensure there is sufficient cash to meet liabilities or for the acquisition of new assets. Often the profit earned will be partially withdrawn, to give the owner at least some cash return and the remainder retained. The £10,000 reported in this case, represents profit which has been retained over the life of the business.

Presentation

The items in the balance sheet are usually shown in order of permanence. Thus for example in Figure 4.2, fixed assets, which may be used for a number of years, precede current assets which will be held for a shorter period of time.

Similarly within the fixed assets section, shop fittings, which we would expect to be used over a longer period than vehicles, are listed first. Within the current assets stocks, which require a sale and the collection of the subsequent debt, may take some time to convert to cash and are therefore listed first. They are followed by debtors, which are only one step away from liquidation and finally the cash/bank balance.

Limitations of Balance Sheets

Although the balance sheet is an important accounting statement containing useful information on the financial position of an organisation, it does have a number of limitations which should be appreciated by those using the information. These include:

1. The Valuation of Fixed Assets

Fixed assets are valued on the basis of their original cost, less an amount representing their depreciation in value over time. The methods generally used to calculate this depreciation (which we will examine in detail in the next chapter) do not take account of changes in market prices. Consequently, the resulting valuation will represent neither the cost of replacement with similar assets nor the current market value of the asset and the value of such information is therefore questionable.

2. The Money Measurement Concept

In Chapter 2 we saw that only those items which can be measured in monetary terms, are reported in accounting statements. However many features of a business cannot be measured in this way. For example the long term success of any undertaking will depend to a large extent, on the skills of those working in it and their commitment to its aims. Accounting statements do not reflect these important factors and will therefore give an incomplete picture of the state of a business.

3. Timeliness

The balance sheet presents a view of the financial position of an organisation at a very precise point in time. As the statement will take some time to prepare, the information produced will be out of date as soon as it is published. A balance sheet representing the financial position of a business as at the end of December, may not be published until perhaps the end of February. Events occurring during the two months elapsing in the meantime, may have affected the financial position reported to such an extent as to make the statement of limited value.

The Profit and Loss Account

The profit and loss account provides a detailed analysis of the profit earned in an accounting period. Whereas the balance sheet looks at the business at a specific point in time, the profit and loss account analyses profits earned throughout a time period, as illustrated in Figure 4.4.

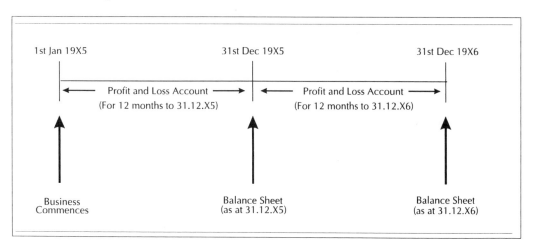

Figure 4.4 Comparison of Accounting Statements

The balance sheet therefore shows the cumulative effect of all activities throughout the life of the business whereas the profit and loss account analyses only the accounting period in question.

Unlike the balance sheet, the profit and loss account forms part of the double entry system. At the end of each period the balances on all income and expense accounts are cleared by transferring them to the profit and loss account in order that the profit for the period can be ascertained. Their opening balances in the following period will therefore be zero, allowing income and expenditure in each period to be separately recorded and analysed. This process is illustrated in Figure 4.5 which relates to Bernian Fashions:

	ACCOUNT TYPES				
	Assets	**Liabilities***	**P & L**	**Income**	**Expense**
Opening balances	17,000	(13,000)	(4,000)	0	0
Effect of activities in the period	9,000	(3,000)	_____	(70,000)	64,000
Closing balances	26,000	(16,000)	(4,000)	(70,000)	64,000
Transfers to P & L account					
– Income accounts			(70,000)	70,000	
– Expense accounts			64,000		(64,000)
Balances shown in balance sheet	26,000	(16,000)	(10,000)	0	0

* i.e. Capital, building society and creditors.
NB. Credit figures are shown with brackets and debits without.

Figure 4.5 The Treatment of Period End Balances

The £70,000 income and £64,000 expenses transferred to the profit and loss account, result in a profit of £6,000 for the period which is analysed in some detail in the profit and loss account as illustrated in Figure 4.6.

This £6,000 is added to the £4,000 which has been transferred in previous periods and the new running total of £10,000 is shown as part of the owner's funds in the balance sheet (as illustrated previously in Figure 4.2).

The Profit and Loss Account Format

The format of the profit and loss account is illustrated in Figure 4.6.

BERNIAN FASHIONS

PROFIT AND LOSS ACCOUNT FOR THE YEAR ENDED 31.12.X6

		£
SALES		70,000
LESS COST OF GOOD SOLD		(47,000)
GROSS PROFIT		23,000
LESS EXPENSES		
Wages	11,000	
Rent	2,000	
Power/heating	1,500	
Maintenance	2,500	(17,000)
NET PROFIT		6,000

Figure 4.6 The Profit and Loss Account

Profit Measurement

In Chapter 2 when examining the matching principle, we saw that the profit earned in a period is ascertained by comparing the sales revenue earned with the costs incurred in generating that income. Consequently in order to measure profit periodically for reporting purposes, revenue and costs must be related to each separate accounting period and we will now consider this process.

Sales Revenue

The revenue reported in the profit and loss account for a period represents the value of goods or services supplied to customers during the period. Note that it is the value of sales which is reported and not cash receipts. Thus goods sold on credit in December 19X6, would be included in the sales figure for 19X6 even if the cash was not received until January 19X7.

Costs

Costs reported in the profit and loss account fall into one of two categories.

- The cost of the goods sold.

- Expenses incurred by the business.

1. The Cost of Goods Sold

The profit and loss account 'matches' the sales for the period with the original cost of those goods, to report the gross profit for the period. This section of the statement is known as the trading account. The matching principle requires that only 'expired' costs are reported in each period. That is to say the benefit arising from the expenditure must have been entirely consumed in the period. The cost of goods sold, having earned sales income, complies with this rule and is therefore reported in the 19X6 profit and loss account.

The goods which are unsold at the end of the year have not yet produced any benefit and their cost is therefore excluded from the profit calculation. They are assets (i.e. they have a future value) and their cost is included in the 'stocks' figure reported in the balance sheet. When they are eventually sold their cost will be reported in the profit and loss account along with the sales proceeds.

Calculating the Cost of Goods Sold

As we saw in the previous chapter the cost of goods sold during a period can be determined using purchases and stock figures which are incorporated in the trading account as shown below.

TRADING ACCOUNT - FOR THE YEAR ENDED 31.12.X6

		£
Sales		70,000
Less Cost of Goods Sold		
Opening stock	7,000	
Purchases	44,500	
	51,500	
Less closing stock	(4,500)	47,000
GROSS PROFIT		23,000

Valuing Stocks

The calculation used in the trading account to determine the cost of goods sold requires the valuation of the opening and closing stocks of finished goods. This value should reflect the lower of their:

- Cost   or,
- Net realisable value

In most cases cost will be the appropriate figure but if for example a number of items held in stock had deteriorated to an extent where they could not be sold, then their scrap value should be used instead.

2. *Expenses*

The expenses included in the profit and loss account should reflect those costs incurred in earning the sales revenue for the period and may include costs such as rent, heating charges, telephone calls and insurance.

Note that it is costs *incurred* which are reported and not payments made. If for example rent is paid in arrears, the cost relating to 19X6 may be not be paid until 19X7. However this cost should be included in 19X6 as the benefit arose in that year. This procedure is known as accruing for the cost and will be examined in more detail in Chapter 5.

Capital and Revenue Expenditure

When measuring profits earned in separate accounting periods it is important to distinguish between two different types of expenditure.

Capital Expenditure

Capital expenditure is incurred in the acquisition of fixed assets such as buildings, vehicles, equipment etc. which are expected to produce benefits over a number of accounting periods. These costs should be spread over those periods in which the assets are used to reflect the benefit derived in each period.

Accounting for fixed assets will also be examined in detail in Chapter 5 when we look at the preparation of accounting statements.

Revenue Expenditure

Revenue expenditure is incurred on the other items and services necessary for the day to day operation of the business. Examples include the cost of the goods sold in a period and the expenses incurred in the period (rent, electricity, insurance etc.). As the benefit from such expenditure is consumed in a single accounting period, the resulting costs are attributed to that period when measuring profit.

The Appropriation of Profit

Cash withdrawals from a business for the owner's personal use are known as 'drawings'. These are not classed as costs but rather a distribution of profit and should therefore be excluded from the expenses reported in the profit and loss account. Their inclusion would result in an over statement of the true costs of operating the business and misleading information on its profitability.

Drawings should be shown as a deduction from the retained profit shown in the balance sheet as illustrated in Figure 4.7.

BERNIAN FASHIONS

BALANCE SHEET AS AT 31.12.X6 (EXTRACT)

OWNERS FUNDS		£
Capital		5,000
Retained profit as at 1.1.X6	4,000	
Net profit for 19X6	6,000	
	10,000	
Less drawings	(1,000)	9,000
		14,000

Figure 4.7 The Appropriation of Profit

In this case, the owner has withdrawn £1,000 of the profit earned during the year for personal use. The remaining £5,000 has been retained by the business and when added to the £4,000 retained in previous years gives a total of £9,000.

An exception to this rule would arise where the cash withdrawn was a salary for work performed in the business. It could be argued in these circumstances that this did represent a business expense and that the £1,000 should therefore be included in the wages figure shown under 'Expenses'.

Summary

- The most important accounting statements are the Balance Sheet and the Profit and Loss Account which are prepared at the end of each accounting period.

- Each period usually covers one year to satisfy external requirements although shorter periods are often used for internal information.

- A *Balance Sheet* gives a 'snapshot' of the financial position of an enterprise at a precise point in time by reporting the value of assets and liabilities.

  - *Fixed assets* are long term assets, which are expected to be used for more than one accounting period.

  - *Current assets* are required to carry out the day to day activities of the business and are expected to be converted to cash relatively quickly.

  - *Current liabilities* are short term debts due for repayment within one year.

  - *Long term liabilities* are due for repayment after more than one year.

  - The *'Owners' funds'* represent investment in the business by the owner. They may include retained profits as well as capital invested.

- A number of limitations should be appreciated by those using Balance Sheets. These include:

  - The valuation of fixed assets is usually based on their historical cost.

  - Only items which can be measured in monetary terms are shown.

  - The figures reflect the position at one precise point in time and will therefore quickly become outdated.

- A *Profit and Loss Account* compares the sales income for an accounting period with the costs incurred in generating that income.

- Income/costs are included in the profit calculation regardless of whether or not the relevant cash receipt/payment occurred in the period.

- Capital expenditure is incurred in respect of fixed assets from which benefits are expected in a number of accounting periods. The cost (known as depreciation) is therefore spread over those periods.

- Revenue expenditure produces benefits which are consumed during the period.

- The owner's drawings should be shown in the balance sheet as a subtraction from retained profit and not as an expense in the profit and loss account. Failure to do so would understate the true profitability of the business.

Questions   (See Appendix C for Answers)

4.1

How would the following items be classified in a balance sheet?

(a)   Amounts owed to suppliers.

(b)   Computers.

(c)   Sums invested by the owner of the business.

(d)   A bank overdraft.

(e)   Goods unsold at the end of a period.

(f)   Profits retained for investment in the business.

(g)   Amounts owed by customers.

(h)   A bank loan due for repayment in 5 years.

4.2

For each of the following state whether the item would be classified as capital or revenue expenditure:

(a)   Purchase of a vehicle.

(b)   Electricity charges for the year.

(c)   Rental of a photocopier.

(d)   Wages paid to staff.

(e)   Purchase of new premises.

(f)   The insurance bill for the year.

(g)   Purchase of production machinery.

(h)   Rental of office accommodation.

(i)   Purchase of office furniture.

(j)   Purchase of a calculator.

4.3

The trial balance of Ashleigh's Fashions at the end of the first year's trading is given below:

Trial Balance as at 31.12.X7

	Dr	Cr
	£	£
Capital		10,000
Bank overdraft		2,100
Shop fittings	11,000	
General expenses	8,400	
Purchases	66,200	
Rent	6,800	
Sales		104,800
Salaries	26,700	
Debtors	4,500	
Creditors		6,700
	123,600	123,600

The stock of goods in the store on 31st December was valued at £10,800.

Required

Prepare a Profit and Loss account for the year and a Balance Sheet as at 31st December 19X7 from the information given.

4.4

Samantha runs a sports shop and the financial position of the business on 30th June 19X8 was as follows:

	£
Motor vehicle	6,000
Cash held	1,450
Capital	7,500
Due from customers	2,100
Stock of goods for re-sale	9,400
Owing to suppliers	7,700
Bank balance	8,450
Shop fittings	10,600
Five year bank loan	4,000

A profit of £6,500 was earned during the year from which Samantha had withdrawn £2,200 for personal use. Retained profits as at 30/6/X7 amounted to £14,500.

Required

Prepare a Balance Sheet for Samantha as at 30th June 19X8.

4.5

(a) Explain the following terms as used by accountants:

(i)   asset

(ii) fixed asset

(iii) current asset

(iv) depreciation.

(b) Do you regard each of the following as an asset of a business for accounting purposes? Explain your answers.

(i)   a screwdriver bought in 19X7

(ii) a machine hired by the business

(iii) the good reputation of the business with its customers.

(c) The fixed assets in the balance sheet of a company have been summarised as follows:

		£m
Land at valuation		3
Buildings at cost		1
Plant and equipment – cost	2	
– depreciation	1.5	0.5
		4.5

Required

Explain the meaning of this £4.5m figure to one of the company's shareholders, and comment on its relevance from a shareholder's point of view.

(ACCA)

Questions Without Answers

4.6

You are required to calculate for each product and for the company as a whole:

(a)   the values of stock at 31st December 19X7, at cost

(b)   the amounts of gross profit, as they would appear in the company's trading account.

The company sell three products, A, B and C on which it earns gross profit percentages, calculated on normal selling prices, of 20, 25 and $33\frac{1}{3}$ respectively. The value of its stock at 1st January 19X7, valued at cost, was:

Product	£
A	24,000
B	36,000
C	12,000

During the year ended 31st December 19X7 the actual purchases and sales were:

Product	Purchases £	Sales £
A	146,000	172,500
B	124,000	159,400
C	48,000	74,600

However, certain items were sold during the year at a discount on the normal selling prices, and these discounts were reflected in the values of sales shown above. The items sold at a discount were:

	Sales	
Product	At normal prices	At actual prices
	£	£
A	10,000	7,500
B	3,000	2,400
C	1,000	600

These discounts were not provided for in the cost values of stock at 1st January 19X7 given above.

(CIMA)

4.7

Patrick runs a business selling pre-recorded videos and has prepared the following trial balance:

Trial Balance as at 31.12.X7

	Dr £	Cr £
Bank	9,120	
Fittings	9,160	
Vehicle	8,400	
Purchases	25,410	
Stock as at 1.1.X7	5,160	
Sales		58,230
Debtors	1,500	
General expenses	5,750	
Premises costs	6,120	
Creditors		2,280
Capital		7,500
Loan		6,000
Cash	860	
Interest payments	550	
Wages	14,200	
Retained profit as at 1.1.X7		12,220
	86,230	86,230

The stock of videos on hand at 31.12.X7 was valued at £5,400.

Required

Compile a profit and loss account for the year ended 31.12.X7 and a balance sheet as at that date.

4.8

Gill commenced business on the 1st April selling gardening equipment and accessories. She initially contributed £30,000 from her own private resources and borrowed £50,000 from the Midshire Bank plc.

The following initial payments were made:

	£
Purchase of business premises	40,000
Purchase of fixtures	10,000
Purchase of a delivery van	12,000

During April the following transactions were incurred:

	£
Purchased stock of gardening equipment and accessories on credit terms from:	
Growmore Ltd.	
T.R. Ellis and Sons	15,000
	17,000
Paid for advertising in the local press	1,000
Paid road tax and insurance in respect of the delivery van	500
Paid for petrol and oil	100
Sold goods on credit to:	
M. J. Kaye	4,000
Ivan Hoe	2,000
Sold goods for cash and banked the proceeds immediately	24,800
Paid miscellaneous expenses	1,000
Paid wages	3,500

On 30th April the unsold stock of gardening equipment and accessories was checked and valued at £10,000.

Required

  (a) Enter the above transactions in appropriate ledger accounts.

  (b) Prepare a trial balance from the information extracted from the ledger accounts.

  (c) Prepare a profit statement for the month of April.

  (d) Prepare a balance sheet as at 30th April.

Chapter 5

The Preparation of Accounting Statements

Learning Objectives

After studying this chapter you should be able to:

- Classify the items shown in a trial balance and determine the accounting statement in which each should appear.

- Explain and demonstrate the accounting treatment of:

    - Fixed assets

    - Payments in arrears

    - Payments in advance

    - Bad debts

- Prepare a profit and loss account and balance sheet from a trial balance and additional relevant information.

- Explain the subjectivity of accounting profit, giving appropriate examples.

Introduction

Having considered the purposes and examined the formats of balance sheets and profit and loss accounts in the previous chapter, we will now look at how they are prepared from accounting records.

The guiding principles studied in Chapter 2 will be reviewed and demonstrated and we will conclude by preparing accounting statements for a business from a trial balance and additional relevant information.

The preparation of accounting statements for a period may be undertaken in the following stages:

1.   Compile a trial balance.

2.   Classify each item within the trial balance.

3.   Make period end adjustments.

4.   Prepare the profit and loss account.

5.   Prepare the balance sheet.

Steps one to three will now be explained in some detail and four and five will be demonstrated using the comprehensive example at the end of the chapter.

Step 1 : Compiling the Trial Balance

The first step is to extract a trial balance from the accounting records. As we saw in Chapter 3, this is a list showing the balance on all the individual accounts at the end of the accounting period. Each item will be included in either the profit and loss account or the balance sheet and the next step is to determine which.

Step 2 : Classifying Items in the Trial Balance

The statement in which each trial balance item appears depends on its nature and is determined as follows:

Item Type	Statement
Assets	
Liabilities	BALANCE SHEET
Capital	
Income	
	PROFIT AND LOSS ACCOUNT
Expenses	

Look at the trial balance given in Example 5.1 and complete the first two columns, classifying each item in terms of the types shown above and determining whether each should appear in the profit and loss account (P&L) or the balance sheet (B/S).

Example 5.1

MORALEE SPORTS SUPPLIES

TRIAL BALANCE AS AT 31.12.X7

Item type	Statement		Debit £	Credit £
		Shop fittings	6,000	
		Sales		93,000
		Wages	12,150	
		Heating	1,400	
		Bank	12,100	
		Capital		4,000
		Telephone charges	1,500	
		Vehicles	9,000	
		Purchases	59,000	
		Retained profit (as at 31.12.X6)		15,500
		Trade creditors		10,700
		Electricity	1,100	
		Stock (as at 31.12.X6	10,000	
		Building society loan		2,000
		Trade debtors	6,200	
		Rent	5,600	
		Cash	1,150	
			125,200	125,200

The stock on hand at 31.12.X7 was valued at £6,000.

Solution

Item	Item Type	Statement
Shop fittings	Asset	B/S
Sales	Income	P&L
Wages	Expense	P&L
Heating	Expense	P&L
Bank	Asset	B/S
Capital	Capital	B/S
Telephone charges	Expense	P&L
Vehicles	Asset	B/S
Purchases	Expense*	P&L
Retained profit (as at 31.12.X6)	Capital	B/S
Trade creditors	Expense	P&L
Electricity	Expense	P&L
Trade creditors	Liability	B/S
Electricity	Expense	P&L
Stock (as at 31.12.X6)	Expense*	P&L
Building society loan	Liability	B/S
Trade debtors	Asset	B/S
Rent	Expense	P&L
Cash	Asset	B/S

These items, which are used to calculate the cost of goods sold, will be shown in the trading account.

NB. *If in doubt as to an item type, their listing as debit and credit balances should help. In Chapter 3 we said that:*
- Debit balances represent assets and expenses.
- Credit balances represent liabilities, capital and income.

As explained earlier, adjustments must be made to the figures in the trial balance before they are incorporated in the final accounting statements for the period. However, before looking at these adjustments in detail you should test your understanding of the principles covered to this point by using the trial balance items as they currently stand to prepare a Profit and Loss Account and Balance Sheet in the formats outlined in the previous chapter.

Check your results with the solutions given below.

MORALEE SPORTS SUPPLIES

PROFIT AND LOSS ACCOUNT FOR THE YEAR ENDED 31.12.X7

		£
Sales		93,000
Less Cost of Goods Sold		
Opening stock	10,000	
Add purchases	59,000	
	69,000	
Less closing stock	(6,000)	(63,000)
GROSS PROFIT		30,000
Less Expenses		
Wages	12,150	
Heating	1,400	
Telephone charges	1,500	
Electricity	1,100	
Rent	5,600	(21,750)
NET PROFIT		8,250

MORALEE SPORTS SUPPLIES

BALANCE SHEET AS AT 31.12.X7

		£
Fixed Assets		
Shop fittings	6,000	
Vehicles	9,000	15,000
Current Assets		
Stock	6,000	
Trade debtors	6,200	
Bank	12,100	
Cash	1,150	
	25,450	
Less: Current Liabilities		
Trade creditors	(10,700)	
Net Current Assets		14,750
Less: Long Term Liabilities		
Building society		(2,000)
Net Assets		**27,750**
Financed by:		
Capital		4,000
Retained Profit		
As at 31.12.X6	15,500	
Profit for the year	8,250	23,750
Owner's Funds		**27,750**

Step 3 : Period End Adjustments

At the end of each accounting period various adjustments will be required to ensure that statements are prepared in accordance with the accounting principles we examined in Chapter 2. As the accounting records have not yet been amended in respect of these adjustments each must be recorded with a double entry. As we shall see, the effect on the various accounts will therefore be twofold in each case.

We will now look in some detail at the period end (or 'post trial balance') adjustments required when accounting for:

- Depreciation of fixed assets.

- Accruals and prepayments.

- Bad and doubtful debts.

Depreciation of Fixed Assets

In the previous chapter, we saw that only expired costs should be included in the expenses for a period. This treatment is in accordance with the matching principle which requires that income be compared with the costs incurred in generating that income when calculating the profit earned in each period.

As capital expenditure on fixed assets is expected to produce benefits over a number of periods there will be an element of unexpired cost at the end of each period representing future benefits anticipated. Some attempt must therefore be made to determine the costs to be included in the current period and those to be withheld for inclusion in future periods.

The cost included in each period in respect of the benefit derived from the use of fixed assets, is called depreciation and the two main methods of determining this cost are:

- The straight line method.

- The reducing balance method.

The Straight Line Method

Using this method the total cost of using an asset over its useful life is estimated by comparing its original cost with any expected residual (re-sale) value at the end of its life. This net cost is then divided equally into each accounting period in which the asset is to be used.

This procedure is illustrated in the following example:

Example 5.2

A business purchases a computer for £24,000 on 1.1.X5 and expects to use it for four years, after which it will be obsolete and worthless.

For each of the next four years, calculate the depreciation cost to be included in the profit and loss account and the unexpired cost at the year end to be carried forward to later periods.

Solution

Net cost of asset   = £24,000

Expected useful life   = 4 years

Cost per year $= \dfrac{£24,000}{4\ years} = £6,000$

Year Ended	Depreciation Included in P&L Account £	Cumulative Depreciation £	Unexpired Cost £
31.12.X5	6,000	6,000	18,000
31.12.X6	6,000	12,000	12,000
31.12.X7	6,000	18,000	6,000
31.12.X8	6,000	24,000	Nil

In this case, as there is no expected residual value, the cost of using the computer for four years is £24,000. This is divided equally into the four years and £6,000 shown as a cost in each year. Another way of expressing this is to say that a depreciation rate of 25% per annum is being used (and hence after four years, 100% of the cost will have been included in the profit and loss account).

To include the entire £24,000 as a cost in the year of purchase would overstate the costs for that year. Benefits are expected in each of the next four years and each must carry its share of the cost to reflect the use of the asset to generate sales revenue in that year. Thus in the first year £6,000 depreciation is included in the expenses reported in the profit and loss account and the unexpired cost of £18,000 is shown as a fixed asset in the balance sheet.

This value is referred to as the net book value (NBV) of the asset and is usually shown as illustrated below:

BALANCE SHEET AS AT 31.12.X5 (£'s)

Fixed Assets	Cost	Accumulated Depreciation	NBV
	£	£	£
Computer Equipment	24,000	6,000	18,000

Before going any further, draft a similar extract showing how the computer equipment would be reported in the balance sheet as at 31.12.X6. Check your answer with the solution given below:

BALANCE SHEET AS AT 31.12.X6 (£'s)

Fixed Assets	Cost	Accumulated Depreciation	NBV
	£	£	£
Computer Equipment	24,000	12,000	12,000

At this stage £12,000 of the cost has been reported as depreciation (£6,000 in each of two profit and loss accounts) leaving £12,000 unexpired cost to be reported in future years.

By the end of the fourth year all £24,000 will have been included in reported costs and the value shown in the balance sheet will therefore be zero.

The Treatment of Residual Values

In the previous example it was assumed that the computer equipment was worthless at the end of its useful life. This will not always be the case and assets of no further use to a business may be sold even if only for scrap. Any such residual value will reduce the net cost of using the asset and must therefore be incorporated in the depreciation calculation. The following example illustrates this:

Example 5.3

The business referred to in Example 5.2 purchased a vehicle on 1.1.X6 for £18,000. It is expected to be used for three years after which time it is anticipated that the re-sale value will be £3,000.

Show the new depreciation costs to be reported in the profit and loss account (in respect of both the computer equipment and the vehicle) for the four years from 19X5 and the fixed asset section of the balance sheet as at 31.12.X7.

Solution

Vehicle Depreciation

Net cost of asset = £18,000 − £3,000 = £15,000

Expected useful life = 3 years

Annual depreciation = $\dfrac{£15,000}{3\ \text{years}}$ = £5,000

Profit & Loss Account

Year ended	Computer £	Vehicle £	Total Depreciation £
31.12.X5	6,000	0	6,000
31.12.X6	6,000	5,000	11,000
31.12.X7	6,000	5,000	11,000
31.12.X8	6,000	5,000	11,000

BALANCE SHEET AS AT 31.12.X7

Fixed Assets	Cost £	Accumulated Depreciation £	NBV £
Computer Equipment	24,000	18,000	6,000
Vehicles	18,000	10,000	8,000
	42,000	28,000	14,000

Hence the total value of fixed assets as at 31.12.X7 is reported as £14,000.

The Timing of Acquisition

For simplicity it has previously been assumed that assets are purchased at the start of a year. Of course in practice this will not necessarily be the case and assets will be acquired during the course of the year. In these circumstances the asset will not be used for the entire accounting period in the year of acquisition and in theory the depreciation charged should reflect this. Thus for an asset purchased midway through a year, the depreciation charged in that year would represent half of the annual amount.

Let us suppose that the vehicle referred to in Example 5.3 was bought not on 1st. January, but on 1st October 19X6. The depreciation charged in each year could be calculated as follows:

Year ended	Deprec'n. For Year £	Accumulated Deprec'n. £	NBV in £	Balance Sheet
31.12.X6	*1,250	1,250	16,750	
31.12.X7	5,000	6,250	11,750	
31.12.X8	5,000	11,250	6,750	
31.12.X9	†3,750	15,000	3,000 (i.e. re-sale value)	

> ** As the asset was used for only approximately three months, the depreciation charge is 3/12 of the annual amount of £5,000 (i.e. £1,250).*

> *† If the vehicle is to be replaced after three years as expected, it will cease to be used on 30th September 19X9. The depreciation charged in that year, representing approximately nine months usage, is therefore 9/12 of £5,000 (i.e. £3,750).*

Although this method can be used to determine depreciation charges by the month as illustrated above, or even by the day if required, it can be a time consuming exercise. Consequently a simplifying depreciation policy is often adopted regarding assets purchased or sold during the course of an accounting period. For instance a business may decide to charge no depreciation in the year of acquisition but a full year's cost in the year of disposal, thereby restricting calculations to full years only.

The Reducing Balance Method

The straight line method applies depreciation at a constant annual rate and therefore assumes that assets depreciate in value at an equal rate over their useful lives. However, the validity of this assumption is questionable for certain assets. For instance it could be argued that the value of the vehicle referred to above will probably diminish at a faster rate in its early years. In year one, removal from the showroom alone (at which point it becomes a second hand vehicle) will probably result in a relatively sharp fall in value. Thereafter, the annual rate of depreciation is likely to fall year by year. This pattern will also be evident for many other assets and the reducing balance method attempts to portray this.

This is done by calculating the depreciation charge for each period as a percentage of the *net book value* (rather than the net cost) of the asset. As this value falls throughout the life of the asset, the annual depreciation cost will diminish year by year. To illustrate this, let us suppose that the business referred to in Example 5.3 depreciated vehicles at a rate of 40% on the reducing balance. The depreciation charged in each year would then be calculated as follows:

		£
Original cost		18,000
Year 1 depreciation (£18,000 x 40%)		(7,200)
NBV at end of year 1		10,800
Year 2 depreciation (£10,800 x 40%)		(4,320)
NBV at end of year 2		6,480
Year 3 depreciation (£6,480 x 40%)		(2,592)
NBV at end of year 3		3,888

The depreciation charge has fallen in each year, reflecting an ever decreasing rate of reduction in value. However, using a rate of 40% the final net book value does not correspond with the residual value of £3,000. The exact percentage required to produce the anticipated residual value can be obtained using the following formula:

$$Depreciation\ rate\ =\ 1\ -\ \sqrt[Useful\ Life]{\frac{Residual\ value}{Cost\ of\ asset}}$$

Applying this in example 5.3:

$$Depreciation\ rate\quad =\ 1\ -\ \sqrt[3]{\frac{3,000}{18,000}}$$

$$=\ 1\ -\ \sqrt[3]{0.1666}$$

$$=\quad 0.4497$$

$$=\quad 45\%$$

Annual Calculations

	£
Original cost	18,000
Year 1 depreciation (£18,000 x 45%)	(8,100)
NBV at end of year 1	9,900
Year 2 depreciation (£9,900 x 45%)	(4,455)
NBV at end of year 2	5,445
Year 3 depreciation (£5,445 x 45%)	(2,450)
NBV at end of year 3	2,995

N.B. A final balance of exactly £3,000 was not obtained due to the rounding of the *depreciation rate to 45%. However, a close enough approximation has been obtained.*

We can now compare the results obtained from the two methods used:

Year	Depreciation (Straight Line) £	Depreciation (Reducing Balance) £
1	5,000	8,100
2	5,000	4,455
3	5,000	2,450
Total	15,000	15,005

Each method has charged the £15,000 net cost of using the vehicle for three years (again subject to a little rounding difference). However, the reducing balance method has charged more in the early years, reflecting a faster depreciation in value in those years.

Which Method Should Be Used?

The reducing balance method could be justified using the argument that the value of certain assets is likely to fall at a greater rate in their early years and that this should be reflected in financial reports. A counter argument is that if an asset provides equal benefit in a number of years then an equal cost should be included in each of those years. However if we accept this argument then surely it extends to the total cost of operating the asset and not merely the purchase price. If maintenance and repair costs were also considered we would probably find that these increase as the asset deteriorates over time. In these circumstances the reducing balance method of depreciation would produce a more even distribution of total costs over time, as illustrated in Figure 5.1. In theory the method chosen should be that deemed most appropriate in the circumstances bearing in mind the nature of the assets. However in practice this is not always the case and the straight line method, perhaps because it is easier to use and understand, tends to be more popular. For simplicity, one rate is often used for all assets falling within a particular category. For example all vehicles may be depreciated (or 'written off') on a straight line basis at a rate of 25% per annum and all computer equipment at 20% (i.e. over a period of four and five years respectively).

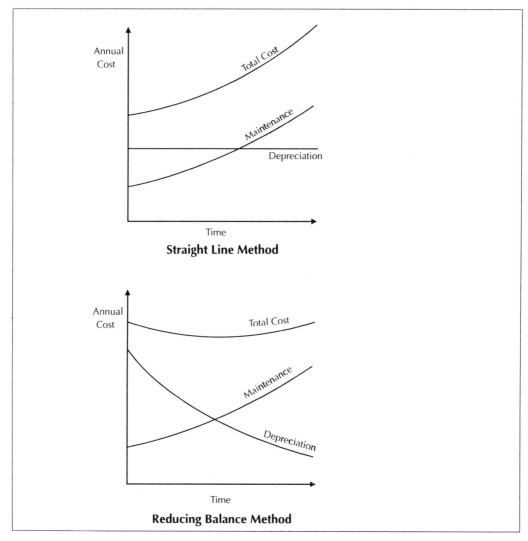

Figure 5.1 Comparison of Depreciation Methods

Determining the Value of Capital Expenditure

Capital expenditure comprises not only the cost of purchasing a fixed asset but also any costs incurred in making the asset operational. Thus for instance where delivery and installation costs are also incurred then these should be added to the purchase price and the full amount depreciated over the life of the asset. Other items which would be treated in this way include any testing or staff training costs necessary to operate the asset.

Bookkeeping Entries

Having looked at methods of depreciating fixed assets we will now consider the appropriate entries in the accounting records, referring to the vehicle in Example 5.3 for illustrative purposes. It was purchased on 1.1.X6 for £18,000 and with an expected residual value of £3,000 after three years, annual depreciation of £5,000 was calculated. We will examine the effect on various accounts, using the worksheet approach used in Chapter 3:

Date		Bank £	Fixed Assets £	Profit £
1. 1.X6	Purchase vehicle	−18,000	18,000	
31.12.X6	Depreciation Yr.1		− 5,000	−5,000
31.12.X6	NBV at end Yr.1		13,000	

You should be familiar with the entries for the purchase from our earlier work. One asset has increased and another decreased by the same amount. As the vehicle was used for the full year in 19X6 depreciation of £5,000 is included in the profit and loss account. At the same time the book value is reduced by £5,000 to reflect a fall in the value of future benefit expected from the vehicle. Thus the value of both an asset and a liability (profit) have fallen by £5,000.

Now complete the entries for the next two years before comparing with the full solution below:

Date		Bank £	Fixed Assets £	Profit £
1. 1.X6	Purchase vehicle	−18,000	18,000	
31.12.X6	Depreciation Yr.1		− 5,000	−5,000
31.12.X6	NBV at end Yr.1		13,000	
31.12.X7	Depreciation Yr.2		− 5,000	−5,000
31.12.X7	NBV at end Yr.2		8,000	
31.12.X8	Depreciation Yr.3		− 5,000	−5,000
31.12.X8	NBV at end Yr.3		3,000	

Over the three years £15,000 depreciation will be included in the expenses section of the profit and loss account, representing the net cost of using the vehicle. The fixed asset account at the end of this time shows the residual value of £3,000.

The Sale of Fixed Assets

In the previous example, it was expected that the vehicle would be sold at the end of the three years for £3,000. If this proved to be the case, the accounting records would appear as follows:

Date		Bank £	Fixed Assets £	Profit £
1. 1.X6	Purchase vehicle	−18,000	18,000	
Various	3 years deprec'n.		−15,000	−15,000
31.12.X8	Sale of vehicle	3,000	−3,000	
31.12.X8	NBV		0	

As the sale proceeds were equal to the net book value at the end of the three year period, the balance on the fixed asset account after the sale would be zero. However, predicting this resale value with complete accuracy at the outset will be difficult and the actual proceeds may not correspond with the final net book value. This would leave a balance on the fixed asset account.

For example, selling for £1,200 would result in the following situation:

Date	Transaction	Bank £	Fixed Assets £	Profit £
1. 1.X6	Purchase vehicle	−18,000	18,000	
Various	3 years deprec'n.		−15,000	−15,000
31.12.X8	Sale of vehicle	1,200	−1,200	
31.12.X8	NBV		1,800	

The sale of an asset with a net book value of £3,000 for only £1,200 has left a balance on the account. This represents a loss made on the sale and must be reported (or 'written off') in the year of sale as follows:

Date	Transaction	Bank £	Fixed Assets £	Profit £
1. 1.X6	Purchase vehicle		18,000	
Various	3 years deprec'n.		−15,000	−15,000
31.12.X8	Sale of vehicle		−1,200	
31.12.X8	NBV		1,800	
31.12.X8	Loss on sale		−1,800	−1,800
			0	−16,800

The £1,800 would be described as 'loss on sale of fixed assets' and shown in the 19X8 profit and loss account, either with the expenses for the year or as a deduction from gross profit before subtracting the expenses.

Although the term 'loss on sale' has been used, the £1,800 actually represents the correction of profits incorrectly reported during the life of the asset. The annual depreciation of £5,000 per annum was based on an incorrect estimation of the resale value. The impact of this can be determined by retrospectively calculating the depreciation which should have been charged in each year, in the light of the information we now have.

Vehicle Depreciation

Cost of using asset = £18,000 − £1,200 = £16,800

Expected useful life = 3 years

Revised annual depreciation = $\frac{£16,800}{3\ yrs}$ = £5,600 p.a.

Revised Profit & Loss Account

Year ended	Vehicle Depreciation £
31.12.X6	5,600
31.12.X7	5,600
31.12.X8	5,600
TOTAL	16,800

The net cost of using the vehicle was actually £16,800 and depreciation of £5,600 per annum would have been required to reflect this. As only £5,000 was charged, costs were understated (and profits overstated) by £600 in each of three years and the £1,800 'loss on sale of fixed assets' reported in 19X8 is the adjustment required to remedy this.

Selling the vehicle for more than the £3,000 originally estimated would have the opposite effect. A 'profit on the sale of fixed assets' would be included in 19X8, compensating for excessive depreciation charged in each of the three years.

Estimation of an Asset's Useful Life

The accuracy of the annual depreciation charged in respect of an asset will be influenced by not only its residual value but also the estimation of its useful life.

Consider for example an asset which is purchased for £40,000 and has an anticipated useful life of five years, with no expected value at the end of that time. The annual depreciation charge would be calculated as follows:

$$\text{Depreciation} = \frac{\text{£40,000}}{5 \ years} = \text{£8,000 per annum.}$$

If the asset only actually lasted four years, the following situation would arise:

	£
Original cost	40,000
Accumulated depreciation after 4 yrs. (£8,000 x 4 years)	−32,000
NBV at end of year 4	8,000

As the asset has no further value at the end of year four, an adjustment will again be necessary to remove the net book value shown in the accounts. As the asset was used for a shorter period than anticipated, insufficient depreciation was charged in the first three years. To compensate for this, as well as the £8,000 annual depreciation charge for the year an additional cost of £8,000 must be included in year four to 'write off' the asset.

Once again, the profits reported in each period have been incorrectly assessed with year four being charged twice as much as the previous three for the use of the same asset.

Intangible Fixed Assets

As mentioned in the previous chapter, as well as "tangible" fixed assets such as vehicles and equipment, a business may also have "intangible" fixed assets such as goodwill and we will now examine this in more detail.

Goodwill

Goodwill is the amount by which the value of a business as a going concern exceeds the value of its net assets. Let us suppose for instance that you own a business which has net assets valued as follows:

	£
Fixed assets	78,000
Stock	6,000
Debtors	5,000
Creditors	(4,000)
Net Assets	85,000

Having decided to dispose of the business you set a selling price of £100,000. The value of goodwill has therefore been estimated at £15,000 and this may be due to factors such as its reputation, its good relationship with customers or the skills and attitude of its employees.

Valuing Goodwill

The valuation placed on goodwill is a matter for negotiation between the buyer and seller of the business. In practice the parties may agree on a price for the business without specifying the value of goodwill. Goodwill is therefore by implication the difference between the agreed selling price and the value of the net assets. In other cases the value of goodwill may be calculated and agreed on before settling on the price of the business. In such instances there are often customary ways of arriving at the goodwill figure in particular types of business. For example, the average weekly sales multiplied by a given figure, or the average annual profit over perhaps the past two or three years multiplied by a given figure.

Let us suppose for instance that the profits for a business over the last three years are as follows:

Year	£
1	30,000
2	35,000
3	37,000

If goodwill is valued at five times the average profit, the figure would be arrived at as follows:

$$\text{Goodwill} = \frac{30,000 + 33,000 + 42,000}{3 \text{ years}} \quad \times \quad 5$$

$$= £35,000 \quad \times \quad 5 \quad = \quad £175,000$$

Alternatively a weighted average could be used in which greater emphasis is placed on profits in the later years:

Year	£		Weight		£
1	30,000	x	1	=	30,000
2	33,000	x	2	=	66,000
3	42,000	x	3	=	126,000
			6		222,000

$$\text{Goodwill} = \frac{222,000}{6} \quad \times \quad 5$$

$$= £37,000 \quad \times \quad 5 \quad = \quad £185,000$$

Another approach is to use the "super profits" method. This approach recognises the fact that the profit figures earned by a business may not allow for two important expenses:

(a)   The services of the owner. (Which may have been recorded as a withdrawal of capital rather than an expense).

(b)   The use of the money invested in the business by the owner.

"Super profits" are the profits remaining after allowing for these two expenses as illustrated below:

	£
Annual profit	37,000
Less - Reasonable salary for owner	(14,000)
- Interest owner could have earned by investing the capital elsewhere	(8,000)
	15,000

Goodwill can then be determined by multiplying this by a given figure.

E.g.: Goodwill = £15,000 x 5 = £75,000

The Accounting Treatment of Goodwill

Although the factors giving rise to goodwill are undoubtedly sources of future benefit, placing an objective valuation on them is difficult and consequently goodwill is usually omitted from the accounts of a business. However, where a business changes hands and the purchaser pays an agreed sum in respect of goodwill a valuation is available and the relevant sum may be shown within the fixed assets section of the balance sheet. If for example a purchaser agrees to buy the business referred to earlier for the £100,000 the opening balance sheet of the newly owned business may be shown as follows:

	£
Intangible fixed assets: goodwill	15,000
Tangible fixed assets	78,000
Stock	6,000
Debtors	5,000
Creditors	(4,000)
Net Assets	100, 000
Capital	100, 000

However, the goodwill acquired at the time of purchase will gradually diminish and in order to maintain the reputation of the business, new goodwill must be created through cultivating relationships with customers, replacing staff when necessary and training employees. Consequently the balance sheet valuation of the goodwill purchased should be depreciated over its estimated useful life in the manner described earlier for tangible fixed assets.

An alternative treatment of purchased goodwill is to take a more prudent approach and rather than spreading its cost over a number of years include all the cost as an expense in the first year of trading. However it could be argued that this does not represent the gradual reduction in value of the goodwill which should be matched against future revenue in accordance with the accruals principle.

The Subjectivity of Profit Measurement

The problems raised above in determining the appropriate depreciation cost in each accounting period demonstrate that the profits reported in each period cannot be described as being totally accurate. The application of accounting concepts often requires judgement in the estimation of various items such as the useful life and residual values of fixed assets. Inevitably estimation errors will occur which will affect the accuracy of profits reported in separate accounting periods. However, it is usually possible to make reasonable estimates and produce results which, although not completely accurate, give a reasonable assessment of the financial position and performance of a business.

If in any doubt when making judgements in the preparation of accounting information, a prudent view should be taken. In respect of fixed assets this may mean using residual values and asset lives which are on the low side. This should prevent the understatement of depreciation costs and ensure a conservative estimate of profit.

Materiality and Depreciation

In compliance with the matching principle the costs of all assets expected to produce benefits for a number of accounting periods should be spread over those periods using the techniques we have examined in this chapter. However, the principle of materiality permits departure from this where the effect of doing so would not materially distort the financial position reported.

Consider for example a calculator which is purchased for £15. Strictly speaking the £15 should be classed as capital expenditure and spread over the useful life of the calculator. However, the effort required to do this for such small items would not justify this treatment. The £15 would therefore usually be treated as revenue expenditure reported in the year of purchase. Although strictly speaking the costs for the year in question would be overstated, the amount involved would not distort the financial situation reported to such an extent as to be misleading.

It is common practice to set a lower limit for the classification of items as capital expenditure with the value chosen depending on the size of the business. A large company may set a limit of £4,000 and write off all items costing less than this as revenue expenditure in the year of purchase. However, in a smaller business where £4,000 may materially affect results, a lower limit of perhaps £1,000 may be imposed.

The Purpose of Depreciation

To conclude this section we will review the purpose of depreciating fixed assets and in doing so, hopefully clear up a common misunderstanding. It is often mistakenly thought that the inclusion of depreciation in the profit calculation results in the accumulation of cash during the life of an asset which can be used to obtain a replacement when required. This is not the case. As we shall see in later chapters, the cash available at any point in time will be influenced by many factors and the inclusion of depreciation will not necessarily produce cash surpluses.

Depreciation is charged in compliance with the matching principle, which requires that sales income in each period be compared with the costs incurred in earning that revenue.

Accruals and Prepayments

Having examined the treatment of capital expenditure on fixed assets, we will now consider revenue expenditure. As we saw in Chapter 4 this is included in the period in which the benefit arose, irrespective of the timing of the payment. Consequently, where payments are made in arrears or in advance, the period in which a cost is reported may differ from the payment period. We will now examine the procedure for dealing with this situation.

Accruals

Where suppliers make charges in arrears or offer credit terms, some of the costs incurred in a period will not be paid until the following period. If for instance, an electricity supplier charges in arrears, the costs for December, 19X6 may not be paid until January 19X7. Nevertheless, the 19X6 profit and loss account must show the electricity cost for the whole year and the cost of December's electricity must be included. This is known as accruing for the cost. If the bill has not been received at the time the accounts are prepared, the charge for December should be estimated.

Here we have further evidence of the subjective nature of accounting profit, with the incorporation of estimated costs in the profit calculation producing an approximate result rather than an absolute figure.

The procedure for the accrual of costs is illustrated in Example 5.4 below:

Example 5.4

The following information was extracted from the trial balance of a business as at 31.12.X6:

	Debit £	Credit £
Electricity costs	20,000	
Creditors		44,000

The electricity bill for December has not yet been received. It is anticipated that the charge for the month will amount to approximately £2,000.

The records are currently incomplete in that they only include eleven months worth of electricity charges. To correct this we must accrue for the cost of electricity in December. The accounting entries required to achieve this are as follows:

	Electricity Charges £	Creditors (Accruals) £
Accrual of electricity charges – December 19X6	2,000	2,000

The £2,000 charged to the electricity account is added to the £20,000 which has already accumulated during the course of the year, to give a total cost of £22,000. The other entry records an estimated debt of £2,000 due to the electricity supplier in respect of December's usage.

This would be reflected in accounting statements as follows:

PROFIT AND LOSS ACCOUNT
FOR THE YEAR ENDED 31.12.X6

Expenses	£	
Electricity	22,000	*(£20,000 + £2,000)*

BALANCE SHEET AS AT 31.12.X6

Current Liabilities	£
Creditors	44,000
Accruals	2,000

The accruals (representing debts for which no bill has yet been received) may be shown separately as illustrated or included in the creditors figure, with a separate note providing a breakdown.

Prepayments

Payments may also be made in advance for goods or services. Compliance with the matching principle requires that these should be excluded from the costs reported in the current period and included in the period to which they relate. Example 5.5 illustrates this principle:

Example 5.5

The trial balance of a business as at 31.12.X6 contained the following information:

	Debit £	Credit £
Premises rental	26,000	
Debtors	30,000	

The figure for premises rental included a payment of £12,000 for the rental of an office for the period 1st. July 19X6 to 30th. June 19X7.

The £12,000 paid for rent included costs in respect of the first six months of 19X7. We must exclude this element and ensure that only 19X6 costs are included. We can ascertain the relevant amount as follows:

Cost per month = $\dfrac{£12,000}{12\ \text{months}}$ = £1,000

19X7 costs   =   £1,000   x   6 months   =   £6,000

This £6,000 is therefore excluded from the costs reported in 19X6. It will be included in 19X7 along with any further costs incurred in that year.

The relevant accounting entries are shown below:

	Premises Rental £	Prepayments £
Office rental paid in advance (Jan - June 19X7)	−6,000	6,000

The £6,000 is deducted from the £26,000 previously recorded in the Premises rental account for inclusion in the following year. The other entry records the prepayment of £6,000.

The accounting statements for 19X6 would reflect this prepayment as shown:

PROFIT AND LOSS ACCOUNT
FOR THE YEAR ENDED 31.12.X6 (£)

Expenses	£	
Premises rental	20,000	*(£26,000 – £6,000)*

BALANCE SHEET AS AT 31.12.X6

Current Assets	£
Debtors	30,000
Prepayments	6,000

Prepayments represent benefits to be enjoyed in the future (in this case in the first six months of the following year) and are therefore reported in the current assets section of the balance sheet. As with accruals they may be shown separately as illustrated or included in the debtors figure and quantified in a separate note in the accounts.

Accounting for Bad Debts

The realisation principle requires that income and any resulting profit are recognised when a sale occurs. This means that where sales are made on credit, profits will be recorded before any cash is received on the assumption that the customer will subsequently pay as agreed. However, offering credit entails a degree of risk and occasionally customers with financial problems may be unable to pay outstanding debts. These are known as bad debts and their effect must be recorded and reflected in accounting statements.

When bad debts are incurred it becomes apparent that income recorded at the time of sale will not materialise. Therefore profits previously recorded will have been overstated. Consider the following example:

Example 5.6

In November 19X6 ABC Limited sold goods on credit to XYZ Limited for £6,000. The goods had originally cost £4,500.

XYZ Limited ceased trading in February 19X7 due to financial problems and as a result, the outstanding debt will not be settled.

The profit recognised at the time of sale and included in the profit and loss account for 19X6 was:

	£
Sales	6,000
Less cost of goods sold	(4,500)
Gross profit	1,500

However as the £6,000 will not be received from XYZ, the sale actually resulted in a loss:

	£
Sales	0
Less cost of goods sold	(4,500)
Gross loss	(4,500)

Consequently, the profit and loss account for 19X6, which included £6,000 worth of income which was not subsequently received, overstated profits by £6,000.

The bad debt should be written off as soon as it is confirmed, in this case February 19X7, with the following entries:

	Debtors £	Profit £
Bad debt incurred in respect of customer XYZ Ltd.	–6,000	–6,000

The debtors balance has been reduced to reflect the fact that the amount expected from customers is now £6,000 lower than previously recorded. The profit figure has been reduced to compensate for its over statement in 19X6 and as the 19X6 profits have already been reported, the adjustment must be reflected in 19X7.

This means that events occurring in one period are being reported in the following period, in contravention of the matching principle. The consequences of selling to bad debtors should in theory be reported in the period in which the sale was made (19X6 in this case). In an attempt to achieve this, an allowance (or 'provision') for doubtful debts is usually made in each period.

Providing for Doubtful Debts

The allowance for doubtful debts is usually calculated as a percentage of debtors outstanding at the end of the period. The percentage figure used tends to be based on past experience of bad debts. As well as matching revenues and costs more closely, this treatment complies with the prudence principle as it will produce a more conservative estimate of profit earned in the period.

The following example illustrates the process:

Example 5.7

G.P. Rafferty commenced trading in January 19X6 and the trial balance at 31.12.X6 showed outstanding debtors of £46,000. This included £6,000 due from Bentons Limited which had recently ceased trading. Rafferty had decided to make a provision of 5% to cover doubtful debts.

The expenses in the profit and loss account for 19X6 would include the following items:

	£
Bad debt written off	6,000
Provision for doubtful debts (£46,000 - £6,000) x 5%	2,000

The £6,000 due from Bentons Limited is written off as a bad debt soon as it is apparent they will not pay. A further sum (5% of the remaining £40,000) is included in the costs to reflect the possibility that a portion of the remaining debts will be irrecoverable.

The debtors recorded in the balance sheet would appear as follows:

Current Assets

	£
* Trade debtors	40,000
† Less Provision for doubtful debts (£40,000 x 5%)	(2,000)
Net debtors figure	38,000

* The debtors figure is shown after deducting £6,000 for the Bentons Limited bad debt. The £40,000 remaining has been reduced further to allow for the additional *bad debts*.

† *This may also be referred to as 'Provision for bad debts'.*

The procedure for dealing with bad and doubtful debts can therefore be summarised as follows:

•   Bad debts should be written off immediately.

- Provision should be made to cover any additional bad debts which may arise in respect of sales made in the period.

We will now look at the treatment of bad debts in Rafferty's accounts in year two.

Example 5.8

In the second year of trading, Rafferty incurred bad debts of £6,000. The net debtors balance at the end of the year (having subtracted the £6,000 for bad debts) was £50,000. The provision for doubtful debts was to be maintained at 5%.

The situation in year two can be summarised as follows:

	£
Bad debts written off in year 2	6,000
Less amount already included in year 1's costs (i.e. the provision at end of year 1)	(2,000)
Bad debts to include in year 2 costs	4,000
Plus 5% provision for doubtful debts	2,500
Costs to be included in year 2	6,500

Of the £6,000 bad debts incurred in year two, £2,000 was anticipated at the end of year one and included in the costs for that year. Consequently, only the remaining £4,000 need be included in the second year. In addition to this, we are prudently allowing £2,500 to cover the probability that further bad debts will arise from the debtors still outstanding at the end of year two. Hence the total charge included in the profit and loss account in year two is £6,500.

The explanation given above should hopefully help you to appreciate the effect of bad debts and related provisions, on the costs reported in each year. However in practice, the charge to the profit and loss account in each year is more commonly and simply calculated by:

1. Writing off all bad debts incurred in the year.

2. Adjusting for any rise or fall in the provision for doubtful debts.

Thus for year two the charge for bad and doubtful debts can be determined as follows:

		£
Bad debts written off		6,000
Increase in Provision for doubtful debts		
- Provision required *(£50,000 x 5%)*	2,500	
- Less existing provision *(£40,000 x 5%)*	(2,000)	500
Charge for bad/doubtful debts in year 2		6,500

As you can see, the same result is obtained and the calculation simplified.

NB. In this case, as the year end debtors rose in year two, an increased provision was necessary. Had debtors fallen, the resulting reduction in the provision would be deducted from the £6,000 giving a lower charge for bad/doubtful *debts*.

Note that the accounting treatment of bad debts provides further evidence of the subjective nature of profit measurement. The costs used in Rafferty's profit calculation for year two include £2,500 representing *expected* bad debts. It is unlikely that this will reflect the actual value of bad debts arising from the year end debtors and the profit reported for the year can therefore be regarded as only an approximation.

A Comprehensive Example

Having examined various techniques to help ensure that accounting statements are prepared in accordance with accepted accounting principles we will now apply these in a comprehensive example.

It is largely based on the trial balance we looked at in Example 5.1 but additional information is supplied which must be incorporated.

Example 5.9

MORALEE SPORTS SUPPLIES

TRIAL BALANCE AS AT 31.12.X7

	Debit £	Credit £
Shop fittings -- Cost	10,000	
-- accumulated deprec'n. at 31.12.X6		4,000
Sales		93,000
Wages	12,150	
Heating	1,400	
Bank balance	12,100	
Capital		4,000
Telephone charges	1,500	
Vehicles – cost	12,000	
– accumulated deprec'n. at 31.12.X6		3,000
Purchases	59,000	
Retained profits (as at 31.12.X6)		15,500
Trade creditors		10,700
Electricity	1,100	
Stock (as at 31.12.X6)	10,000	
Building society loan		2,000
Trade debtors	6,200	
Provision for doubtful debts		400
Rent	5,600	
Cash	1,550	
	132,600	132,600

Additional Information

(a) The stock on hand at 31.12.X7 was valued at £6,000.

(b) Deprecation of fixed assets is to be provided on a straight line basis at the following rates:

-- Shop fittings at 20% of original cost.

-- Vehicles at 25% of original cost.

(c) The amount recorded for rent includes payment in advance for the first four weeks of 19X8.

(d) The electricity bill for December has not yet been received.

(e) The trade debtors figure includes £600 outstanding from a customer with financial difficulties. It is believed that only £400 of this debt will be recoverable.

(f) Provision for bad debts is to be made at a rate of 5% of trade debtors outstanding at the year end.

(g) The owner of the business has withdrawn £1,000 from the business bank account for personal use. This has not yet been recorded in the accounts of the business.

As explained earlier the profit and loss account and balance sheet can be compiled as follows:

STEP 1 : Compile the Trial Balance

This has already been done for us.

STEP 2 : Classify Each Item Shown in the Trial Balance

We did this when working through Example 5.1 earlier in the chapter. The only items which have been added here, are the amounts for accumulated depreciation in respect of shop fittings and vehicles, (which should be shown in the fixed asset section of the balance sheet) and the provision for doubtful debts (which should be used in calculating the bad debt charge for the year).

STEP 3 : Make Any Period End Adjustments

Each adjustment should be dealt with in turn with amendments made to the figures given in the trial balance as required from the additional information given. Remember that each adjustment must be recorded with a double entry and that two accounts will therefore be affected in each case.

The relevant adjustments and explanatory notes are shown below:

Item

(a) Closing Stock

Closing stock (asset)	+ £6,000
Cost of goods sold	− £6,000

Closing stock must be reported as an asset in the balance sheet. It will also be subtracted from the opening stock and purchases in the calculation of the cost of goods sold in the profit and loss account.

(b) Depreciation

Depreciation costs		+ £5,000
Accumulated depreciation	*– Shop fittings*	+ £2,000
	– Vehicles	+ £3,000

Depreciation costs for the year can be calculated as follows:

– Shop fittings (£10,000 x 20%)	£2,000
– Vehicles (£12,000 x 25%)	£3,000
Total charge for year	£5,000

As well as increasing costs (and therefore reducing profit) for the year, the depreciation will reduce the value of fixed assets reported in the balance sheet by £5,000.

(c) Prepayment

Rent	– £400
Prepayments	+ £400

As the £5,600 shown in the trial balance includes four weeks paid in advance for the following year, it must cover a period of 56 weeks. In the absence of any further information we will assume this represents a cost of £100 per week. The four weeks prepaid can therefore be valued at £400 and this amount will be excluded from costs reported in 19X7 and shown as an asset in the balance sheet.

(d) Accrual

Electricity	+ £150
Accruals	+ £150

As the £1,100 shown for electricity excludes the charge for December, it represents the costs for eleven months only. We must therefore estimate the outstanding charge to ensure that the full year's costs are reported. As costs for the previous eleven months were £1,100 the average cost per month was £100. As more electricity may be used in winter months for lighting and any electrical heating appliances, we will prudently allow £150 for December.

This will be added to the £1,100 already recorded in the electricity account. An accrual reflecting the debt to the electricity supplier has also been recorded and will be shown with current liabilities in the balance sheet.

(e) Bad Debts Written Off

Bad/doubtful debts written off	+ £200
Debtors	− £200

As £200 of the amount due from debtors will not be collected, it should be written off in the profit and loss account and the balance on the debtors account reduced by £200 to £6,000.

(f) Provision for Doubtful Debts

Bad/doubtful debts written off	+ £100
Provision for doubtful debts	− £100

In addition to writing off the specific bad debt in e) above, the provision for doubtful debts must also be amended. This can be calculated as follows:

	£
Provision required (£6,000 x 5%)	300
Current provision	400
Reduction in provision	−100

The £100 reduction will be reported with the expenses in the profit and loss account as a negative cost (thereby increasing profit). The current £400 balance on the provision for bad debts account will be reduced by £100 and the revised provision of £300 will be reported as a deduction from trade debtors in the balance sheet.

(g) Owner's Drawings

Drawings	+ £1,000
Bank	− £1,000

If the £1,000 was withdrawn in payment for work performed during the year, it should be shown with other wages costs in the profit and loss account. As we are not told this, we will assume that it represented the withdrawal of profit. As such, it should be reported as 'drawings' and subtracted from the retained profit reported in the balance sheet.

As the transaction has not been recorded, the bank account should be reduced by £1,000 to reflect the withdrawal.

The effect of each adjustment on the figures in the trial balance is shown in Figure 5.2. The final balances listed can be used to compile the profit and loss account and balance sheet.

MORALEE SPORTS SUPPLIES

	Trial Balance as at 31.12.X7		Adjustments	Final Balances	
	Debit £	*Credit* £		*Debit* £	*Credit* £
Shop fittings – cost	10,000			10,000	
– accum. dep'n. as at 31.12.X6		4,000	+2,000 (b)		6,000
Sales		93,000			93,000
Wages	12,150			12,150	
Heating	1,400			1,400	
Bank	12,100		– 1,000 (g)	11,100	
Capital		4,000			4,000
Telephone charges	1,500			1,500	
Vehicles – cost	12,000			12,000	
– accum. dep'n. as at 31.12.X6		3,000	+3,000 (b)		6,000
Purchases	59,000			59,000	
Retained profit (as at 31.12.X6)		15,500			15,500
Trade creditors		10,700			10,700
Electricity	1,100		+150 (d)	1,250	
Stock (as at 31.12.X6)	10,000			10,000	
Building society loan		2,000			2,000
Trade debtors	6,200		–200 (e)	6,000	
Provision for doubtful debts		400	–100 (f)		300
Rent	5,600		– 400 (c)	5,200	
Cash	1,550			1,550	
New Accounts Opened for Adjustments					
Depreciation			+5,000 (b)	5,000	
Prepayments			+400 (c)	400	
Accruals			+150 (d)		150
Bad/doubtful debts written off			+200 (e)		
			– 100 (f)	100	
Drawings			+1,000 (g)	1,000	
	132,600	132,600		137,650	137,650

Figure 5.2 Moralee Sports Supplies – Trial Balance Adjustments

STEP 4 : Prepare the Profit and Loss Account

When compiling the financial statements it is good practice to tick each item as it is included in the profit and loss account or the balance sheet. This should ensure that no items have been omitted.

The profit and loss account, compiled from the revised balances in Figure 5.2, is shown below:

MORALEE SPORTS SUPPLIES
PROFIT AND LOSS ACCOUNT FOR THE YEAR ENDED 31.12.X7

		£
Sales		93,000
Less Cost of Goods Sold		
Opening stock	10,000	
Add purchases	59,000	
	69,000	
Less closing stock	(6,000)	(63,000)
GROSS PROFIT		30,000
Less Expenses		
Wages	12,150	
Heating	1,400	
Telephone charges	1,500	
Electricity	1,250	
Rent	5,200	
Depreciation	5,000	
Bad debts written off	200	
Decrease in provision for doubtful debts	(100)	(26,600)
NET PROFIT		3,400

STEP 5 : Prepare the Balance Sheet

Finally the balance sheet should be prepared incorporating the net profit of £3,400 reported in the profit and loss account.

Moralee's balance sheet, again compiled from the revised balances in Figure 5.2, is shown below:

MORALEE SPORTS SUPPLIES
BALANCE SHEET AS AT 31.12.X7

Fixed Assets

	Cost	Accumulated Depreciation	NBV
	£	£	£
Shop fittings	10,000	6,000	4,000
Vehicles	12,000	6,000	6,000
	22,000	12,000	10,000

Current Assets

Stock		6,000
Trade debtors	6,000	
Less provn. for doubtful debts	(300)	5,700
Prepayments		400
Bank		11,100
Cash		1,550
		24,750

Less: Current Liabilities

Trade creditors	10,700		
Accruals	150	(10,850)	
Net Current Assets			13,900

Less: Long Term Liabilities

Building society	(2,000)
NET ASSETS	**21,900**

Financed by:

Capital		4,000
Retained Profit		
As at 31.12.X6	15,500	
Net profit for the year	3,400	
	18,900	
Less drawings	(1,000)	17,900
OWNER'S FUNDS		**21,900**

The Subjectivity of Profit Measurement

Having incorporated all the information supplied we have reported a net profit of £3,400 for the year in the profit and loss account. However, as we have seen on numerous occasions, accounting profit is not an absolute measure but the best estimate of those preparing the accounts. Judgements are made as to the appropriate costs to include for various items and these will affect the profit reported for a period. Two accountants with the same information could make different assumptions and therefore produce different results.

We will now review these issues, analysing their impact on the net profit reported.

Depreciation

There are three issues relating to depreciation which may affect the accuracy of reported profits:

1. The Depreciation Rate

Shop fittings are being depreciated at a rate of 20% per annum and vehicles at 25%. This is based on an assumption that they will be used for five and four years respectively. Should these predictions prove to be inaccurate, the charges made in each accounting period will be inappropriate. If the vehicles lasted three years and not four as estimated, one third of the cost should have been included in the year rather than one quarter. Costs reported would therefore be higher and profit lower.

2. Residual Values

As the depreciation charge is based on the original cost of the assets, it has been assumed that they will have no residual value at the end of their useful lives. If this assumption was later found to be incorrect with assets being sold after serving their purpose, their net cost would be less than anticipated. However, the resulting benefit would be reported in the year of sale (as a profit on the sale of fixed assets) rather than reducing the costs reported in each year. If for example the shop fittings were sold for £1,000 at the end of year five, this would be reported as a profit in that year. However, in theory the £1,000 should have been spread over the five years and costs in each reduced by £200. In these circumstances, a profit of £3,600 for 19X7 would therefore be more appropriate than the £3,400 reported.

3. The Depreciation Method

The straight line method has been used for depreciation. This assumes that the asset diminishes in value by the same amount each year. Opponents of this method argue that this is not the case for some assets. The value of vehicles for example will tend to fall more sharply in the earlier years. The reducing balance method can be used to reflect this by charging higher costs to the profit and loss account in those early years. Had this method been adopted in our example the depreciation charge for vehicles (which judging from the accumulated depreciation figure shown in the trial balance are relatively new) would have probably been higher and the net profit therefore lower than £3,400.

Accruals and Prepayments

When making the accrual for December's outstanding electricity charge we used an estimate of £150. It is therefore likely that our reported profit for the year (the accuracy of which is subject to any error in this estimate) will not be entirely correct.

In assessing the value of the prepayment for rent we have assumed a cost of £100 per week. Again this may be inaccurate. Perhaps the cost has risen and although less than £100 per week early in the year is now £120 per week. If this were so, the prepayment for the four weeks would be £480 and not the £400 we assumed and profits for 19X7 would be understated by £80. In practice, inspection of invoices and other documentation should help in ascertaining the value of any prepayments made.

Bad Debts

In determining the provision for bad debts we have estimated that 5% of outstanding debtors (i.e. £300) will not be received. Although this is presumably based on past experience and other relevant information, again the assessment (and therefore the reported profit) is unlikely to be completely accurate. If the irrecoverable debts only totalled £200, the costs in 19X7 would be overstated (and profit understated) by £100.

Conclusion

Accounting principles applied in the measurement of profit require estimation in respect of various items. These estimates should be made in the light of information available on the activities of the business and the environment in which it operates. If in doubt a prudent view should be presented and profit measured conservatively. This approach was adopted in the accrual of December's electricity charge when £150 was estimated despite an average monthly cost of only £100.

With the inclusion of such estimates, profit should be regarded not as an absolute measure but rather the best assessment of those preparing accounting statements, given the information available.

Summary

- The preparation of accounting statements may be undertaken in the following stages:

    1. Compile the trial balance.

    2. Classify each item within the trial balance.

    3. Make period end adjustments.

    4. Prepare the profit and loss account.

    5. Prepare the balance sheet.

- Trial balance items should be shown in accounting statements as follows:

    Assets/Liabilities/Capital in the Balance Sheet

    Income/Expenditure in the Profit and Loss Account

- Period end adjustments are required to ensure that statements are prepared in accordance with accepted accounting principles.

- Depreciation is included in the profit and loss account in each period to reflect the cost of using fixed assets.

- The straight line method spreads the net cost of an asset equally over the periods in which it is expected to be used, on the following basis:

$$Depreciation \ per \ period = \frac{Net \ cost \ of \ asset}{No. \ of \ periods}$$

- The reducing balance method calculates depreciation as a percentage of the net book value (rather than the net cost) of the asset. It will therefore charge higher costs in early years.

- Profits or losses made on the disposal of fixed assets should be reported in the year of sale.

- When accounting for revenue expenditure, costs must be reported in the period in which the benefit arose. Therefore costs relating to the period for which payment has not yet been made, should be included and any prepayments excluded.

- Bad debts should be written off in the period in which they are incurred.

- An additional allowance should be made to cover bad debts which may arise from debtors outstanding at the end of the period.

- All estimates required in making period end adjustments should be assessed prudently.

- Periodic profit measurement relies on the subjective assessment of various items. The result should therefore be viewed as an approximation, rather than an absolute measure.

Questions   (See Appendix C for Answers)

5.1

Most balance sheets include 'fixed assets at cost less depreciation' and an item which is usually significant in most profit and loss accounts is 'depreciation'.

You are required to:

    (a)   define the term 'depreciation'

    (b)   explain why it appears in most profit and loss accounts

    (c)   explain the purpose of showing fixed assets at 'cost less depreciation' in the balance sheet

    (d)   describe the usual methods of calculating the annual charge for depreciation for published financial statement purposes.

(ACCA)

5.2

    (a)   Explain clearly the following accounting terms in a manner which an intelligent non-accountant could understand in the context of a profit-oriented organisation:

        (i)   expense

        (ii)   matching

        (iii) prudence

        (iv) objectivity.

    (b)   Your client has received the following invoice, and has come to you for advice.

       'From: Marketing Services plc

       Due for our services for the three months 1st October to 31st December 19X2.

	£
Agreed monthly fee for general advice three months at £1,000 per month.	3,000
Supply of new colour photocopier on 1/10/X2, with five year guarantee, for use by your marketing department.	10,000
Deposit paid by us on your behalf for television advertising time in February 19X3.	5,000
Full cost of advertising campaign in newspaper, from 1st November to 30th November 19X2.	50,000
Payable in total by 31/1/X3.'	

Required

Write a letter to your client suggesting, for each of the four items on the invoice, how each item is likely to affect the expenses figure for the accounting year ended 31st December 19X2. You should explain your suggestions, and justify them by reference to accounting conventions.

(ACCA)

5.3

The charge for depreciation usually represents a significant item in the accounts of most organisations.

Consider a retail organisation which owns office plant and equipment which cost £70,000 in 19X0 and £5,000 p.a. has been spent on maintenance in each year 19X1 to 19X4. After 10 years useful life it is expected that the scrap value will be £10,000

You are required to:

(a) describe the straight line method, the reducing balance method and one other method which may be used for calculating the annual depreciation charge,

(b) calculate the charge using the first two methods in respect of 19X5 for the office plant and equipment described above,

(c) explain, carefully, the purpose of the depreciation charge.

(ACCA)

5.4

The following balances were extracted from the books of Westville plc. as at 1st May 19X4:

	£	
Debtors	330,000	(debit)
Provision for doubtful debts	16,500	(credit)

During the two years ended 30th April 19X6 the following transactions relating to debtors occurred:

	Year ended 30.4.X5 £	Year ended 30.4.X6 £
Credit sales	375,000	347,200
Sales returns	7,500	5,800
Cash received from debtors	347,500	348,700
Discounts allowed	8,000	6,400
Bad debts written off	5,000	6,300

At 30th April 19X5 it was decided to maintain the provision for doubtful debts at the same percentage of debtors as it was at 30th April 19X4, but at 30th April 19X6 it was decided that a provision of 4% of the debtors was adequate.

Required

Calculate the provision for doubtful debts as at 30th April 19X5 and 19X6.

5.5

Vincent operates a business selling paintings for which the following trial balance has been prepared.

Trial Balance as at 31.12.X1

	Dr (£000's)	Cr (£000's)
Capital		20
Wages Costs	38	
Sales		400
Distribution Expenses	4	
Trade Creditors		19
Trade Debtors	40	
Bank Balance	16	
Admin Expenses	32	
Retained profit as at 1.1.X1		18
Vehicles:		
– at cost	10	
– depreciation as at 1.1.X1		2
Office Equipment:		
– at cost	20	
– depreciation as at 1.1.X1		4
Purchases	280	
Stock (as at 1.1.X1)	23	
	463	463

Additional Information

1.   Depreciation for the year should be charged at the following rates:

Vehicles	20% of original cost
Office Equipment	10% of original cost.

2.   The value of stock held at 31.12.X1 was £20,000.

3.   It has been decided to make provision for bad debts at $2\frac{1}{2}$% of the closing debtors figure.

4.   The costs recorded for admin. expenses includes £3,000 in respect of equipment rental for January of the following year.

5.   Bonuses of £2,000 relating to 19X1 have not yet been paid to staff.

Required

Prepare a Profit and Loss Account for the business for the ended 31.12.X1 and a Balance Sheet as at that date.

5.6

On 1 January Mr Bends starts a business buying and selling motor cars. He gives you a summary of the business receipts and payments account as follows, for the year to 31 December (all figures are in £000).

	£000
Receipts	
Capital introduced (1 January)	100
From customers (after deducting worthless cheque,	
see note iii below)	400
10% loan from his mother (1 January)	50
	550
Payments	
To suppliers of new cars	320
To suppliers of second-hand cars	93
Wages	36
Rent	15
Purchase of furniture	5
Purchase of showroom display equipment	5
Insurance, electricity and stationery	7
Bank charges	1
Transfers to private bank account	26
	508

You are informed that:

(i)   Rent payable is £3,000 for each three month period.

(ii)   Mr Bends has bought a total of 37 new cars at a cost of £10,000 each. One of these was destroyed by fire the day before Mr Bends signed his insurance policy, two were taken into use by Mr Bends and his senior salesman, and 27 have been sold at a markup of 20% on cost (one of which has not yet been paid for).

(iii) Mr Bends had a problem with the very first second-hand car which he sold. He accepted a cheque for £5,000 which proved worthless, and he has been unable to trace the customer. Since then all sales of second-hand cars have been for cash. All purchases of second-hand cars have also been for cash.

(iv)   Four second-hand cars remain in stock at 31 December. The cost of these to Mr Bends was £6,000, £6,000, £7,000 and £8,000 respectively.

(v)   All fixed assets are to be depreciated at the rate of 20% for the year.

Required

Prepare in good order:

Trading account for new cars.
Trading account for second-hand cars.
Profit and loss account for the business for the year.
Balance sheet as at 31 December.

Indicate clearly the calculation of all figures in your solution.

(ACCA)

Questions Without Answers

5.7

From the information given below you are required to show the rent, rates and insurance account in the ledger of S. Forshaw for the year ended 30th June 19X6, showing clearly the prepayments and accruals at the that date and the transfer to profit and loss account for the year.

The balances on the account at 1st July 19X5 were:

	£
Rent accrued	200
Rates prepaid	150
Insurance prepaid	180

Payments made during the year ended 30th June 19X6 were as follows:

19X5		£
Aug. 10	Rent, three months to 31st July 19X5	300
Oct. 26	Insurance, one year to 31st October 19X6	600
Nov. 2	Rates, six months to 31st March 19X6	350
Dec. 12	Rent, four months to 30th November 19X5	400
19X6		
Apr. 17	Rent, four months to 31st March 19X6	400
May 9	Rates, six months to 30th September 19X6	350

(CIMA)

5.8

Phil commenced business on 1st January 19X3 and from that date the following transactions relating to fixed assets occurred:

Date	Asset Transaction	Cost £
19X3		
January 7	Purchased vehicle ABC 123	16,000
February 9	Purchased machine no. 1	80,000
19X4		
March 17	Purchased vehicle BBC 789	18,000
June 16	Purchased machine no. 2	64,000
August 18	Purchased machine no. 3	76,000
19X5		
April 6	Purchased vehicle CBC 567	20,000
19X6		
April 8	Sold vehicle ABC123: proceeds of sale being	5,500
April 9	Purchased vehicle DBC 543	17,600
July 22	Purchased machine no.4	56,000

The depreciation policy is as follows:

(a) Motor vehicles will be depreciated at the rate of 25% per annum using the reducing balance method.

(b) Machinery will be depreciated on a straight line basis on the assumption that each machine will have an estimated life of eight years with no residual value.

(c) Depreciation for a full year is charged in the year of purchase but no depreciation is charged in the year of disposal.

Required

(a) Calculate the depreciation charge for each of the four years ended 31st December 19X3 to 31st December 19X6.

(b) Calculate the profit or loss arising on the sale of vehicle ABC 123

(c) Show how the fixed asset section of the balance sheet would appear at the end of each year.

5.9

Marie operates a business selling fashion clothing to department stores and has prepared the following trial balance:

Trail Balance as at 31.12.X8

	Dr £000's	Cr £000's
Turnover		980
Bank Balance	30	
Purchases	750	
Capital		75
Stock as at 1.1.X8	32	
Admin. Expenses	41	
Motor vehicles:		
– at cost	32	
– depreciation as at 1.1.X8		14
Provision for doubtful debts		1
Interest Paid	2	
Distribution Expenses	7	
Fixtures and Fittings:		
– at cost	60	
– depreciation as at 1.1.X8		12
Trade Debtors	79	
Trade Creditors		43
Salaries Costs	126	
Retained Profit as at 1.1.X8		34
	1,159	1,159

Additional Information

1. Stock held at 31.12.X8 was valued at £28,000.

2. Depreciation for the year is to be charged as follows:
   Motor vehicles   25% of original cost
   Fixtures and Fittings   10% of original cost

3. Marie has withdrawn £5,000 during the year for personal use and included this in admin. expenses.

4. A bill for £2,000 in respect of distribution expenses for the month of December 19X8 has not yet been received and no accounting entry has been made in this respect.

5. Admin. expenses includes £3,000 pre-paid in respect of equipment hire.

6. A customer owing £4,000 has been declared bankrupt and this sum is irrecoverable.

7. The provision for doubtful debts is to be adjusted to 4% of trade debtors.

Required

Prepare a Profit and Loss Account for the year ended 31.12.X8 and a Balance Sheet at that date.

5.10

The trial balance of Snodgrass, a sole trader, at 1st January 19X8 is as follows:

	Dr £000	Cr £000
Capital		600
Fixed assets (net)	350	
Trade debtors	200	
Prepayments --rent	8	
– insurance	12	
Trade creditors		180
Accruals --electricity		9
– telephone		1
Stock	200	
Bank	20	
	790	790

The following information is given for the year:

	£000
Receipts from customers	1,000
Payments to suppliers	700
Payments for: rent	30
insurance	20
electricity	25
telephone	10
wages	100
Proprietor's personal expenses	50
Discounts allowed	8
Bad debts written off	3
Depreciation	50

At the 31st December 19X8 the following balances are given:

	£000
Trade debtors	250
Prepayments -- rent	10
-- telephone	2
Trade creditors	160
Accruals -- electricity	7
-- insurance	6
Stock	230

Required

Prepare a trading and profit and loss account for the year, and a balance sheet as at 31st December 19X8.

(ACCA)

Chapter 6

Accounting for Manufacturing Organisations

Learning Objectives

After completing this chapter you should be able to:

- Explain the difference between the trading accounts of manufacturing and trading organisations.

- Explain how product costs may be classified.

- Establish the cost of materials consumed in a period using alternative valuation methods.

- Prepare a manufacturing account ascertaining the cost of goods completed in a period.

- Explain valuation methods for the following types of stock:

  - Materials

  - Work in progress

  - Finished goods

- Compile a Manufacturing, Trading and Profit and Loss Account for a manufacturing organisation.

Introduction

In previous chapters, where the recording of transactions and preparation of accounts were examined, trading organisations engaged in buying and selling goods were used to demonstrate methods and principles. Of course not all businesses operate in this way and we will now consider another common form of business activity, manufacturing. This entails processing the materials purchased in some way before selling them and as we shall see, accounting for this activity is not as straightforward as for traders.

Accounting for Manufacturing Organisations

The accounting principles we have studied previously are as relevant for manufacturers as for traders and in most respects are applied in exactly the same way. The issue which is a little more complicated in manufacturing, is the ascertainment of the cost of goods sold.

For trading organisations, the trading account was compiled as shown in Figure 6.1.

A. TRADER

TRADING ACCOUNT FOR THE YEAR ENDED 31.12.X6

	£	
SALES		195,000
LESS COST OF GOODS SOLD		
Opening stock	25,000	
Add purchases	160,000	
	185,000	
Less closing stock	(20,000)	(165,000)
GROSS PROFIT		30,000

Figure 6.1 A. Trader – Trading Account

In this case, purchases of £160,000 added to the opening stock of £25,000 meant that goods to the value of £185,000 were available for sale in the period. As £20,000 worth of these were still in stock at the end of the year, the cost of the goods sold during the year was £165,000.

In the case of manufacturers, the statement is prepared on the same basis. However, as they *produce* (rather than purchase) the goods they sell, the cost of finished goods produced is used in place of the cost of purchases as illustrated in Figure 6.2.

```
┌─────────────────────────────────────────────────────────────────────┐
│                         A. MANUFACTURER                               │
│                                                                       │
│          TRADING ACCOUNT FOR THE YEAR ENDED 31.12.X6                  │
│                                                            £          │
│   SALES                                                195,000        │
│                                                                       │
│   LESS COST OF SALES                                                  │
│      Opening stock of finished goods         25,000                   │
│      Add cost of finished goods produced    160,000                   │
│                                             185,000                   │
│      Less closing stock of finished goods  ( 20,000)    (165,000)     │
│                                                                       │
│   GROSS PROFIT                                          30,000        │
│                                                                       │
└─────────────────────────────────────────────────────────────────────┘
```

Figure 6.2 A. Manufacturer – Trading Account

The cost of goods sold has essentially been ascertained in the same way as for the trader. Stocks of finished goods valued at £25,000 were on hand at the start of the year. During the course of the year further items were produced at a cost of £160,000 and the value of goods available to sell was therefore £185,000. As £20,000 worth remained unsold at the end of the year, the cost of the goods sold must have been £165,000.

In order to calculate the cost of goods sold for a manufacturer we must therefore determine the cost of products completed in the period as well as the value of opening and closing stocks and we will now consider how this may be ascertained.

Cost Classification

The costs incurred by a manufacturing business may be classified as either direct or indirect.

Direct Costs

Direct costs are those which can be identified with a particular product. They will fall into one of three categories:

1. **Direct materials**. The raw materials and components used.

2. **Direct labour**. The cost of employing those manufacturing the product.

3.   **Direct expenses**. Any other costs incurred as a direct result of producing the product. These are relatively rare but would include royalties payable or the hire of equipment specifically to produce an item or batch of items.

Indirect Costs

Indirect costs are those which cannot be traced to a specific product. They are also known as 'overheads' and are often classified by function (e.g. marketing, distribution, administration, finance and production overheads). Product costs reported in the trading account comprise only those incurred in the production process. Therefore only the production overheads are included in the cost of goods sold with the remainder being reported in the expenses section of the profit and loss account. Examples of production overheads include the rental of production premises, plant maintenance, indirect labour (e.g. supervisory staff) and depreciation of production equipment.

The cost of the goods completed in a period will therefore include:

Direct costs   – Direct materials.

– Direct labour.

– Direct expenses (if any).

Indirect costs – Production overheads.

Product Costing Systems

Many businesses operate sophisticated costing systems to obtain the cost of individual products. This is achieved by recording the following information as products pass through the production process:

1.   *The quantity of materials used on each product*

This can be multiplied by the cost per Kg./litre etc. to obtain the total material cost of the product.

2.   *The labour time spent producing each product.*

The total labour cost for each product can be determined by multiplying by the times recorded by the relevant wage rates.

3.   *Any direct expenses incurred specifically as a result of manufacturing a product.*

4.   *The production overheads assigned to each product.*

Techniques for attributing production overheads to products are rather more complicated and will be examined in some detail in Chapter 10. At this stage it is sufficient to appreciate that product costs include a share of the production overheads incurred as well as direct costs.

Using these costing systems, the cost of goods produced in a period can be obtained by the aggregation of costs recorded for each individual product.

Calculating the Cost of Completed Production

Where detailed costing systems are not operated and the cost of each individual product is therefore not known, the cost of all items completed in the period can be obtained by:

1. Measuring the production costs incurred in the period.

2. Adjusting for work in progress.

Consider the following example:

Example 6.1

A manufacturer has the following information available in respect of production in 19X8:

	£
Factory rent	6,000
Maintenance of machinery	14,000
Direct Materials	
– Purchases in the year	74,000
– Opening stock	8,000
– Closing stock	12,000
Direct labour	50,000
Supervisor's salary	15,000
Depreciation of machinery	10,000

Partially completed goods in the factory at the end of the year were valued at £15,000 and the corresponding figure at the end of 19X7 was £10,000.

Required

Calculate the cost of finished goods produced during the year.

The first step is to ascertain the production costs *incurred* in the year as demonstrated below:

PRODUCTION COSTS INCURRED 19X8

	£	£
Direct Materials*		
Opening stock	8,000	
Purchases	74,000	
	82,000	
Less closing stock	(12,000)	70,000
Direct labour		50,000
Production overheads		
Factory rent	6,000	
Maintenance of machinery	14,000	
Supervisor's salary	15,000	
Depreciation of machinery	10,000	45,000
TOTAL PRODUCTION COSTS INCURRED		165,000

* Note

We must include the value of materials consumed, rather than purchased, in the period. The opening stock was valued at £8,000 and as purchases of £74,000 were added in the year, there was £82,000 worth of materials available. As £12,000 worth was still in stock at the year end, the remaining £70,000 must have been consumed during the year. The £12,000 closing stock will be reported with the current assets in the balance sheet under the heading 'stocks of *Materials*'.

Adjusting for Work in Progress

From the above calculation we can see that the production costs incurred in 19X8 amounted to £165,000. However, we are told that £15,000 of this related to items which were incomplete at the end of the year. This is known as 'work in progress' and as we require cost of finished goods produced in the period, the £15,000 must be excluded.

We are also informed that at the end of 19X7, partially completed goods were valued at £10,000. These would have been completed in 19X8 and the £10,000 should therefore be included in the cost of finished goods produced in the year.

A manufacturing account incorporating these adjustments for opening and closing work in progress is shown below:

A. MANUFACTURER

MANUFACTURING ACCOUNT 19X8

	£	£	£
OPENING WORK IN PROGRESS			10,000
PRODUCTION **COSTS INCURRED**			
Direct Materials			
Opening stock	8,000		
Purchases	74,000		
	82,000		
Less closing stock	(12,000)	70,000	
Direct labour		50,000	
Production overheads			
Factory rent	6,000		
Maintenance of machinery	14,000		
Supervisor's salary	15,000		
Depreciation of machinery	10,000	45,000	165,000
			175,000
LESS CLOSING WORK IN PROGRESS			(15,000)
COST OF FINISHED GOODS PRODUCED			160,000

The opening work in progress valuation of £10,000 is added to the £165,000 production costs incurred in 19X8. However, of the £175,000 resulting cost, £15,000 was incurred on items which were incomplete at the end of 19X8. This amount is therefore excluded and will be incorporated in the cost of goods completed in 19X9. The cost of the goods completed in 19X8 is therefore £160,000.

The closing work in progress of £15,000 will be reported with the current assets in the balance sheet under the heading 'Stocks - Work in progress'.

The Trading and Profit and Loss Account

The cost of finished goods produced can now be incorporated in the trading account for the year as follows:

A. MANUFACTURER

TRADING ACCOUNT FOR THE YEAR ENDED 31.12.X8

	£	£
SALES		195,000
LESS COST OF SALES		
Opening stock of finished goods	25,000	
Add cost of finished goods produced	160,000	
	185,000	
Less closing stock of finished goods	(20,000)	(165,000)
GROSS PROFIT		30,000

A comprehensive breakdown of the net profit earned in the year can be provided in a single statement incorporating the Manufacturing, Trading and Profit and Loss Accounts as illustrated below. (Note that for the purpose of illustration, expenses are assumed to consist of selling and administration costs at £10,000 and £15,000 respectively).

A. MANUFACTURER
MANUFACTURING, TRADING AND PROFIT AND LOSS ACCOUNT 19X8

				£
SALES				195,000
LESS COST OF SALES				
OPENING STOCK OF FINISHED GOODS			25,000	
ADD COST OF FINISHED GOODS PRODUCED				
Opening Work In Progress		10,000		
Production Costs Incurred				
Direct Materials Consumed*	70,000			
Direct Labour	50,000			
Production overheads				
Factory rent	6,000			
Maintenance of machinery	14,000			
Supervisor's salary	15,000			
Depreciation of machinery	10,000	45,000	165,000	
			175,000	
Less Closing Work In Progress		(15,000)	160,000	
			185,000	
LESS CLOSING STOCK OF FINISHED GOODS			(20,000)	(165,000)
GROSS PROFIT				30,000
LESS EXPENSES				
Selling costs			10,000	
Admin. expenses			15,000	(25,000)
NET PROFIT				5,000

*Direct Materials Consumed

	£
Opening stock	8,000
Purchases	74,000
	82,000
Less closing stock	(12,000)
	70,000

Stock Valuation

We have seen that a manufacturer can hold three different types of stock:

- Materials

- Work in progress

- Finished goods

These are assets with a future benefit and their value is therefore excluded from the costs reported for the period. Consequently in order to measure profit for each period an appropriate method of stock valuation must be employed.

The statement of standard accounting practice on stocks and work in progress (SSAP 9) states that the valuation should reflect the lower of cost or 'net realisable value'. In most instances the cost will be used but if for example a quantity of materials in stock is unusable, perhaps through deterioration, they should be valued at their scrap value.

We will now consider how the value of each type of stock may be determined.

Materials

The value of unused materials at the end of a period may be obtained as follows for each type of material held:

Value = No. of items x Cost per item

The number of items held at the end of a period can be determined from stock records or a stock taking exercise in which all items are counted.

The cost per item may be obtained from purchasing records. However where prices are changing, a particular type of material may have been bought at different prices over a period of time and this creates a problem. Consider the following example:

Example 6.2

On 1st. December a business had in stock, 20 items of a material which had been previously purchased for £10 each. The following purchases and issues to production were recorded during December:

Dec. 11   Purchased 60 items @ £12 each.

Dec. 18   Issued 30 items.

The following table shows the stock on hand after purchasing the additional 60 items on the 11th December:

	RECEIPTS			ISSUES			STOCK		
	Units	Price £	Value £	Units	Price £	Value £	Units	Price £	Value £
Opening stock							20	10	200
Dec 11	60	12	720				20	10	200
							60	12	720
							80		920

At this point there were eighty items in stock with a collective value of £920. Thirty of these were subsequently issued in December and the remaining fifty remained in stock at the end of the month. As these were not used, their value must be excluded from the production costs reported for the year. However, purchases were made at £10 and £12 and we need to determine which price should be used for the valuation of the stocks. How many of the fifty items were bought for £10 each and how many for £12?

This is usually determined based on an assumed pattern of stock usage. We will consider three possible methods:

1. First in First Out (FIFO)

This method assumes that the items are issued to production in the order in which they are purchased (i.e. the first ones received are the first ones issued). Those remaining in stock at the end of the period are therefore assumed to be the most recent purchases. Using this method in the earlier example would produce the following situation:

FIFO

	RECEIPTS			ISSUES			STOCK		
	Units	Price £	Value £	Units	Price £	Value £	Units	Price £	Value £
Stock on hand at Dec 11							20	10	200
							60	12	720
							80		920
Dec 18				20	10	200	50	12	600
				10	12	120			
				30		320			

Using the FIFO method the items in stock at the start of the month are deemed to have been issued first. Of the 30 items issued it is therefore assumed that 20 came from the opening stock and the other 10 from the purchases made in the month at £12 each. The costs incurred in the year will therefore include £320 in respect of these materials. The closing stock comprises the most recently acquired items valued at £12 per unit.

2. Last in First Out (LIFO)

This is based on the opposite assumption. The issues to production are deemed to be those most recently received (i.e. the 'last in') and closing stock therefore comprises the earlier purchases. This method would produce the following values for materials issued and stock:

LIFO									
	RECEIPTS			**ISSUES**			**STOCK**		
	Units	Price £	Value £	Units	Price £	Value £	Units	Price £	Value £
Stock on hand at Dec 11							20	10	200
							60	12	720
							80		920
Dec 18				30	12	360	20	10	200
							30	12	360
							50		560

With LIFO the 30 items issued are assumed to be from the most recent batch purchased at £12 each. The closing stock will therefore comprise the other 30 items from this batch and the 20 items which were held at the start of the month.

3. Average Cost (AVCO)

Using this method, the average value of stock on hand is calculated and both issues and stocks remaining are valued at this rate as demonstrated below:

AVCO									
	RECEIPTS			**ISSUES**			**STOCK**		
	Units	Price £	Value £	Units	Price £	Value £	Units	Price £	Value £
Opening stock							20	10	200
Dec 11	60	12	720				80	11.50	920
Dec 18				30	11.50	345	50	11.50	575

Using the average cost method all items held in stock are valued at the same price. Thus after paying £720 for 60 items, the total stock comprised 80 items with a collective value of £920. This represents an average cost of £11.50 per unit and the issues and remaining stock are valued at this price.

Comparison of Methods

The choice of method will influence the costs (and therefore profit) reported for the period as shown:

	Purchase price of Materials £	Cost reported in the period £	Closing Stock £
FIFO	920	320	600
LIFO	920	360	560
AVCO	920	345	575

When prices are rising as in the example used, LIFO which assumes the latest (most expensive) materials are used first, will show higher costs and therefore lower profits. FIFO, which assumes the opposite, results in higher profits and the averaging effect of AVCO will produce a result somewhere between these two extremes.

The LIFO method is not recommended by SSAP 9 and is also unacceptable to the Inland Revenue. Consequently the FIFO and AVCO methods are more widely used.

The Valuation of Work In Progress and Finished Goods

The work in progress valuation comprises the production costs incurred in bringing unfinished items to their state of completion as at the end of the period. These will include a share of production overheads as well as direct costs such as materials, labour and any direct expenses. Where costing systems are used, they may be ascertained as outlined earlier. In the absence of such a system, the unfinished goods may be inspected and an assessment made as to the costs incurred up to that point.

Finished goods should be valued on the basis of the production costs incurred in completing the products. Again these will include direct costs and production overheads.

Summary

- Accounting statements for manufacturing organisations should be prepared in compliance with the principles previously examined for traders.

- The cost of goods sold reported in the trading account is ascertained using the cost of goods produced adjusted for opening and closing stocks:

	£
Opening stock of finished goods	25,000
Add cost of finished goods produced	160,000
	185,000
Less closing stock of finished goods	(20,000)
COST OF GOODS SOLD	165,000

- Product costs include:

    Direct costs – Direct materials.

    – Direct labour.

    – Direct expenses (if any).

    Indirect costs – Production overheads.

- The cost of materials consumed in a period may be based on one of the following assumptions:

    - First in first out (FIFO)

    - Last in first out (LIFO)

    - Average cost (AVCO)

    FIFO and AVCO are most commonly used in practice.

- The cost of finished goods produced should exclude that attributable to work in progress at the end of the period.

- The valuation of work in progress is based on an assessment of the production costs incurred in bringing the products to their state of completion at the end of the period.

- Finished goods are valued at the production costs incurred in their completion.

Questions   (See Appendix C for Answers)

6.1

On 1 January 19X7 a company had 200 units of component X in its stores which were valued in its books at the original cost of £50 per unit. The following purchases were then made:

> 8 January   600 units @ £58 each
> 3 February 400 units @ £64 each
> 11 March   600 units @ £72 each
> 3 April   200 units @ £73 each

Issues of the component to the factory during the first three months of 19X7 were:

> 16 January   400 units
> 12 February 600 units
> 23 March   200 units

You are required to

    (a)   Prepare the stores ledger account for component X showing the receipts, issues and stock in hand in both quantities and values when issues are priced in accordance with the weighted average price method;

    (b)   Describe briefly two other methods of pricing material issues from stock. What effect on the company's reported profit would the application of one of these methods have as compared to the existing weighted average price method?

(CIMA)

6.2

    (a)   A firm has the following transactions with its product R.

        Year 1
        Opening stock: nil
        Buys 10 units @ £300 per unit
        Buys 12 units @ £250 per unit
        Sells 8 units @ £400 per unit
        Buys 6 units @ £200 per unit
        Sells 12 units @ £400 per unit

        Year 2
        Buys 10 units @ £200 per unit
        Sells 5 units @ £400 per unit

Buys 12 units @ £150 per unit
Sells 25 units @ £400 per unit

Required

Calculate on an item by item basis for both year 1 and year 2:

(i)   The closing stock

(ii) The sales

(iii) The cost of sales

(iv) The gross profit

using, separately, the LIFO and the FIFO methods of stock valuation. Present all workings clearly.

(b)   Paragraph 39 of SSAP 9 suggests that the LIFO stock figure at the end of year 1 in (a) above would be a 'misstatement of balance sheet amounts' and would potentially cause a 'distortion of current and future results'.

Required

Comment on these suggestions, using the situation and calculations from part (a) above as an illustration. Your answer should indicate the extent to which you agree with the comment in Paragraph 39 as regards the use of the LIFO method of stock valuation.

(ACCA)

6.3

Laurel Manufacturing has the following information available in respect of the year ended 31.12.X8.

	£
Direct labour	71,300
Opening stocks – Direct materials	27,500
– Work in progress	37,400
– Finished goods	41,500
Closing stocks – Direct materials	30,300
– Work in progress	36,000
– Finished goods	40,600
Selling and distribution expenses	38,000
Administration expenses	79,100
Indirect production expenses	63,200
Sales	415,600
Purchases of raw materials	116,300

Required

Prepare a Manufacturing, Trading and Profit and Loss Account for the year ended 31.12.X8.

6.4

The following information relates to the activities of Amos Manufacturing during the year ended 30th September 19X7.

	£
Sales	250,400
Selling and distribution expenses	12,300
Production overheads	18,500
Opening Stocks	
Raw materials	9,600
Work in progress	23,500
Finished goods	30,800
Closing Stocks	
Work in progress	21,300
Finished goods	29,900
Administration expenses	21,600
Raw materials consumed	102,000
Direct wages	64,200

The sales figure includes £5,000 in respect of goods which were returned by a customer before the end of the financial year. A mark up of 25% had been applied to the cost of producing these goods in determining the selling price.

The following accruals and prepayments have not yet been accounted for:

	Prepayments £	*Accruals* £
Selling and distribution	600	1,500
Administration	–	2,900
Production overheads	300	900

Required

Prepare Amos's Manufacturing, Trading and Profit and Loss Account for the year.

Questions Without Answers

6.5

The following information has been extracted from the accounts of Wardley Manufacturing for the year ended 31.12.X8:

	£
Opening stocks – raw materials	21,250
-- work in progress	26,180
-- finished goods	41,760
Sales	286,400
Raw materials purchased	93,100
Direct wages costs	39,420
Factory indirect expenses	51,640
Administrative expenses	46,730
Selling and distribution expenses	18,670
Closing stocks – raw materials	29,480
– work in progress	21,360
– finished goods	38,410

As at 31.12.X8 £3,200 was outstanding in respect of administrative expenses and £4,100 relating to factory indirect expenses. Selling and distribution expenses included prepayments of £1,400.

Closing stocks include raw materials valued at £830 which have deteriorated to such an extent that they must be disposed of. Their scrap value has been estimated at £100.

Required

Prepare a manufacturing, trading and profit and loss account for the year ended 31.12.X8.

6.6

Rock was the sole proprietor of a sweet manufacturing business and the following trial balance was extracted from his books as on 31st December 19X7:

	Dr £	Cr £
Capital account: Rock		20,400
Freehold land and buildings at cost	15,000	
Plant and machinery at cost	14,500	
Plant and machinery, provision for depreciation		7,000
Travellers' cars at cost	4,000	
Travellers' cars, provision for depreciation		2,800
Loose tools and utensils at valuation on 1 January 19X7	1,200	
Stocks, 1 January 19X7		
Raw materials	3,300	
Finished goods (25 tons)	6,000	
Purchases		
Raw materials	18,500	
Tools and utensils	800	
Sales 210 tons		66,000
Wages		
Factory	13,640	
Administration	5,400	
Sales department	3,000	
Rates and insurance	1,600	
Repairs to buildings	1,000	
Sales expenses including vehicle running costs	1,440	
Electricity and power	6,000	
Administration expenses	2,810	
Provision for doubtful debts		1,000
Sales ledger balances	6,100	
Purchase ledger balances		3,580
Bank		3,610
Cash in hand	100	
	104,390	104,390

You are given the following information:

1.   Closing stocks on 31st December 19X7 raw materials £2,800; finished goods (15 tons) £3,900; loose tools and utensils, £1,600.

2.   Provision is to be made for the following amounts owing on 31st December 19X7: electricity and power £800, new machinery £500.

3. Payments in advance on 31st December 19X7, were as follows: rates £300, vehicle licences £40.

4. Annual depreciation on plant and machinery and travellers' cars to be provided at the rate of 15% and 20% respectively on cost at the end of the year.

5. Bad debts amounting to £500 are to be written off and the provision for doubtful debts reduced to £600.

6. Expenses are to be allotted as follows:

	Works	Administration
Rates and insurance	7/10	3/10
Repairs	4/5	1/5
Electricity and power	9/10	1/10

Adjustments for bad debts and the provision for doubtful debts are attributable to selling and delivery expenses.

You are required to prepare:

(a) the manufacturing, trading and profit and loss accounts for the year ended 31st December 19X7, showing the works cost and administration cost per ton produced, and

(b) the balance sheet as on that date.

(ICAEW)

6.7

The following information has been extracted from the books of account of the Marsden Manufacturing Company for the year to 30 September 19X4:

	£
Advertising	2,000
Depreciation for the year to 30 September 19X4:	
Factory equipment	7,000
Office equipment	4,000
Direct wages	40,000
Factory: Insurance	1,000
Heat	15,000
Indirect materials	5,000
Power	20,000
Salaries	25,000
Finished goods (at 1 October 19X3)	24,000
Office: electricity	15,000
general expenses	9,000
postage and telephones	2,900
salaries	70,000
Raw material purchases	202,000
Raw material stock (at 1 October 19X3)	8,000
Sales	512,400
Work in progress (at 1 October 19X3)	12,000

Notes:

1.   At 30 September 19X4, the following stocks were on hand:

	£
Raw materials	10,000
Work in progress	9,000
Finished goods	30,000

2.   At 30 September 19X4, there was an accrual for advertising of £1,000, and it was estimated that £1,500 had been paid in advance for electricity. These items had not been included in the books of account for the year to 30 September 19X4.

You are required to prepare Marsden's manufacturing, trading and profit and loss account for the year to 30 September 19X4.

(AAT)

Chapter 7

Partnership and Company Accounts

Learning Objectives

After completing this chapter you should be able to:

- Distinguish between sole traders, partnerships and limited companies.

- Describe the typical contents of a partnership agreement.

- Describe the way in which capital and current accounts are used in partnerships.

- Prepare a profit and loss account and balance sheet for a partnership.

- Show how the following changes affect partnership accounts:

  - the admission of a new partner

  - the revaluation of fixed assets

  - the retirement of a partner

  - a change in the profit sharing ratio.

- Explain the concept of limited liability.

- Describe the main sources of capital for a company.

- Outline the main requirements of the Companies Act 1985/89 in respect of the disclosure of accounting information.

Introduction

The accounting reports examined in previous chapters have reflected the activities of sole traders. These businesses are owned by one individual who provides capital, is entitled to any profits earned and is personally liable for the debts of the business. As finance is limited to that provided by, or available to, the owner these businesses tend to be relatively small. To obtain the funds required for growth it may be necessary to widen the ownership of the business by forming a partnership or limited company. In this chapter, we will examine the differences between these types of businesses and sole traders in terms of their legal obligations and the preparation of accounting information.

Partnerships

A partnership is a business owned by more than one person. The maximum number of partners permitted is twenty, although professional firms such as solicitors and architects are allowed to exceed this limit. Establishing a partnership may be preferable to operating as a sole trader for a number of reasons. These may include:

Access to additional finance

Capital can be provided by each partner and if additional investment is subsequently required, partners may be able to provide (or gain access to) further funds.

Extending the range of skills

Each partner may bring to the business particular skills which will enhance the collective expertise of the partnership.

Widening the customer base

Partners may have previously established good relationships with potential customers which can be exploited by the partnership.

Legal Requirements

Partners, like sole traders, are generally legally liable for the actions and debts of the business. However, the Limited Partnership Act 1907 permits a partnership to include some partners whose liability is limited to the amount of capital invested, so long as they are not involved in the management of the business.

As far as accounting is concerned the Partnership Act 1890 requires that accounts are maintained which record for each partner, the capital provided, their share of profits and any drawings.

The Partnership Agreement

The basis on which the partnership is to operate is usually recorded in a legally binding partnership agreement. This will include among other things:

1. Day to day working arrangements

Some partners may play a more active part in the management and day to day operation of the business than others. These arrangements may be recorded formally in the agreement.

2. Salaries

Those partners spending time managing or working in the business may be granted a salary as well as a share of profits.

3. The capital to be provided by each partner

The partners may contribute equally or agree different levels of investment. Those with a higher level of investment may be compensated through the payment of interest on the capital provided or entitlement to a greater share of profits.

4. Interest on capital

Where all partners have contributed capital equally and are entitled to an equal share of profits, the payment of interest may be unnecessary. However where this is not the case, interest on capital may be paid at an agreed rate.

5. Interest on drawings

All businesses must ensure that sufficient cash is available to meet liabilities as they fall due. In addition funds will be required for investment purposes. Consequently, to encourage the retention of funds in the business, partners may be charged interest on drawings, calculated at an agreed rate from the date of withdrawal to the end of the financial year. As well as discouraging the early withdrawal of cash this ensures that the remaining partners are compensated for leaving their entitlement in the business for a longer period.

6. The division of profits and losses between the partners

The risks and rewards arising from the business are shared by the partners and some agreement must be reached on the basis for the division of profits and losses. Those who have contributed greater capital sums and/or spend more time working in the business may be compensated with a greater share of profits. Alternatively, such inequalities may be catered for through the payment of interest on capital and/or salaries as explained above. In these circumstances the remaining profit may be divided equally between the partners or may perhaps reflect other factors such as the relative experience and expertise of each partner. The share of profit to which each partner is entitled also represents the contribution which must be made towards any losses made by the business.

An example illustrating the division of profit is given below:

Example 7.1

Ron, Pat and Jan operate a business in which they have invested £10,000, £20,000, and £20,000 respectively. They have agreed that profits remaining after paying 10% interest on capital and a salary of £15,000 to Jan, will be split on the following basis:

Ron 40%

Pat 30%

Jan 30%

In 19X9 the business made a net profit of £40,000 before allowing for Jan's salary.

This would be distributed as shown:

	Total £	Ron £	Pat £	Jan £
Salary	15,000			15,000
Interest on capital	5,000	1,000	2,000	2,000
Balance for distribution	20,000	8,000 (40%)	6,000 (30%)	6,000 (30%)
Total	40,000	9,000	8,000	23,000

Jan has been paid for her work in the business and each partner compensated for the capital sums invested. The remaining £20,000 has been distributed on the agreed basis with Ron's greater share perhaps reflecting his greater expertise.

Where no partnership agreement exists, the Partnership Act 1890 states that partners are entitled to neither a salary nor interest on capital and that all profits should be shared equally.

Recording Transactions

Transactions in a partnership are recorded in the same manner as for a sole trader as explained in Chapter 3. The only additional complication is the recording of each partner's investment and their entitlement to a share of the profits. This is accomplished through the operation of a capital and current account for each partner.

The Capital Account

The capital account is used to record the long term investment in the business in the same way as a sole trader. The only difference in the case of a partnership is that a separate account will be used to record the investment of each partner.

The Current Account

All other transactions are recorded in a current account for each partner. Any sum to which a partner is entitled is transferred from the profit and loss account to this account and any drawings made by the partner will reduce the balance outstanding. This process is illustrated in the following example:

Example 7.2

The partners in Example 7.1 made the following drawings during 19X9:

> Ron £ 7,000
> Pat £12,000
> Jan £15,000

The balance on Pat's current account at the start of the year was £1,000. The other current accounts had zero balances.

The transactions for the year will be reflected in current accounts as shown below:

	Ron £	Pat £	Jan £
Opening balance	0	1,000	0
Salary	0	0	15,000
Interest on capital	1,000	2,000	2,000
Share of profits	8,000	6,000	6,000
Amount due	9,000	9,000	23,000
Less drawings	(7,000)	(12,000)	(15,000)
Closing balance	2,000	(3,000)	8,000

Ron has withdrawn £7,000 of the £9,000 to which he is entitled and the closing balance on his current account reflects the £2,000 still outstanding. This will be shown with the owners' funds in the balance sheet.

Pat was owed £1,000 at the start of the year and her entitlement for 19X9 increased this to £9,000. However, as her drawings amounted to £12,000 her current account was overdrawn by £3,000 at the end of the year. This represents an advance on future entitlements.

Jan has withdrawn her full salary of £15,000 but none of her interest or profit and is therefore due a further £8,000.

The Retention of Profit

Where the business requires additional long term finance, the partners may decide to reinvest some of the profits rather than withdraw them for personal use. This may be recorded by transferring the relevant amounts from current to capital accounts, reflecting additional long term investment by the partners.

The Preparation of Accounting Statements

Accounting statements are prepared on the same basis as for sole traders. However, they must show that capital is provided by more than one owner and that profits will be distributed to a number of individuals. These factors will affect both the profit and loss account and balance sheet.

The Profit and Loss Account

Each partner's entitlement to a share of profit is shown in an appropriation (distribution) section in the profit and loss account as shown below:

THE RON PAT AND JAN PARTNERSHIP

PROFIT AND LOSS ACCOUNT FOR THE YEAR ENDED 31.12.X9

			£
Sales			220,000
Less cost of sales			(100,000)
Gross Profit			120,000
Less Expenses			(80,000)
NET PROFIT			40,000
Appropriation			
Salaries	–Jan		15,000
Interest on capital	– Ron	1,000	
	– Pat	2,000	
	– Jan	2,000	5,000
Share of profit	– Ron	8,000	
	– Pat	6,000	
	– Jan	6,000	20,000
			40,000

The Balance Sheet

The balance sheet must show the capital provided by each partner, distinguishing between long term investment recorded in capital accounts and short term funds in current accounts:

THE RON PAT AND JAN PARTNERSHIP

BALANCE SHEET AS AT 31.12.X9

		£ Cost	£ Accum. Dep'n	£
Fixed Assets		60,000	20,000	40,000
Current Assets				
Stock			14,000	
Debtors			25,000	
Cash			8,000	
			47,000	
Less: Current Liabilities				
Creditors			(30,000)	17,000
				57,000
Financed by,				
Capital Accounts	– Ron		10,000	
	– Pat		20,000	
	– Jan		20,000	50,000
Current Accounts	– Ron		2,000	
	– Pat		(3,000)	
	– Jan		8,000	7,000
				57,000

Changes in Partnerships

Changes in partnerships may arise due to a change in the number of partners (e.g. a new partner is introduced or an existing partner retires) or an agreement to alter the existing profit sharing ratio. We will now examine the implications of such changes.

Introduction of a New Partner

The admission of a new partner will result in an increase in assets (e.g. the cash paid to join the partnership) and a resulting increase in capital (i.e. the new partner's capital account). This is illustrated in the following example:

Example 7.3

Oliver and Stanley are in partnership sharing profits equally and the following balance sheet has been prepared for the business:

OLIVER AND STANLEY

BALANCE SHEET AS AT 31.12.X8

		£
Fixed assets		60,000
Current assets		
Stock	20,000	
Debtors	10,000	
Cash	10,000	
	40,000	
Current liabilities		
Creditors	(15,000)	
Net current assets		25,000
Net assets		85,000
Capital		
Oliver		45,000
Stanley		40,000
		85,000

Charlie is introduced to the partnership on 31 December 19X8 with capital of £35,000 and the three partners are to share profits equally.

The new balance sheet would appear as shown below:

OLIVER, STANLEY AND CHARLIE

BALANCE SHEET AS AT 31.12.X8

		£
Fixed assets		60,000
Current assets		
Stock	20,000	
Debtors	10,000	
Cash (10,000 + 35,000)	45,000	
	75,000	
Current liabilities		
Creditors	(15,000)	
Net current assets		60,000
Net assets		120,000
Capital		
Oliver		45,000
Stanley		40,000
Charlie		35,000
		120,000

However the situation is complicated if the business is worth more than the value of the net assets shown in the balance sheet.

Let us suppose for example that Oliver and Stanley's partnership had been valued at £100,000 as a going concern. Selling the business for this amount would realise £15,000 more than the value of the net assets, with this sum representing goodwill. Oliver and Stanley would be entitled to half of this each and would therefore each receive £7,500 in addition to their capital entitlements. The £100,000 sales proceeds would therefore be distributed as follows.

	Oliver £	Stanley £	Total £
Capital	45,000	40,000	85,000
Share of goodwill	7,500	7,500	15,000
Amount received	52,500	47,500	100,000

If the business was sold immediately Charlie joined the partnership, the selling price would probably be £135,000 (i.e. the original £100,000 value plus the £35,000 cash introduced by Charlie). As the three partners have agreed that profits should be divided equally, this sum would be distributed as follows:

	Oliver £	Stanley £	Charlie £	Total £
Capital	45,000	40,000	35,000	120,000
Share of goodwill	5,000	5,000	5,000	15,000
Amount received	50,000	45,000	40,000	135,000

Thus Charlie would make a profit of £5,000 on the sale when it could be argued that he had as yet done nothing to warrant this since his injection of £35,000 had done nothing to increase the value of the business. Oliver and Stanley on the other hand would each see their profit fall by £2,500 as their share of the goodwill fell from £7,500 to £5,000. As the goodwill was accumulated before Charlie joined the partnership, it should be attributed only to Oliver and Stanley and the accounts should be adjusted to reflect this.

Accounting Adjustments

To rectify the problem discussed above, the goodwill can be recorded in the accounts and credited to the original partners' capital accounts. This would result in the following balance sheet after the introduction of Charlie:

OLIVER, STANLEY AND CHARLIE

BALANCE SHEET AS AT 31.12.X8

		£
Fixed assets (60,000 + 15,000)		75,000
Current assets		
Stock	20,000	
Debtors	10,000	
Cash (10,000 + 35,000)	45,000	
	75,000	
Current liabilities		
Creditors	(15,000)	
Net current assets		60,000
Net assets		135,000
Capital		
Oliver (45,000 + 7,500)		52,500
Stanley (40,000 + 7,500)		47,500
Charlie		35,000
		135,000

On selling the business now for £135,000 each partner would receive their capital as shown in the balance sheet. Charlie would therefore receive only the £35,000 he invested and the goodwill would be shared equally between Oliver and Stanley.

Revaluation of Fixed Assets

Another reason which could give rise to a business being worth more than the net assets shown in the balance sheet is the possibility that fixed assets such as buildings and equipment etc. which are valued at historical cost less depreciation, may be undervalued. This can be rectified in the same manner as described for goodwill with the asset values being amended in the accounts and the capital accounts of the existing partners increased in accordance with the profit sharing ratios. Note that if the assets were overvalued in the accounts their revaluation would result in a reduction in capital accounts, again in accordance with profit sharing ratios.

Adjustments Through Capital Accounts Only

Where it has been decided not to amend the individual asset accounts to reflect goodwill or asset revaluations it will still be necessary to ascertain the difference between the book value of net assets and their current value. This is to ensure that existing partners are not disadvantaged by the introduction of a new partner. Compensating adjustments can be confined to capital accounts only in these circumstances.

To illustrate this let us suppose that on Charlie joining Oliver and Stanley's partnership it was decided that the accounts should not be amended to show goodwill. As we saw earlier the accounts undervalue net assets by £15,000 and unless capital accounts are amended, Charlie would effectively gain a £5,000 share of this with Oliver and Stanley each losing £2,500. To compensate for this, capital accounts could be amended as follows:

Oliver Capital	+ £2,500
Stanley Capital	+ £2,500
Charlie Capital	− £5,000

The balance sheet after Charlie's introduction would then appear as follows:

OLIVER, STANLEY AND CHARLIE

BALANCE SHEET AS AT 31.12.X8

		£
Fixed assets		60,000
Current assets		
Stock	20,000	
Debtors	10,000	
Cash (10,000 + 35,000)	45,000	
	75,000	
Current liabilities		
Creditors	(15,000)	
Net current assets		60,000
Net assets		120,000
Capital		
Oliver (45,000 + 2,500)		47,500
Stanley (40,000 + 2,500)		42,500
Charlie (35,000 – 5,000)		30,000
		120,000

Charlie's entitlement is therefore £30,000 in respect of capital and a £5,000 share of goodwill (i.e. £15,000 ÷ 3) and as with the previous method is equal to the £35,000 he has invested.

Retirement of a Partner

Any partners leaving a partnership will be entitled to repayment of their capital account. However as described earlier, where the net assets shown in the account are under or over valued, the the capital account will not reflect the partner's true entitlement. Consequently the asset values and capital accounts should be re-stated as explained earlier in order that the true claim of the retiring partner can be ascertained.

Changing Profit Sharing Ratios

Where existing partners agree to change the profit sharing ratio, then again adjustments must be made for goodwill or any under/over valuation of net assets in the accounts.

Let us suppose for instance that Oliver and Stanley decide to change the profit sharing ratio from 1:1 to 2:1 in Oliver's favour. Although Oliver will be entitled to a greater share of profit in the future, it would be unfair to Stanley if this entitlement included goodwill built up during the time during which their entitlements were equal. Therefore an adjustment should be made and as with the introduction of a new partner, there are two ways of dealing with this as shown below:

(a) Recording Goodwill in the Accounts

This would require the following entries crediting each partner with an equal share of goodwill generated to date:

Goodwill	+ £15,000
Oliver Capital	+ £ 7,500
Stanley Capital	+ £ 7,500

(b) Adjustment Through Capital Accounts Only

If a decision was taken not to record goodwill in the accounts then adjustments could be made in capital accounts only as shown below:

	Oliver £	Stanley £	Total £
Share of Goodwill			
Current profit share ratio	7,500	7,500	15,000
Revised profit share ratio	10,000	5,000	15,000
Difference	2,500	2,500	–
	increase	decrease	

Adjustment required to compensate:

Oliver Capital	– £2,500
Stanley Capital	+ £2,500

Stanley is thus compensated for the decrease in his entitlement to goodwill resulting from the change in profit sharing.

Changes During a Financial Year

Where change is made in the partnership structure or profit sharing ratios during the course of a financial year, the profit for the year must be split between those earned before and those after the change. This will enable the profits to be apportioned to the partners in the agreed ratios in each separate period.

Let us suppose for example that Oliver and Stanley's agreement to change profit sharing from an equal basis to 2:1 was to be effective from 1st May and that the profits for the year in question were:

January - April	£ 7,000
May - December	£12,000

These profits would be attributed to the partners as follows:

	Total £	Oliver £	Stanley £
January - April (1:1)	7,000	3,500	3,500
May - December (2:1)	12,000	8,000	4,000
	19,000	11,500	7,500

Limited Companies

One of the drawbacks of operating in partnership or as a sole trader, is that the owner(s) are legally liable for the debts of the business. If it has financial problems they may be forced to sell personal assets such as their home or car to pay creditors. To prevent this from discouraging investment in business, the concept of limited liability has been established.

The main factor distinguishing limited companies from sole traders and partnerships is that they are recognised as having a separate legal identity from their owners. Consequently a company can own assets and incur liabilities in its own name and if creditors are unable to recover debts, it is the company which is sued rather than its owners. The liability of the owners is limited to the amount they have agreed to invest in the business and their personal assets are therefore protected and their risk reduced considerably.

To protect the interests of those trading with, or lending money to, limited companies, they are legally obliged to publish accounting information which can be used by such parties to appraise their financial position. The nature of this information will be explained later in this chapter.

Sources of Capital

As well as the protection of limited liability, another reason for establishing a limited company may be to gain greater access to capital as it is required. A company may raise long term finance by issuing shares or obtaining loans.

Company Shares

The maximum share capital which a company is allowed to issue (known as the 'Authorised Share Capital') is detailed in a document called the Memorandum of Association which must be lodged with the Registrar of Companies when the company is established. Shares may then be sold to satisfy the capital requirements of the business. A company requiring initial capital of £100,000 may for example issue 100,000 shares for £1 each or 200,000 shares at 50p each (this is known as the 'nominal' value of the shares). The shareholders, of whom there must be at least two, share in the risks and rewards of the venture in proportion to the number of shares held. Additional sums may be raised at a later date by further issues to either existing shareholders or new investors.

The parties to whom shares may be offered is determined by the nature of the company.

Public Limited Companies are permitted to offer shares for sale to the general public. These companies must use the term 'Public limited company' (or 'plc') after their names to alert those dealing with them of their limited liability status. They tend to be large organisations and may be either 'listed', in which case the shares are traded on a recognised stock exchange, or 'unlisted'.

Private limited companies use the term 'Limited' ('Ltd.') after their names and are not permitted to offer shares for sale to the public. Consequently, they tend to be smaller businesses which may at some stage 'go public' in order to acquire the additional capital which may be necessary for expansion.

Shareholders wishing to reduce, or relinquish their investment in a company may do so by selling shares. If the company has performed well, the price obtainable may exceed the nominal value of the shares. Although the seller would realise a capital gain on the sale, the increase in the market value of the shares would produce no direct benefit for the company itself with any share dealings after the initial issue being between the individuals concerned.

Dividends

As well as capital gains through rising share prices, shareholders may also receive an annual income from the distribution of profits. As explained in Chapter 4, a portion of profit earned is usually retained within a business for reinvestment and the balance withdrawn by the owners. In the case of a company this takes the form of a dividend payable at a rate per share held. This may be paid in full at the end of the year or alternatively, an 'interim' dividend may be paid during the year with the balance payable at the year end.

In order to protect the interests of creditors, dividends may only be paid from profits. This prevents shareholders in companies with financial problems from withdrawing their capital and depriving the business of the means to pay creditors, employees etc. It is the shareholders who stand to benefit most from the success of a company and it is they who should bear the greatest risk, not the creditors.

The size of the dividend in any year will therefore be influenced by:

- The profits available.

- The future financial requirements of the business (i.e. how much should be retained).

- The availability of liquid funds. As we shall see in the next chapter, profits do not necessarily generate cash.

Classes of Share

The two main types of shares issued by companies are preference and ordinary shares.

Preference Shares

Preference shareholders are entitled to their share of profits before any payment is made to ordinary shareholders. Consequently if profits are low, there may be sufficient to pay only preference dividends, in which case ordinary shareholders will receive nothing. Preference shareholders also rank above ordinary shareholders for repayment of capital when a business is being wound up. If insufficient funds remain after settling liabilities and repaying preference shareholders, ordinary shareholders may not recoup their investment.

As preference shareholders bear less risk than the ordinary shareholders, their returns from the business are restricted. Preference dividends are limited to a fixed annual rate expressed as a percentage of the nominal value of the shares. For example holders of 6% preference shares with a nominal value of £1 will receive a dividend of 6p per annum no matter how successful the company is.

Preference shares may be classed as either cumulative or non-cumulative. In the case of cumulative shares, if the full dividend is not paid in any year the entitlement accumulates and this shortfall must be paid up in subsequent years before any dividends can be paid to ordinary shareholders.

Another consequence of lower risk for preference shareholders is that they may have less influence on company policy than ordinary shareholders. Major decisions such as the appointment of directors, are taken at a company's annual general meeting and preference shareholders may have restricted voting rights on such matters.

Ordinary Shares

To compensate for bearing greater risk, the rewards available to ordinary shareholders are potentially unlimited. They are entitled to the profits remaining after paying preference dividends and if the company is successful may receive substantial returns. As the ultimate risk bearers in a company they are usually entitled to one vote per share held at the annual general meeting.

Loans and Debentures

Another source of long term finance for companies is borrowing. In addition to loans from institutions such as banks, companies may also borrow through issuing debentures. These are documents evidencing a loan made to a company at a specified interest rate. They are transferable in the same way as shares and their market value may also fluctuate over time. Debenture holders are creditors and not members (owners) of a company and are therefore not eligible to vote at the annual general meeting. They are entitled to interest annually and repayment of their capital at the redemption date stated on the debenture document.

Borrowing as a source of company finance has advantages and disadvantages. On the positive side, loans and debentures may represent a relatively cheap way of raising funds. This is because the interest payable is tax deductible (i.e. it is deducted in establishing the profits on which corporation tax is payable, therefore reducing the tax charge). Its disadvantage is that unlike dividends, loan and debenture interest must be paid regardless of whether there are profits available. Consequently excessive debt can place a great burden on a business when profits are low and the level of borrowing should therefore be managed carefully.

Legal Requirements

Companies, should comply with the principles and accounting standards outlined in Chapter 2 in the same way as any other business. However, they differ from other organisations in that they have limited liability status which may have serious implications for those with whom they do business. Where a company has financial problems creditors may be unable to recover outstanding debts and there are many examples of suppliers becoming insolvent as a result of a major customer folding. To protect these and other parties with a financial interest, companies must comply with the legal requirements of the Companies Act 1985/89. Although these are extensive and complex, the most relevant aspects at this introductory level are those relating to the disclosure of information.

The Disclosure of Information

The Act requires that all companies prepare a document known as the annual report and accounts. A copy must be sent to each shareholder and an additional copy filed with the Registrar of Companies. As the documents filed are available to the public, anyone wishing to do business with a company may do so having firstly inspected information relating to its activities and financial position.

The Act prescribes the content of the annual report and accounts and the format in which information must be presented and requires that the following are included:

1. A profit and loss account.

2. A balance sheet.

3. A statement of accounting policies.

4. A directors' report.

5. An auditor's report.

We will consider each of these in turn:

1. The Profit and Loss Account

Both the profit and loss account and the balance sheet must be presented in one of a number of prescribed formats. Two alternatives for the balance sheet are given and four for the profit and loss account.

The profit and loss account looks like those prepared for sole traders or partnerships in most respects with the main differences occurring in the detail which follows the net profit figure. This is best illustrated by looking at an example using one of the prescribed formats:

PRESTWICK LIMITED

PROFIT AND LOSS ACCOUNT FOR THE YEAR ENDED 31.12.X8

		19X8	19X7
	NOTES	£'000	£'000
Turnover	*1*	1,504	1,433
Cost of Sales		(1,182)	(1,092)
GROSS PROFIT		322	341
Distribution Costs	2	(30)	(24)
Administrative Expenses	2	(61)	(48)
OPERATING PROFIT BEFORE INTEREST		231	269
Income From Investments	3	3	6
Interest Payable	4	(79)	(37)
PROFIT BEFORE TAX		155	238
Taxation	5	(29)	(37)
PROFIT AFTER TAX		126	201
Dividends	6	(21)	(25)
RETAINED PROFIT FOR THE YEAR		105	176
Earnings Per Share	7	11.32p	19.64p

NB. *(i) The results for the previous year are also given to permit comparison between the two years.*

(ii) The note numbers refer to fuller explanations given elsewhere in the document which may provide a breakdown of the relevant figure or perhaps the basis on which it has been calculated.

The statement is explained below, using the numbered notes for reference purposes.

Note

1.   Turnover relates to the sales income for the year. The explanatory note may break this down by market segment and/or geographical area.

2.   A detailed analysis of expenses is not required by the Act. They are shown in broad categories as illustrated.

3.   Companies may receive as well as pay interest. Receipts from investments such as bank deposits and shares in other companies will increase the profit for the period.

4.   Interest may be payable on debentures and other types of loan. The note in the accounts will provide a breakdown of the total figure.

5.   Taxation was not shown in the accounts for sole traders and partnerships because the owners are taxed personally on their income from those types of business. As a company has a separate legal identity it pays corporation tax on profits.

6.   The profit remaining after tax is attributable to the shareholders. As explained previously, it is likely that an element will be withdrawn in the form of dividends and the balance retained by the company for reinvestment.

7.   Companies are required to report an earnings per share figure. This shows current and potential shareholders the profit earned by the company in respect of each share issued. The statement may also indicate the portion of earnings which has been distributed, by stating the dividend per share.

2. The Balance Sheet

The balance sheet is also presented in essentially the same manner as for sole traders and partnerships. The main differences occur in the section showing the owners' funds as demonstrated in the following example:

PRESTWICK LIMITED

BALANCE SHEET AS AT 31.12.X8

	NOTES	19X8 £'000	19X7 £'000
FIXED ASSETS			
Tangible Assets	8	2,700	1,768
Investments	9	140	150
		2,840	1,918
CURRENT ASSETS			
Stocks	10	189	195
Debtors	11	186	171
Cash at Bank and in Hand	12	220	85
		595	451
CREDITORS : amounts falling due within one year	13	(350)	(291)
NET CURRENT ASSETS		**245**	**160**
CREDITORS : amounts falling due after more than one year	14	(1,417)	(560)
NET ASSETS EMPLOYED		**1,668**	**1,518**
CAPITAL AND RESERVES			
Called Up Share Capital	15	300	267
Share Premium account	16	120	108
Revaluation Reserve	17	310	310
Profit and Loss account	18	938	833
SHAREHOLDERS' FUNDS		**1,668**	**1,518**

Note

8. The note referring to fixed assets will contain details of the cost, accumulated depreciation and net book value of the various categories of assets.

9. This figure represents long term investments such as shares in other companies.

10. The analysis of the stocks figure in the notes will show values for raw materials, work in progress and finished goods where appropriate.

11. The debtors figure will include any prepayments.

12. Short term investments such as bank deposits are included with the current assets.

13. Creditors may include two items which do not appear in the accounts of sole traders or partnerships:

> **Taxation**. The tax payable on the profit for the year will be paid after the end of the financial year. However, in accordance with the accruals principle, the amount payable should be estimated and included in the year to which it relates. At the year end date it is therefore recorded as a liability in the balance sheet and included with creditors payable within one year.

> **Dividends**. As the full dividend will not be paid to shareholders until after the year end, the outstanding amount will also be reported with the creditors.

14. The longer term creditors figure will include debentures and other long term loans.

15. The share capital represents the nominal value of shares issued by the company. The note to the accounts will provide a breakdown between different types of shares (e.g. ordinary, preference).

16. As explained earlier, the market value of company shares may rise if it performs well. In these circumstances, any subsequent shares issued by the company will be at a price in excess of the nominal value. The additional proceeds from such issues which are attributable to the rise in share price are recorded in a share premium account and reported separately in the balance sheet.

17. Fixed assets such as land and buildings may appreciate in value over time rather than depreciate. This is recorded by increasing fixed asset values and creating a revaluation reserve to reflect the increase in shareholders' funds.

18. The profit and loss account shows the profit retained by the company over its lifetime and effectively represents additional investment by the shareholders.

3. Statement of Accounting Policies

As accounting standards permit some discretion in the treatment of certain items, companies must publish a statement outlining their accounting policies. This will include information such as the depreciation policy for fixed assets and will assist users of accounting statements in their interpretation.

4. The Directors' Report

The directors' report must include:

- A review of the company's activities and developments during the year.

- Details of any important events occurring since the year end.

- Information on planned future developments.

- The names of all directors and details of any shares or debentures they hold.

- The dividend proposed for the year.

- Details of research and development activities.

- The company's employment policy towards disabled persons.

- Details of any donations to political or charitable organisations during the year.

The report should be signed by either one director or the company secretary on behalf of the board of directors.

5. The Auditors' Report

To protect the interests of users of accounting information, all but the smallest limited companies are legally obliged to have their accounts verified by independent accountants acting as auditors who give their opinion as to whether the accounts:

(a) Have been prepared in accordance with the Companies Act.

(b) Represent a true and fair view of the results for the year and the financial position of the business as at the year end.

Any contentious issues are usually discussed prior to publishing the accounts and agreement reached between the auditors and the company's accountants as to the information to be disclosed. In these circumstances the auditors will give a brief report verifying the accounts. Where the auditors are dissatisfied with the information published, a qualified report is produced outlining the items with which they are unhappy.

Audit Exemptions

In 1994 the statutory audit was abolished for companies with a turnover not exceeding £90,000 per annum. For companies with an annual turnover between £90,000 and £350,000 it was replaced with the less onerous requirement for an independent account-ant's report verifying that the accounts correctly reflect the accounting records.

Disclosure of Additional Information

As well as complying with the disclosure requirements of the Companies Act, companies usually publish additional information voluntarily. This may include:

- Promotional material to publicise the company's activities.

- A report from the chairman reviewing the results and commenting on future prospects.

- A cash flow statement. (This is required by accounting standard FRS 1 and will be examined in detail in Chapter 8).

- A summary of financial results over a number of years.

Small and Medium Sized Companies

The Companies Act requires that a full set of accounts, complying with the disclosure requirements outlined above, be sent to each shareholder and that a copy be filed with the Registrar of Companies. However, small and medium sized companies are permitted to file an abridged version (although full accounts must be sent to shareholders).

To qualify as a small or medium sized company, two of the following three conditions must be satisfied for the current and previous year:

Definition of Small and Medium Companies

	Small Companies	Medium Companies
Turnover not exceeding	£2.8m	£11.2m
Total assets at the year end not exceeding	£1.4m	£ 5.6m
Average number of employees not exceeding	50	250

NB. The definition excludes:

    – Public limited companies

    – Banking, insurance and shipping companies (or groups containing these companies).

Small Companies

Small companies are permitted to file an abbreviated balance sheet and are not required to file a profit and loss account, directors' report or statement of accounting policies.

Medium Sized Companies

Medium sized companies are permitted to file an abbreviated profit and loss account and a limited amount of information in the notes to the accounts.

Listed Companies

In addition to complying with the Companies Act, public limited companies listed on the stock exchange must disclose additional information. This includes publishing a half yearly profit report and providing additional information in the annual report and accounts.

Group Accounts

A group of companies exists where a 'holding company' has a majority share holding in one or more 'subsidiary' companies. Subsidiaries may be wholly owned by the group or partially owned, in which case other parties will have a minority interest in the company.

Each company within a group must prepare its own annual accounts in the normal manner. However, the holding company must also publish a 'consolidated' profit and loss account and balance sheet showing the financial position of the entire group. The consolidated balance sheet will therefore show the combined assets and liabilities of the companies within the group. The claim on group assets by any minority interests will be shown separately within the balance sheet.

Summary

- Partnerships are owned by between two and twenty persons who are legally responsible for the actions and debts of the business.

- The basis on which the partnership is to operate is usually recorded in a legally binding partnership agreement. This will usually cover issues such as the division of profits/losses between the partners, the payment of salaries and interest payable on capital.

- Long term investment in the business is recorded in a separate capital account for each partner.

- A current account for each partner is used to record all other transactions (e.g. entitlement to profit and any drawings).

- The profit and loss account for a partnership will include an appropriation account showing the distribution of profits to the partners.

- The balance sheet must show the capital provided by each partner, distinguishing between long term investment recorded in capital accounts and short term funds in current accounts.

- Where there is a difference between the value of a partnership business and the value of net assets shown in the balance sheet, accounting adjustments should be made if:

  - a new partner is admitted

  - an existing partner retires

  - existing partners agree to change the profit sharing ratio.

- Limited companies are recognised as having a separate legal identity from their owners. The liability of the owners is limited to the amount they have agreed to invest in the business and their personal assets are therefore protected.

- Companies may raise capital through issuing shares and/or obtaining loans. Unlike private companies, public limited companies may sell shares to the general public.

- Company shareholders may benefit through a rise in the market price of the shares and/or dividends paid out of profits in proportion to the number of shares held.

- Preference shareholders rank before ordinary shareholders in respect of payment of dividends and repayment of capital on winding up the business. However unlike ordinary shareholders, their dividend is limited to an annual fixed percentage.

- Debentures are documents evidencing a loan made to a company at a specified interest rate. Debenture holders are creditors and not members (owners) of a company and are therefore not eligible to vote at the annual general meeting.

- In compliance with the Companies Act 1985/89, companies must circulate an annual report and accounts to all shareholders and file a copy with the Registrar of Companies. The report should include:

  1. A profit and loss account.

  2. A balance sheet.

  3. A statement of accounting policies.

  4. A directors' report.

  5. An auditor's report.

- Small and medium sized companies are given certain exemptions in respect of the information which must be published.

- Listed companies must comply with the more onerous disclosure requirements of the stock exchange.

- Holding companies are required to publish consolidated accounts for the entire group.

Questions   (See Appendix C for Answers)

7.1

Write short notes on the characteristics of the following sources of finance for a company and highlight the advantages and disadvantages of each to prospective investors in companies:

(a)   Ordinary shares

(b)   Preference shares

(c)   Debentures

7.2

It has been suggested that published accounting statements should attempt to be relevant, understandable, reliable, complete, objective, timely and comparable.

Required

(a)   Explain briefly in your own words, the meaning of these terms as applied to accounting.

(b)   Are there any difficulties in applying all of them at the same time?

(ACCA)

7.3

A friend has bought some shares in a quoted United Kingdom company and has received the latest accounts. There is one page he is having difficulty in understanding.

Required

Briefly but clearly answer his questions:

(a)   What is a balance sheet?

(b)   What is an asset?

(c)   What is a liability?

(d)   What is share capital?

(e)   What are reserves?

(f)   Why does the balance sheet balance?

(g)   To what extent does the balance sheet value my investment?

(ACCA)

7.4

The trial balance as at 30th April 19X2 in respect of Nibble Pie Limited is given below:

	DR (£000's)	CR (£000's)
Bank overdraft		80
Stock (as at 1st May X1)	820	
Turnover		15,150
Distribution costs	410	
Trade creditors		1,060
Trade debtors	1,900	
Fixtures and fittings:		
at cost	1,720	
accumulated depreciation at 1st May X1		400
Purchases	10,800	
Interest paid on overdraft	14	
Salaries -- distribution	120	
-- administration	750	
Called up share capital –		
(500,000 ordinary shares of £1)		500
Office Equipment:		
at cost	940	
accumulated depreciation as at 1st May X1		320
Profit and Loss A/C as at 1st May X1		2,064
Administrative Expenses	2,100	
	19,574	19,574

Further information is available as follows:

1. A dividend of 20p per share has been proposed.

2. There is an estimated liability to corporation tax of £160,000 on the ordinary profits of the year.

3. Estimated costs of £10,000 in respect of outstanding telephone charges for the period 1st February 19X2 - 30th April 19X2 have not yet been accounted for.

4. Depreciation for the year has not yet been accounted for and should be charged on the following basis:

Fixtures and fittings	5% of original cost
Office equipment	10% of original cost.

5.   The value of stock on hand at 30th April 19X2 was £520,000

6.   The figure for administrative expenses includes a prepayment of £30,000 in respect of office rental.

Required

From the above information, prepare a Profit and Loss Account for the year ended 30th April 19X2 and a Balance Sheet at that date in accordance with the Companies Act 1985.

7.5

Rigoletto Limited's Trial Balance as at 31st October 19X5 was as follows:

Trial Balance as at 31st October 19X5

	Debit £'000	Credit £'000
Ordinary Shares of 50p each, fully paid		600
14% Preference Shares of £1 each, fully paid		300
15% Debentures		200
Share Premium Account		100
General Reserve		400
Profit and Loss Account: Balance at 1 November 19X4		40
Stock as at 1 November 19X4	850	
Purchases and Sales	3,000	4,200
Selling and Distribution Costs	310	
Administrative Expenses	240	
Debenture Interest Paid for the half-year to 30 April 19X5	15	
Preference Dividend Paid for the half-year to 30 April 19X5	21	
Freehold Land and Buildings at cost	800	
Office Equipment at cost	360	
Motor Vehicles at cost	200	
Fixtures and Fittings at cost	120	
Provision for Depreciation as at 1 November 19X4:		
Office Equipment		160
Motor Vehicles		100
Fixtures and fittings		50
Debtors and Creditors	780	430
Bank Overdraft		116
	£6,696	£6,696

Additional Notes

1. Stock as at 31 October 19X5 was valued at £795,000.

2. Provision for depreciation of fixed assets is to be charged for the year on the reducing balance basis at the rate of 25% for office equipment; 30% for motor vehicles; and 10% for fixtures and fittings.

3. Selling and Distribution Costs accrued at 31.10.X5 amounted to £15,000. An audit fee of £18,000 has also to be provided for in the Accounts.

4. Administrative Expenses paid in advance at 31.10.X5 amounted to £13,000.

5. Provision is to be made for the second half-year's interest on the debentures.

6. Corporation Tax on the year's profit is calculated at £110,000.

7. The directors recommend that the second half-year's preference dividend be provided and propose to pay a dividend on ordinary shares of 10p per share. The directors also propose to transfer £180,000 to General Reserve.

Required

Prepare the Profit and Loss Account of Rigoletto limited for the year ended 31 October 19X5, together with a Balance Sheet as at that date, using the format laid down in the Companies Act, 1985.

7.6

Al and Bert are in partnership, sharing profits equally. At 30 June they have balances on their capital accounts of £12,000 (A1) and £15,000 (Bert). On that day they agree to bring in their friend Hall as a third partner. All three partners are to share profits equally from now on. Hall is to introduce £20,000 as capital into the business. Goodwill on 30 June is agreed at £18,000.

You are required:

(a) to show the partners' capital accounts for 30 June and 1 July on the assumption that the goodwill, previously unrecorded, is to be included in the accounts.

(b) to show the additional entries necessary to eliminate goodwill again from the accounts.

(c) to explain briefly what goodwill is. Why are adjustments necessary when a new partner joins a partnership?

(ACCA)

7.7

Webb and Guy are partners sharing profits and losses in the ratio 3:1 and the partnership agreement provides for Guy to receive a salary of £2,000 per annum and for interest on capital at 5% per annum. The partners' current accounts for the year ended 31 December 19X8 were as follows:

	Webb £	Guy £		Webb £	Guy £
Drawings	4,280	3,950	Balance at 1 Jan 19X8	900	100
Goods		100	Salary		2,000
			Interest on capital	480	300
			Share of profit	4,500	1,500
Balance at 31 Dec 19X8	1,600		Balance at 31 Dec 19X8		150
	£5,880	£4,050		£5,880	£4,050

The balance sheet as at 31 December 19X8 was:

	£	£		£	£
Premises at cost		10,400	**Capital accounts**		
Equipment at cost	4,000		Webb	8,000	
Less depreciation	2,400	1,600	Guy	5,000	13,000
		12,000			
			Current accounts		
Stock	2,800		Webb	1,600	
Debtors	1,100		Guy	(150)	1,450
Cash	200	4,100			
			Creditors and Accruals		1,650
		16,100			16,100

Investigation of the accounts revealed the following information:

(i) The goods taken by Guy had been charged at selling price rather than at cost (£65).

(ii) The interest on capital had been provided at 6% per annum.

(iii) The closing stock included some items which had been valued at original cost (£550), but which had deteriorated badly while in store and were considered to have a market value of £200.

(iv) The equipment had been depreciated in 19X8 at 10% on original cost, but should have been depreciated at 15% per year of the written down value at 1 January 19X8.

(v) The partnership agreement had been amended on 1 July 19X8 to increase Guy's annual salary to £2,700, with effect from 1 July, but this had not been reflected in the accounts.

(vi) No provision had been made for doubtful debts, but a provision of 3% of debtors is now considered desirable.

(vii) £82 owing for electricity had not been accrued.

Required

(a) A statement showing the revised net trading profit for the year ended 31 December 19X8.

(b) The amended current accounts of the partners, and

(c) A revised balance sheet as at 31 December 19X8.

(ACCA)

Questions Without Answers

7.8

'Limited liability is advantageous to owners and unfair to creditors.'

Required

(a) Explain the meaning and effect of limited liability.

(b) State three mechanisms by which the advantages to owners are restricted.

(c) Do you agree with the quotation?

(ACCA)

7.9

Ben, Ken and Len are in partnership sharing profits and losses in the ratio 3:2:1. The following is the trial balance of the partnership as at 30 September 19X3:

	£	£
Bad debts provision (at 1 October 19X2)		1,000
Bank and cash in hand	2,500	
Capital accounts:		
Ben		18,000
Ken		12,000
Len		6,000
Current accounts:		
Ben		700
Ken	500	
Len		300
Debtors and creditors	23,000	35,000
Depreciation (at 1 October 19X2)		
Land and buildings		12,000
Motor vehicles		8,000
Drawings:		
Ben	4,000	
Ken	3,000	
Len	3,000	
Land and buildings at cost	60,000	
Motor vehicles at cost	20,000	
Office expenses	4,000	
Purchases	85,000	
Rates	4,000	
Sales		150,000
Selling expenses	14,000	
Stock (at 1 October 19X2)	20,000	
	243,000	243,000

You are provided with the following additional information:

1. Stock at 30 September 19X3 was valued at £30,000.

2. Fixed assets are written off at the following rates: Land and buildings 5% per annum on cost; Motor vehicles 20% per annum on cost.

3. At 30 September 19X3 an amount of £1,775 was owing for selling expenses.

4. Rates were prepaid by £2,000 as at 30 September 19X3.

5. A certain bad debt of £500 is to be written off.

6. The bad debts provision is to be 5% of outstanding debtors as at 30 September 19X3.

7. The partnership agreement covers the following appropriations:

   (a) Len is to be allowed a salary of £6,000 per annum.

   (b) Interest of 10% per annum is allowed on the partners' capital account balances.

   (c) No interest is allowed on the partners' current accounts.

   (d) No interest is charged on the partners' drawings.

You are required to:

   (a) prepare the partners' trading, profit and loss and profit and loss appropriation accounts for the year to 30 September 19X3.

   (b) write up the partners' current accounts for the year to 30 September 19X3, and bring down the balances as at 1 October 19X3; and

   (c) prepare the partnership balance sheet at 30 September 19X3.

(AAT)

7.10

Hawes and Peters are partners, sharing profits and losses in the ratio 3:2. The following is the trial balance in the partnership books at 31 December 19X5:

	£	£
Capital account at 1 January 19X5		
Hawes		16,400
Peters		13,200
Drawings		
Hawes	3,600	
Peters	2,400	
Provision for doubtful debts		480
Purchases	101,640	
Sales		131,860
Vans at cost	11,600	
Fittings at cost	2,400	
Provision for depreciation		
Van		5,920
Fittings		1,140
Stock at 1 January 19X5	17,360	
Petty cash	40	
Office expenses	6,400	
Vehicle expenses	3,960	
Motor car at cost (1 January 19X5)	1,600	
Debtors and creditors	12,200	4,200
Bank		540
Wages	7,360	
Insurance	620	
Discounts allowed	2,560	
	173,740	173,740

The following additional information is available:

(i)   Stock at 31 December 19X5 was valued at £26,380.

(ii)   Depreciation is to be provided at 10% per annum on the written down value of the fittings and at 20% per annum on the written down value of the vans and car. Hawes is to bear personally £400 of the vehicle expenses and one-half of the depreciation charge on the car.

(iii) No rent has been paid on the business premises during the year because of a dispute with the landlord. The rental agreement provides for a rent of £928 per year.

(iv)   The partners are entitled to interest on capital at 10% per annum.

(v) Bad debts of £200 are to be written off and the provision for doubtful debts to be adjusted to 2.5% of the remaining debtors.

(vi) Insurance, £70, has been paid in advance at 31 December 19X5.

(vii) Wages, £370, were owing at 31 December 19X5.

(viii) An item of £70 for bank charges appears in the bank statement but has not yet been entered into the partnership bank account.

Required

Prepare the trading, profit and loss account for the year ended 31 December 19X5 and a balance sheet as at that date. (Ignore taxation).

(ACCA)

7.11

Reg, Sam and Ted are in partnership, sharing profits and losses equally. Interest on capital and partnership salaries are not provided. The position of the business at the end of its financial year is:

Balance Sheet June 19X6

		£
Buildings		17,000
Equipment		3,300
Stock		900
Debtors		2,020
Bank		2,840
		26,060

	£	£
Capital Accounts:		
Reg	9,000	
Sam	8,000	
Ted	8,000	
		25,000
Current Accounts:		
Reg	140	
Sam	200	
	340	
Ted (debit)	100	
		240
Creditors		820
		26,060

Reg died suddenly on 31 October 19X6.

The partnership agreement provides that in the event of the death of a partner the sum to be paid to his estate will be the amount of his capital and current balances at the last financial year-end adjusted by his share of profit or loss since that date together with his share of goodwill. A formula for the calculation of goodwill is given, and its application produced a figure of £7,500. No goodwill account is to remain in the books after any change of the partnership constitution.

The stock value at 31 October has been calculated and all other accounts balanced off, including provisions for depreciation, accrued expenses and prepaid expenses. This results in the following position at 31 October.

	£
Buildings	17,000
Equipment (including additions of £400)	3,480
Stock	1,100
Debtors	2,230
Bank balance	3,370
Creditors	980

There were no additions to, or reductions of, the capital accounts during the four months, but the following drawings have been made:

Reg	£2,000
Sam	£1,600
Ted	£1,800

It has also been agreed that the share of a deceased partner should be repaid in three equal instalments, the first payment being made as on the day after the day of death.

The surviving partners agree that Abe (son of Reg) should be admitted as a new partner with effect from 1 November, and it is agreed that he will bring into the business £4,000 as his capital together with a premium for his share of the goodwill (using the existing valuation). The profit-sharing agreement is: Sam, two-fifths; Ted, two-fifths; and Abe one-fifth.

Required

Show the partnership balance sheet as at 1 November 19X6 on the assumption that the above transactions have been completed by that date.

(ACCA)

7.12

The following Trial Balance had been prepared from the books of accounts of Zephyr plc. as at 31st October 19X5, together with additional relevant notes.

Zephyr plc

Trial Balance as at 31st October 19X5

	Debit £'000	Credit £'000
Issued and fully paid Share Capital		600
Share Premium Account		90
15% Debenture Stock		160
Retained Earnings as at 1 November 19X4		460
Stock at Cost as at 1 November 19X4	520	
Freehold Property at Cost	470	
Office Equipment at Cost	315	
Motor Vehicles at Cost	125	
Furniture, Fixtures and Fittings at Cost	50	
Provision for Depreciation as at 1 November 19X4		
Office Equipment		105
Motor Vehicles		61
Furniture, Fixtures and Fittings		20
Purchases and Sales	2,950	3,960
Wages and Salaries	340	
Directors' Fees and Salaries	210	
Advertising	12	
Administrative Costs	50	
Selling and Distribution Costs	75	
Provision for Doubtful Debts		5
Balance at Bank	79	
Cash in Hand	7	
Debenture Interest Paid for the Half-year to 30 April 19X5	12	
Preference Share Dividend Paid on 1 May 19X5	6	
Debtors and Creditors	450	210
	5,671	5,671

Additional Notes

1.   The issued share capital is made up of 2,000,000 ordinary shares and 100,000 preference shares.

2.   Stock at cost as at 31 October 19X5 was valued at £655,000.

3.   Provide for depreciation of fixed assets for the year ended 31 October 19X5, using the reducing balance basis at the following rates:

Office Equipment	20%
Motor Vehicles	25%
Furniture, Fixtures and Fittings	10%

Motor Vehicles are used 75% by the Sales Director and his staff, and the remainder by administrative staff.

4.   Amend the provision for doubtful debts to 4% of the debtors figure.

5.   There are three directors of the company, whose remuneration is as follows:

Managing Director (administrative)	£80,000
Marketing and Sales Director	£75,000
Finance Director	£55,000

6.   Other salaries and wages are to be apportioned, 25% to Selling and Distribution, and 75% to Administration.

7.   Provide for the following:

An audit fee of £10,000
Corporation tax of £70,000
The second half-year's debenture interest
The second half-year's preference dividend
A dividend on ordinary shares of 4p per share

Required

(a)   Prepare the Profit and Loss Account of Zephyr plc. for the year ended 31 October 19X5 using the standard format laid down by the Companies Act 1985.

(b)   Prepare the Balance Sheet of Zephyr plc. as at 31 October 19X5, in accordance with the Companies Act.

7.13

The following trial balance has been extracted from the ledgers of QWS Limited on 31st October 19X2.

	Dr £	Cr £
Premises at cost	180,000	
Equipment at cost	121,200	
Motor vehicles at cost	26,500	
Accumulated depreciation:		
Premises		30,000
Equipment		64,100
Motor vehicles		8,250
Stock at 1 November 19X1	28,500	
Debtors and creditors	7,625	5,430
Cash	100	
Bank	10,295	
PAYE liability		440
VAT liability		625
Ordinary shares of £1 each		100,000
Profit and loss balance, 1 November 19X1		40,180
Sales		379,600
Purchases	132,400	
Discounts		1,570
Carriage outwards	2,325	
Wages and salaries	85,300	
Heat and light	12,650	
Provision for doubtful debts		450
Vehicle expenses	3,600	
Telephone, postage, stationery	2,100	
Business rates	15,400	
Carriage inwards	2,650	
	£630,645	£630,645

The following notes are also relevant:

1. One of the company's customers has been declared bankrupt, owing £600. This is to be written off as a bad debt.

2. The provision for doubtful debts is to be adjusted so that it is equal to 8% of debtors. It is company policy no to use a separate bad debts account.

3.   Closing stock on 31 October 19X2 was valued at cost of £30,750 by a physical stock-taking on that date. It does not include £2,000 of goods which have been supplied on sale or return to L. Brown. These goods were despatched on 28 October 19X2 and L. Brown has not yet indicated whether he intends to retain the goods or not. No entry has been made in the accounts in respect of these goods.

4.   Adjustments need to be made for the following accruals and prepayments at the end of the year:

	Accruals £	Prepayments £
Telephones	150	60
Business rates		1,500
Vehicle expenses	740	
Heat and light	220	

5.   Depreciation is to be provided for the year as follows:

Premises	4% per annum on cost
Equipment	25% per annum reducing balance
Motor vehicles	20% per annum on cost

6.   Taxation of £35,000 is to be provided on the profits of the year.

7.   The directors have proposed a final dividend of 10 pence per share.

You are required

(a)   to show the provision for bad debts account after making the adjustments noted above and to comment on the reasons why a provision for doubtful debts is made;

(b)   to prepare the company's trading and profit and loss account in vertical form for the year ended 31st October 19X2;

(c)   to prepare the company's balance sheet at 31st October 19X2 in vertical form;

(d)   to comment on your treatment of the goods dispatched on sale or return, with reference to accounting concepts as appropriate.

(CIMA)

7.14

The trial balance of Toby Limited at 31st December 19X8 is as follows:

	£	£
Share capital --£1 ordinary shares		10,000
Profit and loss account		19,000
Sales and purchases	61,000	100,000
Sales returns and purchase returns	2,000	4,000
Sales and purchase ledger control A/cs	20,000	7,000
Land and buildings (at cost)	40,000	
Plant (at cost, and depreciation to 1st January 19X8)	50,000	22,000
Debentures (10% p.a. interest)		30,000
Opening stock	15,000	
Operating expenses	9,000	
Administration expenses	7,000	
Selling expenses	6,000	
Bank		8,000
Suspense account		10,000
	210,000	210,000

Notes

(i)   5,000 new shares were issued during the year at £1.60 per share. The proceeds have been credited to the suspense account.

(ii)   Sales returns of £1,000 have been entered in the sales day book as if they were sales.

(iii)   The bookkeeper has included the opening provision for doubtful debts of £800 in the selling expenses account in the trial balance. The provision is required to be 5% of debtors.

(iv)   A standing order payment of £1,000 for rates paid in December has not been entered. This payment covered the half-year to 31st March 19X9.

(v)   Closing stock is £18,000.

(vi)   No debenture interest has been paid.

(vii)   The remaining balance on the suspense account after the above represents the sales proceeds of a fully depreciated item of plant, costing £10,000. No other entries (except bank) have been made concerning this disposal.

(viii) Depreciation at 10% on cost should be provided on the plant.

Required

    (a)   Prepare a trading, profit and loss account for the year, and balance sheet as at 31st December 19X8, in good order, taking account of the above notes.

    (b)   The land and buildings have both been retained at original cost. Neither has been depreciated, or revalued. In each case state with reasons whether you find this reasonable and useful.

(ACCA)

Chapter 8

Cash Flow Statements

Learning Objectives

After completing this chapter you should be able to:

- Appreciate the importance of managing cash in a business.

- Explain the difference between accounting profit and cash flow.

- Prepare and interpret a cash flow statement.

Introduction

The accounting statements we have looked at in previous chapters provide information on the profits earned in a period and the financial position of the business at the end of the period. However, they provide little information on an issue of crucial importance to any business, cash flow. There are many examples of businesses folding despite generating profits, because of liquidity problems. To prevent this situation cash must be carefully managed to ensure that debts can be settled as they become due. This requires the preparation of cash flow forecasts which enable management to plan ahead for any potential problems identified. These forecasts will be considered in Chapter 15 in which the planning process is examined. However external parties such as shareholders and lenders, will also require detailed information concerning the ability of the business to generate cash. Cash flow statements can help in this respect by providing retrospective information on cash movements during an accounting period.

The Distinction Between Profit and Cash

Even a profitable business can experience liquidity problems which if not remedied, may threaten its existence. This can occur because the profit earned in a period will not necessarily produce an equivalent increase in the cash balance. Consider the following example:

Example 8.1

A business selling office equipment offers customers credit of one month. Its purchases are made on cash terms in order to take advantage of attractive discounts from suppliers. In May, sales amounted to £30,000 and the cost of those goods was £20,000.

Sales for April were £15,000.

The gross profit for May can be calculated as follows:

	£
Sales	30,000
Less cost of sales	(20,000)
Gross profit	10,000

However, this £10,000 profit does not generate an equivalent cash sum. In the following table the cash movement for the month has been added:

	May Profit £	May Cash £
Sales	30,000	15,000
Less cost of sales	(20,000)	(20,000)
	10,000	(5,000)

As the sales are made on credit, there is a delay of one month in receiving cash from customers. The goods sold in May will therefore not be received until June and receipts in May relate to April's sales of £15,000. Consequently, the cash balance fell by £5,000 in the month, despite earning a profit of £10,000.

This and other reasons for differences between cash flow and profit are explained below:

Credit Transactions

Any credit transactions will affect profit and cash flows in a period differently. The above example illustrates this for credit sales but the same will be true for purchases. Where an expense is incurred on credit terms the cost will be included in the period and the profit reduced accordingly. However cash will be unaffected by the transaction with the payment being made in a later period.

Stock Movements

Under the matching principle the cost of goods purchased for resale is not included in the profit and loss account until the goods are actually sold. Thus payments made for items remaining in stock at the end of a period will reduce cash but have no effect on profit. When the goods are eventually sold, the profit calculation for the period in which the sale occurs will include their cost but as no payment is made in that period, cash will be unaffected.

Fixed Assets

The accounting treatment of fixed assets will also influence profit and cash flow in different ways as illustrated in Example 8.2:

Example 8.2

An asset is purchased for cash on 1st January for £40,000. It is expected to last for four years and have no residual value at the end of that time. The business uses the straight line method of depreciation.

The impact on profit and cash over the four years is:

Year	Impact on profit £	Impact on Cash £
1	(10,000)	(40,000)
2	(10,000)	0
3	(10,000)	0
4	(10,000)	0

Although the depreciation charge reduces profits by £10,000 in each year this does not represent a cash flow. The inclusion of depreciation in each period is an accounting technique to spread the cost of the asset over its useful life. The cash position will change only at the time of purchase (and sale where the asset has a residual value).

Cash Transactions not Affecting Profits

There are various transactions which affect cash but have no impact on profit at all. These include raising additional capital and obtaining or repaying loans.

For the reasons outlined above, it is dangerous to assume that if sufficient profits are generated the cash situation will take care of itself. Cash must be carefully planned and controlled to ensure that the business can pay its way at all times.

Cash Flow Statements

Cash flow statements show the cash generated in a period from various sources and explain how it was used.

They are prepared by comparing the financial position reflected in the period end balance sheet with the opening balance sheet (i.e. that at the end of the previous period). This procedure is demonstrated in Example 8.3.

Example 8.3

Balance sheets for Sherburn Stores are given below:

SHERBURN STORES
BALANCE SHEETS AS AT 31st. DECEMBER

	19X7 £000	19X6 £000
Fixed Assets		
Cost	500	420
Less accumulated deprec'n.	(250)	(200)
Net book value	250	220
Current Assets		
Stocks	124	112
Debtors	96	90
Cash	25	40
	245	242
Less Current Liabilities		
Trade Creditors	(70)	(82)
Net Current Assets	175	160
Long Term Liabilities		
Long term loans	(25)	(60)
NET ASSETS EMPLOYED	**400**	**320**
OWNER'S FUNDS		
Capital	220	200
Profit and loss account	180	120
	400	**320**

Note. There were no fixed assets sold during the year.

The statements show that although profits increased by £60,000 in 19X7 (from £120,000 to £180,000) the bank balance fell by £15,000. This can be explained by comparing the balance sheet figures for each individual item to identify the cash flowing in and out of the business during 19X7, as follows:

	SOURCES OF CASH		£000	
Note				
	Net Profit		60	*(180 – 120)*
1	Add depreciation		50	*(250 – 200)*
1	Cash generated from trading		110	
2	Capital raised		20	*(220 – 200)*
			130	
	LESS APPLICATIONS			
3	Purchase of fixed assets	80		*(500 – 420)*
4	Stocks	12		*(124 – 112)*
5	Debtors	6		*(96 – 90)*
6	Creditors	12		*(82 – 70)*
7	Long term loans	35	(145)	*(60 – 25)*
8	Reduction in cash balance		(15)	*(40 – 25)*

Notes

1. To determine the cash generated from trading, depreciation must be added back. As we saw in Example 8.2, depreciation does not represent a cash flow and the cash generated in the period therefore exceeded the net profit as shown below:

	£
Cash generated from trading	110,000
Less depreciation	(50,000)
Net profit	60,000

2. As capital has risen from £200,000 to £220,000 an additional sum of £20,000 has been raised during the year.

3. The balance sheet shows that the cost of fixed assets owned has risen by £80,000. As none were sold during the year this figure must represent cash spent on acquiring additional assets.

4.   A further £12,000 has been used to increase the value of stocks held by the business.

5.   The increase in the debtors balance is also an application of funds. The business is allowing customers to hold a greater amount of the income to which it is entitled.

6.   £12,000 has been used to reduce the amount owed to suppliers from £82,000 to £70,000.

7.   Repayment of £35,000 of loans represents another application of cash.

8.   The reduction in cash can now be explained. Although the business generated £130,000 during the course of the year, it used £145,000 for purposes such as acquiring additional fixed assets, repaying loans and increasing the working capital of the business (stocks, debtors etc.) and the cash balance therefore fell by £15,000.

Company Accounts

Financial Reporting Standard No.1 (FRS 1) 'Cash Flow Statements', requires that all medium and large companies publish a cash flow statement in their annual report and accounts in order to show the operation and absorption of cash and highlight changes in liquidity. The presentation method given in FRS 1 analyses cash movements in eight separate categories:

1. Operating Activities

This section includes the cash generated from operations and the impact of movements in working capital (as we saw in Example 8.3, changes in the stock , debtors and creditors will affect cash).

2. Returns on Investments and Servicing of Finance

This category includes payments and receipts in respect of interest and dividends with the exception of equity (i.e. ordinary share) dividends paid, which are reported in section 6 below.

3. Taxation

This section shows the tax paid during the year.

4. Capital Expenditure (and Financial Investment)

The acquisition and disposal of fixed assets are reported in this category.

5. Acquisitions and Disposals

This section includes cash flows arising from the purchase of group entities (i.e. businesses which are associates, joint ventures or subsidiaries).

6. Equity Dividends Paid

Dividends paid to ordinary shareholders are reported in this category.

7. Management of Liquid Resources

This section shows inflows and outflows in respect of short term deposits and investments.

8. Financing

The final section shows the effect of raising capital and obtaining or repaying loans.

If the business in Example 8.3 was a limited company required to adopt the FRS 1 format, the cash flow statement would appear as shown below:

(NB. For the purpose of illustration it has been assumed that Sherburn Stores paid interest of £5,000 in the year and that the operating profit before interest was therefore £65,000).

SHERBURN STORES LIMITED
CASH FLOW STATEMENT FOR THE YEAR ENDED 31.12.X7

Note		£000	£000
1.	Net Cash Inflow from Operating Activities		85
	Returns on Investments and Servicing of Finance		
	Interest paid		(5)
	Taxation		
	Tax paid		--
	Capital Expenditure and Financial Investment		
	Payments to acquire tangible fixed assets		(80)
	Acquisitions and Disposals		--
	Equity Dividend Paid		--
	Net cash inflow before use of liquid resources and financing		--
	Management of Liquid Resources		--
	Financing		
	Issue of capital	20	
	Repayment of loans	(35)	
	Net cash outflow from financing		(15)
2.	Decrease in Cash		(15)

Notes

In order to assist in FRS 1's objective to assess a business's liquidity, solvency and financial adaptability, the following supporting information is disclosed below the cash flow statement.

1.	Reconciliation of operating profit to net cash inflow from operating activities	£000
	Operating profit (before interest and tax)	65
	Add depreciation	50
	Increase in stocks	(12)
	Increase in debtors	(6)
	Decrease in creditors	(12)
	Net cash inflow from operating activities	85

2.   Analysis of changes in Net Debt.

	At 1.1.X7	Cashflows	At 31.12.X7
	£000	£000	£000
Cash in hand and at bank	40	(15)	25
Debt due after 1 year	(60)	35	(25)
Total	(20)	20	–

3.   Reconciliation of Net Cash Flow Movement in Net Debt

	£000
Decrease in cash in the year	(15)
Cash outflow from decrease in debt (loan)	35
Movement in net debt	20
Net debt at 1.1.X7	(20)
Net debt at 31.12.X7	–

The statement explained why cash fell by £15,000 despite operating profits of £65,000. Cash generated from operating activities actually amounted to £85,000 but this has been off set significantly by fixed asset acquisitions and the repayment of loans. In future the business should consider the financing implications of investment in fixed assets carefully. Investing heavily in a period in which loans are repaid can result in liquidity problems. If loans cannot be renewed to help finance such capital expenditure, other measures such as raising more capital (as has occurred in this case) or perhaps leasing the assets could be considered. Sherburn Stores should also review its working capital policy. During the past year it has increased stocks and debtors while reducing the amount owing to creditors, all of which have depleted cash funds.

A Comprehensive Example

To ensure that you fully understand the procedure for the preparation of cash flow statements you should now work through the following example.

Example 8.4

The annual accounts of Beaufront Limited included the following information:

BALANCE SHEET AS AT 31.12.X7

	19X7 £000	19X6 £000
Fixed Assets		
Cost	730	620
Less accumulated deprec'n.	(325)	(250)
Net book value	405	370
Current Assets		
Stocks	250	186
Debtors	121	138
Cash	95	35
	466	359
Less Current Liabilities		
Trade Creditors	(103)	(90)
Dividends	(6)	(15)
Taxation	(14)	(20)
Net Current Assets	343	234
Long Term Liabilities		
Debentures	(170)	(125)
NET ASSETS EMPLOYED	578	479
SHAREHOLDERS' FUNDS		
Share capital	350	320
Share premium account	40	30
Profit and loss account	188	129
	578	479

PROFIT AND LOSS ACCOUNT FOR YEAR ENDED
31.12.X7

(EXTRACT)

	£000
Operating profit before interest and tax	111
Less: Interest	(16)
Tax payable	(24)
Dividends	(12)
Retained Profit for the Year	59
Retained Profit as at 31.12.X6	129
Retained Profit as at 31.12.X7	188

Note. There were no fixed assets sold during the year.

Required

Prepare a cash flow statement for the Company for 19X7 in accordance with FRS 1.

Solution

BEAUFRONT LIMITED
CASH FLOW STATEMENT FOR THE YEAR ENDED 31.12.X7

Note			£000
1.	**Net Cash Inflow from Operating Activities**		152
	Returns on Investments and Servicing of Finance		
	Interest paid		(16)
2.	**Taxation**		
	Tax paid		(30)
	Capital Expenditure and Financial Investment		
	Payments to acquire tangible fixed assets		(110)
	Acquisitions and Disposals		–
3.	**Equity Dividend Paid**		(21)
	Net Cash Outflow before use of Liquid Resources and Financing		(25)
	Management of Liquid Resources		–
	Financing		
4.	Issue of share capital	40	
	Issue of debentures	45	
	Net cash inflow from financing		85
	Increase in Cash		60

Note

1.	Reconciliation of operating profit to net cash inflow from operating activities	£000
	Operating profit (before interest and tax)	111
	Add depreciation	75
	Increase in stocks	(64)
	Decrease in debtors	17
	Increase in creditors	13
	Net cash inflow from operating activities	152

2.   *Tax paid*

	£000
Tax outstanding at the start of the year	20
Tax due for 19X7	24
Total amount payable	44
Less tax outstanding at the end of the year	(14)
Amount paid	30

3.   *Dividends paid*

Remember that it is the amount *paid* in the year which is relevant and not the dividend due for the year. This can be ascertained as follows:

	£000
Dividends outstanding at the start of the year	15
Dividends due for 19X7	12
Total amount payable	27
Less dividends outstanding at the end of the year	(6)
Amount paid	21

4.   *Issue of share capital*

	£000	
Share capital as at 31.12.X7	390	*(350 + 40)*
Share capital as at 31.12.X6	350	*(320 + 30)*
Issued during 19X7	40	

Analysis of Changes in Net Debt

	As at 1.1.X7 £000	Cash Flows £000	At 31.12.X7 £000
Cash in hand and at bank	35	60	95
Due after one year	(125)	(45)	(170)
Total	(90)	(15)	(75)

Reconciliation of Net Cash Flow Movement in Net Debt

	£000
Increase in cash in the year	60
Cash inflow from increase in debt (loan)	(45)
Movement in net debt	15
Net debt at 1.1.X7	(90)
Net debt at 31.12..X7	(75)

The cash flow statement shows that despite generating £152,000 from operating activities, Beaufront Limited had a net cash outflow before financing of £25,000. Although payments in respect of dividends, interest and taxation were partly responsible, substantial investment in fixed assets was the main reason for this. However additional capital from the issue of shares and debentures resulted in a £60,000 increase in cash during the year. Another point worth noting is the significant increase in stocks. There may be a good reason for this, such as a substantial increase in turnover or the expectation of high demand shortly after the year end. If this is not the case the reason for the increase should be investigated to ensure that the business is not over investing in stocks.

The Sale of Fixed Assets

If the proceeds from the sale of fixed assets exceed the net book value, a profit on the sale will be included in the profits reported for the period. As we saw in Chapter 5, this profit is actually the correction of an over provision of depreciation during the life of the asset. It has no impact on cash flow and should therefore be excluded from the net profit shown in the cash flow statement. Only the sales proceeds affect the cash position and they alone should be included.

This procedure is illustrated in Example 8.5:

Example 8.5

Sundridge Limited reported profit before interest and tax of £65,000 in 19X7. This included profit arising from the sale of fixed assets (with a book value of £12,000) for £16,000. Fixed assets were purchased during the year for £25,000.

An extract from the cash flow statement for the year is given below:

SUNDRIDGE LIMITED

CASH FLOW STATEMENT FOR THE YEAR ENDED 31.12.X7

(EXTRACT)

	£000
Operating Activities	
Operating profit (before interest and tax)	65
Less profit on sale of tangible fixed assets (16 – 12)	(4)
Add depreciation	
etc.	
etc.	
Capital Expenditure and Financial Investment	
Payments to acquire tangible fixed assets	(25)
Receipts from sale of tangible fixed assets	16
Net cash outflow from investing activities	(9)

As the operating profit of £65,000 included £4,000 which did not affect cash, this amount is deducted, thus ensuring that only the cash generated in the period is reported.

Where assets are sold for less than their book value a loss will be made on the sale. Again this has no impact on cash and the loss should therefore be added back to the operating profit for the period to determine the cash generated. As before the entire sales proceeds are reported as a source of cash.

Summary

- It is vitally important that businesses carefully manage cash.

- Earning profits does not necessarily increase cash. Profit and cash movements for a period will differ due to:

    (a) *Buying and selling items on credit terms.* For example, income is reported when a sale is made whereas the cash may be received in a later period.

    (b) *Stock movements during the period.* Paying for items held in stock will reduce cash in the period in which the payment is made whereas profit will be unaffected until the goods are sold.

    (c) *The accounting treatment of fixed assets.* Cash is only affected when assets are bought and sold. However, profits are subject to depreciation charged in each accounting period.

    (d) *Cash transactions not affecting profits.* These include raising new capital and obtaining or repaying loans.

- Profit and loss accounts and balance sheets provide little information on the movement of cash during a period.

- Cash flow statements show the sources of cash during a period and the way in which it was used.

- They can be prepared by comparing the balance sheets at the start and at the end of the period in question.

- FRS 1 'Cash Flow Statements' requires that all medium and large companies publish such statements and gives a recommended format which should be used.

Questions   (See Appendix C for Answers)

8.1

The information given below was extracted from the annual accounts of Robson Limited.

Robson Limited

Profit and Loss Account for the year ended 31.12.X6

		£
Sales		280,000
Cost of Sales		(150,000)
Gross Profit		130,000
Less Expenses		
Depreciation on plant and machinery	8,000	
Interest paid	1,000	
Other expenses	75,000	(84,000)
Net Profit		46,000
Taxation		(18,000)
Dividends Proposed		(14,000)
Retained Profit		14,000

ROBSON LIMITED BALANCE SHEETS

	As at 31.12.X6		As at 31.12.X5	
Fixed Assets		£		£
Land and Buildings		95,000		85,000
Plant and Machinery		62,000		65,000
		157,000		150,000
Current Assets				
Stock	30,000		34,000	
Debtors	42,000		32,000	
Cash at bank	13,000		21,000	
	85,000		87,000	
Current Liabilities				
Creditors	(22,000)		(30,000)	
Dividends	(7,000)		(5,000)	
Taxation	(10,000)	(39,000)	(13,000)	(48,000)
Net Current Assets		46,000		39,000
		203,000		189,000
Financed by:				
Ordinary Share Capital		80,000		70,000
Debentures		–		10,000
Profit and Loss Account		123,000		109,000
		203,000		189,000

There were no disposals of fixed assets during the year.

Required

(a) Prepare a cash flow statement for the company for the year ended 31.12.X6

(b) Explain the difference between a cash flow statement and a profit and loss account.

8.2

The following Balance Sheets were prepared for Hartleyburn Limited:

	31.12.X8 £'000s		31.12.X7 £'000s	
Fixed Assets				
Land and Buildings at Cost		240		170
Equipment at Cost	340		280	
Less Depreciation	(190)	150	(150)	130
		390		300
Current assets				
Stocks	105		82	
Debtors	74		58	
Cash and Bank	14		25	
	193		165	
Current Liabilities				
Trade Creditors	(50)		(35)	
Taxation	(20)		(23)	
Proposed Dividend	(5)		(10)	
	(75)		(68)	
Working Capital		118		97
Long Term Liabilities				
Long Term Loans		(30)		(50)
		478		347
Financed by:				
Share Capital		270		200
Share Premium		70		40
Retained Profits		138		107
		478		347

The following extract from the Profit and Loss Account for 19X8 is also available:

	£'000s
Operating profit	84
Less Interest	(12)
Profit before Tax	72
Less Taxation	(16)
	56
Less Dividends	(25)
Retained Profit	31

There were no disposals of fixed assets during the year.

Required

Prepare a cash flow statement for Hartleyburn Limited for the year ended 31.12.X8

8.3

The following information is available in respect of Brioche plc.

Brioche plc
Profit and Loss Account for the year ended 31st March 19X5

	£'000	£'000
Turnover		39,200
Cost of Sales:		
Stock as at 1 April 19X4	1,530	
Purchases	24,900	
	26,430	
Less Stock as at 31 March 19X5	1,930	
		24,500
Gross Profit for the Year		14,700
Selling and Distribution Costs	6,906	
Administrative Expenses	3,200	
Debenture Interest paid	84	
		10,190
Net Profit for the Year Before Tax		4,510
Provision for Corporation Tax		1,344
Net Profit for the Year After Tax		3,166
Proposed Dividend on Ordinary Shares		1,000
Retained Profit for the Year		2,166
Retained Profit Brought Forward from Previous Years		8,594
Retained Profit to be Carried Forward to Next Year		10,760

BRIOCHE PLC BALANCE SHEETS AS AT 31ST MARCH

	19X5		19X4	
	£'000	£'000	£'000	£'000
Fixed assets:				
Freehold land and buildings at cost		15,200		12,600
Motor vehicles at cost	2,750		2,400	
Less: Provision for depreciation	(1,360)	1,390	(900)	1,500
Other equipment at cost	4,000		3,500	
Less: Provision for depreciation	(1,450)	2,550	(1,000)	2,500
		19,140		16,600
Current assets:				
Stock	1,930		1,530	
Debtors	5,160		4,580	
Cash at bank	1,350		524	
	8,440		6,634	
Less: Current liabilities:				
Creditors	(3,076)		(2,780)	
Corporation tax	(1,344)		(1,050)	
Proposed dividend	(1,000)		(810)	
Net current assets		3,020		1,994
Total assets less current liabilities		22,160		18,594
12% Debentures (long term liabilities)		400		1,000
		21,760		17,594
Share capital and reserves:				
Ordinary shares of £1 each, issued and fully paid		10,000		9,000
Share premium account		1,000		
Retained profit		10,760		8,594
		21,760		17,594

Note:

    1.   No fixed assets were sold or otherwise disposed of during the year.

    2.   During the year there had been an issue of 1,000,000 ordinary shares at price of £2.00 per share. Some debentures had also been redeemed.

Required

Prepare a cash flow statement for the year ended 31 March 19X5 in respect of Brioche plc.

Questions Without Answers

8.4

The following balance sheets and additional notes in respect of Lewis plc have been presented to you.

LEWIS PLC BALANCE SHEETS AS AT

	30 November 19X5		30 November 19X4	
	£'000	£'000	£'000	£'000
Fixed assets		2,536		1,830
Current assets:				
Stock	1,219		973	
Debtors	885		1,060	
Balance at bank	–		226	
	2,104		2,259	
Creditors: Amounts due within one year:				
Trade creditors	(576)		(690)	
Bank overdraft	(166)		–	
Provision for corporation tax	(317)		(270)	
Proposed dividend	(144)		(96)	
		901		1,203
		3,437		3,033
Creditors: Amounts due after more than one year – 10% Debenture stock		(240)		(320)
		3,197		2,713
Share capital and reserves:				
Ordinary shares of £1 each, fully paid		1,280		960
15% preference shares of £1 each, fully paid		280		480
Share premium account		128		–
Retained profits		1,509		1,273
		3,197		2,713

Notes

1.   Fixed assets are made up as follows:

	30 November 19X5		30 November 19X4	
	£'000	£'000	£'000	£'000
Freehold property at cost		1,126		712
Plant and machinery at cost	2,016		1,597	
Less: Depreciation to date	(774)	1,242	(637)	960
Motor vehicles at cost	392		326	
Less: Depreciation to date	(224)	168	(168)	158
		2,536		1,830

Plant and machinery which had originally cost £285,000 and which had been written down to £112,000 by 1st December 19X4, had been sold during the year ended 30th November 19X5 for £85,000.

No property or motor vehicles were sold during the year.

2.   On 30th May 19X5 Lewis plc had repaid £80,000 debenture stock. The company had also redeemed 200,000 preference shares at nominal value on 1st August 19X5.

3.   During the year ended 30th November 19X5 an issue of ordinary shares had been made at a price of £1.40 per share.

4.   The summarised profit and loss and appropriation account for the year ended 30th November 19X5 is as follows:

	£'000	£'000
Gross profit		1,463
Less: Expenditure including depreciation, loss on sale of plant, and debenture interest		(677)
Net profit for the year before tax		786
Provision for corporation tax		(344)
Net profit for the year after tax		442
Dividends paid and proposed:		
Preference dividend paid	(62)	
Ordinary dividend proposed	(144)	(206)
Retained profit for the year		236

Required

Prepare the cash flow statement of Lewis plc. for the year ended 30th November 19X5 in accordance with the requirements of FRS 1 and comment on major changes as highlighted by this statement.

8.5

The opening and closing balance sheets of a sports and leisure club, together with the linking income and expenditure account, have been summarised and are shown below:

	Opening £	Closing £
Tangible fixed assets at cost	18,000	27,000
Depreciation provided	(10,000)	(12,500)
Net book amount	8,000	14,500
Current assets		
Stock	4,000	6,000
Subscriptions due	3,500	5,000
Cash	2,500	500
	18,000	26,000
Retained surpluses	6,000	9,500
Creditors due after one year		
Loan from bank	2,500	10,000
Creditors due within one year		
Trade creditors	4,500	3,500
Subscriptions in advance	5,000	3,000
	18,000	26,000

	£
Subscriptions	24,000
Sundry expenses	(18,000)
Depreciation	(2,500)
Retained	3,500

You are required to:

(a) Prepare a statement which shows clearly the reasons for the decline in the cash balance.

(b) Explain why it is considered desirable that such a statement should be compiled.

(ACCA)

8.6

Y Limited's profit and loss account for the year ended 31st December 19X2 and balance sheets at 31st December 19X1 and 31st December 19X2 were as follows:

Y Limited
Profit and loss Account for the year ended 31 December 19X2

	£'000	£'000
Sales		360
Raw materials consumed	35	
Staff costs	47	
Depreciation	59	
Loss on disposal	9	
		150
Operating profit		210
Interest payable		14
Profit before tax		196
Taxation		62
		134
Dividend		36
Profit retained for the year		98
Balance brought forward		245
		343

Y Limited
Balance Sheets

	31 December 19X2 £000	31 December 19X2 £000	31 December 19X1 £000	31 December 19X1 £000
Fixed Assets				
Cost		798		780
Depreciation		159		112
		639		668
Current assets				
Stock	12		10	
Trade debtors	33		25	
Recoverable ACT	5		4	
Bank	24		28	
	74		67	
Current Liabilities				
Trade creditors	6		3	
Taxation	51		43	
Proposed dividend	15		12	
	72		58	
Working capital		2		9
		641		677
Long-term liabilities				
Long-term loans		100		250
		541		427
Share capital		180		170
Share premium		18		12
Profit and loss		343		245
		541		427

During the year, the company paid £45,000 for a new piece of machinery.

Required

Prepare a cash flow statement for Y Ltd. for the year ended 31 December 19X2 in accordance with the requirements of Financial Reporting Standard 1 (FRS 1).

(CIMA)

Chapter 9

The Interpretation of Accounting Statements

Learning Objectives

After completing this chapter you should be able to:

- Explain and use the following techniques for analysing information reported in accounting statements:

  - Horizontal analysis

  - Trend analysis

  - Vertical analysis

- Calculate and interpret ratios which may be used to assess the following aspects of a business:

  - Performance

  - Profitability

  - Productivity

  - Liquidity

  - Capital structure

  - Investment

- Explain the limitations of ratio analysis.

Introduction

In previous chapters we have been concerned with recording business transactions and compiling accounting statements. These statements contain information on the financial position and performance of a business which will be of interest to external parties such as shareholders, lenders, suppliers and customers as well as managers working within the business. The particular interests of each group were considered in Chapter 1 and you may find it useful at this point to review these.

In this chapter we will look at various techniques which may be used to interpret accounting statements and provide useful information for these parties. Although they are applicable for any type of business, we will use the company accounts given in Example 9.1 for demonstration purposes.

Example 9.1

DENSHAW plc

PROFIT AND LOSS ACCOUNT FOR YEAR ENDED 31ST. DECEMBER

	NOTES	19X7 £'000	19X8 £'000
Turnover		2,915	3,874
Cost of Sales	1	(2,011)	(2,819)
GROSS PROFIT		**904**	**1,055**
Distribution Costs		(141)	(224)
Administrative Expenses		(402)	(430)
OPERATING PROFIT BEFORE INTEREST		**361**	**401**
Interest		(26)	(90)
PROFIT BEFORE TAX		335	311
Taxation		(103)	(66)
PROFIT AFTER TAX		232	245
Dividends		(168)	(108)
RETAINED PROFIT FOR THE YEAR		64	137

DENSHAW plc

BALANCE SHEET AS AT 31ST DECEMBER

	NOTES	19X7 £'000	19X8 £'000
FIXED ASSETS		1,568	2,289
CURRENT ASSETS			
Stocks		154	273
Debtors	2	304	488
Cash at Bank and in Hand		37	11
		495	772
Creditors: amounts falling due within one year	3	(226)	(457)
NET CURRENT ASSETS		269	315
LONG TERM LOANS		(320)	(950)
NET ASSETS		**1,517**	**1,654**
CAPITAL AND RESERVES			
Called Up Share Capital (600,000 shares @£1)		600	600
Profit and Loss account		917	1,054
SHAREHOLDERS' FUNDS		**1,517**	**1,654**

Notes

1. Cost of sales

	19X7 £'000	19X8 £000
Opening stock	148	154
Purchases	2,017	2,938
	2,165	3,092
Less closing stock	(154)	(273)
Cost of sales	2,011	2,819

2. Debtors as at 31.12.X6 were £242,000.

3.   Creditors as at 31.12.X6 were £170,000.

Other Information

(a)   Numbers employed:

> as at 31.12.X6 23
> as at 31.12.X7 26
> as at 31.12.X8 30

(b)   Market price of the shares

> as at 31.12.X7 £4.50
> as at 31.12.X8 £4.10

Methods of Analysis

Horizontal Analysis

Horizontal analysis is the comparison of values reported in successive periods. Differences are highlighted by showing the percentage change as demonstrated in Figure 9.1:

DENSHAW plc – HORIZONTAL ANALYSIS			
	19X7	19X8	
	£'000	£'000	Change
Turnover	2,915	3,874	+33%
Cost of Sales	(2,011)	(2,819)	+40%
GROSS PROFIT	904	1,055	+17%
Distribution Costs	(141)	(224)	+59%
Administrative Expenses	(402)	(430)	+ 7%
OPERATING PROFIT BEFORE INTEREST	361	401	+11%

Figure 9.1 Horizontal Analysis

This information may prompt questions such as:

What caused the great increase in turnover?

Why did the cost of sales rise at a greater rate than turnover?

Why did distribution expenses rise at a greater rate than turnover?

Analysis of Trends

Using this method, changes in key figures over a number of years are analysed. A commonly used method is to express the first year as a value of 100 and relate subsequent years to this as demonstrated in Figure 9.2:

Turnover					
	19X4	**19X5**	**19X6**	**19X7**	**19X8**
(£000)	2,000	2,500	2,780	2,915	3,874
19X4 = 100	100	125	139	146	194

Figure 9.2 Trend Analysis

Expressing the figures in this way helps in the identification of trends over the five year period. However, the effect of inflation should be considered when interpreting such figures. Although Figure 9.2 indicates sales growth of 94% over the five years, this may have been partially due to inflation and adjusting the figures to reflect this will produce more meaningful information.

Vertical Analysis

Vertical analysis shows the relative values of a list of figures by expressing them as a percentage of the total. It is often used to highlight changes in the financial position reported in the balance sheet as shown in Figure 9.3:

DENSHAW plc – VERTICAL ANALYSIS BALANCE SHEETS AS AT 31ST. DECEMBER				
	19X7		19X8	
	£'000	%	£'000	%
Fixed Assets	1,568	85	2,289	88
CURRENT ASSETS				
Stocks	154	8	273	10
Debtors	304	17	488	19
Cash at Bank and in Hand	37	2	11	1
	495	27	772	30
Creditors: amounts falling due within one year	(226)	(12)	(457)	(18)
Net Current Assets	269	15	315	12
TOTAL ASSETS LESS CURRENT LIABILITIES	1,837	100	2,604	100
CAPITAL AND RESERVES				
Called Up Share Capital (600,000) shares @ £1)	600	33	600	23
Profit and Loss account	917	50	1,054	41
Shareholders' Funds	1,517	83	1,654	64
Long Term Loans	320	17	950	36
CAPITAL EMPLOYED	1,837	100	2,604	100

Figure 9.3 Vertical Analysis

Note that in order to assess the relative value of each type of asset and each separate component of capital employed, the balance sheet has been re-arranged to show net assets in the first section and capital employed in the other. The percentages shown alongside each item indicate among other things, that in 19X8 the business is financed to a greater degree by long term loans and that a slightly higher proportion of funds are invested in fixed assets.

Vertical analysis of the profit and loss account may provide useful information on changes in profitability, as we shall see later when assessing this aspect of the company in some detail.

Ratio Analysis

The figures reported in accounting statements may be of limited value when considered in isolation. Consider for example a business (Company A), which earned profits of £100,000 last year. Does this represent a satisfactory level of performance? We are not in a position to answer this as we have insufficient information to make a judgement. The profit figure alone is of limited value in assessing the financial performance of a business. Relating it to the capital employed will give a more meaningful figure which can be compared with returns from alternative investment opportunities.

Let us suppose that the capital employed by company A was £400,000. The rate of return on this investment can now be calculated as follows:

$$\text{Annual return} = \frac{Profit}{Capital\,employed} \times 100$$

$$\text{For Company A} = \frac{£100,000}{£400,000} \times 100 = 25\%$$

Compare this with the return from Company B which also earned a profit of £100,000 but used capital of £2,000,000:

$$\text{Annual return Company B} = \frac{£100,000}{£2,000,000} \times 100 = 5\%$$

Although their profits were identical, the financial performance of each (based on the ability to use capital productively) shows a very different picture. Company A used capital of only £400,000 to generate profits of £100,000 and therefore performed five times better than Company B.

Relating figures to each other in this way and assessing the results is known as ratio analysis and we will now consider this technique in detail.

What is a Ratio?

A ratio expresses the relationship between two figures as a proportion. If we are told that the ratio of passes to failures in an examination was 3:1 we know that three times as many people passed as failed (or to put it another way, 75% passed and 25% failed). The majority of the figures derived in ratio analysis are expressed in one of these two ways.

They can be used to identify aspects of a business which warrant further consideration. The reasons for problems identified may be investigated through the calculation of additional ratios or analysis of other available information.

The Interpretation of Ratios

When viewed in isolation ratios are of limited value and to serve any useful purpose must be put into context. For example the 5% annual return calculated for Company B earlier is of little value in itself without a figure with which to compare it. The knowledge that company A achieved a return of 25% puts B's performance into perspective. In order to appreciate the significance of ratios they should therefore be compared with:

1. Plans and Targets

Comparison with pre-determined plans and targets will help to determine the extent to which the business has achieved its financial objectives. This is usually performed by those working within the business as it is unlikely that outside parties will be given access to detailed information on financial plans.

2. Previous Periods

This will indicate whether the performance and financial position of a business has improved or deteriorated over time. Reasons for the trends emerging can then be investigated further.

3. Other Businesses

An indication of performance in relation to other businesses may highlight the scope for improvement or perhaps reveal strengths. However, different types of business are likely to have different characteristics and therefore comparison should only be made with those engaged in similar activities.

Areas for Analysis

Ratios can be used to analyse many aspects of a business's financial position and performance. The major areas are:

1.   Performance

    (a)   Overall performance

    (b)   Profitability

    (c)   Productivity

2.   Liquidity

3.   Capital structure

4.   Investment

The more commonly used ratios in each of these areas will now be calculated and explained using the accounts for Denshaw plc given in Example 9.1.

As you work through each you should ensure that:

(i) You understand how each ratio is derived. (Study the calculation for 19X7 and then calculate the ratio for 19X8 yourself, checking your result with the figure given).

(ii) You are aware of the relevance of each ratio.

Overall Performance

Return on Capital Employed (ROCE)

The financial success of a business depends on its ability to generate satisfactory returns on the funds invested and return on capital employed is the most commonly used method of assessing this. It relates the profit earned in a period to the capital employed and is calculated as follows:

$$\frac{Net\ profit\ (before\ interest\ and\ tax)}{Capital\ employed\ ^*} \quad \text{x} \quad 100$$

* *i.e. shareholders' funds and long term loans*

DENSHAW plc	
19X7	**19X8**
$\dfrac{361}{1{,}517\ +\ 320}$ x 100 = 19.7%	$\dfrac{401}{1{,}654\ +\ 950}$ x 100 = 15.4%

Note that as we are measuring the return earned on all long term capital (whether provided by lenders or the shareholders) we must use the profit before interest. This represents the pre-tax return which is available to reward the providers of long term finance through the payment of interest to lenders and dividends to shareholders.

Return on Shareholders' Funds

This ratio, which is also known as 'return on equity', measures the return earned on behalf of ordinary shareholders and can be calculated as follows:

$$\frac{Net\ profit\ attributable\ to\ ordinary\ shareholders\ ^*}{Ordinary\ Shareholders'\ Funds}\quad x\quad 100$$

*i.e. after interest, tax and any preference dividends (although pre-tax profit may also be used)

19X7	19X8
$\dfrac{232}{1,517}$ x 100 = 15.3%	$\dfrac{245}{1,654}$ x 100 = 14.8%

A deterioration in the return on capital employed, such as that experienced by Denshaw in 19X8, can be caused by:

- *Lower profitability.* (i.e. a reduction in the rate at which profit is earned on sales)

  and/or

- *Lower productivity.* (i.e. a fall in the rate at which the capital employed generates sales income)

Profitability and productivity can each be assessed using further ratios.

Profitability

Net Profit Margin

This net profit margin measures the rate at which profit is generated on sales and is calculated as shown below:

$$\frac{Net\ profit\ (before\ interest\ and\ tax)}{Sales\ revenue}\quad x\quad 100$$

19X7	19X8
$\dfrac{361}{2,915}$ x 100 = 12.4%	$\dfrac{401}{3,874}$ x 100 = 10.4%
(i.e. for every £100 worth of sales net profit of £12.40 was earned).	*(i.e. for every £100 worth of sales net profit of £10.40 was earned).*

Denshaw's reduced return on capital employed in 19X8 was therefore partly due to a fall in the net profit margin from 12.4% to 10.4%. This may have been the result of:

- A reduced gross profit margin

   and/or

- A higher rate of overhead expenses

These can be investigated using two further ratios.

Gross Profit Margin

The gross profit margin assesses trading profitability by indicating the rate at which gross profit is generated. It is calculated as follows:

$$\frac{Gross\ profit}{Sales\ revenue}\ \text{x}\ \ 100$$

19X7	19X8
$\dfrac{904}{2,915}$ x 100 = 31.0%	$\dfrac{1,055}{3,874}$ x 100 = 27.2%
(i.e. for every £100 worth of sales gross profit of £31 was earned).	*(i.e. for every £100 worth of sales gross profit of £27.20 was earned).*

The gross profit margin will be closely monitored by management as small changes in this figure can have a great impact on profit. In Denshaw's case the fall in gross profit margin in 19X8 has contributed to the lower net profit margin.

Expenses to Sales

This ratio shows the relationship between expenses and sales as illustrated below:

$$\frac{Total\ expenses}{Sales\ revenue} \times 100$$

19X7	19X8
$\frac{402\ +\ 141}{2,915} \times 100 = 18.6\%$	$\frac{430\ +\ 224}{3,874} \times 100 = 16.9\%$

Although Denshaw spent relatively less on expenses in 19X8 (i.e. 16.9% of sales revenues) this was insufficient to compensate for the lower gross profit margin. Consequently as we saw earlier, the net profit margin fell in 19X8.

Where the expenses warrant further investigation, each category may be analysed individually as demonstrated below:

Distribution Costs to Sales

19X7	19X8
$\frac{141}{2,915} \times 100 = 4.8\%$	$\frac{224}{3,874} \times 100 = 5.8\%$

Administration Expenses to Sales

19X7	19X8
$\frac{402}{2,915} \times 100 = 13.8\%$	$\frac{430}{3,874} \times 100 = 11.1\%$

Productivity

Having discovered that Denshaw's reduced return on capital employed in 19X8 was at least partially due to lower profitability, we will now consider the other potential cause, a lower level of productivity. Productivity in this context refers to the rate at which assets generate sales revenue and we will examine a number of ratios which can help to assess this.

Asset Turnover

The asset turnover ratio assesses the productivity of the total assets as shown below:

$$\frac{Sales\ revenue}{Capital\ employed\ ^*}$$

* NB. this corresponds with the net value of the assets.

E.g. for Denshaw plc

	19X7
	£000
Fixed assets	*1,568*
Net current assets (i.e. working capital)	*269*
Capital employed (i.e. net assets)	*1,837*

19X7	19X8
$\dfrac{2,915}{1,837}$ = 1.59 times	$\dfrac{3,874}{2,604}$ = 1.49 times
(i.e. for every £1 capital employed sales of £1.59 were generated)	*(i.e. sales of £1.49 were generated for every £1 capital employed).*

We can now see that Denshaw's lower ROCE in 19X8 was due not only to a reduction in profitability but also lower productivity with asset turnover falling from 1.59 to 1.49.

The utilisation of assets may be examined more closely by analysing fixed and net current assets (working capital) separately using the following ratios.

Fixed Asset Turnover

$$\frac{Sales\ revenue}{Fixed\ assets}$$

19X7	19X8
$\dfrac{2,915}{1,568}$ = 1.9 times	$\dfrac{3,874}{2,289}$ = 1.7 times

With additional information on the values of each type of fixed asset, this performance could be examined in even more detail by assessing each type separately.

Working Capital Turnover

$$\frac{Sales\ revenue}{Working\ capital}$$

19X7	19X8
$\dfrac{2,915}{269}$ = 10.8 times	$\dfrac{3,874}{315}$ = 12.3 times

Again the items comprising working capital may be analysed individually using the ratios explained below.

Stock Turnover

This is a measure of how effectively stock has been used and is calculated as follows:

$$\frac{Cost\ of\ goods\ sold}{Average\ stock\ ^*}$$

* *For convenience the average stock held in a period is usually estimated as follows:*

$$Average\ stock = \frac{Opening\ stock + closing\ stock}{2}$$

19X7	19X8
$\dfrac{2{,}011}{(148 + 154) \div 2}$ = 13 times	$\dfrac{2{,}819}{(154 + 273) \div 2}$ = 13 times
(i.e. the average stock on hand was sold 13 times in each year).	

These results can be expressed another way by calculating the average length of time goods were held in stock:

$$\text{Average time in stock} \ = \ \frac{365 \text{ days}}{13 \text{ times}} \ = \ 28 \text{ days}$$

As holding stocks ties up funds which may be required for other purposes, businesses often seek to increase stock turnover by reducing stock levels.

Debtor Collection Period

The debtor collection period measures the average delay between making a sale and collecting the cash from the customer. It is calculated as shown:

$$\frac{\textit{Average trade debtors}^{\,*}}{\textit{Average credit sales per day}}$$

* The average trade debtors may be estimated in the same manner as described for stock above. If there is insufficient information available to calculate this, the year end debtors shown in the balance sheet may be used.

19X7	19X8
$\dfrac{(242 + 304) \div 2}{2{,}915 \div 365 \text{ days}}$ = 34 days	$\dfrac{(304 + 488) \div 2}{3{,}874 \div 365 \text{ days}}$ = 37 days
(i.e. on average debts are collected 34 days after the goods are sold).	(i.e. on average debts are collected after 37 days).

NB. In the absence of further information it has been assumed that:

(i)   Denshaw's sales are all made on credit.

(ii)   *The debtors figure comprises only trade debtors (with a full set of accounts the relevant figure could be determined by referring to the note on debtors).*

Denshaw has taken slightly longer to collect its debts in 19X8 and although the rise is not drastic, the ratio should be monitored closely. Allowing excessively long credit periods can cause liquidity problems which may ultimately lead to insolvency. On the other hand, offering terms which are less favourable than competitors may deter customers and lead to a reduction in sales revenue. Consequently, credit terms are often based on those generally available in the industry in which a business operates and success in collecting debts monitored using indicators such as the collection period.

Creditor Payment Period

This measures the average time taken to pay credit suppliers and is calculated as follows:

$$\frac{Average\ trade\ creditors}{Average\ credit\ purchases\ per\ day\ ^*}$$

* As the purchases figure may not be available in published accounts, the cost of sales may be substituted. Although not as appropriate as purchases, the result should at least provide an indication of the trend.

19X7	19X8
$\dfrac{(170\ +\ 226)\ \div\ 2}{2{,}017\ \div\ 365\ days}$ = 36 days *(i.e. on average suppliers are paid 36 days after goods are purchased).*	$\dfrac{(226\ +\ 457)\ \div\ 2}{2{,}938\ \div\ 365\ days}$ = 42 days *(i.e. on average suppliers are paid after 42 days).*

NB.   *It has been assumed that:*

(i)   *All purchases are made on credit.*

(ii)   *Expenses do not include goods/services obtained on credit.*

(iii)   *The creditors figure comprises only trade creditors (again with a full set of accounts the value could be determined by referring to the relevant note).*

An increase in the creditor payment period such as Denshaw has experienced, often reflects difficulties in paying suppliers and may be an indication of liquidity problems.

Employee Ratios

These ratios relate key figures to the average numbers employed in the period. A commonly used example is sales per employee:

Sales per Employee

$$\frac{Sales\ revenue}{Average\ number\ of\ employees}$$

19X7		19X8	
$\dfrac{2,915}{(23+26) \div 2}$ = £119,000 (rounded)		$\dfrac{3,874}{(26+30) \div 2}$ = £138,000 (rounded)	

Although the higher figure for 19X8 suggests greater productivity, care should be taken in interpreting these results. If selling prices had risen in 19X8, higher sales revenue per employee may be due to this rather than selling more goods.

Other employee ratios include gross profit, net profit and total expenses per employee.

The Relationship Between Performance Ratios

As explained previously, fluctuations in overall performance (as measured by the return on capital employed) are due to changes in:

- The net profit margin
- The asset turnover ratio

The relationship between these three ratios can be expressed as follows:

Return on capital employed   =   Net profit margin x Asset turnover ratio

$$\frac{Net\ profit}{Capital\ employed} = \frac{Net\ profit}{Sales\ revenue} \quad \text{x} \quad \frac{Sales\ revenue}{Capital\ employed}$$

Thus for Denshaw in 19X7:

$$\frac{361}{1,837} \quad = \quad \frac{361}{2,915} \quad x \quad \frac{2,915}{1,837}$$

$$19.7\% \quad = \quad 12.4\% \quad x \quad 1.59$$

As we have seen, changes in the two sub-ratios can be investigated through further ratio analysis as illustrated in Figure 9.4:

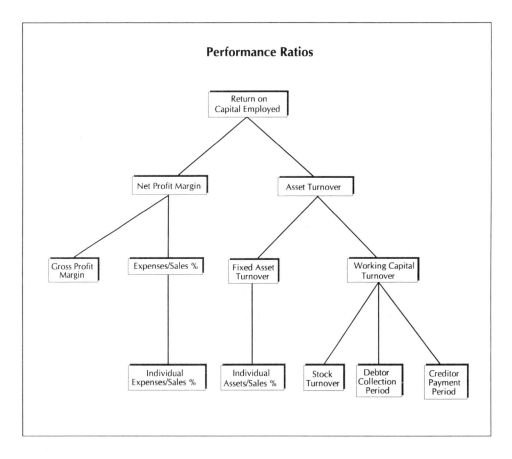

Figure 9.4 Performance Ratios

Liquidity

As we saw in Chapter 8, it is important that liquidity is managed as well as profitability. All parties with an interest in a business will be concerned with this as a poor liquidity position may eventually result in insolvency. As a result shareholders may lose their investment, lenders and suppliers on credit may be unable to recover outstanding debts and employees may lose their jobs.

As we have already seen, the creditor collection period may give some insight into the liquidity position and we will now consider two other ratios which can also help in this respect.

Current Ratio

The current ratio assesses the ability to meet short term liabilities from the most immediate source of cash, current assets. It is expressed as a ratio as shown below:

$$\frac{Current\ assets}{Current\ liabilities} : 1$$

19X7	19X8
$\dfrac{495}{226}$ = 2.2 : 1	$\dfrac{772}{457}$ = 1.7 : 1
i.e. There are £2.20 worth of current assets to cover each £1 worth of current liabilities.	*i.e. There are £1.70 worth of current assets to cover each £1 worth of current liabilities.*

Although Denshaw has insufficient cash at the end of each year to pay short term liabilities, it has stocks and debtors which can be converted into cash. Provided this occurs before creditors are due to be paid, the business should remain solvent.

A low current ratio may suggest liquidity problems whilst a particularly high figure may indicate over-investment in current assets (e.g. carrying too much stock or allowing customers too much credit). It is not possible to give an ideal or acceptable figure as the ratio will vary according to the type of business. Supermarkets for example, which may have little or no debtors, tend to have lower ratios than manufacturing companies. The ratio obtained should therefore be assessed by comparing with previous periods or businesses engaged in similar activities.

Liquidity Ratio

The liquidity ratio which is also known as the 'Quick assets' or 'Acid test' ratio takes a more cautious view of the liquidity position. It recognises that as it may take some time to sell the stock on hand, it may not be converted into cash quickly enough to pay the current liabilities as they fall due. The ratio therefore assesses the ability to meet short term liabilities from the more liquid assets (i.e. cash and debtors). It is expressed as follows:

$$\frac{Current\ assets - stock}{Current\ liabilities} : 1$$

19X7	19X8
$\dfrac{495 - 154}{226} = 1.5 : 1$	$\dfrac{772 - 273}{457} = 1.1 : 1$
i.e. There are £1.50 worth of liquid assets (debtors and cash) to cover each £1 of current liabilities.	i.e. There are £1.10 worth of liquid assets to cover each £1 of current liabilities.

Again the size of the ratio will be influenced by the type of activity the business is engaged in.

Other Indicators of Liquidity

Another relevant issue when assessing liquidity is access to alternative sources of finance. Liquidity ratios assess the ability to meet short term liabilities from current assets. However a business with other sources of finance, such as an overdraft facility, will not be so reliant on its current assets and may have little cause for concern even with poor liquidity ratios.

A true assessment of liquidity requires a more sophisticated approach than the rough indications provided by ratios. For example, Denshaw's liquidity ratio at the end of 19X8 indicates that liquid assets are sufficient to cover short term liabilities. However, this will only be the case if outstanding debtors can be collected quickly enough to meet the liabilities as they fall due. Comprehensive assessment of liquidity therefore entails detailed forecasting of the timing and value of expected future cash flows. Any projected shortfalls can then be addressed in advance to ensure that funds will be available as and when required. Such cash flow forecasts are an essential aid for managers responsible for financial management and will be examined in detail in Chapter 15 when we look at short term planning.

Capital Structure

Companies may be financed by capital provided by both the owners and lenders. Where finance is mainly provided by the owners, a company is said to be low geared and where a greater proportion of debt is used, it may be referred to as highly geared. A company which is highly geared is considered to be a riskier investment for shareholders as the interest on debt must be paid regardless of the level of profit. Consequently in lean years there may be insufficient remaining after paying interest to pay dividends to shareholders. As far as ordinary shareholders are concerned, the level of preference capital also increases the degree of risk as preference shareholders are entitled to dividends before ordinary shareholders.

The degree to which a company is financed by 'prior charge capital' (i.e. debt and preference shares) is measured using the gearing ratio.

Gearing Ratio

$$\frac{Long\ term\ loans + preference\ share\ capital}{Capital\ employed}$$

19X7	19X8
$\frac{320 + 0}{1,837}$ × 100 = 17%	$\frac{950 + 0}{2,604}$ × 100 = 36%

Additional borrowing in 19X8 has increased Denshaw's gearing ratio. To compensate for the additional risk this entails, shareholders may require a higher return on their investment.

Interest Cover

This looks at the extent to which interest payments are covered by profit. It is ascertained as follows:

$$\frac{Net\ profit\ (before\ interest\ and\ tax)}{Interest\ charge}$$

19X7	19X8
$\frac{361}{26}$ = 14 times	$\frac{401}{90}$ = 4 times

Interest payable on the additional borrowing in 19X8 has resulted in a sharp decrease in Denshaw's interest cover. This ratio is of particularly interest to lenders as a company with low interest cover may be unable to meet interest charges in the future if profits were to fall.

Investment

Investment ratios can help current and prospective investors to assess the performance of companies from a shareholder's point of view.

Earnings Per Share (EPS)

This shows amount earned by the company in respect of each ordinary share issued and is obtained as follows:

$$\frac{Profit\ attributable\ to\ ordinary\ shareholders}{Average\ number\ of\ shares\ in\ issue}$$

19X7		19X8	
$\frac{232}{600}$ = £0.39		$\frac{245}{600}$ = £0.41	

A proportion of these earnings is usually paid to shareholders in the form of a dividend and the balance retained for investment in the business.

Earnings Yield

This relates the earnings per share to the market value of the shares and is obtained as follows:

$$\frac{Earnings\ per\ share}{Market\ price\ per\ share}\ \ \text{x}\ \ 100$$

19X7	19X8
$\frac{0.39}{4.50}$ x 100 = 8.7%	$\frac{0.41}{4.10}$ x 100 = 10%

The earnings yield can be compared with that available from other shares or the return from alternative investments. However, in the case of the latter, it should be remembered that as a portion of the earnings is usually retained by the business, the earnings yield is unlikely to reflect the cash received by shareholders. The cash return can be assessed using the dividend yield.

Dividend Yield

This relates the dividend income of investors to the value of their investment as follows:

$$\frac{Dividend\ per\ share}{Market\ price\ per\ share}$$

19X7	19X8
$\frac{0.28^*}{4.50}$ × 100 = 6.2%	$\frac{0.18^*}{4.10}$ × 100 = 4.4%
$\frac{* £168,000}{600,000\ shares}$	$\frac{* £108,000}{600,000\ shares}$

When comparing this return with that available from alternative investments it should be remembered that as well as income, investors in companies may also benefit from a rise in the market price of the shares.

Dividend Cover

Dividend cover measures the extent to which dividends are covered by profits. It is calculated as follows:

$$\frac{Profit\ attributable\ to\ ordinary\ shares}{Dividend\ for\ the\ year}$$

19X7	19X8
$\frac{232}{168}$ = 1.4 times	$\frac{245}{108}$ = 2.3 times

The ratio gives some indication of the prospects for maintaining dividends at the current level . A company with low cover may have difficulty in doing so if profits were to fall in future years.

Price Earnings (PE) Ratio

The PE ratio measures the number of years' earnings covered by the market price of the shares. It is expressed as the inverse of the earnings yield:

$$\frac{Market\ price\ per\ share}{Earnings\ per\ share}$$

19X7			19X8		
$\dfrac{4.50}{0.39}$	=	11.5	$\dfrac{4.10}{0.41}$	=	10

A high PE ratio means that investors are willing to pay a high price for the shares in relation to the current level of earnings and may indicate that they anticipate favourable returns in the future.

Denshaw's Performance and Financial Position

The ratios calculated for Denshaw plc are summarised in Figure 9.5.

	19X7	19X8
OVERALL PERFORMANCE		
Return on capital employed	19.7%	15.4%
Return on shareholders' funds	15.3%	14.8%
PROFITABILITY		
Net profit margin	12.4%	10.4%
Gross profit margin	31.0%	27.2%
Expenses to sales	18.6%	16.9%
Distribution costs to sales	4.8%	5.8%
Administration expenses to sales	13.8%	11.1%
PRODUCTIVITY		
Asset turnover	1.59 times	1.49 times
Fixed asset turnover	1.9 times	1.7 times
Working capital turnover	10.8 times	12.3 times
Stock turnover	13 times	13 times
Debtor collection period	34 days	37 days
Creditor payment period	36 days	42 days
Sales per employee	£119,000	£138,000
LIQUIDITY		
Current ratio	2.2 : 1	1.7 : 1
Liquidity ratio	1.5 : 1	1.1 : 1
CAPITAL STRUCTURE		
Gearing ratio	17%	36%
Interest cover	14 times	4 times
INVESTMENT		
Earnings per share	£0.39	£0.41
Earnings yield	8.7%	10%
Dividend yield	6.2%	4.4%
Dividend cover	1.4 times	2.3 times
PE ratio	11.5	10

Figure 9.5 Denshaw plc – Summary of Ratios

Using these ratios the performance and financial position of the company can be analysed as follows:

Overall Performance

Although sales have risen by 33% in 19X8, return on capital employed has fallen from 19.7% to 15.4% because:

(a)   Sales were less profitable in 19X8.

(b)   Assets were utilised less effectively in 19X8, generating sales of £1.49 per £1 capital employed compared to £1.59 in 19X7.

Profitability

Figure 9.6 provides a vertical analysis of Denshaw's profitability in each year rounded to the nearest 1%:

		19X7		19X8
		(%)		(%)
Sales		100		100
Cost of sales		(69)		(73)
Gross profit margin		31		27
Less expenses				
Distribution	(5)		(6)	
Administration	(14)	(19)	(11)	(17)
Net profit margin		12		10

Figure 9.6 Denshaw plc – Profitability Analysis

Lower profitability in 19X8 was due to a substantial fall in the gross profit margin. As sales income rose by 33% the lower margin may have been due to a reduction in selling prices in order to boost sales.

Although the rise in sales revenue did not produce a corresponding rise in the cost of administration, distribution costs increased at a greater rate than sales and may require further investigation.

Productivity

A substantial investment was made in fixed assets during 19X8. However, the company was unable to maintain productivity with fixed asset turnover falling from 1.9 to 1.7. It may be that the company is not yet reaping the full benefit of the newly acquired assets and that performance will improve in the future.

In terms of working capital, the increase in the debtor collection period in 19X8 may indicate that better credit terms have been used as a means of attracting new customers. The longer creditor payment period may have been due to the deterioration in the liquidity position.

Liquidity

Although the liquidity ratios show that short term assets exceed current liabilities, the cash balance is low at the end of 19X8 and the liquidity position has deteriorated during the year. The ability to meet short term liabilities depends on collecting cash from debtors before creditors are due for payment. If it has not already done so, Denshaw may need to negotiate an overdraft facility or consider an alternative source of finance. The position should be monitored closely and cash flow forecasts prepared to ensure that cash will be available to meet future requirements.

Capital Structure

The acquisition of fixed assets has been financed by additional borrowing. This has reduced the interest cover considerably although the gearing ratio does not appear to be excessively high.

Investment

Although earnings per share have increased, the share price has fallen. This may reflect investors' perception of greater financial risk due to the higher level of gearing.

The dividend per share has fallen from 28p to 18p and yield has also fallen. Dividend cover is greater in 19X8 due to a combination of the lower dividend and slightly higher profits.

Further Points on the Interpretation of Ratios

When interpreting ratios derived from accounting statements it is worth bearing the following points in mind:

- A number of ratios should be used to investigate a particular aspect of the business rather than looking at one in isolation. As we saw when analysing Denshaw plc, this can provide further clues as to the reasons for features identified.

- Consulting other available information will give a more complete picture of the company's activities. Sources of information include the chairman's statement in the annual accounts and information in trade journals and the financial press.

- Comparing with other companies in the same line of business can be useful.

- Ratios should be used in the light of the limitations identified below.

Limitations of Ratio Analysis

Although ratio analysis is a useful means of interpreting accounting statements, it does have its limitations. These include:

Inconsistency

Meaningful comparison of ratios, with previous periods or other businesses, requires a degree of consistency in the preparation of accounting information. Although accounting principles and standards have evolved in an attempt to ensure that this is the case, there is still scope for a degree of inconsistency. Examples include depreciation (where differing rates and methods may be used) and stock valuation (where FIFO or AVCO principles may be employed).

When comparing results for a business over a number of periods the problem should not be too great as accounting policies should be consistently applied from one period to the next. However, when comparing different businesses there is no such guarantee.

Subjectivity

In Chapter 5 we saw that the measurement of profit is a subjective exercise requiring judgement in the estimation of certain figures. Consequently conclusions drawn from accounting information will reflect judgements made by those preparing it.

Seasonality

Ratios derived from information available in the balance sheet tend to use year end figures. Where a business is seasonal this approach may produce a distorted view of the business. For example, using year end stock balances to ascertain the average stock level will be inappropriate if the business always carries high stocks at that time of year to meet high demand shortly after the year end.

Inflation

When using ratios to assess trends over a number of years, fluctuations may result from inflation rather than the performance of the business. To compensate, figures should be adjusted to reflect the rate of inflation during the periods in question.

To summarise, ratio analysis is a useful means of assessing the financial position and performance of a business. However, it has limitations and a clearer picture is likely to emerge from supplementing ratio analysis with information available from other sources.

SUMMARY OF ACCOUNTING RATIOS

Aspects of Business Analysed	Parties Most Interested	Ratio	Method of Calculation	Meaning
Overall Performance	Shareholders Management Competitors Lenders	Return on Capital Employed (%)	$\dfrac{\text{Net Profit (before tax and interest)}}{\text{Capital Employed}^*} \times 100$ (*Owners funds and long term liabilities)	The key ratio relating profit earned to the amount of long term capital invested in the business. (This can be compared to alternative investments).
		Return on Shareholders' Funds (%)	$\dfrac{\text{Net Profit Attributable to Ordinary Shareholders}^*}{\text{Ordinary Shareholders' Funds}} \times 100$ (*i.e. After interest tax and preference dividends)	Relates profit earned on behalf of ordinary shareholders to the value of the capital they have provided.
Profitability	As above	Gross Profit Margin (%)	$\dfrac{\text{Gross Profit}}{\text{Sales Revenue}} \times 100$	Assesses the trading profitability of the business.
		Net Profit Margin (%)	$\dfrac{\text{Net Profit (before tax and interest)}}{\text{Sales Revenue}} \times 100$	Measures the final profit made on sales after expenses have been deducted from the gross profit.
		Expenses to Sales (%)	$\dfrac{\text{Total Expenses}}{\text{Sales Revenue}} \times 100$	Indicates why the net profit margin may have improved/deteriorated.
Productivity	As above	Asset Turnover (times)	$\dfrac{\text{Sales Revenue}}{\text{Capital Employed}}$	Measures the sales income generated in relation to the assets employed in the business.
		Fixed Asset Turnover (times)	$\dfrac{\text{Sales Revenue}}{\text{Fixed Assets}}$	Measures the sales income generated in relation to the fixed assets
		Working Capital Turnover (times)	$\dfrac{\text{Sales Revenue}}{\text{Working Capital}}$	Measures the sales income generated in relation to the investment in working capital.
		Stock Turnover (times)	$\dfrac{\text{Cost of Goods Sold}}{\text{Average Stock}}$	Measures how effectively stock has been used.
		Debtor Collection Period (days)	$\dfrac{\text{Average Trade Debtors}}{\text{Average Credit Sales per Day}}$	Indicates the speed with which debts are collected from credit customers.
		Credit Payment Period (days)	$\dfrac{\text{Average Trade Creditors}}{\text{Average Credit Purchases per Day}}$	Indicates the speed with which suppliers are paid.
		Sales per Employee	$\dfrac{\text{Sales Revenue}}{\text{Average No. of Employees}}$	Measures the sales income generated per employee.

SUMMARY OF ACCOUNTING RATIOS

Aspects of Business Analysed	Parties Most Interested	Ratio	Method Of Calculation	Meaning
Liquidity	Management, Lenders, Trade creditors	Current Ratio	$\dfrac{\text{Current Assets}}{\text{Current Liabilities}} : 1$	Indicates the ability of the business to meet short term debts from short term assets.
		Liquidity Ratio	$\dfrac{\text{*Liquid Assets}}{\text{Current Liabilities}} : 1$ (*Current assets – stock)	Indicates the ability to meet short term debts from liquid assets (i.e. recognises that it can take some time to convert stock into cash).
Capital Structure	Shareholders, Management, Lenders	Gearing Ratio (%)	$\dfrac{\text{Long Term Loans} + \text{Preference Share Capital}}{\text{Capital Employed}}$	Indicates the extent to which the company is financed by "prior charge capital".
		Interest Cover (%)	$\dfrac{\text{Net Profit (Before Interest and Tax)}}{\text{Interest Charge}}$	Indicates the extent to which interest payments are covered by profit.
Investment	Shareholders, Management	Earnings per Share	$\dfrac{\text{Profit Attributable to Ordinary Shareholders}}{\text{Number of Shares Issued}}$	Shows the amount earned by the company in respect of each share issued.
		Earnings Yield (%)	$\dfrac{\text{Earnings per Share}}{\text{Market Price per Share}}$	Shows the rate of earnings in relation to the market price of shares.
		Dividend Yield (%)	$\dfrac{\text{Dividend per Share}}{\text{Market Price per Share}}$	Relates the dividend income of investors to the value of their investment.
		Dividend Cover (times)	$\dfrac{\text{Profit Attributable to Ordinary Shareholders}}{\text{Dividend for the Year}}$	Indicates the extent to which dividends are covered by profits
		Price/Earnings (PE) Ratio	$\dfrac{\text{Market Price per Share}}{\text{Earnings per Share}}$	Measures the number of years' earnings covered by the market price of the shares.

Figure 9.7 Summary of Accounting Ratios

Summary

- The information reported in accounting statements can be used to analyse the financial position and performance of a business using a number of techniques.

- *Horizontal analysis* highlights differences in figures reported in successive periods.

- *Trend analysis* shows changes occurring over a number of periods.

- *Vertical analysis* shows the relative values of a list of figures by expressing them as a percentage of the total. The results may be compared with previous periods or other similar businesses.

- *Ratios* show the relationship between various figures reported in accounting statements. They can be used to analyse:

  1. Performance

     (a) Overall performance

     (b) Profitability

     (c) Productivity

  2. Liquidity

  3. Capital structure

  4. Investment

- The most commonly used ratios are summarised in Figure 9.7

- They are most useful when compared with:

  - Plans and targets

  - Previous periods

  - Other similar businesses

- Although providing useful indicators, ratio analysis has limitations and is best used with other available information to build up a more complete picture of the performance and financial position of a business.

Questions   (See Appendix C for Answers)

9.1

You are given below, in summarised form, the accounts of Algernon Ltd. for 19X6 and 19X7.

	19X6 Balance Sheet			19X7 Balance Sheet		
	Cost £	Depn £	Net £	Cost £	Depn £	Net £
Plant	10,000	4,000	6,000	11,000	5,000	6,000
Building	50,000	10,000	40,000	90,000	11,000	79,000
			46,000			85,000
Investments at cost			50,000			80,000
Land			43,000			63,000
Stock			55,000			65,000
Debtors			40,000			50,000
Bank			3,000			–
			237,000			343,000
Ordinary shares £1 each			40,000			50,000
Share premium			12,000			14,000
Revaluation reserve			–			20,000
Profit and loss account			25,000			25,000
10% Debentures			100,000			150,000
Creditors			40,000			60,000
Proposed dividend			20,000			20,000
Bank			–			4,000
			237,000			343,000

	19X6 **Profit and Loss A/c** **£**	**19X7** **Profit and Loss A/c** **£**
Sales	200,000	200,000
Cost of sales	100,000	120,000
	100,000	80,000
Expenses	60,000	60,000
	40,000	20,000
Dividends	20,000	20,000
	20,000	–
Balance b/f	5,000	25,000
Balance c/f	25,000	25,000

(a)   Calculate for Algernon Ltd., for 19X6 and 19X7 the following ratios:

Return on capital employed;
Return on owners' equity (return on shareholders' funds):
Debtors turnover;
Creditors turnover:
Current ratio;
Quick assets (acid test) ratio;
Gross profit percentage;
Net profit percentage;
Dividend cover;
Gearing ratio.

(b)   Using the summarised accounts given, and the ratios you have just prepared, comment on the position, progress and direction of Algernon Ltd.

(ACCA)

9.2

You are given summarised information about two firms in the same line of business: A and B, as follows.

Balance sheets at 30th June	A			B		
	£000	£000	£000	£000	£000	£000
Land			80			260
Buildings		120			200	
Less: Depreciation		40	80		–	200
Plant		90			150	
Less: Depreciation		70	20		40	110
			180			570
Stocks		80			100	
Debtors		100			90	
Bank		–			10	
		180			200	
Creditors	110			120		
Bank	50			–		
	160			120		
		20			80	
		200			650	
Capital b/forward		100			300	
Profit for year		30			100	
		130			400	
Less: Drawings		30			40	
		100			360	
Land revaluation		–			160	
Loan (10% p.a.)		100			130	
		200			650	
Sales		1,000			3,000	
Cost of sales		400			2,000	

Required

(a)   Produce a table of eight ratios calculated for both businesses.

(b)   Write a report briefly outlining the strengths and weaknesses of the two businesses. Include comment on any major areas where the simple use of the figures could be misleading.

(ACCA)

9.3

You are given summarised results of an electrical engineering business, as follows. All figures are in £000.

Profit and loss account

	Year ended	
	31.12.X1	31.12.X0
Turnover	60,000	50,000
Cost of sales	42,000	34,000
Gross profit	18,000	16,000
Operating expenses	15,500	13,000
	2,500	3,000
Interest payable	2,200	1,300
Profit before taxation	300	1,700
Taxation	350	600
(Loss) profit after taxation	(50)	1,100
Dividends	600	600
Transfer (from) to reserves	(650)	500

Balance sheet

Fixed assets		
Intangible	500	–
Tangible	12,000	11,000
	12,500	11,000
Current assets		
Stocks	14,000	13,000
Debtors	16,000	15,000
Bank and cash	500	500
	30,500	28,500
Creditors due within one year	24,000	20,000
Net current assets	6,500	8,500
Total assets less current liabilities	19,000	19,500
Creditors due after one year	6,000	5,500
	13,000	14,000
Capital and reserves		
Share capital	1,300	1,300
Share premium	3,300	3,300
Revaluation	2,000	2,000
Profit and loss	6,400	7,400
	13,000	14,000

Required

(a)   Prepare a table of the following 12 ratios, calculated for both years, clearly showing the figures used in the calculations.

    current ratio
    quick assets ratio
    stock turnover in days
    debtors turnover in days
    creditors turnover in days
    gross profit %
    net profit % (before taxation)
    interest cover
    dividend cover
    ROOE (before taxation)
    ROCE
    gearing

(b)   Making full use of the information given in the question, your table of ratios and your common sense, comment on the apparent position of the business and on the actions of the management.

(ACCA)

Questions Without Answers

9.4

Business A and Business B are both engaged in retailing, but seem to take a different approach to this trade according to the information available. This information consists of a table of ratios, shown below:

Ratio	Business A	Business B
Current ratio	2:1	1.5:1
Quick assets (acid test) ratio	1.7:1	0.7:1
Return on capital employed (ROCE)	20%	17%
Return on owner's equity (ROOE)	30%	18%
Debtors turnover	63 days	21 days
Creditors turnover	50 days	45 days
Gross profit percentage	40%	15%
Net profit percentage	10%	10%
Stock turnover	52 days	25 days

Required

(a) Explain briefly how each ratio is calculated.

(b) Describe what this information indicates about the differences in approach between the two businesses. If one of them prides itself on personal service and one of them on competitive prices, which do you think is which and why?

(ACCA)

9.5

The abbreviated accounts for Backwell Limited are given below. Backwell is a private manufacturing firm operating wholly within the UK.

Backwell Limited
Profit and Loss Accounts for the years ending 31st December

	19X6		19X5		19X4	
	£000	£000	£000	£000	£000	£000
Sales		660		620		600
Cost of sales		(330)		(300)		(300)
Gross profit		330		320		300
Operating expenses	60		100		85	
Depreciation	105		65		65	
Interest	20		–		–	
		(185)		(165)		(150)
Net profit before tax						
and dividend		145		155		150
Tax		(50)		(50)		(50)
Net profit after tax		95		105		100
Dividend proposed		(45)		(40)		(40)
Profit retained for year		50		65		60

Balance Sheets as at 31st December

	19X6		19X5		19X4	
	£000	£000	£000	£000	£000	£000
Fixed assets: Cost		1,050		650		650
Depreciation		(460)		(355)		(290)
		590		295		360
Current assets						
Stocks: Raw materials	60		55		50	
Finished goods and work in progress	140		80		40	
Debtors	160		120		80	
Cash	130		155		100	
	490		410		270	
Less:						
Creditors due within one year						
Trade creditors	90		70		60	
Tax	50		50		50	
Dividend	45		40		40	
	185		160		150	
Net current assets		305		250		120
Less:						
Creditors due after more than one year						
Loan stock		(200)		--		--
		695		545		480
Capital and reserves						
Ordinary shares of £1 fully paid		350		300		300
Share premium		50		--		--
Retained profits		295		245		180
		695		545		480

Required

Using the above statements and any ratios you consider helpful, comment on the performance of Backwell Limited from the viewpoint of:

(i)   a small shareholder in the company;

(ii)   a small company about to supply goods and become a creditor of Backwell Limited.

(ACCA)

9.6

The following balance sheet and profit and loss account have been prepared together with information regarding the revaluation of assets during the year.

Balance Sheet at 30th November

	19X3 £	19X3 £	19X3 £	19X4 £	19X4 £	19X4 £
Fixed assets						
Tangible assets						
At valuation			–			55,000
At cost			100,000			115,000
Depreciation			(45,000)			(60,000)
			55,000			110,000
Current assets						
Stock	16,500			21,760		
Trade debtors	26,750			42,150		
Cash	7,236			27		
		50,486			63,937	
Less						
Creditors due within one year						
Trade creditors	20,000			14,569		
Taxation	7,462			2,785		
Dividend	5,000			5,000		
Bank overdraft	36,087			14,365		
		68,549			36,719	
Net current assets			(18,063)			27,218
Less						
Creditors due after more than one year						
Debentures						
			–			(20,000)
			36,937			117,218

	19X3 £	19X4 £
Capital and reserves		
Share capital paid up	20,000	50,000
Share premium account	10,000	20,000
Revaluation reserve	–	40,000
Profit and loss account	6,937	7,218
	36,937	117,218

At 30th November 19X4 buildings which originally cost £20,000, with a net book value of £15,000, were revalued on a going concern basis at £55,000.

Profit and Loss Account year ended 30th November

	19X3 £	19X4 £
Sales turnover	278,942	421,265
Cost of sales, and operating expenses after charging depreciation (£15,000 and £20,000)	253,781	408,202
Profit before interest and tax	25,161	13,063
Interest payable, Debentures (£0 and £2,800)		
Bank (£8,427 and £2,765)	8,427	5,565
Profit before tax	16,734	7,498
Tax	7,113	2,217
Profit for the financial year, after tax	9,621	5,281
Dividends paid and proposed	5,000	5,000
Retention	4,621	281

You are required to:

(a) calculate the following ratios for 19X4 using the closing balance sheet values.

(i) Return on capital employed.

(ii) Return on shareholders' funds.

(iii) A gearing ratio based on the balance sheet.

(iv) Sales turnover ratio.

(v)   Profit margin.

(b)   explain the relationship between ratios (i), (iv) and (v), and the effect of this relationship on the pricing policy of the organisation.

(c)   comment upon the performance of the company from the viewpoint of

(i)   the management

(ii)   the bank

(You may need to calculate further ratios)

(ACCA)

Part 3

Management Accounting

Chapter 10

Costing

Learning Objectives

After completing this chapter you should be able to:

- Explain how costing information may be used.

- Describe how costs may be recorded and analysed using a cost coding system.

- Explain how the direct cost of a product or service may be ascertained.

- Describe the process through which indirect costs may be assigned to products.

- Calculate the total cost of a product.

- Explain the treatment of under/over absorbed overheads.

- Discuss the limitations of absorption costing.

- Explain the benefits which Activity Based Costing (ABC) may provide.

- Outline costing methods suitable for various types of business activity.

Introduction

In Part Two we considered the provision of accounting information for interested parties operating outside the business. Although accounting statements such as profit and loss accounts, balance sheets and cash flow statements may also be used by managers working within the business, their information needs are unlikely to be entirely satisfied by such reports. To operate effectively more detailed management accounting information will be required to assist in managing activities and influencing future performance rather than merely reporting the consequences of past events. As we saw in Chapter 1, management accounting is unconstrained by the legal and regulatory requirements we encountered when studying financial accounting in Part Two. The information provided should reflect the particular requirements of those for whom it is intended. However there are various techniques and methods which are commonly used in practice and in Part Three we will consider these in some detail. The first topic we shall examine is costing which is concerned with the ascertainment of costs for departments, activities, processes, products and services.

As we will see in this chapter, information may be compiled using alternative methods and techniques which vary in terms of their sophistication and according to the type of business in which they are most suitable. This information may be used for various management purposes which we will now consider.

Using Costing Information

The information derived from costing systems can provide useful guidance for management in the following functions:

Planning

Costing information can be used to estimate future costs for departments, activities and products/services. This can help managers to ensure that plans should produce acceptable levels of profit and cash flows which enable the business to pay liabilities as they fall due.

Control

Having established business plans, steps must be taken to control activities in order to attain the objectives set. Measuring actual costs and comparing with those planned can give some indication of activities which are not proceeding according to plan and which may require some remedial action.

Decision Making

Most decisions have a cost implication and the provision of relevant cost information can provide useful guidance when addressing questions such as:

Should we produce a particular product/service?

Where competitive forces create a market price for a product the ability to earn an acceptable profit at that price will be a factor in deciding whether or not to produce it. To determine this the cost of producing the item must be known.

At what price should a product/service be sold?

Some businesses use 'cost plus' pricing methods in which selling prices are set by applying a percentage mark-up to the product cost. Again the aim is to ensure that products are sold at a price at which an acceptable profit is earned. We will look at examples of this technique later in the chapter.

Should methods of operation be changed?

Where new methods are proposed the financial consequences of the changes will inevitably influence the decision. This will require cost information in respect of both existing and proposed methods.

Cost Analysis

In order to provide the information required for the purposes described above, costs must be analysed in a meaningful way. To do this they may be classified according to:

1. Their nature (i.e. what was the money spent on?).

2. Their purpose (i.e. which department, product or activity incurred the cost?).

To facilitate this analysis coding systems are commonly used to record and process cost data. An extract from such a system is given in Figure 10.1.

Cost Coding System (Extract)	
Code	**Nature of Cost**
TB92	Timber (9cm x 2cm)
TB94	Timber (9cm x 4cm)
PB00	Paint (Black)
PW00	Paint (White)
ST00	Stationery
SA00	Salaries
Code	**Purpose of Cost**
0001	Job No.1
0002	Job No.2
0003	Job No.3
1001	Maintenance Dept.
1002	Admin. Dept.
1003	Sales Dept.

Figure 10.1 A Cost Coding System

Using the system illustrated, an invoice received for stationery to be used in the sales dept would be coded:

1003   /   ST00

White paint to be used on job no.2 would be coded:

0002   /   PW00

These codes can be input to a computer which will include the relevant amounts in the sales department's stationery costs and the material cost of Job No.2. The total costs incurred by each department/product can then be analysed by type through the aggregation of data recorded over a period of time.

Product Costing

Product costing is the ascertainment of the cost of individual items produced or services rendered. These units of product/service are known as cost units and will differ according to the nature of the organisation. Typical examples are shown in Figure 10.2:

Typical Cost Units	
Organisation	**Cost Unit**
Car manufacturer	Car
Construction business	Construction contract
TV Production company	Television programme
Hospital	Bed occupied
College	Student
Hotel	Room night

Figure 10.2 Typical Cost Units

As we saw in Chapter 6, costs incurred in the production of these cost units may be classed as either direct (ie. identifiable with a specific unit produced) or indirect (those not directly associated with the production of goods/services). In order to ascertain the cost of the units produced, these cost inputs must be assigned to cost units as illustrated in Figure 10.3:

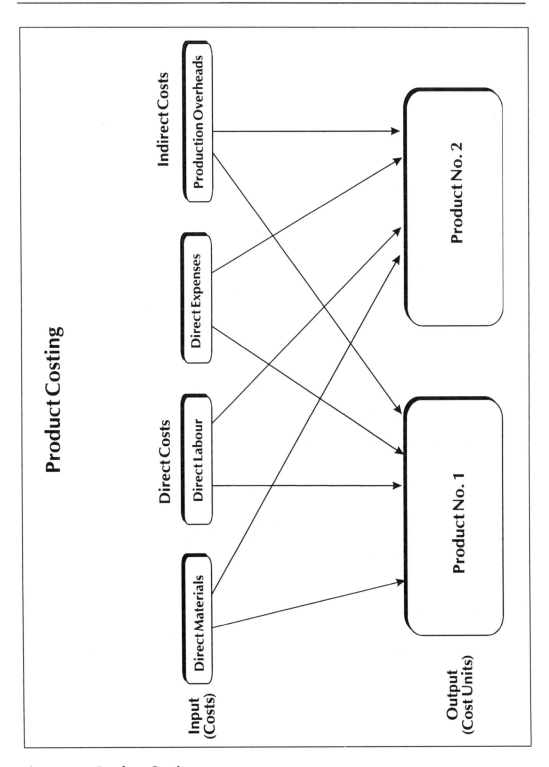

Figure 10.3 Product Costing

The production cost for each unit will therefore comprise the following elements:

Direct costs

- Direct materials ⎫
- Direct labour ⎬ Prime Cost
- Direct expenses ⎭

Indirect costs

- A share of production overheads

Production Cost

We will now examine the way in which the total production cost of a unit may be ascertained by considering each of the above elements in turn.

Note that although a manufacturing organisation is used for demonstration purposes, as we shall see later the same techniques may be applied in service organisations.

Direct Costs

Direct Materials

The material cost of a product may be obtained as follows:

$$\text{Cost} = \text{Quantity used} \times \text{Price}$$

E.g. Product Manufactured - Garden Bench

				£
Timber	– 4 sq. m	x £6.50 per m^2	=	26.00
Paint	– 1 litre	x £2.00 per litre	=	2.00
Total material cost				28.00

Recording Materials Usage

To obtain the total material cost of each product the quantity of each material used must be determined. This can be recorded using material requisition forms as illustrated in Figure 10.4.

```
┌─────────────────────────────────────────────────────────────────────┐
│                        Material Requisition                           │
│                                                                       │
│  Job No.              Quantity            Description    Material Code │
│   0034                 4 m.          Timber (9cm.x 2cm.)     TB92      │
│   0038                 7 m           Timber (9cm.x 4cm.)     TB94      │
│                                                                       │
│                                                                       │
│  Authorised By ..................      Date ........                  │
└─────────────────────────────────────────────────────────────────────┘
```

Figure 10.4 A Material Requisition

Materials are issued from stores only on receipt of an authorised requisition which can be used to update the stock records and charge the relevant job with the cost of the materials. After processing the requisition shown:

- The stock records for materials TB92 and TB94 would be reduced by 4 and 7 metres respectively.

- The cost of job nos. 0034 and 0038 would include the cost of the timber used by multiplying the quantities shown by the relevant price per metre for each type of material.

Pricing Materials Used

As we saw in Chapter 6, determining the price of materials used on a particular job is not straightforward where purchases are made over a period of time at different prices. You may find it useful at this point to review the alternative pricing methods (FIFO, LIFO and AVCO) outlined in Chapter 6. When deciding which of these is to be used in a costing system the following advantages and disadvantages should be considered:

FIFO (First in first out)

Advantages

1. It is a realistic method. It assumes that the oldest stock is issued first.

2. Stock is valued at current prices. As stock held is deemed to be that most recently purchased it is valued at the most recent prices.

3. The method is acceptable to the Inland Revenue and the accounting standard on stocks (SSAP 9).

Disadvantages

1. Product costs may be out of date. Issues of materials to production are deemed to be those acquired earliest. Product costs are therefore based on older material prices and may be out of date.

2.   Comparing the costs of jobs can be difficult. Two identical products could be charged different prices for the same materials. One will therefore have a higher reported cost merely because its materials were deemed to be from a batch purchased at an earlier date.

LIFO (Last in first out)

Advantage

Product costs are based on current prices. As materials used are deemed to be those most recently acquired, costs reported are more up to date.

Disadvantages

1.   The method is unacceptable to the Inland Revenue and SSAP 9. Consequently although it may be used to generate internal management information (perhaps to ensure up to date product costs are available) it should not be used as a basis for determining the costs reported in the year end Profit and Loss Account. As most businesses use computerised costing systems it should be possible to produce information for different purposes, perhaps using FIFO for published accounts and LIFO for up to date product costs for management.

2.   Stock is valued at out of date prices. As stock held is deemed to comprise the earlier purchases, it is valued at outdated prices.

3.   Again comparing the costs of jobs can be difficult, for the same reasons outlined for FIFO.

AVCO (Average cost)

Advantages

1.   It is logical. It assumes that identical materials are of equal value.

2.   It is acceptable to the Inland Revenue and SSAP 9.

3.   Comparison of product costs is easier as identical materials are charged to cost units at the same price.

Disadvantage

It has been argued that the price used, being an average, is not based on any actual purchase price. However as we have seen, using actual prices can create problems and an average price may be an acceptable compromise.

Direct Labour

The labour cost of a product may also be obtained using the formula:

$$\text{Cost} \quad = \quad \text{Quantity used} \quad \text{x} \quad \text{Price}$$

In the case of labour, the quantity refers to hours worked on the product and the price reflects the wage rate. Therefore:

$$\text{Cost} \quad = \quad \text{Hours worked} \quad \text{x} \quad \text{Wage rate}$$

E.g. Product – Garden Bench

Joiners	– 2 hours	x £8.00 per hour	= £16.00
Painters	– 1 hour	x £7.50 per hour	= £ 7.50
Total labour cost			£23.50

Recording Direct Labour Costs

The time spent on each product may be ascertained using a booking system through which individuals record how they have spent their time. Time sheets such as that illustrated in Figure 10.5 may be used for this purpose.

Time Sheet

Week No. : 24

Employee Name: F. Craig   Employee No.:417

Department: Assembly

		Code	Hours
	Job Nos.	0032	14.50
		0037	6.00
		0043	9.00
	Idle Time	IT01	3.50
		IT04	1.25
		IT05	0.75
Total Hours attended			35.00

Authorised By

....
               (Dept. Supervisor)

Figure 10.5 A Time Sheet

To ascertain the labour cost to be charged to each job the time recorded is multiplied by the relevant wage rate. The total labour cost for a job can be obtained through the aggregation of amounts charged on all time sheets completed.

Another method of recording labour time is to use job cards for each separate job rather than employee time sheets. These accompany each job as it passes through the production process and employees record the time spent on it. The total time taken can be obtained on completing the job and the cost obtained using the appropriate wage rates.

In some organisations labour times are entered directly to computerised systems by production workers rather than via time sheets or job cards processed by clerical staff. This may prove a more effective method of data collection and should enable detailed costing information to be produced more quickly.

Idle Time

It is unlikely that direct production workers will spend all their time manufacturing products. Machine breakdowns, material shortages and many other causes may prevent them from being continually occupied on production work. Any time which is not spent productively is known as 'idle time' or 'lost time' and information on the level of idle time will be of great interest to production management who will be keen to utilise employees as productively as possible. An example of an idle time report is given in Figure 10.6:

Idle Time Report				
	Week 7		**Year to Date**	
	Hours	*%*	*Hours*	*%*
Attendance Hours	2,000	100	15,000	100
Idle Time				
Waiting for work	60	3.0	365	2.4
Waiting for materials	34	1.7	268	1.8
Waiting for equipment	19	1.0	134	0.9
Machine breakdown	26	1.3	201	1.3
Training	32	1.6	84	0.6
Other causes	9	0.4	84	0.6
Total Idle Time	180	9.0	1,136	7.6

Figure 10.6 Idle Time Report

Direct Expenses

Any other costs incurred as a direct consequence of producing a particular item or batch of items should be included in the product cost via the cost coding system.

This type of cost is relatively rare but the hire of specialised equipment for a particular job would fall into this category.

Indirect Costs (Overheads)

As we saw in Figure 10.3, all production costs should be assigned to the cost units produced in order to obtain the cost of producing each unit. These costs include production overheads such as:

- *Premises costs*. Maintenance, rent, cleaning, heating etc.

- *Equipment costs*. Depreciation, maintenance, power etc.

- *Employment costs*. Indirect labour such as supervisors not directly engaged in producing units, maintenance staff etc.

In order to obtain the full production cost these overheads must be related to the units produced in some way. However as there is no direct relationship between the overheads incurred and units produced, the technique for dealing with overheads is not as straightforward as for direct costs.

Overhead Absorption

The process through which overheads are related to cost units is called 'overhead absorption' (i.e. the units produced each absorb a share of overheads). The aim is to assign all production overheads incurred in a period to the units produced in order to obtain the full cost of production. This could be achieved by simply dividing the costs into the total output as follows:

$$\text{Overhead cost per unit} = \frac{\text{Total overheads incurred}}{\text{No. of units produced}}$$

However, as the actual costs and number of units produced would not be known until the end of the period, it would be impossible to calculate product costs until this time.

This would be unacceptable for managers who require estimated costs before commencing production for planning and pricing purposes and details of actual costs throughout the period for control purposes.

To satisfy these requirements overhead costs attributable to products must be determined using estimates rather than the actual figures for a period as demonstrated in the following example:

Example 10.1

The management team at Garden Furnishings Limited have estimated that production overheads of £240,000 will be incurred during the forthcoming year. They expect to produce 12,000 units and to work 40,000 direct labour hours.

The overheads can be assigned to the units by dividing the £240,000 equally among the 12,000 units:

$$\text{Overhead cost per unit} = \frac{\textit{Estimated total overheads}}{\textit{Estimated no. of units produced}}$$

$$= \frac{£240,000}{12,000 \ \textit{units}} = £20 \text{ per unit}$$

The resulting figure provides a basis for assigning (or 'charging') overheads to the units produced and is known as the overhead absorption rate (OAR). In this case each unit will be charged with overheads of £20 in addition to the direct costs incurred.

From this information and the direct costs we saw earlier the total production cost for a garden bench can now be calculated as follows:

```
┌─────────────────────────────────────────────────────────────┐
│              Production Cost – Garden Bench                    │
│                                                                │
│  Direct Materials                                         £    │
│    Timber    –    (4 sq.m.  x  £6.50 per m²)    26.00         │
│                                                                │
│    Paint     –    (1 litre  x  £2.00 per litre)  2.00   28.00 │
│                                                                │
│  Direct Labour                                                 │
│    Joiners   –    (2 hours  x  £8.00)           16.00         │
│                                                                │
│    Painters  –    (1 hour   x  £7.50)            7.50   23.50 │
│                                                                │
│  Prime Cost                                             51.50 │
│                                                                │
│  Overheads (@ £20 per unit)                             20.00 │
│                                                                │
│  Production Cost                                        71.50 │
└─────────────────────────────────────────────────────────────┘
```

Where all units produced are identical, this simple approach to sharing out the overheads is acceptable. However where a variety of different products are produced, charging an equal amount of overhead to each unit will be inappropriate.

Let us suppose for example that as well as benches Garden Furniture Ltd. also produces tables, which take 6 hours to make. Using the OAR of £20 per unit obtained above, overheads of £20 would be assigned to both a table and a bench. However, as benches are produced in only 3 hours each table takes twice as long to produce. Consequently tables are likely to have a greater influence on the level of overheads incurred and the cost assigned to each product should reflect this in some way.

This can be achieved by charging overheads in proportion to the number of labour hours required as follows:

1. Calculate the OAR

The OAR is calculated as before but this time labour hours are used instead of the number of units:

$$\text{OAR} = \frac{\textit{Total estimated overheads}}{\textit{Estimated no. of labour hours}}$$

$$= \frac{£240,000}{40,000 \; hours} = £6 \text{ per labour hour}$$

2. Charge overheads to products

Overheads can now be charged at a rate of £6 for every labour hour spent working on a product:

Overhead Costs:

Benches – 3 labour hours x £6 per hour = £18 per bench

Tables – 6 labour hours x £6 per hour = £36 per table

Using labour hours as the basis for absorbing overheads, tables which take twice as long to produce, are assigned double the overhead cost.

Using Departmental OAR's

Using the method described above, the absorption rate of £6 per labour would be used to charge overheads to all units produced by the business. Although this ensures that the most time consuming units are assigned higher overhead costs, it fails to recognise the fact that the time may be spent in a number of different departments, some of which may incur more overheads than others. Where two products take the same time to produce but one is produced in a more costly department, this should be reflected in the product cost.

This can be achieved by using a separate OAR for each production department rather than a single rate for the entire business.

The OAR for each department is derived as follows:

$$\text{OAR} = \frac{\textit{Estimated overheads} \text{ for } \textit{the dept.}}{\textit{Estimated no. of labour hours} \text{ for } \textit{the dept.}}$$

The rate calculated is used to charge overheads to all units spending time in that department. Thus a unit produced in a number of departments will be charged overheads by each, using the departmental OAR.

This approach will be demonstrated using further information relating to Garden Furnishings Ltd.:

Example 10.2

Garden Furnishings Limited has analysed the production overheads estimated for the year as follows:

	£
Indirect labour	
Joinery Dept	23,500
Painting Dept.	10,100
Stores Dept.	22,400
Maintenance Dept	32,000
Factory rent	40,000
Building insurance	16,000
Depreciation	60,000
Machinery insurance	24,000
Staff welfare costs	12,000
	240,000

The following additional information is available:

	* Cost Centres				
	Production Depts.		Service Depts.		
	Joinery Dept.	Painting Dept.	Stores Dept.	Maint'ce Dept	Total
Estimated direct labour hours	24,000	16,000			40,000
No. of employees	15	9	3	3	30
Floor area (m²)	10,000	5,000	3,000	2,000	20,000
Value of machinery (£'s)	240,000	80,000			320,000
Use of stores dept.	50%	40%		10%	

* A 'cost centre' is a department in which costs are collected for analysis.

Required

Calculate an overhead absorption rate for each of the two production departments.

Solution

$$OAR = \frac{Estimated\ overheads\ for\ the\ dept.}{Estimated\ no.\ of\ labour\ hours\ for\ the\ dept.}$$

We have been provided with the estimated number of labour hours for the year in each production department:

Joinery Dept.   24,000 hours

Paint Dept.   16,000 hours

To calculate the estimated overheads for each production department we must divide the total overhead costs of £240,000 between them following steps 1 to 3 below :

STEP 1 -- Allocate Costs Across All Four Departments

Some costs are readily identifiable with departments and can be easily assigned. This is called 'allocating' the cost and in the example indirect labour, for which we are given the amount attributable to each department, can be allocated as follows:

		Production Depts.		Service Depts.	
	Total	Joinery	Painting	Stores	Maintenance
	£	£	£	£	£
Indirect labour					
Joinery Dept.	23,500	23,500			
Painting Dept.	10,100		10,100		
Stores Dept.	22,400			22,400	
Maintenance Dept.	32,000				32,000

STEP 2 -- Apportion the Remaining Costs

As we are not given specific figures for each department in respect of the remaining costs they must be apportioned between the departments on some reasonable basis. The basis of apportionment chosen for each cost should reflect the nature of the cost and the manner in which it is incurred.

For example a suitable basis for the apportionment of factory rent would be floor area as the rent charge will probably be influenced by the size of the premises. Using this basis the cost relating to each department can be calculated as follows:

Joinery Dept.

$$\frac{10,000 \text{ m}^2}{20,000 \text{ m}^2} \quad \times \quad £40,000 \quad = \quad £20,000$$

Painting Dept.

$$\frac{5,000 \text{ m}^2}{20,000 \text{ m}^2} \quad \times \quad £40,000 \quad = \quad £10,000$$

Stores Dept.

$$\frac{3,000 \text{ m}^2}{20,000 \text{ m}^2} \quad \times \quad £40,000 \quad = \quad £ 6,000$$

Maintenance Dept.

$$\frac{2,000 \text{ m}^2}{20,000 \text{ m}^2} \quad \times \quad £40,000 \quad = \quad £ 4,000$$

Total Cost Apportioned   £40,000

The Joinery Department which occupies half the space, is apportioned half of the rent cost, the Maintenance Department which occupies 10% of the area, receives 10% of the cost and so on.

The overhead analysis below shows the allocation and apportionment of the entire £240,000 across the four departments using suitable bases of apportionment for individual costs.

			Production Depts		Service Depts	
Cost		Basis for Apportionment	Joinery Dept.	Painting Dept.	Stores Dept.	Maint'ce Dept.
	£		£	£	£	£
Indirect labour						
Joinery Dept	23,500	Allocate	23,500			
Painting Dept.	10,100	"		10,100		
Stores Dept.	22,400	"			22,400	
Maintenance Dept.	32,000	"				32,000
Factory rent	40,000	Floor area	20,000	10,000	6,000	4,000
Building insurance	16,000	"	8,000	4,000	2,400	1,600
Depreciation	60,000	Value of machinery	45,000	15,000	0	0
Machinery insur-ance	24,000	"	18,000	6,000	0	0
Staff welfare	12,000	No. of employees	6,000	3,600	1,200	1,200
	240,000		120,500	48,700	32,000	38,800

We can check that the entire £240,000 has now been allocated and apportioned by adding up the total cost shown under each department. You should find that all £240,000 has been accounted for.

STEP 3 -- Re-apportion Service Department Costs to Production Departments

The ultimate aim in absorption costing is to charge the overhead costs to cost units as they are produced. However as stores and maintenance are service departments they do not produce any units and are unable to pass on a share of their overheads to products in this way. We must therefore assign all costs to production departments by re-apportioning the service department costs.

In the case of the Stores Department, we are given an indication of the use of its services by other departments and can use this as the basis for apportionment. For the Maintenance Department it could be argued that there is likely to be a relationship between the service provided and the value of machinery in each department and the costs can therefore be apportioned accordingly.

Re-apportionment of the service department costs using these bases is demonstrated below:

			Production Depts		Service Depts	
Cost		**Basis for Apportionment**	**Joinery Dept.**	**Painting Dept.**	**Stores Dept.**	**Maintenance Dept.**
	£		£	£	£	£
Costs originally allocated/apportioned	240,000		120,500	48,700	32,000	38,800
Re-apportionment of Stores dept.		Stores usage	16,000	12,800	(32,000)	3,200
	240,000		136,500	61,500	0	42,000
Re-apportionment of Maintenance dept.		Value of machinery	31,500	10,500	0	(42,000)
	240,000		168,000	72,000	0	0

Note that the department providing a service to other service departments is re-apportioned first. In this case Stores, which provides a service to the Maintenance Department as well as production departments, is dealt with first.

We have now allocated and apportioned the overheads of £240,000 to the two production departments and can now calculate an OAR for each department using these figures:

$$\text{OAR} = \frac{\textit{Estimated overheads for the dept.}}{\textit{Estimated no. of hours for the dept.}}$$

Joinery dept. $\quad = \dfrac{£168,000}{24,000 \textit{ labour hrs.}} \quad = £7 \text{ per labour hour}$

Painting dept. $\quad = \dfrac{£72,000}{16,000 \textit{ labour hrs.}} \quad = £4.50 \text{ per labour hour}$

Charging Overheads to Products

These OAR's can now be used to charge overheads to the products passing through each department. For example in the case of a garden bench, overheads would be charged as follows:

Charged by Joinery Dept.   £

   2 labour hours.   x   £7 per hour   14.00

Charged by Painting Dept.

   1 labour hour   x   £4.50 per hour   4.50

Total overhead cost   18.50

The full production cost of a bench using the direct costs ascertained earlier is shown below:

Production Cost – Garden Bench

			£
Direct materials			28.00
Direct labour			23.50
PRIME COST			51.50
OVERHEADS			
Joiners –	(2 hours x £7.00 per hour)	14.00	
Painters –	(1 hour x £4.50 per hour)	4.50	18.50
PRODUCTION COST			70.00

Note that the time spent working on the product is used as a basis for not only charging labour cost but also overheads, using the absorption rates calculated for each department. Thus for each labour hour in the Joinery Department a product will be charged not only £8 for the labour cost but also £7 for overheads.

The compilation of the production cost of a garden bench using absorption costing is illustrated in Figure 10.7.

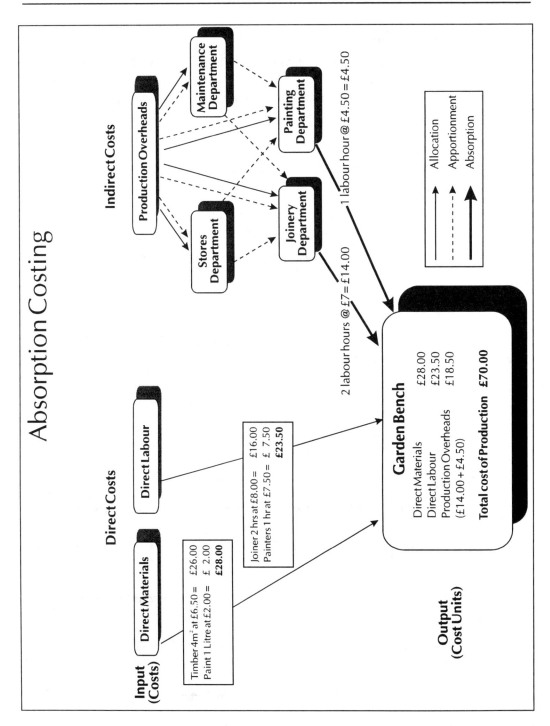

Figure 10.7 Absorption Costing Overview

Why use Departmental OAR's?

Earlier it was suggested that departmental OAR's reflecting the overheads attributable to each production department, were preferable to a single rate. The reason for this will now be demonstrated using an example based on the OAR's we have calculated:

	Joinery	Painting	Total
Estimated overheads	£168,000	£72,000	£240,000
Estimated labour hours	24,000	16,000	40,000
OAR (per labour hour)	£7	£4.50	£6

Departmental Rates   Single Rate

Example 10.3

Garden Furnishings has produced two products for which the following information has been obtained.

	Labour hours Product A	Labour hours Product B
Joinery Department	6	2
Painting Department	2	6
Total hours	8	8

Required

From this information calculate the overhead cost of each product using:

(a)   A single overhead absorption rate.

(b)   Departmental rates.

Having done so check your results with the solution given below.

Solution

(a)   Single Rate

	Product A £		Product B £	
Overhead cost	48	(8 hrs x £6)	48	(8 hrs x £6)

Using the single rate, overheads are charged at a rate of £6 per hour regardless of where this time was spent and each product is therefore charged an equal overhead cost of £48. This is despite the fact that product A spent most of its time in the more costly Joinery Department whereas product B was mainly produced in the cheaper Painting Department.

(b)   Departmental Rates

	Product A		Product B	
	£		£	
Joinery	42	(6 hrs x £7)	14	(2 hrs x £7)
Painting	9	(2 hrs x £4.50)	27	(6 hrs x £4.50)
Overhead cost	51		41	

Using departmental rates, time spent in the more expensive Joinery Department is charged at a higher hourly rate. Consequently, the use of more costly resources in producing A is reflected in the product cost which is now substantially higher than for product B.

Alternative Absorption Bases

In the examples we have looked at, overhead absorption has been based on labour hours. This may be appropriate in labour intensive departments where many overheads may relate to the employment of direct labour. However in machine intensive departments, where the majority of overheads are likely to be related to the operation of machines (depreciation, maintenance, power etc.) overhead absorption on the basis of machine hours will be more appropriate. Overheads are absorbed as described earlier but a rate per machine hour is used and products are charged in accordance with the length of time they spend on the machines rather than the number of labour hours taken.

This should help to ensure that overheads are charged on a reasonable basis. If operating machinery has the greatest influence on the level of overheads incurred, then the products making most use of the machines should be charged a greater proportion of the associated costs.

Other possible bases for overhead absorption include direct labour cost, direct material cost and units produced (as described earlier). However these have a number of disadvantages and are not widely used. Time based systems using labour and/or machine hours are more commonly used in practice.

Absorption of Non-Production Overheads

As well as production, businesses incur overheads in other functions such as selling, distribution and administration. Where the total cost of a product is required, perhaps for pricing purposes, these 'general overheads' can also be absorbed using the principles described for production overheads. Absorption is commonly based on either production cost or selling price and expressed as a percentage as demonstrated in Example 10.4.

Example 10.4

Garden Furnishings Limited absorbs general overheads on the basis of production cost and has made the following estimates for the coming year:

Estimated general overheads   £840,000

Estimated total production costs   £1,200,000

Required

From this information determine:

(a)   The overhead absorption rate for general overheads.

(b)   The total cost of the garden bench for which we earlier obtained a production cost of £70.

Solution

(a)   OAR $= \dfrac{Estimated\ general\ overheads}{Estimated\ production\ costs} \times 100$

$= \dfrac{£840,000}{£1,200,000} \times 100 = $ 70% of production cost

(b)

	£	
Production cost	70	
General overheads	49	(£70 x 70%)
Total cost	119	

A Comprehensive Example

To test your understanding of the principles covered to this point you should now attempt the following example. Check your results by referring to the solution given:

Example 10.5

A manufacturing company has made the following estimates for the forthcoming year:

Production overheads

		£
Indirect labour	– Machine Dept.	23,910
	– Assembly Dept.	31,880
	– Paint Dept.	49,090
	– Maintenance Dept.	68,630
	– Canteen	14,020
Heating and lighting		18,000
Factory rent		52,000
Machine depreciation		44,000
Machine power		16,800
Machine insurance		37,500
Factory cleaning		13,800
Total		£369,630

General overheads are absorbed as a percentage of production cost and the following estimates have been made for the period:

Estimated general overheads   £459,200

Estimated total production cost   £1,640,000

The following information is also available:

	Total	Production Departments			Service Departments	
		Machine	Assembly	Painting	Maintenance	Canteen
Area occupied (m^2)	10,000	3,000	3,000	1,500	1,500	1,000
Value of machinery (£'s)	550,000	440,000	66,000	44,000		
Number of employees	42	10	17	8	5	2
Direct labour hours	32,100	7,500	13,500	11,100		
Machine hours	26,000	22,100	2,600	1,300		
Direct wage rate per hr.		£8.00	£8.35	£6.50		

Selling prices are determined by applying a 25% mark up on total cost.

Required

(a) Prepare a production overhead analysis showing the bases of apportionment used.

(b) Calculate appropriate overhead absorption rates for:

   (i)   Each of the three production departments.

   (ii)   General overheads.

(c) Determine the selling price for job no. 846 for which the following estimates have been made:

   – Direct material £515

   – Direct labour/machine hours required:

	Labour hrs	Machine hrs
Machine dept.	5	10
Assembly dept.	8	–
Painting dept.	4	–

Solution

(a) Production Overhead Analysis

	Total	Basis of Apportionment	Production Departments			Service Departments	
			Machine	Assembly	Painting	Maintce.	Canteen
Indirect labour	187,530	Allocate	23,910	31,880	49,090	68,630	14,020
Heating and lighting	18,000	Area	5,400	5,400	2,700	2,700	1,800
Factory rent	52,000	Area	15,600	15,600	7,800	7,800	5,200
Machine depreciation	44,000	Machine value	35,200	5,280	3,520	--	--
Machine power	16,800	Machine hours	14,280	1,680	840	--	--
Machine insurance	37,500	Machine value	30,000	4,500	3,000	--	--
Cleaning	13,800	Area	4,140	4,140	2,070	2,070	1,380
	369,630		128,530	68,480	69,020	81,200	22,400
Re-apportion canteen		No. of employees*	5,600	9,520	4,480	2,800	(22,400)
	369,630		134,130	78,000	73,500	84,000	0
Re-apportion maintenance		Machine hours†	71,400	8,400	4,200	(84,000)	0
	369,630		205,530	86,400	77,700	0	0

*Excluding the two persons employed in the canteen (including these would result in costs remaining in the canteen department).

†NB. Re-apportioning the maintenance department costs on the basis of machine values would also be reasonable.

(b) Overhead absorption rates

(i) Production Departments

	Machine Dept.	Assembly Dept.	Painting Dept.
Basis of absorption	Machine hours	Labour hours	Labour hours

$$\text{OAR} = \frac{£205,530}{22,100 \text{ machine hrs.}} \quad \frac{£86,400}{13,500 \text{ labour hrs.}} \quad \frac{£77,700}{11,100 \text{ labour hrs.}}$$

$$= \quad \begin{array}{c} £9.30 \\ \text{per machine hour} \end{array} \quad \begin{array}{c} £6.40 \\ \text{per labour hour} \end{array} \quad \begin{array}{c} £7.00 \\ \text{per labour hour} \end{array}$$

Note that as most of its overheads are machine rather than labour related, the machine department uses a machine hour rate.

(ii) General Overheads

$$\text{OAR} \quad = \quad \frac{\textit{Total estimated general overheads}}{\textit{Total estimated production costs}} \quad \text{x} \quad 100$$

$$= \quad \frac{£459,200}{£1,640,000} \quad \text{x} \quad 100$$

$$= \quad 28\% \quad \text{of production cost}$$

(c) *Selling Price Job No. 846*

			£	£
Direct Materials				515.00
Direct Labour	Machine Dept.	(5 hours x £8.00 per hour)	40.00	
	Assembly Dept.	(8 hours x £8.35 per hour)	66.80	
	Painting Dept.	(4 hours x £6.50 per hour)	26.00	132.80
PRIME COST				647.80
Production Overheads	Machine Dept.	(10 machine hrs. x £9.30 per hour)	93.00	
	Assembly Dept.	(8 labour hrs. x £6.40 per hour)	51.20	
	Painting Dept.	(4 labour hrs. x £7.00 per hour)	28.00	172.20
PRODUCTION COST				820.00
General Overheads		(820.00 x 28%)		229.60
TOTAL COST				1,049.60
Mark-Up		(1,049.60 x 25%)		262.40
SELLING PRICE				1,312.00

Over/Under Absorption of Overheads

As we saw earlier, in order to obtain product costs before the end of a period, overheads are absorbed using a pre-determined OAR. As this rate is based on the *estimated* overheads for the period and the *estimated* number of labour/machine hours, overheads will only be fully absorbed by units produced if these estimates are completely accurate.

In our earlier example, if the estimated overheads and labour hours for the Joinery Department were accurate, the overheads would be fully absorbed by the units produced as shown below:

	£	
Actual overheads	168,000	
Overheads absorbed	168,000	(24,000 labour hours x £7 per hour)
Balance	0	

However in practice completely accurate estimates are highly unlikely and it is probable that the overheads absorbed will not correspond with those incurred. Let us suppose that the actual overheads incurred by the Joinery Department were £172,000 and that 23,000 labour hours were worked. This would result in the following situation:

	£	
Actual overheads	172,000	
Overheads absorbed	161,000	(23,000 labour hours x £7 per hour)
Under absorption of overheads	11,000	

Overhead costs of £161,000 have been absorbed by the units produced and will be included in the costs reported in the profit and loss account when those units are sold. However, the actual costs incurred were £172,000 and the product costs were therefore understated by £11,000. To compensate for this and to ensure that all costs are accounted for, this £11,000 should be included as a cost for the period and the profit and loss account will therefore include this amount reported as 'under absorption of production overheads'.

Incorrect estimates may also lead to over absorption of overheads. If actual overheads incurred were £170,000 and 25,000 hours were worked, the following situation would arise:

	£	
Actual overheads	170,000	
Overheads absorbed	175,000	(25,000 labour hours x £7 per hour)
Over absorption of overheads	5,000	

In this case, as overheads of £175,000 were absorbed when actual costs were only £170,000, the cost of units produced has been overstated. To correct this £5,000 must be deducted from the costs reported for the period.

Limitations of Absorption Costing

Although absorption costing is widely used for purposes such as setting selling prices and profit measurement it is an imprecise exercise. As overheads have no direct relationship with output, relating them to cost units in a meaningful way is a difficult task.

Choosing bases for the apportionment of overhead costs between departments is not always easy and in many cases one factor cannot satisfactorily explain the way in which costs are incurred. In earlier examples maintenance costs were apportioned on the basis of the value of machinery in one case and the number of machine hours in another. In reality, maintenance costs are likely to be influenced by both factors and using only one will not give a true indication of the service provided to each department.

In another example canteen costs were apportioned on the basis of the number of employees in each department. However, this may not reflect the actual use of the canteen. It may be that no-one in the Stores Department actually uses the canteen in which case the cost should have been apportioned only to the other three departments. However, obtaining precise information on the use of the canteen would be would be very difficult and time consuming. The number of employees provides a simple basis for apportionment which may give a reasonable indication of the influence of each department on the costs incurred in the operation of the canteen.

There are similar problems in using one absorption base in each production department. For example, absorption on the basis of machine hours assumes that overheads vary in proportion to the number of hours used. Even in machine intensive departments this is unlikely with at least some overheads being affected by other factors. No single factor can accurately reflect the influence units produced have on overhead costs incurred and the basis used for absorption is therefore a compromise.

For these reasons we cannot describe product costs compiled using absorption costing systems as being completely accurate. However the information generated can provide guidance for activities such as planning and pricing as well as financial reporting and the technique is widely used for these purposes.

Recent Developments

Conventional absorption costing systems have come under increasing criticism in recent years. Modern machine intensive manufacturing methods have resulted in lower levels of direct labour cost and higher overheads (machine depreciation, maintenance etc.) many of which are not volume related. Absorbing overheads using volume related bases such as labour and machine hours may therefore produce misleading information, leading to poor management decisions. The following example illustrates the problems which a traditional absorption costing system can create in the provision of management information:

Example 10.6

A production department produces two products in respect of which the following information is available for a period:

	Product A	Product B
Production volume (units)	1,000	100
No. of batches to achieve production	5	5
Machine hours per unit	2	2

The overheads assigned to the department include £1,100 in respect of production scheduling (planning which batches will be produced when and on which machines etc.).

A conventional absorption costing system would assign the overhead costs to the products as follows :

$$\text{Overhead absorption rate} = \frac{Total\ overheads}{Total\ machine\ hours}$$

$$= \frac{£1,100}{(2\ hrs \times 1,000\ units) + (2\ hrs \times 100\ units)}$$

$$= \frac{£1,100}{2,200\ hrs} = £0.50\ per\ machine\ hour$$

Overheads assigned to product lines:

Product A

2 machine hours x £0.50 per hour = £1 per unit x 1,000 units = £1,000

Product B

2 machine hours x £0.50 per hour = £1 per unit x 100 units   = £ 100

Total   £1,100

Thus, although the products are each produced in five batches and therefore place equal demands on the production scheduling activity, Product A is assigned ten times as much of the scheduling cost as Product B. This occurs because Product A's production volume and therefore the number of machine hours required, is ten times that of B. Absorbing the overhead costs on the basis of machine hours effectively implies that there is a relationship between the costs incurred and the number of hours the machines are in operation. In the case of production scheduling however this is unlikely to be the case and the cost is more likely to be influenced by the number of batches which must be scheduled.

In terms of unit costs, each product has been assigned the same amount (£1 per unit) despite the fact that Product A is produced in average batch sizes of 200 (1,000 ÷ 5) and B in batches of 20 (100 ÷ 5). The costing system does not highlight the fact that in reality larger batches are likely to reduce unit costs by spreading scheduling costs over a greater number of units. Thus with no cost advantage there is no incentive to produce in larger batches and any potential savings are lost. Management may in fact decide to produce in small batches for other reasons such as reducing stock levels but they should be provided with information which makes them aware of the cost implications of doing so and as we have seen, conventional costing systems may let them down in this respect.

Activity Based Costing

Growing dissatisfaction with traditional methods has led to the emergence of alternative techniques such as activity Based Costing (ABC) in an attempt to produce more meaningful cost information. ABC aims to charge costs to products on the basis of benefits received rather than using only volume related absorption bases such as labour or machine hours. Costs are collected by activity and the most significant factor influencing the cost of the activity is determined. This is known as the "cost driver" and is used to assign the costs of each activity to products as demonstrated below using the information supplied in Example 10.6:

$$\text{Overhead absorption rate} = \frac{Total\ overheads}{Total\ number\ of\ batches}$$

$$= \frac{£1,100}{5+5} = £110 \text{ per batch}$$

Overheads assigned to products

				Cost per Unit	
Product A	5 batches x £110 per batch	=	£550	£0.55	(£550/1,000)
Product B	5 batches x £110 per batch	=	£550	£5.50	(£550/100)
Total			£1,100		

Using ABC, as both product lines require the same effort from production scheduling (i.e. 5 batches) each is assigned an equal share of the cost. However as Product A had ten times as much output to spread this cost over, its unit cost is ten times lower than that of Product B. The costing system now highlights that production in small quantities has cost implications and allows management to take more informed production planning decisions.

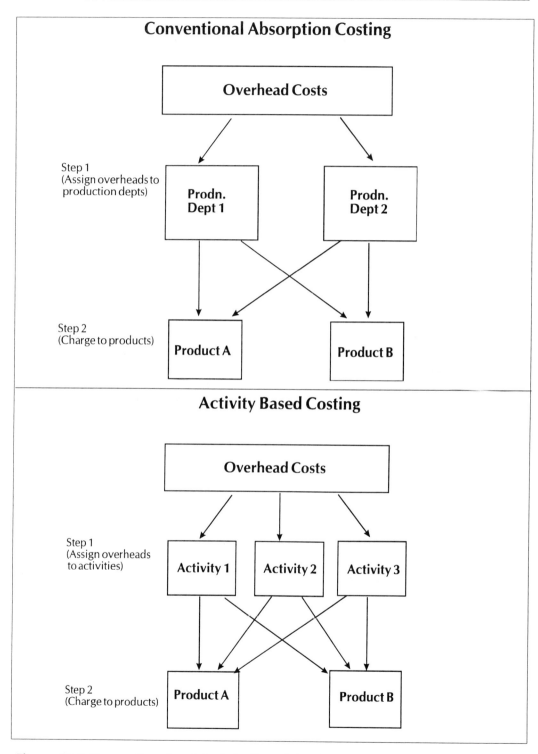

Figure 10.8 Conventional and Activity Based Costing

In terms of its application, activity based costing is, like conventional absorption costing, a two stage process as illustrated in Figure 10.8. However, they differ in both the way costs are collected and analysed and the basis on which they are related to products as follows:

	Cost Focus	**Absorption Bases**
Conventional Methods	By department/function	Volume related only (units/labour hrs./machine hrs.)
Activity Based Costing	By activity	Many (i.e. uses "cost driver" of each activity)

As well as providing better product cost information, the activity based approach can also help in managing costs. Focusing on activities and their cost drivers makes the activities more visible and should help managers to gain a better understanding of costs incurred and more importantly, their causes. This can lead to questioning whether activities are cost effective or in some cases, necessary at all. Attention can be focused on managing cost drivers as means of reducing costs. For example The B & D Tool Company in the USA identified the number of unique parts used in production as a significant cost driver for activities such as purchasing, inspection, receiving and storage. This caused designers to re-design products to use more common parts and in three years the number of parts used fell from 5,000 to 800 the number of suppliers fell from 1,200 to 100 and the costs "driven" by parts fell by 70%.

Other Costing Methods

Although all costing systems are based on the same principles, the costing methods employed will depend on the way in which goods are manufactured or services provided. The method described earlier is known as 'job costing' and is suitable where individual, identifiable cost units are produced.

We will now briefly consider some of the alternative costing methods applicable in other situations:

Batch Costing

This method is used where batches of identical products are produced rather than individual units. In these circumstances each batch is treated as being one job for which the cost is determined as in job costing. Direct costs are allocated and overheads absorbed as described earlier and the resulting figure can be divided by the number of units in the batch to obtain the cost per unit.

Contract Costing

This method is used for long term contracts such as major construction works (buildings, roads etc.). As with job costing, the aim of the costing system is to ascertain the cost of each cost unit, which in this case is each individual contract. As the work is often performed on a site many costs which are normally considered indirect may be classed as direct for a contract. For example supervisors' salaries and site electricity costs, which must be absorbed by many cost units in job costing, can be charged directly to the contract to which they relate. Overheads such as head office costs may be apportioned to each contract on some suitable basis such as costs incurred or hours worked on the contract.

Process Costing

Process costing is suitable in situations where identical units are produced from a series of processes and is used in the food and drink and chemical industries.

The output from one process becomes an input to the next until completed units emerge from the final process. As the units produced are identical there is no need to assign costs to individual products. The cost of each unit may be determined by:

1.   Recording all costs incurred by each process department.

2.   Dividing the total cost for a period by the number of units produced by the process.

This method is illustrated in Figure 10.9.

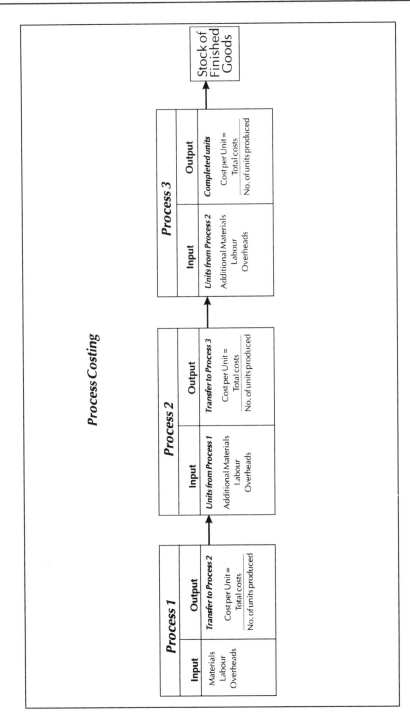

Figure 10.9 Process Costing

Service Industries

Where services are provided rather than goods manufactured, the same costing principles apply and costs can be ascertained using the same techniques.

Where a service organisation provides similar or identical 'service units' (E.g. a restaurant providing meals) the cost per unit may be determined as described above for process costing:

$$\text{Cost per unit} \; = \; \frac{Total\ costs \text{ for } the\ period}{No.\ of\ service\ units\ in\ the\ period}$$

Where the service units are distinct and separately identifiable such as in management consultancy where a service is provided to meet a customer's specific requirements, job costing may be used. Direct costs specific to the job can be allocated and overheads absorbed on a suitable basis as demonstrated below:

Example 10.6

Wren Associates, a management consultancy firm, charges customers on the basis of total cost plus a mark up of 25%. The following estimates have been made in respect of a job for which a quotation has been requested from a prospective client.

Direct Costs

Consultancy time	24 days @ £160 per day
Materials (training booklets)	£48

Overheads are absorbed on the basis of consultancy time and the following estimates have been made for the current period:

Total overheads	£44,820
Consultancy time to be sold	540 days

Required

Prepare a quotation for the client.

Solution

Overhead Absorption Rate

$$\text{OAR} \quad = \quad \frac{\textit{Total estimated overheads}}{\textit{Total estimated consultancy days}}$$

$$= \quad \frac{£44,820}{540 \; \textit{days}} \quad = £83 \text{ per day}$$

Quotation

	£
Direct Costs	
Consultancy time (24 days @ £160)	3,480
Materials	48
Overheads	
24 days @ £83 per day	1,992
Total cost	5,520
Add mark-up (£5,520 x 25%)	1,380
Price Quoted	6,900

Summary

- Costing information can be useful in planning, control and decision making.

- Costs may be analysed according to their nature and purpose and recorded using a cost coding system.

- The objective in product costing is to ascertain the cost of producing each unit. This cost may include:

    Direct costs   - Direct materials

                    - Direct labour

                    - Direct expenses

    Indirect costs - A share of production overheads.

- The direct material cost of each unit may be obtained by recording the quantity of each material used and multiplying by the appropriate prices.

- Direct labour costs can be determined by recording the labour hours worked on each unit and multiplying by the relevant wage rates.

- Any direct expenses should be charged to the relevant cost unit using a cost coding system.

- Overheads are absorbed by cost units through the application of pre-determined overhead absorption rates (OAR's) calculated as follows:

$$\text{OAR} \; = \; \frac{\textit{Estimated overheads for the period}}{\textit{Estimated no. of labour hours for the period}^{*}}$$

* Absorption may also be based on other factors such as machine hours.

- The total cost of a unit may be ascertained by charging general overheads using a suitable basis of absorption.

- Under absorbed overheads must be included in the costs reported for a period. Where overheads are over absorbed the relevant amount should be subtracted from the costs for the period.

- Absorption costing relies on arguable bases of overhead apportionment and absorption. Consequently information derived cannot be described as a completely accurate representation of costs incurred in the production of individual cost units.

- Activity Based Costing (ABC) attempts to relate costs to products or services on the basis of benefits received. Costs are collected by activity rather than department and a specific "cost driver" is used to charge them to products.

- Although costing systems are based on common principles, the costing methods employed will depend on the way in which goods are manufactured or services provided.

Questions   (See Appendix C for Answers)

10.1

Contrast the use of:

    (i)   Blanket as opposed to departmental overhead absorption rates;

    (ii)   Predetermined overhead absorption rates as opposed to rates calculated from actual activity and expenditure.

(ACCA)

10.2

"It is probably impossible to obtain an absolutely accurate true cost of a product or service" said a speaker at a students' society meeting.

You are required to comment on the above statement, referring in your answer to

    (a)   The definition of 'cost' as a noun and as a verb;

    (b)   Whether or not you are in agreement with the statement, supporting your conclusion with an explanation;

    (c)   Three purposes for which costs are needed by a business.

(CIMA)

10.3

The AAT company has two departments A and B engaged in manufacturing operations and they are serviced by stores, a maintenance department and a tool room. The following has been budgeted for the next financial period:

Overhead (£000s)

	Total	A	B	Stores	Main tenance	Tool Room
Indirect labour	1,837	620	846	149	115	107
Supervision	140					
Power	160					
Rent	280					
Rates	112					
Plant insurance	40					
Plant depreciation	20					
	2,589					

Additional information available includes:

	A	B	Stores	Main tenance	Tool Room
Floor area (square metres)	1,000	2,500	1,100	600	400
Number of employees	30	50	10	20	30
Power (kilowatt hours)	60,000	30,000	3,000	15,000	12,000
Number of material requisitions	5,000	6,000	–	2,000	3,000
Maintenance (hours)	8,000	9,000	–	–	6,000
Plant valuation (£)	50,000	40,000	–	5,000	5,000
Tool room hours estimated	7,000	10,000	–	–	–
Machine hours estimated	55,200	99,000	–	–	–

(a)   You are required to calculate appropriate machine hour overhead absorption rates for both manufacturing departments in which all overheads will be recovered, and to show clearly the method of overhead allocation.

(AAT)

10.4

A furniture making business manufatures quality furniture to customers' orders. It has three production departments and two service departments. Budgeted overhead costs for the coming year are as follows:

	Total (£)
Rent and Rates	12,800
Machine insurance	6,000
Telephone charges	3,200
Depreciation	18,000
Production Supervisors' salaries	24,000
Heating & Lighting	6,400
	70,400

The three production departments – A, B and C and the two service departments – X and Y, are housed in the premises, the details of which, together with other statistics and information, are given below.

	Departments				
	A	B	C	X	Y
Floor area occupied (sq. metres)	3,000	1,800	600	600	400
Machine value (£000)	24	10	8	4	2
Direct labour hrs budgeted	3,200	1,800	1,000		
Labour rates per hour	£3.80	£3.50	£3.40	£3.00	£3.00
Allocated Overheads:					
Specific to each department (£000)	2.8	1.7	1.2	0.8	0.6
Service Department X's costs apportioned	50%	25%	25%		
Service Department Y's costs apportioned	20%	30%	50%		

Required:

(a) Prepare a statement showing the overhead costs budgeted for each department, showing the basis of apportionment used. Also calculate suitable overhead absorption rates.

(b) Two pieces of furniture are to be manufactured for customers. Direct costs are as follows:

	Job 123	Job 124
Direct Material	£154	£108
Direct Labour	20 hours Dept A	16 hours Dept A
	12 hours Dept B	10 hours Dept B
	10 hours Dept C	14 hours Dept C

Calculate the total costs of each job.

(c) If the firm quotes prices to customers that reflect a required profit of 25% on selling price, calculate the quoted selling price for each job.

(AAT)

10.5

A company manufactures and sells two products, X and Y whose selling prices are £100 and £300 respectively, and each product passes through two manufacturing processes, A and B. In process A, product X takes two hours per unit and product Y takes four hours.

In process B, product X takes one hour per unit, and product Y takes three hours. Labour in process A is paid £4 per hour, and in process B £5 per hour.

The two products are made out of materials P, Q and R, and the quantities of each material used in making one unit of each product are:

	Product X	Product Y
Material P	37 Kg	93 Kg
Material Q	10	240
Material R	20 m^2	75 m^2

Material prices are £1 per Kg for P, £2.40 per dozen for Q and £0.20 per m^2 for R.

Salesmen are paid a commission of 5% of sales. The packing materials are £1 for X and £4 for Y. Costs of transporting the goods to the customer are £2 for X and £5 for Y.

Other annual costs are:

	£	£
Indirect wages – Process A	25,000	
Process B	40,000	
Stores	20,000	
Canteen	10,000	
		95,000
Indirect materials -- Process A	51,510	
Process B	58,505	
Stores	1,310	
Canteen	8,425	
		119,750
Rent and rates		450,000
Depreciation of plant and machinery		140,000
Power		50,000
Insurance – Fire on buildings		3,750
Workmen's compensation @ 2% of wages		12,000
Heating and lighting		4,500
Advertising		90,000

A royalty of £1 per unit is payable on product X. The annual quantities sold are 15,000 units of X and 10,000 units of Y.

Other relevant information is:

Cost centre	Area in square feet	Book value of plant and machinery £	Horsepower of machinery %	Direct labour Hours	Number of employees	Number of stores issue notes
Process A	100,000	1,000,000	80	70,000	40	10,000
Process B	50,000	200,000	20	45,000	30	5,000
Stores	100,000	150,000			10	
Canteen	50,000	50,000			5	
	300,000	1,400,000	100	115,000	85	15,000

You are required to:

(a) Prepare a production overhead analysis and appointment sheet, showing clearly the bases of apportionment used.

(b) Calculate appropriate rates of overhead recovery for processes A and B.

(c) Calculate the full (absorption) cost of making and selling one unit of each product.

(d) Calculate the unit profit or loss for each product.

(CIMA)

10.6

A manufacturing company has three production departments (A, B and C) and one service department in its factory. A predetermined overhead absorption rate is established for each of the production departments on the basis of machine hours at normal capacity. The overheads of each production department comprise directly allocated expenses and a share of the overheads of the service department, apportioned in the ratio 3:2:5 to departments A, B and C respectively. All overheads are classified as fixed.

The following incomplete information is available concerning the apportionment and absorption of production overhead for a period.

	Production Department		
	A	B	C
Budgeted allocated expenses (£)	143,220	125,180	213,700
Budgeted service department apportionment (£)	i	ii	66,300
Normal machine capacity (hours)	15,000	iii	v
Predetermined absorption rate (£ per machine hour)	vi	8.2	iv
Actual machine utilisation (hours)	vii	19,050	19,520
Over/(under) absorption of overhead (£)	(3,660)	viii	(6,720)

Actual overhead incurred in each department was as per budget.

Required

(a) Calculate the missing figures for (i) to (viii) in the above table.

(b) Comment briefly on the possible treatment of the over/under absorbed overhead balances at the end of the period.

(ACCA)

Questions Without Answers

10.7

PTS Limited is a manufacturing company which uses three production departments to make its product. It has the following factory costs which are expected to be incurred in the year to 31st December 19X2:

		£
Direct wages	Machining	234,980
	Assembly	345,900
	Finishing	134,525

		£
Indirect wages and salaries	Machining	120,354
	Assembly	238,970
	Finishing	89,700

	£
Factory rent	12,685,500
Business rates	3,450,900
Heat and lighting	935,350
Machinery power	2,890,600
Depreciation	600,000
Canteen subsidy	256,000

Other information is available as follows:

	Machining	Assembly	Finishing
Number of employees	50	60	18
Floor space occupied (m^2)	1,800	1,400	800
Horse power of machinery	13,000	500	6,500
Value of machinery (£000)	250	30	120
Number of labour hours	100,000	140,000	35,000
Number of machine hours	200,000	36,000	90,000

You are required

(a) To prepare the company's overhead analysis sheet for 19X2;

(b) To calculate appropriate overhead absorption rates (to two decimal places) for each department.

(CIMA)

10.8

LMN Limited has the following budgeted overhead costs and related data for the year to 31st March 19X9.

	Machining	Assembly	Finishing
Overhead costs	£175,500	£56,450	£98,750
Number of employees	16	7	12
Labour hours	32,540	14,000	26,000
Machine hours	30,000	2,400	NIL
Wages cost	£142,400	£43,600	£91,500
Material cost	£94,500	£32,560	£43,575

During September 19X8 Job 123 was completed. Direct costs and related data were as follows:

	Machining	Assembly	Finishing
Material cost	£1,369	£124	£93
Labour cost	£608	£90	£251
Labour hours	52	30	70
Machine hours	147	25	NIL

You are required to

   (a)   calculate an appropriate overhead absorption rate for each of the three departments (to the nearest £0.01) giving reasons for your choice of method;

   (b)   use these rates to calculate

       (i)   the total cost of Job 123, and

      (ii)   the selling price if a gross profit of 40% on selling price is applied.

(CIMA)

10.9

SM Limited make two products, Exe and Wye. For product costing purposes a single cost centre overhead rate of £3.40 per hour is used based on budgeted production overhead of £680,000 and 200,000 budgeted hours given as below.

	Budgeted Overhead £	Budgeted Hours
Department 1	480,000	100,000
Department 2	200,000	100,000
	680,000	200,000

The number of hours required to manufacture each of the products is as follows.

	Exe	Wye
Department 1	8	4
Department 2	2	6
	10	10

There were no work in progress or finished goods stocks at the beginning of the period of operations but at the end of the period 10,000 finished units of Exe and 5,000 finished units of Wye were in stock. There was no closing work in progress.

The prime cost per unit of Exe is £30. The pricing policy is to add 50% to the production cost to cover administration, selling and distribution costs and to provide what is thought to be a reasonable profit.

Required

(a) Calculate what the effect is on the company's profit for the period, by using a single cost centre overhead rate compared with using departmental overhead rates.

(b) Show by means of a comparative statement what the price of Exe would be using:

(i) single cost centre overhead rate; and

(ii) departmental overhead rates.

(c) Discuss briefly whether the company should change its present policy on overhead absorption, stating reasons to support your conclusion.

(CIMA)

10.10

Gloucester Manufacturing Limited produces two products for which the following information is available for the month of January:

Product	A	B
Output (units)	200	500
Machine hours per unit	6	9
No. of production runs to produce January's output	5	6
No. of material components per unit	4	3

Overhead Costs	£	Cost Driver
Machine depreciation/maintenance	23,598	Machine hours
Production scheduling costs	7,392	Production runs
Materials handling costs	6,486	No. of components
Machine set up costs	3,168	Production runs
	40,644	

Required

(a) Calculate the overhead cost per unit for each product using:

   (i) Conventional costing (absorbing overhead on the basis of machine hours).

   (ii) Activity based costing using the cost drivers given.

(b) Comment on the differences in the results using the two methods and the implications of these differences for decision making.

Chapter 11

Cost Behaviour

Learning Objectives

After completing this chapter you should be able to:

- Distinguish between fixed and variable costs.

- Ascertain the fixed cost per period and variable cost per unit from total costs incurred at various levels of activity.

- Use this information to estimate costs for future periods.

- Explain the limitations of the methods used.

- Describe curvilinear and stepped costs giving practical examples of each.

- Explain the limitations of historical cost information.

Introduction

In the previous chapter we saw how costs may be ascertained for departments and individual products or services. The remainder of the book is concerned with how costing information may be used in planning, control and decision making. To guide them in the performance of these functions, managers require information on the cost implications of their actions. Although other factors may affect costs a major influence will be changes in the level of activity, perhaps as a result of introducing a new product line, dropping an existing product or accepting a new contract. In this chapter we will look at the way in which costs respond to changes in activity and how an understanding of their behaviour can help in predicting costs for future periods.

Cost Classification

We have already seen that costs may be classed as either direct or indirect and will now look at another means of classification based on their behaviour in response to changes in activity levels. When analysing costs in this way a distinction can be made between those which may be described as variable and those which are fixed.

Variable Costs

Variable costs change in response to changes in the level of activity. Direct material costs, which rise and fall with the number of units produced, display this type of behaviour which can be illustrated graphically as shown in Figure 11.1.

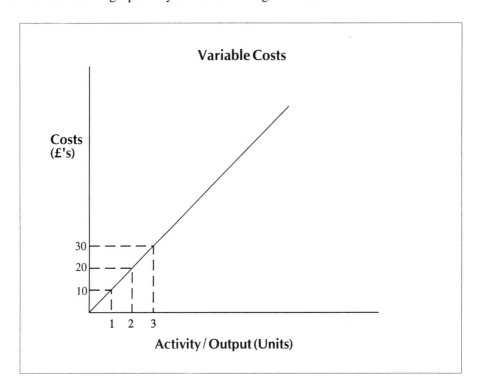

Figure 11.1 Variable Costs

In this case direct material costs are £10 per unit and will rise and fall with the level of activity at this rate. The variable costs incurred at any activity level can therefore be estimated as follows:

Variable cost incurred = Variable cost per unit x Activity level

E.g. The direct material cost for 150 units:

$$= \quad £10 \quad x \quad 150 \quad units$$

$$= \quad £1,500$$

In this example the cost may be described as being both direct and variable but this is not always the case. For example power for production equipment may also be a variable cost but as in most cases it could not be identified with individual cost units, it would be classed as indirect.

Fixed Costs

Fixed costs are those which, within certain output limits, are unaffected by changes in activity. They are incurred in relation to the passage of time rather than volume of output and are therefore also known as 'period costs'. An example would be the rental of premises which would incur the same cost regardless of the activity level as illustrated in Figure 11.2.

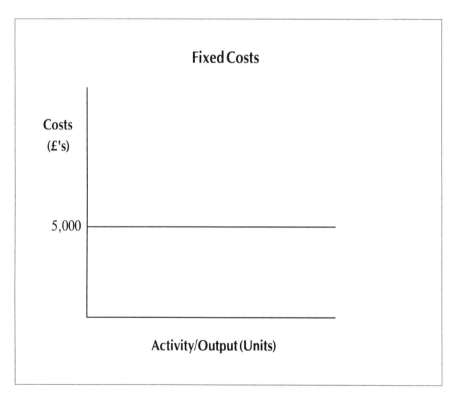

Figure 11.2 Fixed Costs

Note that this is not to say that fixed costs will not change. All costs change over time and a price review may result in a higher rent cost. However in the case of fixed costs the change is not attributable to a change in the level of activity.

Total Cost

Having distinguished between fixed and variable costs, total costs can be determined as follows:

$$\text{Total cost} = \text{Fixed costs} + \text{Variable costs}$$

$$= \text{Fixed costs} + (\text{Variable cost per unit} \times \text{Activity level})$$

This is demonstrated in the following example which you should attempt before referring to the solution given:

Example 11.1

A business has estimated that fixed costs are £25,000 per month and variable costs £10 per unit.

Required

Estimate the total costs for a month in which expected output is 3,000 units.

Solution

$$\text{Total cost} = \text{Fixed costs} + (\text{Variable cost per unit} \times \text{Activity level})$$

$$= £25,000 + (£10 \times 3,000 \text{ units})$$

$$= £55,000$$

This may be depicted graphically as shown below:

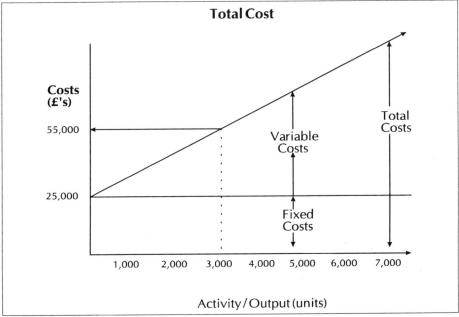

Figure 11.3 Total Cost

The estimation of total costs in this way may be useful in short term planning where they can be compared with the income expected from the sale of 3,000 units in order to predict the profit for the period.

Unit Costs

As fixed costs do not respond to changes in activity level, unit costs will fall as activity rises. An example should help to explain this:

Example 11.2

Chris Graham sells car alarms from a number of small retail outlets. He obtains them at a cost of £50 each and fixed costs (premises, wages etc.) amount to £8,000 per month.

Required

Estimate the total cost per alarm at the following activity levels:

(a) 400 alarms per month.

(b) 800 alarms per month.

Solution

	400 Alarms		800 Alarms	
	£		£	
Cost per unit				
Variable cost	50		50	
Fixed cost	20	(£8,000 ÷400)	10	(£8,000 ÷800)
Total cost	70		60	

From this we can see that as the activity level rises:

(i) The variable cost per unit remains constant.

(ii) The fixed cost per unit falls. As fixed costs do not change with activity, increasing the number of units sold means each receives a smaller share of the costs.

(iii) The total cost per unit therefore falls.

These relationships are illustrated in Figure 11.4.

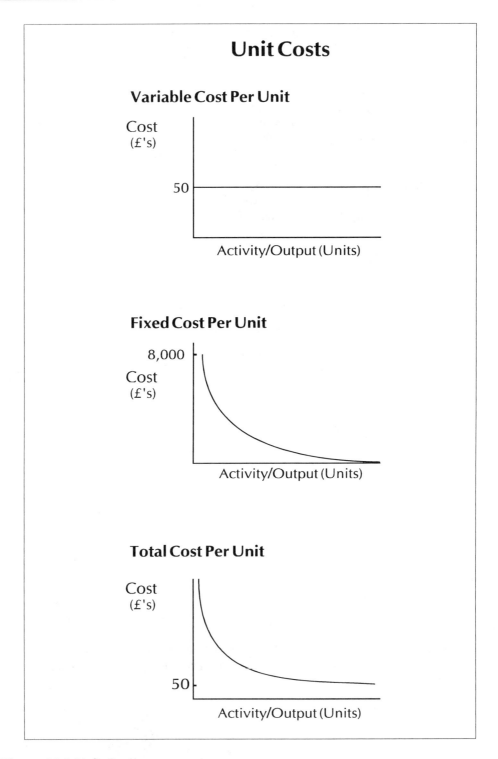

Figure 11.4 Unit Costs

Because the total cost per unit falls as the level of activity rises, a business increasing output may be in a position to:

- Maintain current selling prices and earn a greater profit per unit.   or,

- Reduce selling prices and maintain the current profit per unit. This may produce higher total profits through increased sales volume.

Semi-variable Costs

Semi-variable costs have both a fixed and variable element and are therefore partly affected by changes in activity levels.

Typical examples are illustrated in Figure 11.5.

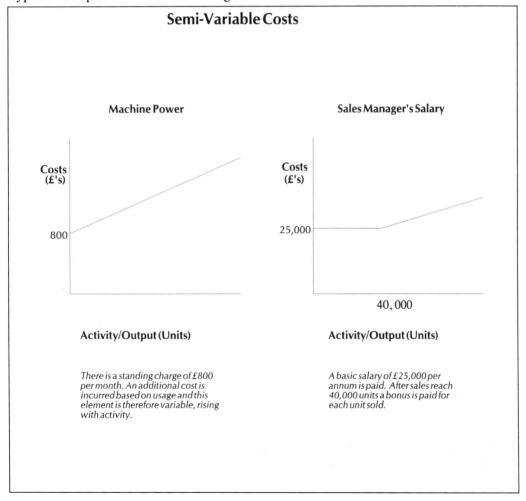

Figure 11.5 Semi-variable Costs

Ascertaining Fixed and Variable Costs

As we saw earlier, total costs for a particular activity level can be predicted using the fixed costs per period and variable cost per unit. Where this information is not available the figures can be estimated from total costs recorded in previous periods and we will now examine two methods which may be used to do this.

Example 11.3

A business has recorded the following information over the past six months:

	Total Costs	Output
	£	Units
January	48,100	4,200
February	49,900	4,700
March	50,500	4,800
April	54,700	5,400
May	54,400	5,100
June	48,500	4,500

Required

Estimate costs expected for the next three months in which the following activity levels are anticipated:

July	4,400	units
August	4,200	units
September	3,600	units

The Range Method

Using this method the highest and lowest cost months are selected and the costs and output for each compared as shown below:

	Total Costs £	Output Units
Highest cost - April	54,700	5,400
Lowest cost - January	48,100	4,200
Difference	6,600	1,200

Additional output of 1,200 units in April caused costs to rise by £6,600. As only variable costs vary in response to changes in activity, the additional £6,600 must be variable. The variable cost per unit can therefore be estimated by dividing this figure by the number of extra units produced as shown below:

$$\text{Variable cost per unit} = \frac{Additional\ cost}{Additional\ units} = \frac{£6,600}{1,200\ units}$$

$$= \text{£5.50 per unit}$$

Having determined the variable element, we can estimate the fixed costs using information relating to one of the months as follows:

	£
Total costs for January	48,100
Less variable element (4,200 units x £5.50 per unit)	23,100
Fixed cost	25,000

Costs for July to September can now be predicted using this information:

	Fixed Costs	+	Variable Costs	=	Total Cost
July	£25,000	+	(4,400 units x £5.50)	=	£49,200
August	£25,000	+	(4,200 units x £5.50)	=	£48,100
September	£25,000	+	(3,600 units x £5.50)	=	£44,800

The Scattergraph Method

Using this method the cost and output information provided for each of the six months is plotted on a graph as shown in Figure 11.6.

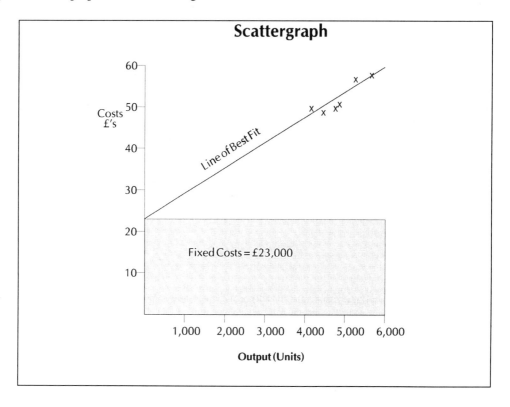

Figure 11.6 Scattergraph

A line known as the 'line of best fit' has been drawn as close as possible through the middle of the points plotted and the point at which this strikes the vertical axis (i.e. *£23,000*) represents fixed costs.

As before, once we have one element we can deduce the other from information relating to one of the months:

	£
Total costs for January	48,100
Less fixed costs	(23,000)
Variable costs	25,100

Variable costs incurred in January have been estimated at £25,100 and the cost per unit can be obtained by dividing this by the number of units produced in the month:

$$\text{Variable cost per unit} \quad = \quad \frac{£25,100}{4,200 \; units}$$

$$= \quad £5.98$$

Limitations of the Methods Used

Reviewing the figures obtained from each method we can see that the results differ:

	Fixed Costs per Month	Variable Costs per Unit
Range method	£25,000	£5.50
Scattergraph method	£23,000	£5.98

This occurs because each method is relatively crude and will only provide rough estimates.

The range method does not use all information available. Estimates are based on information from only two of the six months and if for any reason they were not typical (perhaps an unusual 'one off' cost was incurred) the results would be distorted. Consequently the time periods used should be chosen with care and any which are not typical ignored.

The scattergraph method uses all available information but relies on an accurate line of best fit. It can be difficult to determine precisely where this should be drawn and two people would probably obtain slightly different results from the same information.

Where results obtained differ materially further analysis will be required to determine the appropriate costs.

Better result can be obtained using a statistical technique known as regression analysis. This technique is beyond the scope of this introdutory text and readers interested in studying statistical approaches to cost estimation should refer to texts on statistics or those covering management accounting at a more advanced level.

Curvilinear Variable Costs

When looking at variable costs it was assumed that there is a linear relationship between activity and cost (i.e. that costs change in direct proportion to changes in activity). However this is not always true and for some variable costs the relationship may be described as curvilinear. Examples are given in Figure 11.7.

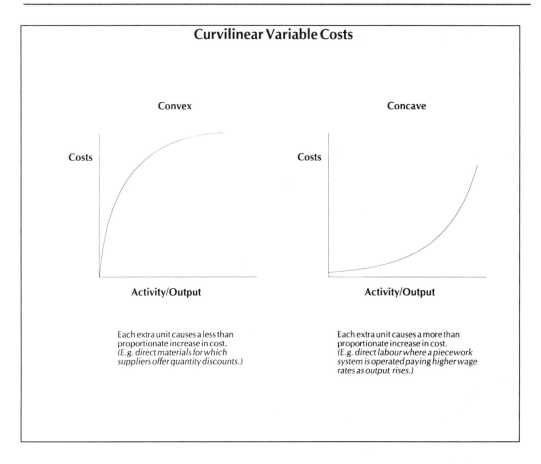

Figure 11.7 Curvilinear Variable Costs

To simplify calculations it is often assumed that all variable costs are linear and over a limited range of activity this may provide acceptable estimates. However, beyond this range the increasing influence of curvilinear costs can distort results and a more detailed analysis of cost behaviour may be necessary.

Stepped Costs

Fixed costs were earlier described as being unaffected by changes in activity level *within certain output limits*. Rent was used as an example and it was suggested that if activity increased the rent cost would remain unchanged. Although this may be true up to a point, it would not be possible to continually increase output without affecting the cost. There would come a point where the premises would be incapable of supporting the higher level of activity and additional space would be required. This would increase costs to a new level which would remain fixed until output once again reached a point where additional space was required.

Costs which behave in this manner are known as 'stepped costs' as they can be depicted graphically as shown in Figure 11.8.

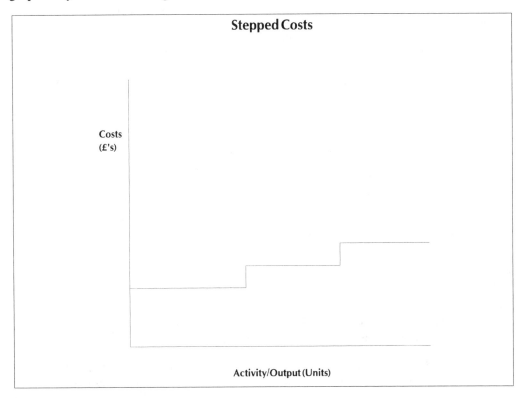

Figure 11.8 Stepped Costs

The majority of fixed costs are likely to behave in this manner and for this reason most costs can be described as being variable in the long run.

As with curvilinear costs, the impact of stepped costs tends to be greater at higher activity levels and more detailed cost analysis may be necessary when predicting costs at these levels.

Using Historical Costs

In this chapter costs recorded for previous periods have been used as a basis for making predictions about the future. Although historical costs may be a useful source of information, it should be remembered that they were incurred under specific operating conditions which are likely to change over time. Price rises, the adoption of new methods, the availability of new resources and many other changes are likely to affect future costs and predictions based on past information should be adjusted to reflect such factors.

Summary

- Variable costs change in response to changes in the level of activity.

- Fixed costs are incurred in relation to the passage of time and are (within certain output limits) unaffected by changes in activity.

- Total cost = Fixed costs + (Variable cost per unit x Activity level)

- Assuming that fixed costs remain constant, unit costs will fall as output rises.

- Semi-variable costs have both a fixed and variable element and are therefore partly affected by changes in activity levels.

- Fixed costs per period and variable costs per unit may be estimated using either the range or scattergraph methods. Each will give only a rough estimate and further analysis may be required to improve the accuracy of the results obtained.

- Variable costs which do not change in direct proportion to changes in activity are known as curvilinear costs.

- Stepped costs remain constant across a range of activity and rise to a new level when certain activity levels are reached.

- When using historical costs to make predictions about the future, adjustments should be made to reflect any known changes in conditions.

Questions (See Appendix C for Answers)

11.1

(a) Describe each of the following types of cost, illustrating your explanation with a small hand drawn graph in each case. (Graph paper need not be used).

- stepped costs

- curvilinear costs

- variable costs

- fixed costs

- semi-variable costs

(b) For a business of your choice give an example of each of the cost types referred to in (a) above.

11.2

The following data relating to monthly costs at differing levels of activity was recorded in respect of a company engaged in selling television sets:

	Activity Level (No of TV's Sold)	
	600	900
Costs	£	£
Delivery costs	3,000	4,500
Postage	750	1,050
Admin Salaries	1,900	1,900
Insurance	6,600	8,400
Cost of purchasing TV sets	186,000	279,000
Telephones	3,900	5,250

Required

(a) (i) For each item listed state whether you believe it to be fixed, variable or semi-variable, giving reasons for your conclusions.

(ii)   Where appropriate, separate the fixed and variable elements giving estimates of each.

(iii) Assuming that the pattern of cost behaviour remains the same calculate the expected cost of all six items at a sales level of 1,050 TV sets.

(b)   Explain the importance of ascertaining the way in which costs behave over different levels of activity, illustrating your answer with examples of how the company in part (a) may use such information.

11.3

A hotel has the following information available in respect of weekly costs:

Catering

Three catering staff are employed at a cost of £250 per week each and food and drink costs £8.00 per guest per day.

Maintenance

Maintenance costs have been estimated at £150 per week.

Management

The hotel manager is paid £500 per week plus an additional bonus of £2 per guest for each room booked in excess of 200 rooms per week.

Other Staff

Four other staff are employed on a permanent basis at a cost of £300 per week each. When the number of rooms booked in a week exceeds 200, an extra person is employed from a local agency for every additional 50 rooms per week. The agency charges £400 per person per week.

Laundry

Linen is changed every day and is cleaned by a local firm who charge £2 per room. This charge reduces by 25% for any rooms in excess of 100 per week.

NB A room booked refers to one person occupying a room for one night.

Required

(a)   Classify each cost in terms of its behaviour.

(b)   Prepare an estimate of the expected costs in each category resulting from the following activity levels:

(i)   150 rooms per week

(ii)   250 rooms per week.

Questions Without Answers

11.4

Active Breaks Limited sells adventure holidays in single room accommodation and its costs include the following:

- The cost of sending tickets to individual customers by first class mail.

- The cost of providing accommodation, where discounts offered by the hotel result in a cheaper room rate as the number of rooms booked increases.

- Brochure costs. The printer charges £300 to provide a sample brochure and £0.10 for each copy subsequently printed.

- The hire of a photocopier at an annual cost of £1,200.

- Salary of the sales manager. A basic salary and a bonus of £2 per holiday payable on all holidays sold in excess of 5,000 per annum.

- Administration staff. One person is required for every 3,000 holidays sold.

- Insurance. An initial premium of £7,000 is payable but once 5,000 holidays are sold in a year, a further premium of £1.10 per holiday is payable until sales reach 10,000 holidays, after which no further costs are incurred.

You are required to:

(i)   Classify each cost in terms of its behaviour, giving reasons for your answers.

(ii)   Identify which of the following graphs best represents each one. (NB each graph may be used more than once).

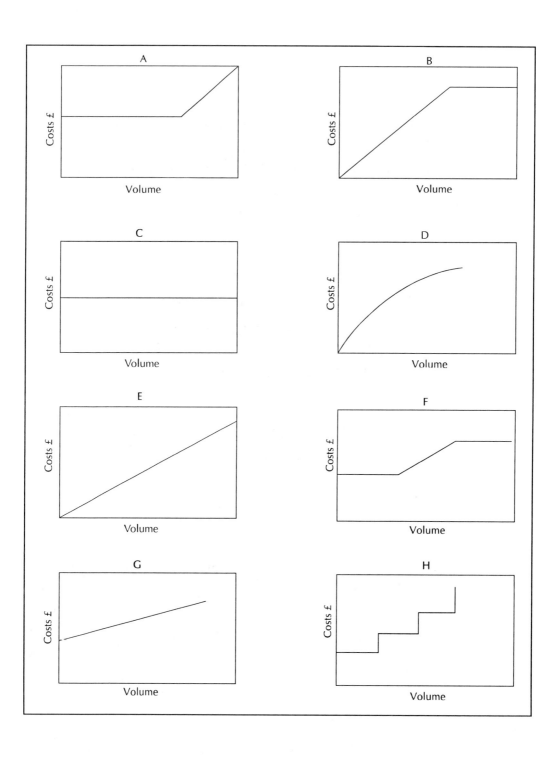

11.5

An airline recorded the following costs in two consecutive weeks:

	Week 1	Week 2
No. of seats sold	4,000	6,000
Costs	£	£
Wages	12,000	12,000
In flight magazine	1,000	1,500
Catering	14,000	20,000
Depreciation	5,000	5,000
Administration	10,500	14,500
Other costs	5,000	6,000

Required

(a) For each cost item, state with reasons whether you believe it to be fixed, variable or semi-variable.

(b) Estimate for each of the semi-variable costs, the fixed cost per week and the variable cost per seat.

(c) Assuming that the pattern of cost behaviour remains the same, calculate the expected cost for each item in a week in which 6,500 seats are sold.

11.6

Data:	£
Cost of motor car	5,000
Trade-in price after 2 years or 60,000 miles is expected to be	1,500
Maintenance -- 6 monthly service costing	60
Spares/replacement parts, per 1,000 miles	20
Vehicle licence, per annum	80
Insurance, per annum	150
Tyre replacements after 25,000 miles, four at	37.50 each
Petrol, per gallon	1.90

Average mileage from one gallon is 25 miles.

(a)   From the above data you are required:

    (i)   To prepare a schedule to be presented to management showing for the mileages of 5,000, 10,000, 15,000 and 30,000 miles per annum:

        (1)   total variable cost

        (2)   total fixed cost

        (3)   total cost

        (4)   variable cost per mile (in pence to nearest penny)

        (5)   fixed cost per mile (in pence to nearest penny)

        (6)   total cost per mile (in pence to nearest penny)

    If, in classifying the costs, you consider that some can be treated as either variable or fixed, state the assumption(s) on which your answer is based together with brief supporting reason(s).

    (ii)   On the graph paper provided, to plot the information given in your answer to (i) above for the costs listed against (1), (2), (3) and (6).

    (iii)   To read off from your graph(s) in (ii) and state approximate total costs applicable to 18,000 miles and 25,000 miles and the total cost per mile (in pence) at these two mileages.

(b)   'The more miles you travel, the cheaper it becomes.' Comment briefly on this statement.

(CIMA)

Chapter 12

Marginal Costing and Decision Making

Learning Objectives

After completing this chapter you should be able to:

- Identify relevant costs and revenues for decision making.

- Explain the limitations of absorption costing information for decision making purposes.

- Apply marginal costing techniques in business decisions.

- Understand the concept of opportunity costs and explain their relevance in decision making.

Introduction

Decision making entails choosing from a range of alternatives, the option which best satisfies an aim or objective. For most businesses the primary objective is to maximise net cash flows (i.e. revenues less costs) and alternative courses of action will be judged accordingly. To assist decision makers in this process, information will be required on the financial consequences of each alternative and in this chapter we will consider how the relevant costs and revenues for short term decision making may be determined. Long term decisions affecting cash flows over more than one year create additional problems and will be examined in detail in Chapter 14.

Relevant Costs and Revenues for Decision Making

The costs and revenues relevant to any decision are those which are expected to change as a result of that decision. These are referred to as incremental (or differential) cash flows. Those which are not expected to alter are irrelevant and should be ignored. This principle is illustrated in the following example:

Example 12.1

Matthew owns a car in which he expects to travel 10,000 miles per annum for personal use. He has estimated the following annual costs at this mileage rate:

	£
Insurance	500
Road Tax	200
Petrol	800
Loan repayment	2,000
Total costs	3,500

$$\text{Total cost per mile} \quad = \quad \frac{£3,500}{10,000 \ miles} \quad = \quad 35\text{p per mile}$$

Matthew's employer has offered him an allowance of 30p per mile to use his car for business purposes.

Required

Should the offer be accepted?

At first glance it may appear that the offer is not worthwhile as the allowance falls short of the cost per mile. However the only incremental cost in this case is petrol, which will rise as a result of the extra mileage. Insurance, road tax and loan repayments, are all fixed costs which will be unaffected by extra mileage and are therefore irrelevant (it has been assumed for simplicity that using the vehicle for business purposes would not affect the insurance premium).

The incremental cost per mile can be calculated as follows :

$$\text{Incremental cost per mile} \quad = \quad \frac{£800}{10,000 \ miles}$$

$$= \quad 8\text{p per mile}$$

As 30p will be received for each mile covered and additional costs amount to only 8p, Matthew will benefit by 22p per mile and should accept the offer.

Marginal Costing

Marginal costing is a decision making technique based on the principle that in the short term, only variable costs (also known as 'marginal costs') change with output. As fixed costs do not alter they should be ignored when taking decisions affecting the level of activity.

This principle was used in the previous example and can be applied in many business situations. We will now consider some typical examples.

Discontinuing a Product Line

Where a business has a range of products, profitability is likely to be a major factor in assessing the viability of each product line. However where profit is calculated using absorption costing, the results can be misleading. As we saw in Chapter 10, absorption costing assigns fixed as well as variable costs to units produced in order to determine the total cost of production. As fixed costs are irrelevant for short term decision making, the resulting cost information will be inappropriate for this purpose and could be misleading.

Consider the following example:

Example 12.2

Chris Gibson Kitchenware Limited sells kitchen appliances to department stores. Product costs are ascertained using an absorption costing system from which the following statement has been prepared in respect of the business's three product lines:

	Dishwashers £000's	Fridges £000's	Ovens £000's	Total £000's
Sales income	180	330	270	780
Less total costs	(200)	(250)	(220)	(670)
Profit/(Loss)	(20)	80	50	110

It has been estimated that costs are 60% variable and 40% fixed.

Required

Advise whether dishwashers should be dropped from the product range in order to improve profitability.

Solution

It may appear from the statement that dishwashers should be discontinued as they are operating at a loss. However the costs assigned to the product include a share of fixed overheads and these will be incurred whether dishwashers are produced or not. Only variable costs will be saved as a result of discontinuing any product line and information used for decision making purposes should reflect this. This can be achieved by re-drafting the original statement in a marginal costing format, assigning only variable costs to products.

To do this the costs must firstly be split into their fixed and variable elements as follows:

	Dishwashers £000's	Fridges £000's	Ovens £000's	Total £000's
Total costs	200	250	220	670
Variable (60%)	120	150	132	402
Fixed (40%)	80	100	88	268

The original statement can now be re-drafted in a marginal costing format as shown below:

	Dishwashers £000's	Fridges £000's	Ovens £000's	Total £000's
Sales Income	180	330	270	780
Less variable costs	(120)	(150)	(132)	(402)
Contribution	60	180	138	378
Less fixed costs				(268)
Profit				110

In this statement only variable costs are assigned to individual products. These are subtracted from sales income to show the 'contribution' made by each product towards fixed costs and profit. In this case the three products generate total contribution of £378,000. The fixed costs of £268,000 must be paid out of this and the remaining £110,000 represents profit.

Product lines should be judged on the basis of their contribution rather than profits. Any product which generates a contribution earns income in excess of its incremental cost and is therefore worth retaining. Ceasing production of dishwashers would reduce total contribution (and therefore profit) by £60,000 as shown below:

	Dishwashers £000's	Fridges £000's	Ovens £000's	Total £000's
Sales Income	0	330	270	600
Less variable costs	0	(150)	(132)	(282)
Contribution	0	180	148	318
Less fixed costs				(268)
Profit				50

Income of £180,000 from dishwashers has been lost and only the variable costs of £120,000 saved. The fixed costs are unaffected and profits have therefore fallen by £60,000.

The initial statement showed total costs of £200,000 for dishwashers and may have given the false impression that this could be saved by discontinuing the product line. Consequently, although absorption costing principles must be used for measuring profits reported in financial accounts, marginal costing is more appropriate for decision making.

Other Considerations

Before making a final decision as to whether dishwashers should be dropped or retained, other factors may be worth investigating. These include:

(a) The Behaviour of Fixed Costs

The decision to retain dishwashers is based on the assumption that fixed costs will not change as a result of halting production. However, this may be not always be true and before a decision is reached the following issues may be worth considering:

(i) Specific Fixed Costs

Some of the fixed costs may be specific to dishwashers and may be avoidable if the product was discontinued. Suppose for instance that the fixed costs included £65,000 in respect of premises which are used only for the production of dishwashers and which could be vacated if their production was discontinued. Under these circumstances such a decision would result in the following situation:

		£
Cost	: Lost contribution from dishwashers	(60,000)
Benefit	: Premises costs saved	65,000
Net savings		5,000

As the benefit arising from vacating the premises exceeds the lost contribution, closing the product line would save £5,000. In these circumstances unless there are sound non-financial reasons for producing dishwashers, they should be discontinued.

(ii) Stepped Costs

As we saw in the previous chapter, fixed costs may be stepped and therefore liable to change when certain activity levels are reached. If for example fewer administrative were required due to ceasing production of dishwashers the resulting cost savings should be considered when assessing the viability of the product.

(b) Alternative Products

Although dishwashers generate a contribution, the return is relatively low compared to the other two products. It may be worth investigating whether dishwashers could be replaced by another product line which could generate higher returns.

Pricing Decisions for Special Orders

When setting selling prices for special 'one off' orders, provided that the price exceeds variable costs (i.e. a contribution is made on the sale) profit will increase. Consider the following example:

Example 12.3

Capital Tours Limited sells weekend tours of London for £200 per person. Last month 1,000 tours were sold and costs were £180,000 (representing a total cost per tour of £180). These costs included £60,000 which were fixed.

A local college wishing to send 200 students on an educational trip has offered Capital Tours £140 per tour.

Required

Should Capital Tours accept the offer?

Solution

At first glance it may appear that the offer, which falls below the total cost of £180 per tour should be rejected. However the decision should be based on the contribution expected from the offer which can be calculated as follows:

Contribution = Sales income - Variable costs

We know the sales income for each tour and the variable cost per tour can be obtained from the previous month's costs:

	£
Total costs for the month	180,000
Less fixed costs	(60,000)
Variable costs for the month	120,000

$$\text{Variable cost per tour} = \frac{£120,000}{1,000 \ tours} = £120$$

We can now calculate the contribution per tour at the proposed selling price:

Contribution per tour = £140 – £120

= £20

As the proposed selling price exceeds the cost of providing each tour by £20, the offer should be accepted, increasing profits by £4,000 (200 tours @ £20). In fact any price above the marginal cost of £120 per tour would earn a contribution and therefore be financially acceptable.

However, when considering selling at below normal selling prices, other factors should also be assessed. These include:

Existing Customers

Customers paying the full price may be unhappy to discover others paying less. If discounts are offered for purchasing in large quantities as in the example, the pricing policy may be easily defended. However where this is not the case, existing customers may request a similar discount or seek alternative suppliers in future.

Competitors

Competitor reaction to lower selling prices should also be considered. They may respond by cutting their own prices and perhaps starting a price war in which consumers benefit but suppliers lose out through falling revenue.

Alternative Uses of Spare Capacity

Where capacity is limited, other potential customers should be considered before selling at a discount.

Let us suppose that Capital Tours has a maximum of 1,200 tours per month available and has already sold 1,000 of next month's tours at the normal selling price. Before selling the remaining 200 tours at £140 each, the company should investigate the possibility that others may be willing to pay a higher price.

The Dangers of Pricing Based on Marginal Cost

Although basing prices on marginal costs may be suitable for special orders or where there is spare capacity, pricing all output in this manner can be dangerous. In the long run, to ensure profitability sales revenue must be sufficient to cover all costs and not just the marginal element.

To illustrate this we will refer back to Capital Tours. Having concluded earlier that £140 per tour was an acceptable selling price, let us now consider the effect of selling the normal monthly output of 1,000 tours at this price:

> *Selling 1,000 tours at £140 each*

	£	
Sales income	140,000	(1,000 x £140)
Less variable costs	(120,000)	(1,000 x £120)
Contribution	20,000	
Less fixed costs	(60,000)	
Profit/(loss)	(40,000)	

At this selling price the business would lose £40,000 per month. How can this be when we have already decided that £140 is an acceptable selling price?

The loss has arisen because although selling at £140 per tour does generate a contribution, it is insufficient to cover the fixed costs. In the earlier example when setting a price for the extra 200 tours we could do so in the knowledge that fixed costs had already been covered by selling 1,000 tours at the normal price of £200. Any additional contribution from selling to the college would therefore increase profits and this could be achieved at any selling price above the marginal cost of £120 per tour.

Decision Making with Limiting Factors

In the short term the output of any business will be constrained by the limited availability of resources such as machine capacity, labour hours, space etc. There will come a point where the supply of one of these becomes exhausted, preventing further expansion of output. This is known as the limiting factor.

Where this prevents the business from satisfying customer demand the most profitable product mix must be determined. To maximise profit, production should be concentrated on those products which make the best use of the scarce resource.

Consider the following an example:

Example 12.4

A company manufactures four products for which the following information is available:

	A £	B £	C £	D £
Selling price per unit	67	100	85	56
Less variable costs	(45)	(60)	(55)	(35)
Contribution per unit	22	40	30	21
Machine hours per unit	2	10	5	3

The estimated demand for next month is 600 units of each product. However due to essential maintenance work, machine capacity in the month will be limited to 9,000 hours.

Required

Determine the most profitable product mix for the month.

Solution

As all four products generate a healthy contribution the ideal situation would be to produce enough of each to satisfy total demand. However as shown below, this is not possible given the limitation on machine hours:

Machine Hours Required to Satisfy Demand:

Product	Demand (Units)	Machine hours per unit	Total machine hours required
A	600	2	1,200
B	600	10	6,000
C	600	5	3,000
D	600	3	1,800
			12,000

As there are only 9,000 machine hours available in the month total demand cannot be satisfied and we must determine which products should be produced.

It may appear that priority should be given to product B which generates the highest contribution per unit at £40. However it also uses more machine hours than any other product and will therefore deplete the scarce resource more quickly. To ensure that the maximum benefit is derived from this resource the products should be ranked according to their contribution per machine hour rather than per unit. This can be calculated as follows:

Contribution per Machine Hour

	A	B	C	D
Contribution per unit	£22	£40	£30	£21
Machine hours per unit	2	10	5	3
Contribution per machine hour	£11	£4	£6	£7
Ranking	*1*	*4*	*3*	*2*

Relating contribution to the limiting factor we can see that due to its high machine hour requirement, Product B is actually ranked last with a contribution of only £4 per machine hour. Product A makes best use of the limiting factor, earning £11 for each machine hour used and should be given priority.

The most profitable product mix for the month, based on these figures is given below:

Product	Units	Machine hours used
A	600	1,200
D	600	1,800
C	600	3,000
B	300	3,000
		9,000

Producing 600 units each of Products A, D and C uses 6,000 machine hours leaving 3,000 hours for the production of B. This is sufficient for only 300 units and the demand for the remaining 300 units of B will be unsatisfied.

This product mix will generate the following total contribution which represents the highest possible return given the shortage of machine hours:

	£
600 units of A @ £22 per unit	13,200
600 units of D @ £21 per unit	12,600
600 units of C @ £30 per unit	18,000
300 units of B @ £40 per unit	12,000
Total contribution	55,800

Although this method will identify the most profitable mix with one limiting factor, it cannot be used where there is more than one constraint (e.g. if labour hours were also scarce). In these circumstances a mathematical technique called linear programming must be employed.

Make or Buy Decisions

Manufacturing organisations may be faced with a choice between buying a component part from a supplier or producing it themselves. In assessing the two options it should be remembered that only incremental costs are relevant and fixed costs should be ignored. The following example demonstrates this principle:

Example 12.5

M. Milne Limited uses 40,000 units of component X per annum which it currently produces at the following cost:

	£
Direct materials	7.20
Direct labour	3.30
Variable overheads	2.00
Fixed overheads	5.50
Total cost of production	18.00

A supplier has offered to supply the component at a price of £15 each.

Required

State whether the component should be bought from the supplier or manufactured.

Solution

It may appear that as the cost of production exceeds the supplier's price, component X should be purchased. However, only variable costs increase as a result of manufacturing the part. The fixed overheads of £5.50 per unit merely represent part X's share of the total fixed overheads of the business and ceasing to produce it would not affect those costs. Part X's share would simply be re-distributed, increasing the fixed overheads absorbed by the other products/components manufactured. The fixed element should therefore be ignored and the purchase price should be compared with the marginal cost per unit:

Marginal cost of manufacturing X:

	£
Direct materials	7.20
Direct labour	3.30
Variable overheads	2.00
	12.50

This represents a saving of £2.50 per unit when compared with the purchase price of £15 and the component should therefore be manufactured.

Note that as explained earlier, it may be worth analysing the fixed costs more closely before making a final decision. Any specific to component X may be avoidable if production was halted and may make purchasing a more attractive proposition.

Opportunity Costs

Opportunity costs arise where benefits available from a particular course of action are sacrificed in order to take advantage of an alternative option. If for example you decide to take time off from a part-time job to see a rock concert, the opportunity cost of attending is the wages lost. These should be added to the ticket price, travel costs etc. to calculate the true cost of attending the concert.

In business situations opportunity costs may occur when scarce resources prevent a firm from exploiting all opportunities available to it. This is illustrated in the following example:

Example 12.6

Let us suppose that in Example 12.5 the production capacity currently used to manufacture component X could otherwise be used to produce 25,000 units of product Z per annum at a marginal cost of £8 per unit and that these could be sold for £14 per unit.

As producing X would deprive the company of the opportunity to earn contribution from product Z, the opportunity cost must be incorporated as follows:

	£	
MANUFACTURING X		
Marginal cost of production	500,000	(40,000 units @ £12.50)
Opportunity cost - loss of contribution from Z	150,000	(25,000 units x £14 - £8)
Net cost of manufacture	650,000	
PURCHASING X	(600,000)	(40,000 units @ £15)
Saving through purchasing	50,000	

The cost of purchasing is lower by £50,000 and the company should therefore purchase 40,000 units of component X and manufacture 30,000 units of Product Z with the resulting spare production capacity.

Relevant Costs - A Comprehensive Example

In the examples we have looked at, decisions have been based on the assumption that as fixed costs do not change with activity, they are irrelevant and should be ignored. However as explained earlier, all incremental cash flows should be considered and in certain circumstances these may include fixed costs. To test your understanding of this principle you should now work through the following example:

Example 12.7

A building company has estimated the following costs in respect of a contract for which it will be paid £120,000:

Direct Materials

Material costs for the work have been estimated at £46,000.

Direct Labour

The contract would require four persons for 32 weeks. These are already employed on a permanent basis at a cost of £350 per week and if not used on the new contract would perform general maintenance work. If the employees were used on the contract a local firm would perform this maintenance for £22,000.

Estimation Costs

The estimating department has already incurred costs of £6,000 in respect of the contract.

Administration Costs

The contract would require the recruitment of an additional person to work in the administration department for 40 weeks at a cost of £250 per week. In addition, overtime costs in the department would increase by £6,000 as a consequence of accepting the contract.

Equipment Hire

The work would require additional equipment which could be hired for the duration of the contract for £12,000.

Head Office Costs

Head office costs of £18,000 would be charged to the contract.

Required

Advise the company whether or not the contract should be accepted.

Solution

The relevant costs and revenues are listed below with explanatory notes:

Note			£
	Income		120,000
	Less Incremental Costs		
	Direct materials	46,000	
1	Direct labour	-	
2	Maintenance	22,000	
3	Estimation costs	-	
4	Administration	16,000	
	Equipment hire	12,000	
5	Head office costs	-	(96,000)
	NET BENEFIT		24,000

As the contract is expected to produce a net benefit of £24,000 it should be accepted.

Explanatory notes

(1) As the direct workers are permanently employed by the company they will be paid regardless of whether the contract is accepted and the cost is therefore irrelevant.

(2) The incremental cost arising from the use of the employees on the contract is the £22,000 required to pay contractors for maintenance work and this should be included.

(3) As the estimation costs have already been incurred they will not be influenced by acceptance of the contract. Past costs are irrelevant for decision making purposes and should be ignored.

(4) Although administration costs are often classed as fixed, in this case the additional costs are specific to the contract and should be included as noted below:

	£	
Additional person	10,000	(40 weeks x £250)
Additional overtime	6,000	
Total	16,000	

(5) As explained in Example 12.5, changing the level of activity will merely result in the re-distribution of existing fixed overheads and in the absence of any information to the contrary, it should be assumed that the actual costs incurred remain unchanged. In this case the £18,000 charged represents the contract's share of head

office overheads and not additional costs incurred and should therefore be excluded.

Non-financial Implications of Decisions

In the course of this chapter the relative merits of alternative courses of action have been assessed on the basis of their financial consequences. However decisions should be taken in the light of all available information and non-financial factors should also be considered. If for example a plan to change operating methods was expected to affect employee morale, then the implications of this should be assessed as well as the effect on costs. Although financial information can provide useful guidance for those responsible for taking decisions, it is no substitute for sound management judgement. Failure to consider wider implications may result in short term financial gains at the expense of long term objectives.

Summary

- The costs and revenues relevant to any decision are those which are expected to change as a result of that decision (i.e. incremental cash flows).

- Marginal costing is a technique based on the principle that fixed costs, which remain constant with changes in output, are irrelevant for short term decision making.

- Consequently absorption costing information in which fixed costs are assigned to products, can be misleading if used for decision making.

- Any product generating contribution earns income in excess of the variable costs incurred and will therefore increase profit.

- Selling prices should be set high enough initially to ensure that all costs are covered. Having achieved this, selling additional output at any price above marginal cost will increase profit.

- Where potential demand cannot be satisfied due to a single scarce resource, the most profitable product mix can be determined by ranking products on the basis of their contribution per unit of scarce resource.

- Opportunity costs represent the benefit sacrificed by pursuing an alternative course of action.

- Those responsible for taking decisions should consider non-financial factors as well as the financial consequences of alternative courses of action.

Questions   (See Appendix C for Answers)

12.1

The managing director of a company has stated that if price levels are always set at a level which exceeds marginal cost, income must exceed expenditure and therefore the company must be profitable. State whether or not you agree giving your reasons.

12.2

Mediterranean Tours Limited sells cruises and has produced the following statement in respect of last month's activity.

	Spanish Islands	Greek Islands	Total
Selling Price per cruise	£700	£900	
	£	£	£
Sales revenue	77,000	180,000	257,000
Total costs	(90, 000)	(130,000)	(220,000)
Profit/(Loss)	(13,000)	50,000	37,000

Costs for the business are 30% fixed and 70% variable.

Required

(a) (i)   It has been suggested that Spanish cruises should be discontinued to improve the profitability of the business. State, giving reasons, whether or not you agree with this proposal.

(ii)   What other factors may be worth considering when taking such a decision?

(b) (i)   Mediterranean Tours have received an enquiry from a school wishing to buy 40 Greek cruises for £700 each. State, giving reasons, whether or not you believe the tours should be sold at this price.

(ii)   What other factors should be considered when taking such a decision.

12.3

A company specialising in the production and installation of kitchens incurs costs on its product range as follows:

	Country Manor	De-Luxe	Continental
	£	£	£
Materials:			
Wood	80.00	120.00	70.00
Fittings	26.80	27.40	18.80
Labour:			
Constructors	109.20	159.60	67.20
Installers	90.00	180.00	20.00
Selling Price	800.00	1,000.00	400.00
Expected Annual Demand (units)	750	350	800

Fixed Costs are £400,000 per annum.

Constructors are currently paid £8.40 per hour and are difficult to recruit. Consequently it is estimated that only 18,240 constructor hours will be available next year.

Required

(a) Determine the most profitable mix for the year and calculate the resulting profit.

(b) Awarding constructors a pay rise of £2 per hour would enable the company to attract sufficient additional labour to enable the demand for the products to be satisfied. Evaluate this option in terms of:

    (i) Profitability

    (ii) Any other factors which should be considered.

12.4

(a) Explain the meaning of the terms 'sunk' and 'opportunity' costs and assess their relevance in decision making.

(b) Depreciation is an important concept in determining profit. Discuss its relevance in decision making.

(c) Although marginal costing treats 'fixed costs' as being irrelevant for decision making this is not always the case in practice. Describe circumstances in which such costs may be relevant, using an example to illustrate your answer.

12.5

HGC Limited, a small construction business has been asked to build an extension for a sports club for £20,000. The estimating department has completed the following estimate in respect of the contract:

	£	Note
Estimating costs	750	1
Materials	11,600	2
Direct labour		
4 Craftsmen for 15 days @ £60 per day	3,600	3
2 Labourers for 15 days @ £35 per day	1,050	4
Supervision costs	580	5
Plus overheads (see note 6)		

Additional notes

1. Estimating costs include materials costing £80 and £300 overtime costs which were specifically incurred for the contract. The remainder are fixed staff related costs.

2. Material costs include 30 metres of timber (currently held in stock) at its historical cost of £8 per metre. This is commonly used on building work and HGC Limited has recently negotiated a price of £7.50 per metre from a new supplier. Other materials would be obtained locally and have been costed at current prices.

3. The craftsmen to be assigned to the contract are currently employed on a full time basis and to complete the contract for the sports club would have to be transferred from other work. Temporary staff employed to complete this work would be provided by an agency at a cost of £75 per day.

4. The labourers to be assigned to the contract are both employed on a full-time basis. If the job for the sports club is not undertaken one would have no work during the period in question. The other would be hired out to a small building business for £45 per day.

5. Supervisors work on a number of jobs at any one time.

6. Overheads are assigned to contracts at a rate of £55 per direct labour day. 80% of overheads are fixed and 20% variable.

Required

    (a)   Advise HGC Limited's' management team as to whether or not they should proceed with the contract. Your recommendation should be accompanied by relevant cost figures.

    (b)   Explain the relevance of the following terms in the context of decision making and provide an illustration of each in the information relating to HGC Limited:

        (i)   Sunk costs

        (ii)   Incremental costs

        (iii) Opportunity costs

12.6

Company A expects to have 2,000 direct labour hours of manufacturing capacity (in normal time) available over the next two months after completion of current regular orders. It is considering two options in order to utilise the spare capacity. If the available hours are not utilised direct labour costs would not be incurred.

The first option involves the early manufacture of a firm future order which would as a result reduce the currently anticipated need for overtime working in a few months time. The premium for overtime working is 30% of the basic rate of £4.00 per hour, and is charged to production as a direct labour cost. Overheads are charged at £6.00 per direct labour hour. 40% of overhead costs are variable with hours worked.

Alternatively, Company A has just been asked to quote for a one-off job to be completed over the next two months and which would require the following resources:

    1.   Raw materials:

        (i)   960 kgs of Material X which has a current weighted average cost in stock of £3.02 per kg and a replacement cost of £3.10 per kg. Material X is used continuously by Company A.

        (ii)   570 kgs of Material Y which is in stock at £5.26 per kg. It has a current replacement cost of £5.85 per kg. If used, Material Y would not be replaced. It has no other anticipated use, other than disposal for £2.30 per kg.

        (iii) Other materials costing £3,360.

    2.   Direct labour: 2,200 hours.

Required:

(a) Establish the minimum quote that could be tendered for the one-off job such that it would increase Company A's profit, compared with the alternative use of spare capacity. (Ignore the interest cost/benefit associated with the different timing of cash flows from the different options).

(b) Explain, and provide illustrations of, the following terms:

   (i)   sunk cost,

   (ii) opportunity cost,

   (iii) incremental cost.

(ACCA)

Questions Without Answers

12.7

Happyhols Limited sells Mediterranean cruises from its sales office directly to the public for £500 each and expects to sell 1,000 cruises in the forthcoming year. It has forecast that total costs for the year will amount to £480,000 of which 25% will be fixed and the remainder variable.

Two organisations have expressed interest in buying holidays in bulk as detailed below:

Comprehensive School

A school has offered to buy 80 cruises at a discount of 20% on the normal selling price.

Daily Newspaper

A newspaper wishes to purchase 50 cruises to offer as competition prizes and has requested a discount of 30% on the normal selling price. Satisfying the newspaper's demand would involve additional costs of £20 per cruise in respect of a special welcome banquet to be provided for each prize winner.

Required

(a) Advise Happyhols as to whether each of the two offers should be accepted, giving reasons for your decisions.

(b) Explain any changes in your advice in (a) if the bulk purchases replaced existing sales.

(c) What other factors should be considered whenever taking decisions on selling at below normal selling prices.

12.8

The following cost information has been prepared in respect of a research project undertaken on behalf of a client and due to be completed in one year's time:

	£
Costs to date	40,000
Estimated costs to completion	
- Materials	75,000
- Staff costs	110,000
- Other costs	80,000
Total	305,000

As the total costs exceed the contracted value of £220,000 for the completed research you have been asked to review the project. If it is abandoned the client will receive compensation of £25,000.

The following information has also been supplied regarding the estimated costs to complete the work:

Materials

Contracts have already been exchanged for the purchase of materials to the value of £20,000. These have no alternative use and if not used on the project would be disposed of at a cost of £2,000.

Staffing

Four researchers each receive a salary of £25,000 p.a. The other £10,000 represents a portion of the salary of a supervisor who is in charge of several projects. If the project is abandoned the researchers would be declared redundant, each receiving £10,000 in compensation.

Other Costs

Depreciation charges of £20,000 in respect of equipment are included in the estimated costs. This equipment is highly specialised and has no alternative use and its disposal value is:

Now   £18,000

In one year   £6,000

Required

(a)   Give your recommendation whether on financial grounds the project should be continued or abandoned. Your calculations should be supported by clear statements of the reasons why a particular figure is included or excluded.

(b) Briefly explain any non-financial considerations which should be considered before deciding to abandon such a project.

12.9

A small company is engaged solely in the automated production of a standard product by a special extrusion process. The direct material cost of each product is £8, machine time is 1 hour per unit. The direct labour cost is embraced within other variable costs which amount to £2 per machine hour. The availability of the raw material is of concern to the management of the company. There seems no way to increase the available quantity above £80,000 per month. There are no capacity or labour problems in fully utilising the monthly quantity. Sales demand at £20 per item is very heavy. Fixed overhead, based on the volume indicated above is £4 per hour.

A potential customer has approached the company with a special order worth £8,000 for a one off product using the same material. The quantity of material required will cost £3,520 and the necessary machine time of 500 hours is available. A special component costing £600 will need to be purchased by the company to adapt its extrusion equipment. This is easily assembled and dismantled, but it results in £80 of material being wasted due to the interruption of the production run.

Required

(a) Distinguish between:

(i) variable cost and fixed cost,

(ii) opportunity cost and sunk cost.

(b) Tabulate the expected results per unit and per month if the standard product only is made.

(c) What contribution is offered by the special order? Should the company accept the order? What minimum price would you apply to the order? Explain your answer.

(ACCA)

12.10

RC Limited manufactures materials handling equipment and has been offered £3,000 to supply a conveyor system. Estimates relating to the proposal are given below.

Materials:	£	Note
25 metres of M1 @ £14.20 per metre	355	1
12 Kg. of M2 @ £18.50 per Kg.	222	2
1 part no. P3	125	3
Direct Labour:		
50 hours of skilled staff @ £22 per hour	1,100	4
38 hours of unskilled staff @ £14 per hour	532	5
Production Overheads:	1,408	6
	3,742	
Administration overheads @ 8% of the above costs	299	
	4,041	

Additional notes:

1. The current purchase price of material M1 is £15.20 per metre. However, 10 metres are currently held in stock. These were originally bought for £14.20 per metre and as they have no alternative use will be sold back to the supplier for £10 per metre if not used on the conveyor contract.

2. Material M2 is used continually by RC Limited and the requirements for the contract can be met from current stock which has been purchased for £18.50 per Kg. The current purchase price of M2 is £19.75 per Kg.

3. Part no. P3 can be purchased at a cost of £150. Two are currently held in stock and these were originally bought at a cost of £125 for a contract which was subsequently terminated. The company has no further use for these items.

4. The skilled work would be performed during overtime hours at a cost of £22 per hour.

5. The unskilled work would be undertaken by a person who would otherwise be employed on essential maintenance work. A local firm would be willing to perform this maintenance at a cost of £430.

6. Production overheads are absorbed on the basis of direct labour hours at a rate of £16 per hour, of which £11.50 is fixed and the remainder variable.

Required

(a) State whether or not the contract should be accepted, supporting your recommendation with figures and explaining your treatment of each cost.

(b)   Comment briefly on two other factors which the management of RC
Limited should consider which may influence the decision.

12.11

A small company is engaged in the manufacture of three products – P, S and V. Production
and sale of 5,000 units of each are forecast during the following budget period
(January–December 19X1). The unit prices at which the products will be sold are £19,
£30 and £18 respectively for P, S and V.

The direct costs are as follows:

	P	S	V
	£	£	£
Material	6	8	3
Labour	4	7	5

Material cost is based on the common raw material used in all three products.

Overhead recovery is based on 200% of labour cost. Half of the overhead is variable in
relation to labour cost, the remainder is fixed. At the forecast level given above fixed
overheads for the period are fully absorbed.

The material is imported and the company face a problem of quotas imposed by the sole
supplier and a long lead-time for delivery. Orders are placed about one year in advance
and cannot be increased. The forecast production plan for 19X1 uses to the full the present
quota.

The marketing director has determined that, because of a sudden change in forecast
conditions, it would be possible to expand the sales of any or all of the products by 20%,
at current prices and has enquired if, and to what extent, the profit would change. She
also has a prototype of a new product ready for production. It uses the same material and
costs have been estimated at material £12, labour £7. Early indications are that the selling
price would not exceed £35.

Required

As the management accountant, taking a short-term view, and bearing in mind the limited
quantity of material available, prepare a report to the marketing director:

(a)   responding to her enquiry regarding the forecast product mix;

(b)   making reference to the profitability of the new product.

(ACCA)

12.12

A business has been offered £12,000 to repair a building which is currently unused. The estimating department has recently completed the following estimate for the job.

Materials:	£	Note
58 metres of Material A @ £33.50 per metre	1,943	1
10 Kg. of Material B @ £29.70 per Kg.	297	2
Windows - 8 @ £320 each	2,560	3
- 2 @ £260 each	520	
Direct Labour:		
86 hours of Grade 1 staff @ £18 per hour	1,548	4
73 hours of Grade 2 staff @ £15 per hour	1,095	5
Estimating Costs:		
20 hours @ £30 per hour	600	
Production Overheads:	4,611	6
	13,174	
Administration overheads @ 15%	1,976	
	15,150	

Additional notes:

1. The current purchase price of Material A is £33.50 per metre. However, 24 metres are currently held in stock. These were originally bought for £31.00 per m. and as they have no alternative use will be sold back to the supplier for £25 per m. if not used on the repair contract.

2. Material B is used continually by the business and the requirements for the contract can be met from current stock which has been purchased for £29.70 per Kg. The current purchase price of this material is £27.80 per Kg.

3. The windows can be purchased at a cost of £320. Two are currently held in stock and these were originally bought at a cheaper rate of £260 for a contract which was subsequently terminated.

   If these two windows are not used on the repair contract they will be converted at a cost of £20 each and used on another job in place of windows which would otherwise be obtained for £110 each.

4.   The Grade 1 work would be performed during overtime hours at a cost of £22 per hour.

5.   The Grade 2 work would be undertaken by staff who would otherwise be employed on essential maintenance work. A local firm would be willing to perform this maintenance at a cost of £850.

6.   Production overheads are absorbed on the basis of direct labour hours at the following rates:

     Fixed overheads £22 per hour

     Variable overheads £7 per hour

Required

(a)   State whether or not the repair contract should be accepted, supporting your recommendation with figures and explaining your treatment of each cost.

(b)   Comment briefly on two other factors which management should consider which may influence the decision.

Chapter 13

Cost Volume Profit Analysis

Learning Objectives

After studying this chapter you should be able to:

- Explain how cost volume profit analysis may be used to produce information for short term planning.

- Calculate and explain the:

    - Contribution/sales (C/S) ratio.

    - Break even point.

    - Output required to achieve a profit target.

    - Margin of safety.

- Compile and interpret break even charts and profit charts.

- Explain the limitations of cost volume profit analysis and identify the circumstances in which it is likely to be most useful.

Introduction

In this chapter we will examine the relationship between output and revenue, costs and profit. This is known as 'Cost Volume Profit (CVP) Analysis' (or 'Break Even Analysis') and can assist in planning decisions by providing an overview of the financial implications of short term plans. Information may be compiled using two alternative approaches and each will be explained and demonstrated. The first is a mathematical approach using formulae and in the second, information is presented visually using graphs.

These techniques can be used to determine, among other things:

- The number of units which must be sold to break even.

- The number of units which must be sold to achieve a profit target.

- The profit expected from selling a specified number of units.

- The effect on profit of changes in selling prices, costs or output.

The chapter concludes by assessing the limitations of CVP analysis and the conditions under which it is likely to be most appropriate.

The Mathematical Approach

The use of formulae to generate planning information will be demonstrated and explained using the following example:

Example 13.1

Ashday Limited markets a single product which is sold for £10 per unit and has a marginal cost of £6 per unit. Fixed costs are expected to be £140,000 per annum.

The Contribution/Sales (C/S) Ratio

The C/S ratio shows the relationship between contribution and sales revenue and is ascertained as follows :

$$\text{CS ratio} \quad = \quad \frac{Contribution\ per\ unit}{Selling\ price\ per\ unit} \quad \text{x} \quad 100$$

Remembering that contribution is obtained by subtracting marginal costs from sales income, the ratio for Ashday can be calculated as follows:

$$\text{CS ratio} \quad = \quad \frac{£10 - £6}{£10} \quad \text{x} \quad 100$$

$$= \quad \frac{£4}{£10} \quad \text{x} \quad 100 \quad = \quad 40\%$$

This indicates that for every £100 of sales revenue contribution of £40 will be earned and enables management to predict the contribution expected in future periods. If for example sales of £60,000 have been forecast for a particular month, contribution of £24,000 (£60,000 x 40%) can be anticipated.

The Break Even Point

The break even point is the activity level at which neither a profit nor a loss is made. Total contribution from this level of output will therefore be just enough to cover fixed costs, with nothing left over for profit. The number of units which must be sold to achieve this can be calculated using the following formula:

$$\text{Break even point} \quad = \quad \frac{Fixed\ Costs}{Contribution per\ unit}$$

Thus for Ashday Limited:

$$\text{Break even point} \quad = \quad \frac{£140,000\ p.a.}{£4}$$

$$= \quad 35,000\ units\ per\ annum$$

Note that the result is expressed in the same terms as the fixed costs. In this case as fixed costs per annum have been used, the result is expressed in units per annum. Using fixed costs per month would show the break even point in terms of units per month.

The break even point can also be expressed in terms of sales revenue by multiplying by the selling price per unit:

$$\text{Break even point (sales value)} \quad = \quad 35,000\ units\ x\ £10\ per\ unit$$

$$= \quad £350,000$$

These results can be proved by calculating the profit expected from the sale of 35,000 units:

	£	
Sales revenue	350,000	(35,000 units x £10)
Less variable costs	(210,000)	(35,000 units x £6)
Contribution	140,000	
Less fixed costs	(140,000)	
Profit	0	

The contribution earned is exactly enough to cover fixed costs, leaving nothing for profit and the business will therefore break even.

Alternative Formula

The break even point may also be calculated as follows:

$$\text{Break even point (sales value)} \quad = \quad \frac{Fixed\ cost}{C/S\ ratio}$$

$$\text{i.e. for Ashday Limited} \quad = \quad \frac{£140,000}{0.40} \quad = \quad £350,000$$

This can be expressed in units by dividing by the selling price per unit:

$$\text{Break even point (units)} \quad = \quad \frac{£350,000}{£10\ per\ unit} \quad = \quad 35,000\ units$$

Sales Required For a Target Profit

To attain a specific profit figure, sufficient contribution must be generated to not only cover fixed costs but also provide the required profit. The number of units required to achieve this can be ascertained as follows :

$$\text{Units required for target profit} \quad = \quad \frac{Fixed\ Cost + Target\ profit}{Contribution\ per\ unit}$$

Thus if Ashday Limited requires profits of £60,000 per annum:

$$\text{Units required for target profit} \quad = \quad \frac{£140,000 + £60,000}{£4}$$

$$= \quad 50,000\ units$$

Again this can be expressed in terms of sales value by multiplying by the selling price per unit:

Sales value required for £60,000 profit   =   50,000 units x £10 per unit

$$= \quad £500,000$$

These results can be proved as before, by calculating the profit arising from the sale of 50,000 units:

	£	
Sales revenue	500,000	(50,000 units x £10)
Less variable costs	(300,000)	(50,000 units x £6)
Contribution	200,000	
Less fixed costs	(140,000)	
Profit	60,000	

The Margin of Safety

The margin of safety (MOS) provides an assessment of risk by indicating the extent to which expected output can fall before a loss will be made. It is calculated as follows:

MOS = Expected activity level - Break even point

Assuming that Ashday Limited expect output of 50,000 units per annum, the margin of safety would be:

= 50,000 units - 35,000 units

= 15,000 units

Expected output could fall by 15,000 units (i.e. to the break even point of 35,000 units) before the business would make losses.

This may also be expressed as a percentage of expected output as demonstrated below:

$$\text{MOS} \quad = \quad \frac{15,000 \; units}{50,000 \; units} \quad x \quad 100$$

$$= \quad 30\%$$

Thus expected output would have to fall by 30% before losses would be incurred.

The Graphical Approach

The information derived using the formulae explained above can also be obtained from graphs showing the relationship between output, revenue, costs and profit. These take several forms and can provide a quick visual indication of the impact of changes in selling prices, costs and activity levels. We will look at these using the information relating to Ashday Limited in Example 13.1.

Break Even Charts

Figure 13.1 shows a break even chart for Ashday Limited which can be constructed as explained below:

1.   **Draw the axes**

The X (horizontal) axis should accommodate the range of activity for which information is required and the Y (vertical) axis is used to show costs and revenue.

2.   **Draw the Fixed Cost Line**

Fixed costs are depicted by a horizontal line drawn from the point on the Y axis representing their value (i.e. £140,000 for Ashday Limited).

3.   **Draw the Total Cost Line**

This is a diagonal line starting on the Y axis at the point representing fixed costs and passing through a second point which can be determined as follows:

(a)   Estimate the total costs for any chosen activity level. E.g. for 60,000 units:

Total cost = Fixed costs + Variable costs

= £140,000 +(60,000 units x £6 per unit)

= £500,000

(b)   Plot a point on the graph (P1) representing this information (i.e. 60,000 units = £500,000).

4.   **Draw the Total Revenue Line**

This is another diagonal line starting at the origin of the graph and passing through a point which is determined by calculating total revenue for a chosen activity level as demonstrated below:

Total revenue (60,000 units) =	60,000	x	£10 per unit
=	£600,000		

The point (P2) is therefore plotted at the intersection of 60,000 units and £600,000.

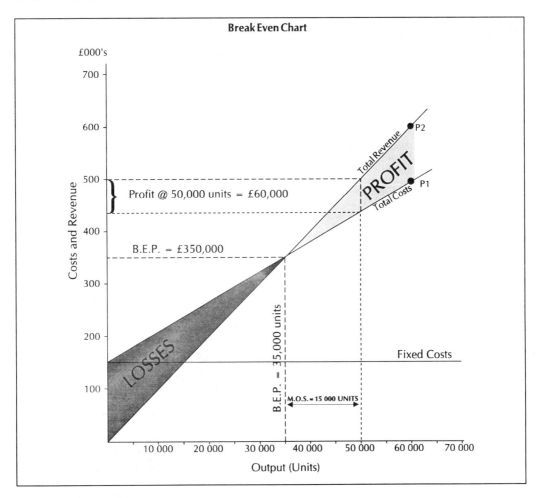

Figure 13.1 Break Even Chart

From this chart we can see that:

- The break even point occurs at the point where total cost and total revenue are equal and confirms the results obtained using the formula (i.e. 35,000 units or £350,000).

- At activity levels above this, total revenue exceeds total costs and profit will be earned. This can be quantified by measuring the distance between the total cost and revenue lines. The graph shows profit of £60,000 from the sale of 50,000 units, again confirming our earlier result.

- For output levels below the break even point total costs exceed total revenue and losses will occur. Again the relevant figure can be obtained by measuring the distance between the total cost and revenue lines.

- The margin of safety is 15,000 units.

Changing Costs and Selling Prices

The break even chart can be easily altered to show the effect of changes in costs or the selling price as illustrated in Figure 13.2.

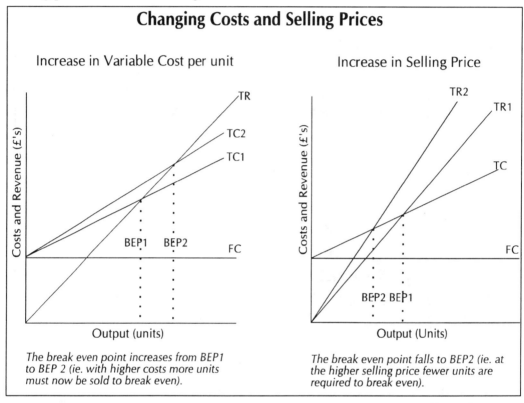

Changing Costs and Selling Prices

Increase in Variable Cost per unit

The break even point increases from BEP1 to BEP 2 (ie. with higher costs more units must now be sold to break even).

Increase in Selling Price

The break even point falls to BEP2 (ie. at the higher selling price fewer units are required to break even).

Figure 13.2 Changing Costs and Selling Prices

Contribution Break Even Charts

On contribution charts variable costs are plotted first (rather than fixed costs as in the traditional method) and fixed costs added to produce a total cost line as illustrated in Figure 13.3:

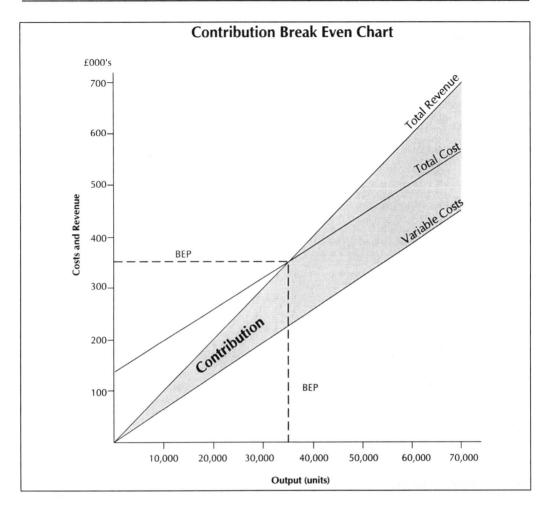

Figure 13.3 Contribution Break Even Chart

This chart provides all the information available from the traditional chart but in addition, contribution can be estimated for any activity level.

Profit Charts

Profit charts are simpler to construct but will show only the profit or loss for a given activity level as illustrated in Figure 13.4.

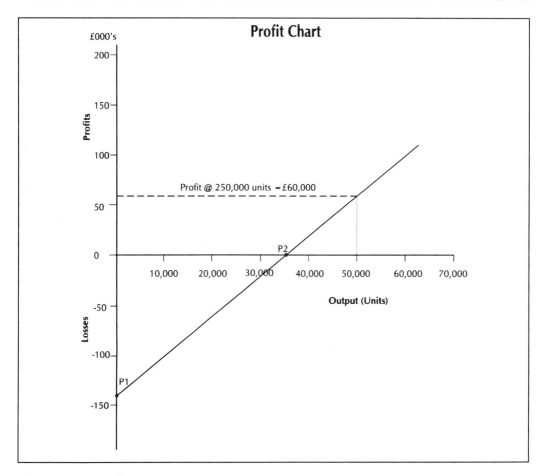

Figure 13.4 Profit Chart

The profit line has been drawn through two points plotted as follows :

P1   As fixed costs must be paid regardless of the activity level, a loss of £140,000 will be incurred when output is zero.

P2   We calculated earlier that the break even point is 35,000 units, therefore profit is zero at this output level.

Multi Product Charts

The charts we have prepared so far have represented a company selling a single product. However, many businesses sell a range of items and we will now look at a chart from which profits earned from selling a variety of products can be estimated:

Example 13.2

Ryholme Limited produces three products for which the following sales mix has been planned for the forthcoming year:

Product	Sales	Contribution	C/S Ratio
	(£)	(£)	
A	80,000	40,000	50%
B	125,000	50,000	40%
C	60,000	15,000	25%
Total	265,000	105,000	

Fixed costs have been estimated at £60,000.

The profit chart shown in Figure 13.5 has been compiled from this information as follows:

1. Draw the axes of the graph with profits/losses on the Y axis and activity measured in terms of sales revenue, on the X axis.

2. Calculate the cumulative sales and profit figures for the products as shown below:

Product	Cumulative Sales	Cumulative Profit*	
	£000's	£000's	
A	80	(20)	40 - 60
B	205	30	(40 + 50) - 60
C	265	45	(40 + 50 +15) - 60

*(i.e. total contribution less fixed costs)

3. Plot this information on the graph as shown.

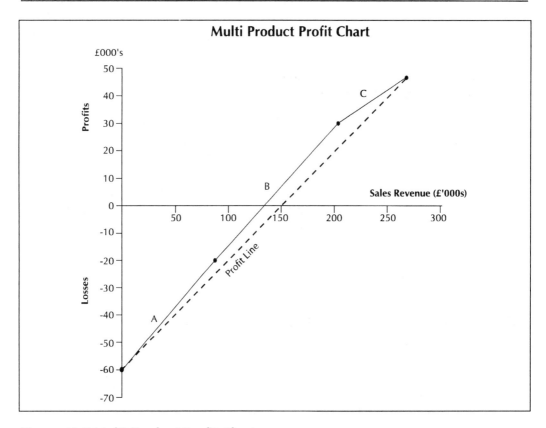

Figure 13.5 Multi Product Profit Chart

The solid lines represent the profit earned by each product and the broken line the average profitability of all three. The break even point in terms of sales revenue occurs where the latter cuts the zero profit line (i.e. £150,000) and this result can be proved as follows:

$$\text{Break even point (sales revenue)} \quad = \quad \frac{Fixed\ costs}{C.S\ ratio}$$

$$= \quad \frac{£60,000}{0.4 \ ^*} \quad = \quad £150,000$$

$$^*\quad \text{C/S ratio for product mix} \quad = \quad \frac{Total\ contribution}{Total\ sales} \quad = \quad \frac{£105,000}{£265,000} \quad = \quad 0.4$$

Note that information obtained from the graph is reliable only for the specific product mix and C/S ratios given. To evaluate other possibilities a number of charts must be compiled reflecting alternative mixes and ratios.

Limitations of CVP Analysis

Cost volume profit analysis is based on the following assumptions which are unlikely to be entirely valid in practice and which therefore limit its effectiveness.

Costs Can be Accurately Divided Into Their Fixed and Variable Elements

This may not be easy in practice where for example the fixed and variable elements of semi-variable costs may be difficult to determine accurately.

The Business Has a Single Product or a Constant Product Mix

Many firms produce more than one product and although multi product profit charts may be used, they are reliable for only a specific sales mix and stated C/S ratios.

Output is the Only Factor Influencing Costs and Revenues

CVP analysis shows how costs and revenues are affected by changes in activity. However they may also be affected by factors such as efficiency and alternative methods of production. Assessing the effect of changes in these variables would require separate CVP analysis for each set of circumstances.

There is a Linear Relationship Between Output and Costs/Revenues

The techniques we have examined are based on the assumptions that as output changes:

- Fixed costs will be unaffected.

- The variable cost per unit will remain constant.

- Selling prices will remain constant.

However in practice, some of the fixed costs are likely be stepped, variable costs per unit may fall as output rises due to economies of scale and selling prices may be reduced at higher activity levels to stimulate demand.

These factors would be more likely to produce the 'economist's break even chart' shown in Figure 13.6 than the straight line version we saw earlier:

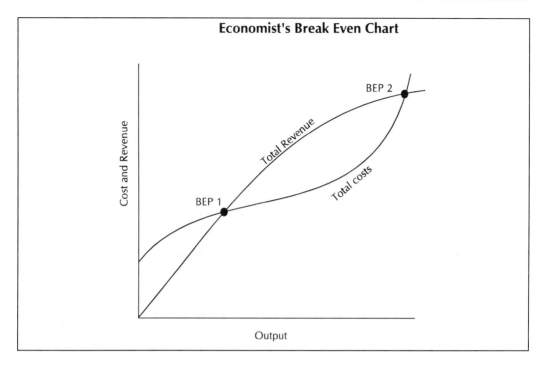

Figure 13.6 Economist's Break Even Chart

The revised chart shows that as output rises:

- The slope of the cost line reduces initially, reflecting economies of scale arising from quantity discounts, greater efficiency etc. However at higher activity levels it rises more steeply due to stepped costs and diminishing returns from operating at an activity level for which the business is not well equipped (perhaps causing breakdown of equipment, scheduling problems etc.).

- The revenue line eventually falls away as selling prices are reduced as a means of increasing sales volume.

- A second break even point is eventually reached as declining revenue becomes insufficient to cover total costs.

Figure 13.7 compares the accountant's break even chart with the curvilinear version and shows that they are similar across a range of activity known as the 'relevant range'. Consequently, CVP analysis will be more reliable within this range and should not be used at extreme levels of activity where linear estimates of costs and revenues will distort results.

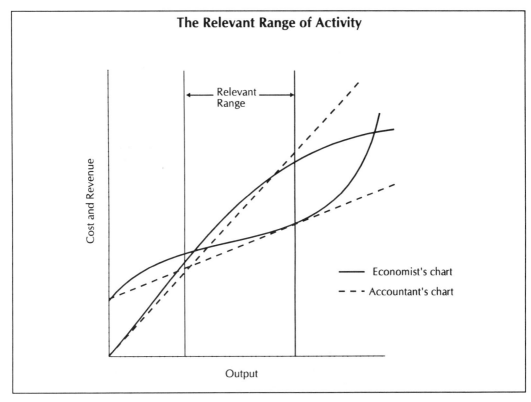

Figure 13.7 The Relevant Range of Activity

When used within the relevant range, CVP analysis can enhance the understanding of the relationship between output, costs, revenue and profit and may provide useful information for short term planning. The effect of changes in selling prices, variable costs, fixed costs and output can be quickly estimated and the identification of the margin of safety provides an assessment of risk. However as we have seen, there are limitations which should be recognised when using the technique and results should be regarded as estimates to guide decision making.

Summary

- Cost volume profit (CVP) analysis is the study of the relationship between output, revenue, costs and profit and can provide useful information for short term planning.

- The following formulae can be used:

$$\text{C/S ratio} = \frac{\textit{Contribution per unit}}{\textit{Selling price per unit}} \text{ x } 100$$

$$\text{Break even point (in units)} = \frac{\textit{Fixed costs}}{\textit{Contribution per unit}}$$

$$\text{Units required for target profit} = \frac{\textit{Fixed Costs + Target Profit}}{\textit{Contribution per unit}}$$

$$\text{The Margin of Safety} = \text{Expected activity level - Break even point}$$

- The following graphs may also be used to provide information on the effect of changes in activity levels, costs and revenues:

  - Break even charts

  - Contribution break even charts

  - Profit charts

- Multi profit charts can be used where more than one product is sold but are only valid for a specific sales mix and given C/S ratios.

- The reliability of CVP analysis is limited by the following assumptions which are unlikely to be entirely valid in practice:

  - Costs can be accurately divided into their fixed and variable elements.

  - The business has a single product or a constant product mix.

  - Output is the only factor influencing costs and revenues.

  - There is a linear relationship between output and costs/revenues.

- CVP analysis is best used within the 'relevant range' of activity as a rough indicator of expected outcomes for a particular set of circumstances.

Questions (See Appendix C for Answers)

13.1

Jean runs a shop selling telephones and has made the following estimates for next year:

Average selling price per telephone	£40
Average cost per telephone	£25
No. of telephones to be sold	24,000
Staff costs for the year	£100,000
Premises costs for the year	£90,000
Administration costs for the year	£50,000

Required

(a) Calculate the number of telephones to be sold to break-even and the margin of safety.

(b) Prepare a break-even graph showing both of these features

(c) Calculate the number of telephones to be sold to earn a profit of £30,000

(d) Briefly discuss the advantages and disadvantages of break-even analysis.

13.2

Family Tours Limited offers one week package holidays each summer on a campsite in France. The following information relates to their operations for the forthcoming season of 20 weeks duration:

- The company has agreed to hire 120 tents from the campsite owners for the entire season at a cost of £300 per tent per week.

- It is expected that on average, throughout the season 80% of the tents will be rented out to customers and that eight persons will occupy each tent.

- Family tours will pay £75 per person for flight charges.

- Guests are to be provided with a 'welcome pack' of groceries on arrival in France. The estimated cost of this is £5 per person.

- The company employs two resort representatives who are paid a salary of £250 per week each.

- A weekly one day excursion is to be provided free of charge and it is expected that all guests will take advantage of this offer. The company will incur costs of £2,400 per week for coach hire and £10 per guest for refreshments.

- Office administration costs amount to £12,000 per week.

- The price of the package holiday is £200 per person (inclusive of flights, excursion etc.).

Required

(a) (i) Calculate the break even point in terms of customers per season.

(ii) Calculate the margin of safety in customers per season and in % terms and explain your results.

(b) (i) Show the break-even point on a graph from which profits can be read at activity levels up to 18,000 customers per season.

(ii) Mark on your graph, the profit/loss expected from the following activity levels:

- the expected activity level

- 275 customers per week

- 60% renting of tents available (at the occupancy given).

13.3

Armoury Limited manufactures a single product and has produced the following information based on its anticipated level of production and sales of 4,000 units per annum.

		£ per unit
Selling price		60
Less Costs		
Direct materials	20	
Direct Labour	8	
Variable overhead	7	
Fixed overhead	10	45
Profit		15

Required

(a) Prepare a chart from which profit and contribution can be read for activity levels up to 6,000 units and show:

(i) The break-even point (in units and £'s)

    (ii)   The anticipated profit/loss at an activity level of 3,000 units per annum.

  (b) Due to world-wide shortages there is a possibility that the price of raw materials used by Armoury may increase.

    (i)   Show on your chart any adjustment(s) necessary to reflect an increase in direct materials of 10% and a decrease in selling price of 5%.

    (ii) State the revised break-even point.

  (c) Calculate the additional units which must be sold to maintain Armoury's current level of annual profit as a result of the changes referred to in (b).

Questions Without Answers

13.4

Claude operates a nightclub which he opens five nights per week for 50 weeks of the year. He charges £20 per person admission fee and for this price customers are provided with a meal, drinks and entertainment from a dance band.

It is anticipated that on average the club will attract 110 persons per night and that costs will be incurred as follows:

Entertainment

An agreement has been reached with an entertainment agency to provide a dance band each evening for the entire 50 weeks for a price of £80,000.

Power/Light/Heat

Costs are expected to be £16,000 per annum.

Loan Repayments

Claude must repay £2,000 per month on the loan he took out to buy the club.

Refreshments

It is estimated that the cost of providing food will be £8 per customer per night and drink £4 per customer per night.

Staff Costs

Four staff have been employed at a rate of £9,000 per annum each to perform catering, cleaning and other general duties.

Claude hopes to generate a profit of £70,000 per annum from the club.

Required

(a) (i) Calculate the break-even point in terms of customers per night.

(ii) Explain the meaning of the term margin of safety and calculate Claude's margin of safety (expressed in number of customers per night and in percentage terms).

(iii) Calculate the number of customers per night required in order to achieve Claude's target profit level.

(b) (i) Construct a break-even chart from which annual profit can be read and mark the break-even point.

(ii) Estimate from your chart the profit or loss arising from the following activity levels:

25,000 customers per annum
10,000 customers per annum
30,000 customers per annum

13.5

CS Limited manufactures miniature radios and has produced the following information:

	£ per radio
Selling price	40
Direct material cost	10
Direct labour cost	8
Variable overhead cost	7

Total annual fixed costs

Advertising	£40,000
Salaries	£100,000
Other fixed costs	£100,000

Current sales volume is 25,000 radios per annum.

Required

(a) Prepare a chart from which contribution and profit can be read at activity levels up to 30,000 radios per annum.

(b) On your chart label and quantify:

      (i)   The number of radios to be sold to break even.

      (ii) The profit/loss incurred on selling 20,000 radios per annum.

      (iii) The margin of safety.

  (c)   Show on your chart the adjustments necessary to reflect:

      (i)   An increase of £20,000 in advertising costs and

      (ii) an increase of 5% in the selling price.

  (d)   Calculate the annual sales volume which would be necessary to maintain the company's annual profit taking into account the charges referred to in (c) above.

13.6

European Villas Limited rents out villas in Italy to British holiday makers for 2 week periods each summer. It rents 25 villas from Italia Ltd. at £250 per week for 20 weeks each summer for this purpose.

The villas are marketed by advertising in newspapers at a total cost of £15,600 and it is expected that 80% of the available capacity will be utilised. In addition, general administration expenses of £40,000 will be incurred and maintenance fees of £60 per week per villa occupied are payable to Italia Ltd.

Required

  (a) (i)   If European Villas wishes to make profits of £30,000 for the season, at what price should it rent out the villas per booking?

      (ii) What would the total turnover be?

  (b)   A chain of travel agents has agreed to market the bookings on behalf of European Villas for a commission of 10% of the selling price and expects to achieve 90% utilisation of the villas.

      (i)   What should the selling price be in these circumstances if European Villas wished to increase its profits to £37,500?

      (ii) What would the revised total turnover be?

Chapter 14

Investment Appraisal

Learning Objectives

After completing this chapter you should be able to:

- Describe the problems associated with taking decisions which have long term implications for a business.

- Apply the following investment appraisal methods and explain their advantages and limitations:

    - The payback period.

    - The accounting rate of return.

    - The net present value.

    - The internal rate of return.

- Explain the concept of the time value of money.

Introduction

Having looked at information for short term planning and decision making in the previous two chapters we will now consider decisions with longer term implications, such as offering a new product or service, purchasing new equipment or acquiring new premises.

Undertaking such projects often requires the initial investment of a large sum of money in the hope that future benefits will justify this outlay. Decisions taken can be difficult to reverse and may incur costs and produce benefits over many years. Consequently they may have a crucial bearing on the long term success of an organisation and it is essential that adequate information is available to guide those responsible for taking such long term investment decisions.

As with short term decision making the basic decision rule is that the benefits arising from the decision taken should exceed the associated costs. However the long term implications of investment decisions pose particular problems and in this chapter we will consider these and examine various methods which may be used to evaluate investment opportunities.

Appraisal Methods

We will consider the following four methods of investment appraisal:

- The payback period

- The accounting rate of return

- The net present value

- The internal rate of return

Each will be demonstrated and explained using the information given in Example 14.1 below:

Example 14.1

Gibson Limited is considering marketing a new product which would require an initial investment of £100,000 in production equipment.

It has been estimated that each unit produced could be sold for £10 and that variable costs will amount to £5 per unit. The following sales forecast has been prepared for the next 5 years:

Year	Units
1	6,000
2	10,000
3	8,000
4	4,000
5	2,000

After five years demand is expected to fall below the level which would justify further production and the product would be discontinued.

Required

On the basis of this information determine whether the company should accept the proposal and make the necessary investment.

The first task is to assess the incremental cash flows resulting from the proposed investment as shown below:

Year	Cash Inflows* £	CashOutflows† £	Net Cash Flow £
1	60,000	30,000	30,000
2	100,000	50,000	50,000
3	80,000	40,000	40,000
4	40,000	20,000	20,000
5	20,000	10,000	10,000
			150,000
Initial investment	0	100,000	(100,000)
Total	300,000	250,000	50,000

* units sold x £10 *each*

† units sold x £5 *each*

Cash inflows have been compared with outflows to show the projected 'net cash flow' in each year. The resulting figures show that the initial investment of £100,000 is expected to produce additional net cash flows of £150,000 over the next five years and that a surplus of £50,000 is therefore anticipated. This may give the impression that the proposal must be worthwhile but as we shall see later in the chapter, this is not necessarily true.

The Payback Period

The payback period considers the length of time the project will take to return the original investment. To calculate this we must project the cumulative return at the end of each year as shown below:

Year	Net Cash Flow £	Cumulative Net Cash Flow £
1	30,000	30,000
2	50,000	80,000
3	40,000	120,000
4	20,000	140,000
5	10,000	150,000

This shows that by the end of year two net returns will amount £80,000 which will be insufficient to repay the original £100,000 invested. By the end of the third year cumulative returns are expected to reach £120,000 and repayment of the investment is therefore expected to occur at some time during the third year.

A more precise figure can be estimated as follows:

$$\text{Payback period} \quad = \quad 2 \quad + \quad \frac{£20,000}{£40,000} \quad \text{Years}$$

$$= \quad 2.5 \text{ years} \quad \text{(ie. 2 years 6 months)}$$

As net returns of £80,000 are anticipated in the first two years, only £20,000 of the £40,000 expected in year 3 is needed to recover the £100,000 investment. Note that this estimate assumes that cash flows occur evenly throughout year 3 (ie. half of the net cash flow will arise exactly halfway through the year).

Accept or Reject Decisions

When deciding whether or not an investment opportunity should be approved (as in Example 14.1) the payback period is compared with a pre-determined target. If for example Gibson Limited required all investments to pay back within 3 years the project in question, with a payback period of 2.5 years, would be approved.

Choosing Between Alternative Investments

Where there are a number of alternative investment opportunities from which a choice must be made, those which pay back quickest are preferable.

Evaluation of the Payback Period

Advantages

1. *It is simple to understand and use.*

2. *It promotes caution in appraisal as it favours those projects which return the initial investment quickest.*

Limitations

1. *It ignores any cash flows occurring after the payback period.*

    We will examine this problem by considering another example:

Example 14.2

Gibson Limited has an alternative opportunity also requiring an initial investment of £ 100,000 with the following projected net cash flows:

OPTION 2

Year	Net Cash Flow £	Cumulative Net cash Flow £
1	30,000	30,000
2	50,000	80,000
3	20,000	100,000
4	120,000	
5	110,000	

Payback period = 3 years

This second option with its longer payback period of 3 years would be rejected in favour of the first. However it produces far greater returns than Option 1 in years 4 and 5 which would more than compensate for the slightly lower returns in year 3 and is therefore likely to prove a more attractive investment. Using the payback period would therefore produce a misleading result in this case.

2. *It ignores the timing of cash flows within the payback period.*

Again this will be illustrated using an example:

Example 14.3

A third option for Gibson Limited, also requiring an investment of £100,000 is expected to produce the following net cash flows:

OPTION 3

Year	Net Cash Flow £
1	60,000
2	20,000
3	40,000
4	20,000
5	10,000

The payback period in this case is 2.5 years and Option 3 would be therefore be ranked equally with Option 1.

However, if we look at the cash flows in years 1 and 2 we can see that although in each case £80,000 is earned over the two years, the timing of the flows differs:

	OPTION 1	OPTION 3
	Net Cash Flow	Net Cash Flow
Year	£	£
1	30,000	60,000
2	50,000	20,000
Total	80,000	80,000

Option 3 generates returns more quickly than Option 1 with twice as much in the first year and would therefore be more attractive. However the payback period, which does not consider these timing differences, fails to indicate this.

We will consider the implications of these timing differences in more detail later in the chapter.

The Accounting Rate of Return (ARR)

The accounting rate of return (or 'return on capital employed') assesses the profitability of an investment by expressing the average profit per annum as a percentage of the sum invested.

Applying this to Option 1 from Example 14.1:

$$\text{ARR} = \frac{Average\ profit\ p.a.}{Initial\ investment} \times 100\ \%$$

$$= \frac{£10,000\ ^*}{£100,000} \times 100$$

$$= 10\%$$

Working

$$^*\ Average\ profit\ p.a. = \frac{Total\ profit}{No.\ of\ years}$$

$$= \frac{(£30,000+£50,000+£40,000+£20,000+£10,000) - £100,000}{5\ years}$$

$$= \frac{£50,000}{5\ years} = £10,000$$

Note that the £100,000 investment must be included as a cost when determining total profit.

Alternative ARR Calculation

An alternative method of calculating the ARR is to express the average profit per annum as a percentage of the *average* (rather than total) investment as demonstrated below:

$$\text{ARR} \quad = \quad \frac{£10,000}{£50,000^{\,*}} \quad \text{x} \quad 100 \quad = \quad 20\%$$

* *The investment is assumed to expire at a constant rate over time and the average investment can*
   therefore be estimated by halving the total figure (ie. £100,000 ÷ 2 = £50,000).

Although either may be used, the method chosen should be applied in all cases to ensure that projects are evaluated consistently.

Accept or Reject Decisions

When determining whether or not an investment proposal should be accepted, a target is established and approval given only for projects expected to attain this rate.

Choosing Between Alternative Investments

When choosing between alternatives, investments are ranked in order of their ARR with the highest first.

Evaluation of the ARR Method

Advantages

1. *It is relatively easy to understand and use.*

2. *It incorporates all returns from the investment (Unlike the payback period).*

Limitations

1. *It ignores the timing of Cash Flows.*

    To illustrate this problem we will compare the original proposal with a fourth option, details of which are given below:

Example 14.4

	OPTION 1	OPTION 4
Year	Net Cash Flow £	Net Cash Flow £
0	(100,000)	(100,000)
1	30,000	5,000
2	50,000	5,000
3	40,000	5,000
4	20,000	5,000
5	10,000	130,000
Net Return	50,000	50,000

NB. The present is referred to as year 0 (i.e. before any time has elapsed).

As the investment and total cash flows for Option 4 are equal to Option 1, the ARR will also be 10% and the proposals would be ranked equally. However the timing of the cash flows is very different and Option 1, from which far higher returns are expected in earlier years, would be a more attractive proposition.

We will now consider the implications of these timing differences in some detail.

The Time Value of Money

To establish the importance of differences in the timing of cash flows we will look at another example:

Example 14.5

Keith and Gary have been asked to do a little promotional work for a local sports club over the next year for which each will be paid £1,000.

The club have offered to pay Gary on completion of the work in one year's time but Keith is to be paid immediately.

Who has the better offer?

Most people would choose to take the money now, even if they had no pressing requirement for it. Why is this?

The reason is that there is a benefit in holding money for a period of time, known as the time value of money. Choosing to take the money now would enable Keith to bank it for the next year and earn interest. Assuming that interest rates are 10% per annum, the relative financial positions at the end of the year would therefore be as follows:

	Keith	**Gary**
From Club	£1,000	£1,000
Interest @ 10%	£100	0
Cash held at end of year	£1,100	£1,000

Although each receives an equal amount from the club, Keith is in a better position at the end of the year with £1,100 compared to the £1,000 held by Gary. To compensate for receiving his payment later Gary would require £1,100 from the club at the end of the year. As the £1,000 received by Keith immediately is worth more than an equal sum received in one year's time, we can conclude that the timing of cash flows is important and should be considered when determining their value.

Net Present Value

Having established that the timing of cash flows is important, we will now see how this factor can be incorporated in the appraisal of Option 1 given in Example 14.1 for which the following projections were made:

Year	Net Cash Flow £
0	(100,000)
1	30,000
2	50,000
3	40,000
4	20,000
5	10,000
Net return	50,000

The addition of expected cash flows shows that a net surplus of £50,000 is anticipated over the five year period. However as we have seen, sums arising in different time periods are not comparable. Adding them in this way is like adding pounds and dollars. To do this they would have to be expressed in common terms by converting the dollars to pounds using the exchange rate. Similarly, before adding cash flows occurring in different time periods they must also be converted into a comparable measure and the most popular method is to express the value of all cash flows in today's terms. This is known as their 'net present value' (NPV).

Calculating the Net Present Value

To calculate net present values a conversion factor must be used (The equivalent of the exchange rate used for comparing currencies). This is known as the discount factor and can be used to determine the NPV of cash flows as shown below:

$$\text{NPV} \; = \; \text{Cash flow} \; \text{x} \; \text{Discount Factor}$$

The relevant discount factor (DF) can be obtained using discount tables which you will find in Appendix A at the back of the book. These give the factor for any year at a given interest rate and if you look up the factor for year 1 at a rate of 10% you will see that it is 0.909. The net present value of cash flows occurring at the end of one year can therefore be obtained by multiplying by 0.909.

So for example, a receipt of £1,100 in one year's time expressed in today's terms with interest rates at 10% is:

$$
\begin{aligned}
\text{NPV} \; &= \; \text{Cash flow} \; \text{x} \; \text{Discount Factor} \\
&= \; £1,100 \quad \text{x} \quad 0.909 \\
&= \; £1,000
\end{aligned}
$$

i.e. receiving £1,100 in one year's time is equivalent to receiving £1,000 today (as we saw earlier in Example 14.5).

Turning now to Gibson Limited's Option 1 and again assuming an interest rate of 10%, the NPV of the £30,000 expected in year 1 is:

$$
\begin{aligned}
\text{NPV} \; &= \; \text{Cash flow} \; \text{x} \; \text{Discount Factor} \\
&= \; £30,000 \quad \text{x} \quad 0.909 \\
&= \; £27,270
\end{aligned}
$$

i.e. £30,000 received in one year's time is equivalent to a receipt of £27,270 immediately.

The NPV for the net cash flows expected in the remaining years can be ascertained in the same way as illustrated below:

Year	Net Cash Flow £	10% D.F.	NPV £
1	30,000	0.909	27,270
2	50,000	0.826	41,300
3	40,000	0.751	30,040
4	20,000	0.683	13,660
5	10,000	0.621	6,210
NPV of future cash flows			118,480
Original investment			(100,000)
NPV of project			18,480

For each year the cash flow has been multiplied by the relevant discount factor obtained from Appendix A to obtain the net present value. Note that the further into the future the cash flows are expected, the less they are worth in today's terms. For example the £10,000 anticipated in year 5 is worth little more than half that amount in today's terms.

Having expressed all future cash flows in today's terms they can then be compared with the £100,000 investment required to generate those returns. The resulting NPV of £18,480 for the project indicates that expected future returns (when expressed in today's terms) exceed the investment required to generate those returns by £18,480 and that the investment is therefore financially acceptable. If the cash flow forecasts were to prove accurate, investing in the project would be equivalent to receiving a sum of £18,480 immediately.

Any project with a positive NPV is expected to provide a net benefit and is therefore financially acceptable.

To test your understanding of this technique you should now calculate the NPV of Option 4, for which the following cash flows were given earlier. Check your result with the solution supplied:

Year	Net Cash Flow £
0	(100,000)
1	5,000
2	5,000
3	5,000
4	5,000
5	130,000
Total	50,000

Solution

Year	Net Cash Flow £	10% D.F.	NPV £
0	(100,000)	1.000	(100,000)
1	5,000	0.909	4,545
2	5,000	0.826	4,130
3	5,000	0.751	3,755
4	5,000	0.683	3,415
5	130,000	0.621	80,730
NPV of project			(3,425)

Note that a discount factor of 1 issued for year 0 as the cash flow is already expressed in today's terms.

In this case the negative NPV of the project indicates that the present value of expected future returns falls below the £100,000 investment required and that the proposal should therefore be rejected on financial grounds.

Annuities

An annuity is a cash flow of the same amount for a number of successive years. An example can be seen in the above solution where there is a net cash outflow of £5,000 in years 1-4. The net present value of these cash flows was determined by multiplying the cash flow in each year by the discount factor for that year and amounts to £15,845 for the four years (£4,545 + £4,130 + £3,755 + £3,415). However with annuities a quicker method can be used in which, instead of performing calculations for each year and adding the results, the cash flow is multiplied by the sum of the discount factors for the year in question as follows:

Year	Cash Flow £	Annuity Factor	NPV £
1-4	5,000	3.169*	15,845

*(0.909 + 0.826 + 0.751 + 0.683)

Rather than adding up discount factors for each year, the relevant annuity factor can be determined using an annuity table which you will find in appendix B at the back of the book.

Choosing Between Alternative Investments

When evaluating alternative investments there may be more than one with a positive NPV, indicating that each is financially worthwhile. Where a choice must be made the alternatives should be ranked in order of their NPV with the highest first.

Evaluation of the Net Present Value Method

Advantages

1. *It incorporates all cash flows expected from the investment.*

2. *The timing of the cash flows is recognised.*

Limitations

1. *It assumes that all cash flows occur at the end of the relevant year.* Clearly this will not be the case in practice where revenues will be received and costs incurred throughout the year. The year end assumption will therefore show cash flows later than they actually occur and the resulting NPV is likely to be understated. In theory the precise timing of cash flows could be incorporated using amended discount factors but for simplicity year end flows tend to be assumed.

The Internal Rate of Return

Sources and Cost of Capital

The capital used to finance long term investment projects, whether obtained from a bank or other sources, will have a cost. In order to increase the value of the business and therefore the wealth of its owners, investments must generate returns which exceed this cost. Thus for a business using funds supplied by a bank charging interest at 10% per annum, only investments generating a return in excess of 10% p.a. will be worthwhile. Hence another method of investment appraisal is to calculate the anticipated rate of return (known as the 'internal rate of return') and compare this with the cost of capital used by the business.

Calculating the Internal Rate of Return (IRR)

The IRR is the discount rate which when applied to estimated cash flows, would result in a NPV of zero. To demonstrate its calculation we will consider Option 1 once again. Having earlier calculated that the NPV at an interest rate of 10% is £18,480 we have established that the project is acceptable at this rate. We can therefore conclude that its return must exceed 10%.

We can now choose another discount rate and by re-calculating the NPV, determine the acceptability of the investment at this rate. We will try using 25%:

Year	Net Cash Flow £	25% D.F.	NPV £
0	(100,000)	1.000	(100,000)
1	30,000	0.800	24,000
2	50,000	0.640	32,000
3	40,000	0.512	20,480
4	20,000	0.410	8,200
5	10,000	0.328	3,280
NPV of project			(12,040)

As the NPV is negative, the project would no longer be worthwhile if the capital used cost 25% p.a. Consequently it must generate a return of less than 25%.

We now know that the return is greater than 10% but below 25% and the actual figure can be estimated by plotting the NPV's obtained using these rates on a graph as illustrated in Figure 14.1.

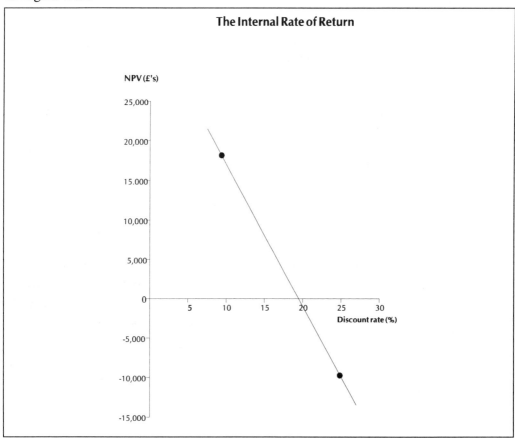

Figure 14.1 The Internal Rate of Return

The line drawn between the two points plotted shows that the discount rate producing a NPV of zero (i.e. the IRR) is a little under 20%. This estimation technique is called interpolation and a more exact figure can be obtained using the following formula:

$$IRR = DR1 + \frac{Positive\ NPV}{Positive\ NPV + Negative\ NPV} \quad x \quad (DR2 - DR1)$$

Where, DR1 is the lower discount rate

DR2 is the higher discount rate

Applying this to the example:

$$IRR = 10\% + \frac{18{,}480}{18{,}480 + 12{,}040} \quad x \quad (25\% - 10\%)$$

$$= 10\% + (0.6 \quad x \quad 15\%)$$

$$= 19\%$$

As the finance is costing only 10% p.a. and the project has an estimated return of 19% we can conclude that it is financially acceptable. This confirms the result of our earlier NPV calculation where the positive figure indicated that the project was worthwhile.

To summarise, the IRR can be determined by:

(a) Identifying by a process of trial and error, a cost of capital which generates a positive NPV and one which produces a negative result.

(b) Calculating the IRR (which must lie between these percentage rates) using interpolation.

We now have two discounted cash flow (DCF) methods which can be used to determine whether an investment is financially acceptable. We can either prove that it has:

- A positive NPV   or,

- An IRR in excess of the cost of capital.

Evaluation of the IRR Method

Advantages

Like the NPV method, the IRR incorporates all cash flows arising from the investment and takes account of their timing.

Limitations

The IRR may give misleading results when choosing between alternative investments. This can occur for two reasons:

1. *Differing investment values.*

   This point is best explained using an example:

Example 14.6

The following information has been prepared in respect of two investment proposals:

	Project A	Project B
Initial investment	£20,000	£90,000
IRR	40%	30%

Appraising the investments on the basis of the IRR, Project A would be ranked higher with a 40% return. However a 30% return on an investment of £90,000 may be preferable to 40% on £20,000 and using the IRR may therefore be misleading.

2. *The results obtained using the IRR may contradict those produced using the NPV.*

   When appraising alternative investments one project may have a higher IRR and another a greater NPV. The reasons for this are beyond the scope of this text but you should note that the NPV is a theoretically sounder method and consequently the IRR should not be used to rank alternative investments.

Which Method Should be Used?

Having now considered four different appraisal methods you may be wondering which should be used. In practice many organisations use more than one method when evaluating investment opportunities. This was confirmed in a survey of methods used by 100 large UK firms carried out by R H Pike in 1992 which produced the following results:

	Total	Always	Mostly	Often	Rarely
Firms using	%	%	%	%	%
Payback	94	62	14	12	6
Accounting rate of return	50	21	5	13	17
Internal rate of return	81	54	7	13	7
Net present value	74	33	14	16	11

Source: Pike & Neale, *Corporate Finance and Investment*

Results indicated that almost two thirds of those surveyed reported using three or more appraisal techniques. The most popular method was the payback period, despite the limitations identified earlier. This method is often used as a screening device providing a first hurdle for potential investments. Only projects paying back within a specified time period are considered and those expected to do so are further evaluated using perhaps the NPV or IRR methods. The payback period is also popular where investments are particularly risky and the business is seeking projects which return the initial outlay as soon as possible.

In respect of the two discounted cash flow (DCF) methods, Pike's survey indicated a preference for internal rate of return despite the fact that net present value is theoretically a better method. This may be due to the fact that IRR results, indicating a percentage return on investment are perhaps more easily understood and communicated than a net present value figure.

Limitations of all Methods

The results obtained from all four methods are based on predictions of future costs and revenues through the estimation of selling prices, sales volume, costs, etc. However making predictions many years in advance is a difficult task and the results produced by any method will be of little value if projections are wildly inaccurate. Consequently the data used and results obtained should be considered carefully and any doubts about their validity investigated before important long term decisions are taken.

Non-Financial Considerations

In the course of this chapter we have examined various methods which may be useful in assessing the financial implications of investment opportunities. However there are likely to be other non-financial factors which also merit consideration and projects which may be financially worthwhile may be rejected for other reasons. For example changing an operating method may result in very poor staff morale and perhaps industrial action and approval for such a project may be delayed or postponed even where attractive returns are anticipated.

Although financial implications are important there are other factors influencing the long term success of a business and the appraisal techniques we have considered should be used in conjunction with other available information to inform managers of the expected consequences of their actions.

Project Control and Review

The techniques we have examined in this chapter are concerned with the provision of information which may assist management when taking investment decisions. However, appraising the viability of investment opportunities is only the starting point and in order to ensure that projected benefits are realised it is important that they are effectively managed and controlled. Actual outcomes should therefore be monitored and compared with those predicted and action taken to remedy any problems arising.

Having completed a project its final results should be compared with those predicted in its initial appraisal. Although at that stage it is too late too affect the outcome of the project itself, reviewing results in this way may help in planning future projects of a similar nature. The reliability of forecasting techniques can also be assessed and operational inefficiencies which could affect other activities may be highlighted. A formal review process can also help to promote a more effective appraisal system. If managers are held accountable for actual results they may be more inclined to investigate proposals thoroughly at the outset and investment in dubious projects may be discouraged.

Summary

- The long term success of a business depends on its ability to identify and take advantage of profitable investment opportunities.

- Decision makers need information for guidance when assessing potential investments.

- The Payback Period measures the time taken to repay the original investment. Its biggest drawback is its failure to recognise the 'time value of money'.

- The Accounting Rate of Return indicates the profitability of an investment. However the timing of cash flows is again ignored.

- Discounted cash flow (DCF) methods allow for timing differences by expressing all cash flows in today's terms.

- The net present value (NPV) method expresses the value of expected future cash flows in today's terms and compares these with the initial investment to show the anticipated net benefit or deficit. Proposals with a positive NPV are expected to generate returns which exceed the initial investment and are therefore financially acceptable.

- The internal rate of return (IRR) measures the expected return from an investment. Where this exceeds the cost of capital the project is financially worthwhile.

- As investment appraisal methods are based on projections of future events, the data used and results obtained should be carefully considered before taking important long term decisions.

- Non-financial implications of investment decisions may have a great bearing on the success of an organisation and should be considered fully.

- Once approved, the implementation of investment projects should be carefully managed and final outcomes reviewed.

Questions   (See Appendix C for Answers)

14.1

The following estimates have been made concerning two possible investment projects, which are mutually exclusive.

	Project A £	Project B £
Initial capital expenditure	200,000	200,000
Net cash inflows Year 1	100,000	30,000
2	80,000	50,000
3	60,000	80,000
4	20,000	120,000
Estimated scrap value at end of year 4	40,000	20,000

The organisation's cost of capital is 10%

Required

(a)   For each project calculate the accounting rate of return, the payback period and the net present value.

(b)   Explain which project you would recommend for acceptance.

14.2

International Engineering plc is considering marketing a new product for which it would require an investment of £460,000 in production equipment.

The product would be sold for £20 per unit and forecast demand over the next five years is as follows:

Year	Demand(units)
1	40,000
2	45,000
3	55,000
4	35,000
5	35,000

After this period it is expected that demand will fall below the point at which production would be viable and the equipment would therefore be sold for £100,000.

Other information is given as follows:

Estimated Costs

- Direct Costs   £12 per unit
- Promotion Costs   £108,000 (year one only)
- Other Costs (including depreciation)   £280,000 per annum

Depreciation Policy

Depreciation is provided for on a straight line basis.

Cost of Capital

International Engineering's cost of capital is 12%.

Required

  (a) Calculate:

    (i) The net present value of the project

    (ii) The payback period.

  (b) State whether or not you believe the project should be approved, giving reasons for your conclusion.

14.3

A hotel is considering whether to replace a vending machine. The existing machine could be sold for £8,000 and a replacement obtained for £22,000. This would allow the hotel to sell a greater variety of snacks and sweets and it is anticipated that as a result net cash flows would increase by £4,000 per year for the next four years. At the end of this period the machine would be bought back by the original supplier for £6,000.

The hotel is able to borrow from the bank at an interest rate of 12% per annum.

Required

  (a) Calculate the payback period, net present value and internal rate of return of the proposal.

  (b) Explain how each of these might assist the hotel in making a decision and state whether or not you would recommend purchasing the new machine.

14.4

Ryan is considering operating a catering outlet on a retail park and has two options, details of which are given below:

Option 1

This entails purchasing a van for £8,000 payable immediately from which the following sales are expected over the next four years.

Year	Sales (£)
1	80,000
2	100,000
3	72,000
4	68,000

A mark up of one third will be applied to the cost of goods when setting selling prices.

Annual running costs of the van have been estimated at £3,000 and it is expected to be sold for £2,000 at the end of year 4. One person will be employed to operate the van for an annual salary of £12,000.

Option 2

This would involve leasing a unit on the site for a four year period for an immediate payment of £5,000 and an annual rent of £2,500. Annual wage costs are expected to amount to £10,000. A mark up of 50% on cost will be applied to determine selling prices and the following sales forecast has been made:

Year	Sales (£)
1	60,000
2	54,000
3	54,000
4	42,000

Ryan can obtain the necessary finance from a bank at an interest rate of 15% per annum.

Required

(a)   Calculate the payback period and net present value of each proposal.

(b)   Advise Ryan as to which option should be chosen.

Questions Without Answers

14.5

Middletower Limited owns a caravan park which it will operate for the next four years before selling the land to a local golf club.

In recent years it has suffered dwindling occupancy rates and the company is considering two alternative proposals to remedy this.

Proposal A

This entails refurbishment of the park at a total cost of £60,000, of which half would be payable immediately and the remainder after one year. It is thought that this measure would attract net additional income of £20,000 in each of the next four years.

Proposal B

This would involve paying a marketing agency £60,000 immediately and £5,000 per year in each of the next four years. The increased customer awareness resulting from this arrangement is expected to produce additional net cash flows of £20,000 per annum for the next two years, £30,000 in year 3 and £45,000 in year 4.

Middletower could obtain the necessary finance at an interest rate of 10% per annum.

Required

(a) Calculate the payback period and the net present value for each proposal and state, with reasons, which you would recommend.

(b) Discuss the merits and limitations of the two investment appraisal methods used in (a).

(c) Briefly highlight any other factors which may be worth considering before Middletower makes a decision.

14.6

Fiona's Fashions a national fashion store with its own production facilities is considering investing in one of the two following projects:

Project 1

The first option is the exploitation of an opportunity to market 'Razza' sweatshirts taking advantage of the current popularity of a sports personality. The initial investment required to establish additional production and merchandising facilities is £100,000 and the estimated sales volumes (at a selling price of £20 each) are as follows:

Year	Units
1	10,000
2	15,000
3	5,000
4	3,000

At the end of year four the demand is expected to cease at which time the production facilities will be sold for £10,000.

It is estimated that the labour costs of the sweatshirts will be £4.50 each, materials will amount to £5.50 each, licensing fees will be £3.25 per sweatshirt sold and variable overheads will amount to £2.75 each.

Project 2

The second alternative is to produce and sell denim ties. It is believed that at a selling price of £10 each sales volume will be 10,000 per annum for the next six years but will fall below the level at which production would be viable after that period. The production facilities (which would cost £100,000 initially) would therefore be sold for £30,000 at the end of year 6.

Should the project be accepted, variable costs will amount to £7 per tie and the allocation of existing fixed costs will be at a rate of £1 per tie.

The projects are believed to have an equal level of risk attached to them and Fiona could obtain the necessary finance at an interest rate of 15% per annum.

You are required to:

(a) Appraise the projects using:

(i)   A DCF method.

(ii) Any other method of investment appraisal.

(b) State, giving your reasons, which project you believe should be accepted.

14.7

Beacon Chemicals plc is considering the erection of a new plant to produce a chemical named X14. The new plant's capital cost is estimated at £100,000 and if its construction is approved now, the plant can be erected and commence production by the end of 19X4. £50,000 has already been spent on research and development work. Estimates of revenues and costs arising from the operation of the new plant appear below:

	19X5	19X6	19X7	19X8	19X9
Sales price – £ per unit	100	120	120	100	80
Sales volume – units	800	1,000	1,200	1,000	800
Variable costs – £ per unit	50	50	40	40	40
Fixed costs £000's	30	30	30	30	30

If the new plant is erected sales of some existing products will be lost and this will result in a loss of contribution of £15,000 per year over its life.

The accountant has informed you that the fixed costs include depreciation of £20,000 per annum on the new plant. They also include an allocation of £10,000 for fixed overheads. A separate study has indicated that if the new plant was built, incremental overheads, excluding depreciation, arising from its construction would be £8,000 per year.

The plant would require additional working capital of £30,000.

For the purposes of your initial evaluation ignore taxation.

Required

(a) Prepare a statement of the incremental revenues, costs and net cash flows arising from a decision to build the plant.

(b) Calculate the payback period to the nearest year.

(c) Compute the net present value of the project using an 8% discount rate.

(d) Write a short report to the managing director recommending acceptance or otherwise of the project. Explain the reasons for your recommendation and state what further investigations may be necessary.

(ACCA)

14.8

Orwell Chemicals Ltd. has recently received an offer to produce a new type of synthetic fibre for a large international company. The offer is to produce 14,000 tonnes of the new fibre each year for a three-year period at a price of £44 per tonne. The directors of Orwell Ltd. are currently considering the offer and have collected the following information:

(i) New equipment costing £85,000 will be required immediately in order to commence production. The equipment required is highly specialised and can only be used by the company for production of the new fibre. At the end of the three-year period the equipment will be sold for an estimated £6,000.

(ii) Eleven new workers will be required to help produce the fibre. The wage costs for the additional workforce is expected to be £200,000 in the first year and will rise at a compound rate of 10% per annum. Recruitment and selection costs, to be paid at the outset, are expected to be £15,000. At the end of the three-year contract the workers will no longer be required and redundancy payments of £2,000 per worker will be paid.

(iii) Overheads relating to the contract are estimated at £60,000 per annum. One third of this figure is arrived at by the reallocation of existing overheads to the contract.

(iv) The production process requires the use of 6,000 tonnes chemical XT3 each year in order to produce the required amount of fibre. The company already has 3,000 tonnes of this chemical in stock. The original cost of this stock was £16 per tonne, however, if the contract is not undertaken the chemical could not be used in any other of the company's production processes or resold in the market. The directors have agreed that, if the new fibre is not produced, the existing stock of XT3 will be disposed of immediately at a cost to the company of £2 per tonne. The replacement cost of the chemical is £20 per tonne.

(v) The production process also requires the use of 8,000 tonnes of chemical ZF6 each year to produce the required amount of fibre. The company has 4,000 tonnes of this chemical already in stock. The original cost of this stock is £22 per tonne and the replacement cost is £25 per tonne. This chemical is widely used in other production processes of the company.

The directors of Orwell Chemicals believe that successful execution of the contract may result in further contracts being offered by the same company. Orwell Chemicals has an estimated cost of capital of 12%. Ignore taxation.

Required

(a) Prepare a statement showing those incremental cash flows which are relevant to a decision concerning whether or not to accept the offer.

(b) Calculate the net present value of the offer.

(c) State whether or not you believe the offer should be accepted.

(d) Outline the basic principles to be applied when identifying relevant costs and benefits relating to the offer.

(ACCA)

14.9

Aquaplan Limited is considering investing in a second-hand marine cruiser which will be used to take tourists on one-day pleasure cruises. The initial cost of the vessel is expected to be £600,000 and maintenance costs £16,000 per annum. It is anticipated that after three years it will no longer be possible to operate the boat and it will be sold for £60,000

Forecasts indicate that demand will amount to 12,000 cruises per annum of which 20% will be taken by children receiving a 50% discount on the normal cruise price of £30. Each person (including children) will receive refreshments included in this price and it has been estimated that these will cost Aquaplan £3 per person.

Staff cots for the venture are expected to amount to £35,000 per annum in year 1 and wage rises of 10% per annum are expected for the following two years. Other costs and revenues (excluding the re-sale of the cruiser) are expected to rise at a rate of 5% per annum.

Advertising posters are to be purchased on the first day of each year for £3,000 and the supplier has agreed to hold this price constant for the three year period.

Aquaplan's cost of capital is 10%.

Required

(a)   Calculate the net present value of the project and advise Aquaplan as to whether or not they should proceed.

Chapter 15

Budgetary Control

Learning Objectives

After completing this chapter you should be able to:

- Explain the purpose of budgetary control.

- Describe how a budget may be compiled.

- Prepare a cash budget and explain the purpose of such a statement.

- Explain the budgetary control process.

- Demonstrate how flexible budgeting can be used to generate effective information for control purposes.

- Describe the potential benefits and problems associated with budgetary control systems.

Introduction

One of the main responsibilities of managers is planning for the future by deciding what should be done and how it will be achieved. This will require detailed analysis of the organisation itself and the environment in which it operates in order to determine the best way forward. Having developed long term strategies and compiled detailed plans, control procedures must be established which help to ensure that activities proceed as intended and objectives are ultimately realised. These planning and control activities occur in the following four stages:

1. Setting Objectives

The first stage in the process is to determine the objectives of the business. Establishing objectives gives decision makers a basis for evaluating alternative courses of action. If for example the primary aim of a business is to maximise profits, decision makers can assess alternatives according to their effect on profit. In the case of non-profit making organisations such as hospitals or local authorities the objective may be to provide the best level of service given the resources available and decisions can be taken accordingly.

Assessing performance in terms of achieving objectives can be facilitated by expressing the objectives in measurable terms such as a target rate of return on capital or a target market share. Actual results can then be measured in the same terms and compared with targets to assess the extent to which they have been achieved.

2. Long Term Planning

Policies for the attainment of long term objectives are determined in the strategic planning process. This is also known as 'corporate' planning and normally covers a period of at least 3-4 years. It is normally undertaken by senior management and will include:

(i)   *An internal audit* of the business identifying strengths and weaknesses in areas such as financial performance, management skills, employee morale and physical resources.

(ii)   *An external audit* of the environment in which the business operates to identify potential opportunities and threats. This will involve investigation of factors such as competition, government policy, economic issues and social trends.

From these studies strategies must be drawn up to capitalise on strengths identified, overcome weaknesses, counter threats and take advantage of any opportunities. These strategies may be concerned with issues such as the products or services to be offered, the markets they are to be sold in and the means of providing them.

Advantages of Long Term Planning

- **It focuses attention on the long term.** It is all too easy for managers to concentrate on the short term problems and issues affecting the business. Although these may be important it is essential that the longer term issues affecting the organisation are also fully addressed.

- **Polices and strategies are clarified for those expected to carry them out.**

- **It should help to co-ordinate activities.** Clear guidance in terms of the proposed direction of the business should help to ensure that managers plan activities which complement one another.

Potential Problems in Long Term Planning

As well as the advantages described above, senior managers should consider the following possible problems associated with long term planning:

- **It may cause inflexibility.** Rigid adherence to long term plans may create problems when circumstances change. However, a successful business should be flexible enough to adapt to change.

- **Unrealistic objectives can de-motivate.** In order to motivate those expected to achieve them, objectives set should be seen as reasonable and achievable.

- **Time and cost.** Appraising internal factors and the external environment, drawing up alternative proposals and evaluating these can be very time consuming and expensive. This time and resulting cost should be evaluated in terms of the benefits expected from the process.

3. Short Term Planning

Having determined long term strategies, detailed plans must be prepared indicating the action to be taken in the short term. Short term 'operational' planning is usually carried out by functional managers under the guidance of senior management and may cover a period of approximately one to two years.

4. Control

The compilation of plans provides guidance for subsequent decision making but will not necessarily ensure the attainment of objectives. Activities must be continually monitored to ensure that they proceed as planned. Any which do not should be investigated promptly in order that any necessary remedial action can be taken.

Budgeting

In this chapter we will examine the most widely used technique for short term planning and control, budgeting.

A budget is a financial or quantitative expression of a plan of action prepared and approved prior to the period to which it relates.

As stated earlier, expressing plans in measurable terms helps in the control process in which the results of activities can be measured in the same terms to identify any deviations between planned and actual outcomes.

Organising for Control

To facilitate short term planning and control, organisations are usually divided into specific functions or departments for which a manager is assigned responsibility. To enable managers to control the activities for which they are responsible, authority for decision making must be delegated. This is known as de-centralisation and when determining the extent to which responsibility is to delegated in this way the following benefits and potential drawbacks should be considered.

Advantages of Decentralisation

- *More effective decision making*. Decisions taken by junior managers will be supported by more detailed knowledge of the activities for which they are responsible. In addition, as decisions need not be referred to senior management they can be taken more quickly.

- *Motivation.* Delegating authority and responsibility is often an effective means of increasing motivation as employees feel more involved in the management of the business.

- *Management development.* Assigning responsibility for a specific function or activity can help in developing the management skills which will be necessary for more senior roles.

- *Strategic implications.* Curtailing senior management's operational responsibilities should create more time to devote to strategic planning.

Disadvantages of Decentralisation

- *Loss of control.* By delegating authority senior management run the risk that their subordinates do not necessarily act in the best interests of the organisation. However this can be overcome by providing junior managers with adequate guidance in terms of explicit objectives and regularly monitoring activities through performance reports indicating any potential problems.

- *Cost of information.* One consequence of decentralisation is a greater need for control information to meet the specific requirements of those involved. Although computers help in this respect, management information systems can still be time consuming and expensive to operate.

The extent to which authority is delegated may depend not only on the issues discussed above but also the nature of the responsibility centre. Where for example a department generates sales revenue, the manager may be responsible for income as well as costs. Figure 15.1 shows different types of responsibility centres with the associated level of management authority and a performance indicator for each.

Responsibility Centres		
Type	**Level of Authority**	**Performance Indicator**
Cost Centre	Costs	Controllable Costs
Profit Centre	Costs Sales Revenue	Controllable Profit
Investment Centre	Costs Sales Revenue Investment	Controllable Return on Capital Employed

Figure 15.1 Responsibility Centres

Note that in each case the manager should be accountable for only controllable items. For instance a cost centre manager with no authority over staffing levels should not be held accountable for staff costs. In investment centres where the manager has authority to take decisions on capital expenditure, return on capital employed provides a comprehensive performance indicator incorporating both profit and investment values.

Preparing the Budget

Detailed budgets for each responsibility centre are prepared for a specific period of time known as the 'budget period'. A period of one year is common but it will usually be divided into shorter control periods of perhaps one month to enable activities to be closely controlled through regular monitoring. A simple means of compiling a budget would be to use the budget or actual results from the previous period adjusted for inflation. Using this method and assuming an inflation rate of 5% per annum, the budget for a cost centre could be compiled as follows:

	Expenditure Last year £	Budget This year* £
Staff costs	80,000	84,000
Travelling expenses	14,000	14,700
Equipment rental	4,200	4,410
Consumables	5,800	6,090
Total budget	104,000	109,200

*Last year's expenditure plus 5%

This approach is known as incrementalism and its advantage is that it allows budgets to be compiled very quickly and easily. However it has a number of disadvantages as described below:

Changes in Conditions are Ignored

Expenditure in the previous period was incurred under a specific set of circumstances which may change in the forthcoming period, making the budget inappropriate. Perhaps the most influential change will be a difference in the level of activity. If output is expected to differ from the previous period activities must be planned and budgets amended to reflect this.

Inefficiencies are Perpetuated

Any inefficiencies or wastage in current operating methods may continue if budgets are based on previous spending patterns and current methods remain unchallenged.

Managers May Avoid Underspending

Where budgets are determined on the basis of previous expenditure managers may deliberately avoid underspending to prevent budgets being reduced. This often results in expenditure on non-essential items towards the end of the budget period in an attempt to secure a generous budget for the following period. This practice is obviously not in the best interests of the organisation and every effort should be made to prevent it.

Zero Based Budgeting

To help overcome the problems of incrementalism a technique known as zero based budgeting may be used. Using this approach activities are planned as if they were being performed for the first time. Current practices are therefore challenged and budgets compiled reflect the resources required to achieve the objectives for the forthcoming period in the expected operating conditions.

Using this method budgets can be prepared following the steps illustrated in Figure 15.2 and explained below:

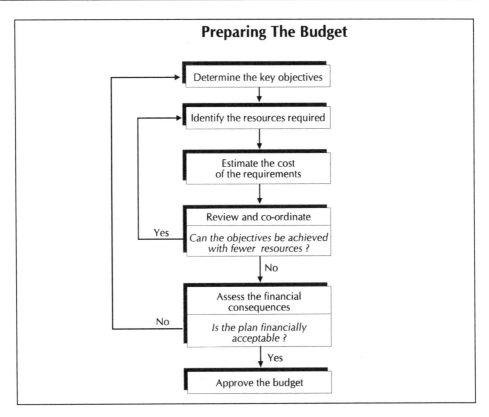

Figure 15.2 Preparing the Budget

1. Determining the Key Objectives

Budgeting is a means of planning and controlling activities to achieve organisational objectives. Consequently the first step must be to determine the objectives for the period in question and inform those involved in the budgeting process in order that supporting departmental objectives can established.

An important factor which should be determined at this stage is the planned level of activity for the period. In the short term output will be constrained by a key factor known as the 'limiting factor' which must be identified in order to determine the expected activity level. It may be a shortage of a resource such as finance, space, skilled labour or perhaps machine capacity. However the most common limiting factor is sales demand and for many organisations the starting point in budgeting is the compilation of a sales forecast for the period. The satisfaction of this demand, through the production of the required output and provision of necessary support services can then be incorporated in departmental objectives.

2. *Identifying the Resources Required*

Having established departmental objectives each manager should identify the resources required to achieve them. These will include people, materials, equipment and services and comprise direct costs and overheads.

Direct Costs

The direct resources required by those departments producing goods or services will depend on planned output for the period as illustrated in the following example:

Example 15.1

Output at Samora Limited, a small company producing kitchen tables is limited by sales demand. The sales department has forecast sales of 300 units in January.

The following requirements have been estimated in respect of each table:

Direct Materials

Wood	3 sq.m.	@	£4 per m^2
Steel tubing	8 m.	@	£2 per m.

Direct Labour

Joiners	4 hours	@	£8 per hour
Assemblers	1.5 hours	@	£6 per hour

Due to an anticipated increase in demand the company wishes to increase stocks from their current levels as detailed below:

	Opening stock at 1st. Jan.	Closing stock required at 31st. Jan.
Completed tables	25	50
Wood	80 m^2	125 m^2
Steel tubing	220 m.	340 m.

Required

From this information prepare the following for January :

(a)   A production budget

(b)   A materials usage budget

(c)   A materials purchases budget

(d)   A labour usage budget

Solution

(a) Production Budget

	Units
Sales forecast	300
Add closing stock requirement	50
Total required	350
Less opening stock	(25)
Production requirement	325

Although 350 tables are required to satisfy sales demand and closing stock requirements, 25 are on hand at the start of January and only the remaining 325 must be produced in the month.

The other budgets can now be compiled on the basis of this planned activity level.

(b) Materials Usage Budget

| Wood | 325 tables x 3 m^2 | = | 975 m^2 |
| Steel tubing | 325 tables x 8 m. | = | 2,600 m. |

(c) Materials Purchases Budget

To determine the materials which must be purchased, adjustments must again be made for stocks.

	Wood m^2	£	Steel Tubing m.	£
Usage	975	3,900	2,600	5,200
Add closing stock	125	500	340	680
Total required	1,100	4,400	2,940	5,880
Less opening stock	(80)	(320)	(220)	(440)
Purchase requirement	1,020	4,080	2,720	5,440

NB. The cost has been calculated by multiplying by the relevant price (i.e. wood £4 per m^2 – steel tubing £2 per metre).

(d) Labour Usage Budget

| Joiners (325 units @ 4 hrs. per unit) | = | 1,300 hours |
| Assemblers (325 units @ 1.5 hrs. per unit) | = | 487.5 hours |

These figures can be used for manpower planning purposes.

Overheads

Overhead costs have a less direct relationship with output and consequently the establishment of resources required is not as straightforward. However with detailed knowledge of the department's functions and given the anticipated activity level for the period, each manager should be able to identify the resources required to satisfy departmental objectives.

Reviewing operating methods and seeking alternatives in this way could prove to be a huge time consuming exercise involving many people. For this reason it may not be performed throughout the entire organisation each year but rather by rotation with each department undergoing a thorough review every few years. In the intervening years circumstances may not change sufficiently to justify such a detailed exercise and an incremental approach may suffice, with overhead budgets based on the previous period and direct costs on planned output.

3. Estimating the Cost of the Requirements

Having established the resources required throughout the organisation the next step is to estimate their cost. This task is usually performed by the finance department and as plans evolve the financial consequences of various alternatives may be prepared. This can be very time consuming and computerised spreadsheet models, which can quickly recalculate the effect of changes, are often used to produce the relevant information.

4. Review and Co-ordination

The plans prepared by each manager and their associated costs should then be reviewed by senior management to ensure that they are realistic and do not conflict with those proposed by other departments or the overall objectives of the organisation.

Another purpose of reviewing proposals is to establish whether objectives could be achieved using fewer resources. The senior management team should consider the proposals carefully and discuss them with departmental managers to establish whether all resources identified are essential. At the first time of asking managers may propose an ideal situation rather than a practical plan. If objectives can be achieved with fewer resources the process reverts back to step two with the identification of those resources and the process is repeated until senior management are satisfied that a true indication of resource requirements has emerged. Questioning proposals in this way should help to eliminate any inefficiencies and produce a plan showing the most cost effective means of achieving objectives. When this stage has been reached the financial consequences of the plan can be assessed.

5. Assessing the Financial Consequences

The financial aspects of the plan can be evaluated using master budgets as described below. Where the plans are financially acceptable the budget can be approved and circulated. Where this is not the case, the objectives must be reviewed. As pursuing them would result in an unsatisfactory financial position the business may have to consider less ambitious objectives which can be afforded in the short term. Perhaps the replacement of equipment should be postponed or the launch of a new product delayed until a later date. Having established revised objectives the budgeting process can recommence and continue until a satisfactory position is attained.

Master Budgets

Master budgets comprise the following three statements :

(a) A Forecast Profit and Loss Account

This will show the profit expected from successfully implementing the plan. This must be sufficient to provide an adequate return for shareholders/owners after the retention of adequate funds for reinvestment in the business.

(b) A Forecast Balance sheet

This will reflect the financial position anticipated at the end of the period as a result of following the plan. It can be used with the forecast profit and loss account to assess factors such as projected return on capital, asset turnover and liquidity.

(c) A Cash Budget

As we saw in Chapter 8, earning profit in a period does not necessarily generate cash. Consequently as well as assessing profitability, the cashflows expected as a result of following the plan must be forecast to ensure that the business will be able meet liabilities as they fall due. To do this the value and timing of receipts and payments expected during the period must be estimated and incorporated in a cash budget (also known as a 'cash flow forecast'). This process is illustrated in the following example:

Example 15.2

Brittney Sports Limited sells sports goods from small retail outlets and has a bank balance of £3,000 as at 1st May.

Sales and purchases figures recorded for the previous two months are shown below:

	Sales £	Purchases £
March	40,000	28,000
April	50,000	30,000

The following forecasts have been made for the following three months :

	Sales £	Purchases £
May	55,000	33,000
June	60,000	36,000
July	65,000	38,000

- 20% of sales are made to sports clubs on credit terms of two months and the remainder are for cash.

- Suppliers allow credit of one month.

- General expenses are expected to amount to £9,000 per month (including £2,000 in respect of depreciation).

- Shop fittings are to be purchased for £45,000 in May and the supplier has offered credit terms of one month.

- Proceeds from the sale of premises for £20,000 are to be received in two equal instalments commencing in July.

Required

Prepare a cash budget for the business covering May, June and July.

Solution

Brittney Sports Limited

Cash Budget May-July

Note		May £000's	June £000's	July £000's
a	Opening Balance	3	18	(9)
	ADD RECEIPTS			
b	Sales- cash	44	48	52
c	- credit	8	10	11
	Sale of premises			10
d	Amount Available	55	76	64
	LESS PAYMENTS			
e	Purchases	30	33	36
f	General expenses	7	7	7
	Shop fittings		45	
	Total Payments	37	85	43
g	CLOSING BALANCE	18	(9)	21

Explanatory Notes

(a) The opening balance for May was given in the information supplied. The figures for June and July correspond with the closing balance at the end of the preceding month.

(b) i.e. Sales for the month x 80%.

(c) As clubs are allowed credit of two months, the cash receipts expected in each month from credit sales is 20% of the sales made two months previously.

(d) i.e. Opening balance plus receipts.

(e) As suppliers offer credit of one month, payments made in each month are for purchases made in the previous month.

(f)   General expenses exclude depreciation which has no impact on cash. Depreciation is an accounting technique to spread the cost of fixed assets over the periods in which they are used. Cash flows occur only when assets are bought or sold.

(g)   The closing balance represents the cash remaining after subtracting payments from the amount available.

The statement indicates that the bank account is expected to be overdrawn by the end of June and this early indication of a potential problem should prompt some action now. The situation could be improved by measures such as delaying the purchase of fittings (or asking for a longer credit period), selling the premises at an earlier date, requesting early payment from credit customers or delaying payments to suppliers. If these cannot be arranged, a temporary overdraft facility should be requested from the bank to cover the expected shortfall or additional funds sought from another source.

Budgetary Control

Having prepared plans and budgets, activities must be controlled in an attempt to ensure that the plans are carried out and objectives for the period achieved. The budgetary control process is illustrated in Figure 15.3 and explained below:

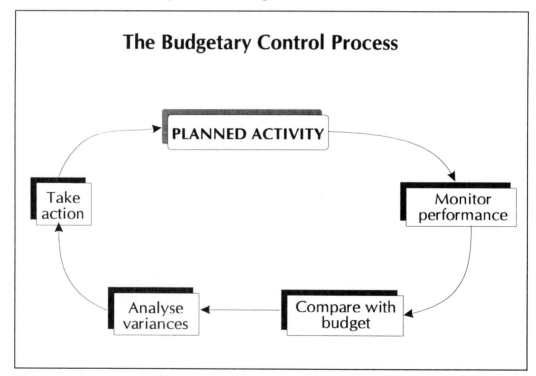

Figure 15.3 The Budgetary Control Process

1. Monitor Performance

The first step is to find out what is actually happening by monitoring activities and quantifying them in the same terms as the budget. This may entail recording costs incurred, income earned or resources used (Kgs of materials, number of labour hours etc.).

2. Compare With Budget

These results should be regularly compared with those planned in order to highlight activities which are not proceeding according to plan. This information may take the form of a monthly budget report as shown in Figure 15.4 or where closer control is required over potentially volatile activities, weekly or daily feedback perhaps via computer terminals.

CAPITAL COACH TOURS LIMITED

BUDGET REPORT - MAY 19X6 (£000's)

	THIS MONTH			YEAR TO DATE		
	Actual	Budget	Variance	Actual	Budget	Variance
SALES	79	80	(1)	301	280	21
LESS COSTS						
Staff costs	50	41	(9)	141	129	(12)
Depreciation	11	11	–	55	55	–
Maintenance	2	6	4	15	21	6
Admin. expenses	8	9	1	42	35	(7)
Advertising	3	3	–	10	10	–
PROFIT	5	10	(5)	38	30	8

NB Adverse variances are shown in brackets.

Figure 15.4 Budget Report

For each item the actual result has been compared with the budget and the difference between the two (the 'variance') shown. Favourable variances occur where costs are less than planned or income higher than estimated. Adverse variances indicate higher costs or lower income than planned.

The figures for the year to date represent the cumulative position in respect of each item and the monthly figures give an indication of the current trend. For example in the case of administration expenses, although the costs incurred for the first five months of the year exceed those planned by £7,000, they were less than expected in May, perhaps indicating that corrective action has prevented further overspending.

3. Analyse Variances

Variances indicate deviations from plans which may require remedial action. The appropriate action will depend on the cause of the variance and some investigation will therefore be necessary to determine the reason for its occurrence. This can be time consuming and in some cases the size of the variance may not justify the time incurred in investigation. In Figure 15.4 for example, the manager may investigate only staff costs and coach maintenance both of which show significant variances for May. The other items, which show only small variances, appear to be proceeding roughly according to plan and may not warrant investigation. This principle is known as 'management by exception' and ensures that attention is directed to the most important issues.

Note that favourable as well as adverse variances should be investigated. In the example given, although maintenance costs were less than planned this is not necessarily a good sign. The low cost may be due to inadequate maintenance of vehicles rather than any efficiency gains and should be reviewed. Any variance reported reflects something which is not proceeding as planned and where the deviation is significant it should be investigated.

4. Take Action

Having discovered the reasons for variances, steps should be taken to remedy any problems identified. However in some cases variances may be due to an inappropriate budget rather than any operational inefficiency. If for example employees are awarded a pay rise in excess of that expected or the price of materials rises unexpectedly, adverse variances will arise which cannot be controlled by the manager concerned. In such circumstances, although the variance may not be preventable, the effect on the costs estimated for the period should at least be recognised and the projected profit amended accordingly.

Flexible Budgeting

Budgets reflect costs and revenues expected from the planned activity level for the period. If however the actual activity level differs from that planned the budget will be inappropriate and using it could produce misleading information. Consider the following example:

Example 15.3

Costs estimated for a production department included the following:

Direct labour	£2 per unit
Direct materials	£4 per unit
Supervision	£3,000 per month

The following budget was prepared for the month of February on the basis of the planned production level of 5,000 units:

Budget
£

Direct labour	10,000	(5,000 units @ £2 per unit)
Direct materials	20,000	(5,000 units @ £4 per unit)
Supervision	3,000	(£3,000 per month)
Total	33,000	

During February 4,000 units were actually produced and at the end of the month the following operating statement was produced:

PRODUCTION DEPARTMENT

OPERATING STATEMENT - FEBRUARY

	Budget £	Actual £	Variance £
Direct labour	10,000	8,800	1,200
Direct materials	20,000	16,000	4,000
Supervision	3,000	3,200	(200)
	33,000	28,000	5,000

This shows that expenditure was £5,000 less than planned for the month, giving the impression that the department has performed well with savings made on labour and in particular, material costs.

However the operating statement is misleading as it compares the planned costs for one activity level (5,000 units) with the actual costs incurred for another (4,000 units). The £5,000 savings reported will therefore be at least partially due to producing fewer units than planned rather than any greater efficiency.

A more meaningful exercise would be the comparison of the actual costs for the 4,000 units produced with a revised budget reflecting the costs expected for that activity level. This would produce the following information:

PRODUCTION DEPARTMENT
OPERATING STATEMENT - FEBRUARY

	Flexed Budget	Actual	Variance
Output (units)	4,000	4,000	
	£	£	£
Direct labour	8,000*	8,800	(800)
Direct materials	16,000†	16,000	0
Supervision	3,000	3,200	(200)
	27,000	28,000	(1,000)

* 4,000 units @ £2 per unit

† 4,000 units @ £4 per unit

Budgets for the variable costs, direct labour and materials, have been adjusted to reflect the cost expected for the production of 4,000 units. A budget revised in this way is called a 'flexed budget' and provides a more meaningful standard with which actual costs can be compared.

The revised statement shows that as the expected cost for 4,000 units was only £27,000 the department actually spent £1,000 more than expected. This information gives a better indication of the performance of the department and will be more useful for control purposes.

Behavioural Aspects of Budgeting

Business objectives are attained by those working within the organisation and it is therefore essential that they are motivated to act in its best interests. Budgetary control systems can play an important part in achieving this provided that their behavioural impact is considered and the following issues are important in this respect:

Setting Targets

Performance targets set in the budgeting process can increase the motivation of managers to achieve their full potential. However care should be taken when establishing the target. If it is perceived as too difficult to meet it will tend to demotivate and may result in a poor performance. On the other hand faced with a target which is easily achieved, managers may do no more than is necessary to attain the standard set and again fail to achieve their potential. Ideally performance standards should be challenging but acceptable to those expected to meet them.

Participation

An effective method of ensuring that targets are acceptable is to involve managers in setting them. Allowing managers to participate in the budgeting process indicates that their contribution is valued and they will generally be more motivated to achieve targets they have set themselves than those imposed by senior management.

Senior Management Attitude

The attitude of senior management towards the budgeting system will have a great bearing on the way it is perceived by those using it. Where a negative approach is adopted, using budgeting information as a means of condemning those not achieving targets, the system will be ruled by fear. Managers may attempt to negotiate easily attainable targets rather than stimulating challenges and make every effort to achieve these even where the best interests of the business are not served. For example a maintenance manager in danger of overspending may provide a dangerously inadequate service in an attempt to reduce costs or a sales manager may attempt to sell defective goods to achieve a sales target. Budgeting systems tend to be most effective when used in a positive way to help managers to perform better through their involvement in planning and controlling the activities of the organisation.

One important point to bear in mind when considering behavioural factors is that the complexity of human nature makes predicting the response to a particular approach very difficult. However as the success of a budgetary control system depends on individuals acting in the best interests of the organisation, the behavioural impact of such systems should not be ignored.

Requirements for Effective Budgetary Control

Although budgeting systems evolve to meet the specific requirements of individual businesses, successful systems tend to include a number of common features. Examples include the following:

Involvement and Support of Senior Management

Where senior managers shows little interest in budgetary planning and control it is unlikely to be a priority for operational managers. If they are truly committed to the process, senior management should make everyone aware of its importance.

Clear Definition of Long Term Objectives

As the aim of budgetary control is to assist in the ultimate achievement of long term objectives it is important that these are clearly defined and communicated.

Clearly Defined Responsibilities

Having determined clear long term objectives, everyone working within the business should be made aware of the part they are expected to play in their achievement.

Participation of all those involved

As explained earlier, participation tends to increase motivation and may play an important part in the achievement of business objectives.

An Effective Information System

Having secured the commitment of those involved, they must be provided with relevant, up to date and accurate information to help assess the results of their actions and prompt any necessary remedial action.

A Flexible Approach

Better results are often achieved in circumstances where individuals are not too constrained by budgets. The acceptance of occasional failure may encourage managers to adopt challenging targets which may produce better performance in the long run.

Benefits of Budgeting

Operating an effective budgeting system incorporating the features outlined above can produce a number of benefits as described below:

Planning

Although an important part of a manager's job is to plan future activities, they often become too engrossed in day to day operational issues to spend sufficient time on planning. Through the preparation of budgets they are forced to consider the future rather than concentrating solely on current issues.

Co-ordination

Left to their own devices individual functions or departments pursuing their own objectives may conflict with one another. For example a sales department's plan to offer generous credit terms in an effort to increase sales volume may conflict with the aims of the finance department, which may be trying to generate cash quickly or the production department, which may be unable to cope with the extra demand. Budgeting helps to ensure that departments work in harmony to attain the overall objectives of the organisation. Communication between departments when compiling budgets and a subsequent review by senior management should help to resolve inter-department conflict at an early stage and ensure that plans are complementary.

Communication

As we have seen, the first step in budget preparation is to establish and communicate organisational and departmental objectives for the period. This should help to develop a sense of purpose by ensuring that everyone is aware of their role in the organisation. Progress made towards the achievement of these objectives can be subsequently communicated through the regular provision of feedback information.

Control

As described earlier, the comparison of actual results with budgets provides managers with useful control information.

Motivation

Provided that objectives are reasonably attainable they can help to motivate managers to perform to the best of their ability.

Performance appraisal

Budgeting systems are often used as a basis for performance appraisal with managers being rewarded for achieving targets.

Potential Problems in Budgeting

Although budgeting can be very useful for short term planning and control, it can also present problems which should be considered when operating budgeting systems. These include:

Inflexibility

Having established short term plans there may be a tendency to rigidly adhere to them rather than consider other courses of action which may be more appropriate. Successful organisations adapt to changing circumstances and if necessary, budgets should be revised to reflect the planned response to such changes.

Performance Appraisal

An effective performance appraisal system must be seen to be fair with reasonably attainable targets and assessment based only on controllable factors. Care must be taken when using budgets for this purpose as variances reported may be due to poor forecasting or changing conditions as well as operational issues. An attempt should therefore be made to isolate the variance attributable to operating performance using techniques such as flexible budgeting.

Behavioural Aspects

Many budgeting systems fail because their behavioural implications are not given the attention they deserve. An effective information system providing up to date, accurate information will be of little use if managers are not motivated to take the action necessary to improve performance. If budgeting systems are to achieve their potential it is crucial that behavioural issues are fully addressed.

Non Financial Performance Indicators

In this chapter we have seen how financial performance indicators such as sales revenue, costs and profit can help in controlling activities. However they may provide an incomplete picture and a more comprehensive view may be obtained by also considering non-financial indicators. For instance measuring the rate of repeat business may indicate the degree of customer satisfaction with a product or service offered and the staff turnover rate may give some indication of employee morale within the organisation. These issues may have an important bearing on the long term success of an organisation and should be closely monitored.

Summary

- Business planning and control occurs in four stages:

    (1)   Setting objectives

    (2)   Long term planning

    (3)   Short term planning

    (4)   Control

- The most popular technique for short term planning and control is budgeting.

- An incremental approach to setting budgets fails to recognise changing conditions and may perpetuate existing inefficiencies.

- When adopting a zero base approach existing methods are challenged by planning activities as if they were being performed for the first time.

- Budgets may be prepared using following steps:

    (1)   Setting objectives

    (2)   Identifying resources required.

    (3)   Costing the requirements.

    (4)   Reviewing and co-ordinating proposals.

    (5)   Assessing the financial consequences.

    (6)   Approving the budget.

- Master budgets consist of a forecast profit and loss account, forecast balance sheet and a cash budget showing expected receipts and payments for the budget period.

- To control planned activities they must be closely monitored with actual results being compared with those planned. Significant variances should be investigated and any necessary remedial action taken.

- A flexible budget is one which is retrospectively adjusted to reflect the actual activity level for a period. Using such a budget will provide useful information for performance appraisal and control.

- As the success of budgetary control systems depends on individuals acting in the best interests of the business, the behavioural impact of budgeting should be fully addressed.

- Budgeting can produce numerous benefits for an organisation but may also present potential problems.

- For a comprehensive evaluation of business performance, non-financial as well as financial indicators should be assessed.

Questions   (See Appendix C for Answers)

15.1

Explain how a decision to prepare and use budgets could be beneficial to a small business. Include in your answer an indication of how a micro-computer could be used to improve the implementation and effectiveness of this decision.

(ACCA)

15.2

(a) In the context of budget preparation explain the term 'limiting factor' illustrating your response by describing three possible examples.

(b) Having established short term plans and budgets a business must exert control over subsequent activities to ensure, as far as possible, that objectives are achieved.

Describe the four steps a business may take in order to exert this 'budgetary control'.

(c) Describe the benefits likely to result from using a budgeting system.

15.3

Summer Camping Limited offers one week package holidays each summer on a campsite in Spain. The following information relates to its operations:

- The Company hires 120 tents from the campsite owners at a cost of £300 per tent per week.

- Each tent can accommodate 10 persons.

- It is expected that during July:

    - 80% of the tents will be rented out.

    - on average eight persons will occupy each tent.

- Summer Camping, in negotiations with an airline company, has guaranteed that it will book a minimum of 3,500 seats per month to Spain. On this basis, the airline has offered the flights at a price of £75 per person.

- Guests are provided with a 'welcome pack' of groceries on arrival in Spain. The estimated cost of this is £5 per person.

- The company employs two resort representatives for every 50 tents hired out per week. They are paid a salary of £220 per week each.

- A weekly one day excursion is offered from the campsite and it is expected that 25% of guests will book this each week. These excursions entail the following:

  - booking price is £20 per customer

  - coaches with a 60 seat capacity are hired at a cost of £120 per day.

  - refreshments are provided and cost Summer Camping £6 per guest.

- Office administration costs amount to £32,000 per week.

- The price of the package holiday is £200 per person.

Required

(a) Prepare the Company's budget for the month of July (assuming there are four weeks in the month).

(b) The Company is considering mounting an extensive advertising campaign at a cost of £22,500 per week. It is hoped that this would result in renting out 95% of tents available. Re-draft the budget incorporating this information and recommend whether or not the advertising campaign should be undertaken.

15.4

You are required, from the data given below, to prepare next year's budgets for:

(a) production;

(b) purchases;

(c) production cost.

Standard cost data are as follows:

	Product	
	Aye (£)	Bee (£)
Direct materials:		
X 24kg at £2	48	
30kg at £2		60
Y 10kg at £5	50	
8kg at £5		40
Z 5kg at £6	30	
10kg at £6		60
Direct wages:		
Unskilled 10 hours at £3 per hour	30	
5 hours at £3 per hour		15
Skilled 6 hours at £5 per hour	30	
5 hours at £5 per hour		25

Production overhead is absorbed on the basis of direct labour hours, while overhead is recovered on the basis of 20% of production cost. Profit is calculated at 20% of sales price.

Budgeted data for the year:

		Material X (£)	Material Y (£)	Material Z (£)
Stock at standard price				
1st January		60,000	125,000	72,000
31st December		70,000	135,000	75,000
Product overhead	£900,000			
Labour hours	75,000			

	Product	
	Aye (£)	Bee (£)
Finished goods stock at production cost		
Opening stock	152,000	256,000
Closing stock	190,000	352,000
Sales at standard sales price	1,368,000	1,536,000

(CIMA)

15.5

A company's opening cash balance on the 1st January is expected to be £30,000. The sales budget is shown below:

	£
December	90,000
January	75,000
February	75,000
March	80,000

Analysis of records shows that customers settle according to the following pattern:

 60% within the month of sale.

 40% the month following.

Extracts from the Purchases budget are given below:

	£
December	60,000
January	55,000
February	45,000
March	55,000

All purchases are on credit and past experience shows that 90% are settled in the month of purchase and the balance settled the month after.

Wages are £15,000 per month and overheads of £20,000 per month (including £5,000 depreciation) are settled monthly.

Taxation of £28,000 must be paid in February and the company will receive settlement of an insurance claim of £30,000 in March.

Required

(a) Prepare a cash budget covering January, February and March.

(b) Explain the benefits of preparing such a statement and advise the company in question based on your results in (a).

15.6

At 1st May Peter's bank overdraft stood at £2,000, well below his agreed limit of £10,000.

His business had been doing so well lately that he decided to request a loan from the bank to buy some new equipment. To support his request he prepared the budgeted profit and loss account shown below. The bank manager refused to grant the loan until Peter had estimated his cash requirement

Budgeted Profit and Loss Account

For 3 Months Ended 31 July (£000's)

	May		June		July		Total
Sales		20		5		30	55
Less Cost of Sales							
Opening Stock	4		6		43		4
Add Purchases	15		40		0		55
	19		46		43		59
Less Closing Stock	6	13	43	3	23	20	23	36
Gross Profit		7		2		10		19
Less Expenses							
Wages		2		1		2	5
Rent		1		1		1	3
Depreciation		1		1		1	3
Net Profit		3		(1)		6	8

Other information

- 10% of sales are for cash and the remainder on two months credit terms (total sales for February were £20,000, March £21,000, and April £20,000).

- It is estimated that 90% of purchases will be paid for on a cash basis and the remainder on credit terms of one month (purchases in April were £20,000).

- Wages are paid in the month incurred.

- Rent is paid half yearly on 1st January and 1st July.

- Tax of £5,000 is payable in June.

Required

(a) Explain the importance of cash budgets in the planning process.

(b) Prepare for Peter, a cash budget covering May, June and July.

(c) Outline areas for concern highlighted by your answer to (b) above and suggest ways of dealing with them.

15.7

The following estimates have been made in respect of monthly costs incurred by a small hotel:

Catering	£2,000 per month plus £10 per room occupied
Staffing	£8,500 per month for occupancy levels up to 750 rooms per month rising to £12,000 per month for occupancy beyond this
Premises	£5,000 per month
Laundry	£3 per room occupied
Equipment depreciation	£4,000 per month

The hotel manager has been provided with the following statement from group headquarters and was recently asked to explain the adverse variance of £4,900 for the month:

BUDGET STATEMENT – MAY

	Budget	Actual	Variance
Rooms Occupied	700	800	100
COSTS	£	£	£
Catering	9,000	10,400	(1,400)
Staffing	8,500	11,700	(3,200)
Premises	5,000	4,300	700
Laundry	2,100	2,300	(200)
Depreciation	4,000	4,800	(800)
Total	28,600	33,500	(4,900)

(Adverse variances are shown in brackets)

NB. The hotel manager has not authority to purchase equipment for the hotel as such decisions are taken by senior staff at group headquarters.

Required

(a) Comment on the effectiveness of the statement provided for control purposes and as a means of appraising the manager's performance.

(b) Re-draft the statement in a format which you consider to be more appropriate and explain the advantages your revised version has over the original statement.

15.8

(a) Budgetary control systems often fail to fulfil their potential due to a reluctance to consider their impact on the behaviour of those working in the organisation.

Discuss the behavioural issues which should be addressed when using such a system.

(b) Briefly explain the benefits and drawbacks which may result from decentralising decision making in an organisation.

Questions Without Answers

15.9

An airline company has made the following estimates in respect of monthly costs:

	Fixed £000's	Variable per seat £
Wages	50	–
In flight magazine	–	0.25
Catering	8	3.00
Depreciation	10	–
Admin. costs	10	2.00
Other costs	12	0.50

In the month of December the company planned to sell 16,000 seats. Actual sales were 20,000 seats and the following costs were incurred:

	£000's
Wages	60
In flight magazine	2
Catering	60
Depreciation	10
Admin. costs	52
Other costs	20

Required

(a)   Prepare an operating statement for December based on

   (i)   The original budget.

   (ii)   A flexed budget.

(b)   Comment on the information produced in each case.

(c)   In respect of the 'flexed' statement, suggest possible reasons for the three largest variances.

15.10

R Limited manufactures three products: A, B and C. You are required:

   (a)   using the information given below, to prepare budgets for the month of January for:

       (i)   sales in quantity and value, including total value;

       (ii)   production quantities;

       (iii) material usage in quantities;

       (iv) material purchases in quantity and value, including total value;

(N.B. Particular attention should be paid to your layout of the budgets.)

   (b)   to explain the term principal budget factor and state what it was assumed to be in (a) of this question.

Data for preparation of January budgets

Sales	Product	Quantity	Price each £
	A	1,000	100
	B	2,000	120
	C	1,500	140

Materials used in the company's products are:

Material	M1	M2	M3
Unit cost	£4	£6	£9

Quantities used in:	units	units	units
Product: A	4	2	–
B	3	3	2
C	2	1	1

Finished stocks:

Product	A	B	C
Quantities			
1st January	1,000	1,500	500
31st January	1,100	1,650	550

Material stocks:	M1 units	M2 units	M3 units
1st January	26,000	20,000	12,000
31st January	31,200	24,000	14,400

(CIMA)

15.11

Multisport Limited a retailer of sports equipment has an agreed overdraft facility of £25,000 and the bank account as at 1st May 19X2 was overdrawn by £24,000.

The following additional information is also available:

• Sales in March and April were £40,000 and £50,000 respectively and the following forecast has been made:

May £50,000
June £60,000
July £65,000

- 20% of the sales are made to clubs on a credit basis (payable one month after the sale is made) and the remainder are for cash.

- The cost of sales is 60% of sales value.

- Goods are sold one month after purchase.

- Suppliers extend credit of one month.

- General expenses are expected to amount to £5,000 per month (including £1,500 in respect of depreciation).

- A tax liability amounting to £17,000 is payable in May.

- Proceeds from the sale of shop premises for £80,000 are to be received in four monthly instalments from July onwards.

- A transport vehicle is to be replaced during May at a cost of £20,000 payable in two equal monthly instalments commencing in May.

Required

(a) Prepare a cash budget for Multisport Limited for May, June and July 19X2.

(b) Explain the chief benefits to be obtained by an organisation preparing cash budgets (your answer should be illustrated by commenting on the budget prepared in (a) above and suggesting how Multisport may use this information).

(c) Comment on the statement that "profitable companies have no need for cash budgets as generating profit ensures that cash is available as and when required".

15.12

The following figures have been extracted from a manufacturing company's budget schedules:

	Sales including VAT £000	Wages and salaries £000	Purchases of materials £000	Production overhead £000	Selling and administration overhead £000
19X2 Oct	1,200	55	210	560	125
Nov	1,100	50	280	500	125
Dec	1,000	65	240	640	125
19X3 Jan	1,400	60	210	560	125
Feb	1,200	60	240	500	130
Mar	1,100	60	230	560	130

Other relevant information:

1. All sales are on credit terms of net settlement within 30 days of the date of the sale. However,

    • only 60% of indebtedness is paid by the end of the calendar month in which the sale is made;

    • another 30% is paid in the following calendar month;

    • 5% in the second calendar month after the invoice date;

    • and 5% become bad debts.

2. Assume all months are of equal number of 30 days for the allocation of the receipts from debtors.

3. Wages and salaries are paid within the month they are incurred.

4. Creditors for materials are paid within the month following the purchase.

5. Of the production overhead, 35% of the figure represents variable expenses which are paid in the month after they were incurred. £164,000 per month is depreciation and is included in the 65% which represents fixed costs. The payment of fixed costs is made in the month in which the cost is incurred.

6. Selling and administration overhead which is payable is paid in the month it is incurred. £15,000 each month is depreciation.

7. Corporation tax of £750,000 is payable in January.

8. A dividend is payable in March: £500,000 net. (Ignore advance corporation tax.)

9. Value added tax (VAT), payable monthly one month later than the sales are made, is to be calculated as follows:

    Output Tax
    7/47 ths of the sales including VAT figure
    less Input Tax of £136,000 for January
    £125,000 for February and
    £121,000 for March.

10. Capital expenditure commitments are due for payment:

    £1,000,000 in January and £700,000 in March.

    Both are payments for machinery to be imported from Japan and thus no VAT is involved.

11. Assume that overdraft facilities, if required, are available.

12. The cash at bank balance at 31st December is expected to be £1,450,000.

You are required

(a) to prepare, in columnar form, cash budgets for each of the months of January, February and March (working to nearest £000);

(b) to recommend action which could be suggested to management to effect

   (i) a permanent improvement in cash flow, and

   (ii) a temporary solution to minimise any overdraft requirements revealed by your answer to (a) above.

(CIMA)

15.13

The manager of an established transport fleet has consulted you regarding the preparation of a flexible budget for the department under his control. One purpose of the budget is to compile an average cost per mile for charging to user departments.

The fleet consists of eight similar vehicles of which two are replaced at the commencement of each year in a cycle which assumes they have a four year life. Each vehicle's current cost is £45,000 with an estimated residual value of £9,000.

Typical maintenance costs for each vehicle consist of a service every six months or 10,000 miles (whichever occurs first) costing £250 and spare parts costing £50 in the first year. The cost of spares becomes greater with the age of each vehicle. It has been observed to double with each year of vehicle life.

On consulting other records the manager is able to establish that annual licence and insurance costs £300 per vehicle. Tyres costing £80 each are changed every 20,000 miles on these four-wheeled vehicles. Fuel is estimated at £1.80 per gallon and each vehicle can achieve 20 miles per gallon.

The annual administration cost of the transport department is part fixed and part variable in relation to the annual mileage covered by all vehicles. The following table shows the prediction of this cost taken from a study recently undertaken.

Mileage travelled per annum	Total administration cost £
175,000	55,000
200,000	60,000
250,000	70,000

The manager is undecided about the annual workload of his department and for the purpose of budget discussion has put forward three possible levels – namely 20,000, 25,000 and 30,000 miles per vehicle.

Required

(a) Prepare flexible budgets for the transport department covering one year taking account of the possible range of vehicle mileage. Provide explanations or workings where you consider it appropriate and comment where you consider further information would improve the accuracy of budget preparation.

(b) The manager has read in a recent transport journal 'the more miles travelled the cheaper it becomes'. Comment on this statement.

(ACCA)

15.14

You are approached by a colleague who knows you are acquainted with accounting for planning and control. He has noted from an article, two extracts, on which he would like more information:

(a) participation in budget setting has both desirable and undesirable effects for an organisation;

(b) a variance indicates a deviation from a plan, but not all variances should be investigated.

Required

Elaborate on, in order to explain to your colleague, the two extracts provided.

(ACCA)

15.15

A local authority provides residential training courses and has made the following estimates in respect of the monthly costs of the training department.

	Fixed £	Variable per course £
Accommodation	5,000	600
Training Materials	–	280
Catering	300	540
Wages	*	*
Other Costs	3,600	450

*Wages costs have not yet been analysed in terms of their behaviour. However the following information is available in respect of the previous two months:

	Wages Cost	No. of Courses
Month 1	£9,280	7
Month 2	£7,600	5

When budgets were originally compiled it was anticipated that eight courses would be offered during month 3. However, six courses were actually delivered and the following costs incurred:

	£
Accommodation	8,900
Training Materials	1,440
Catering	3,100
Wages	10,200
Other Costs	6,400
	30,040

Required

(a) Prepare a budgetary control statement showing variances in month 3 based on:

    (i)   The original budget

    (ii) A flexed budget

(b)   Comment on the information produced in each case.

(c)   In respect of the "flexed" statement suggest two possible reasons for each of the two largest variances.

Chapter 16

Standard Costing

Learning Objectives

After completing this chapter you should be able to:

- Explain how standard costing may be used for short term planning and control.

- Describe how standard costs are established.

- Calculate variances for direct materials, direct labour, production overheads and sales.

- Compile an operating statement showing how these variances explain the difference between planned and actual profit for a period.

- Explain the benefits and potential problems of using standard costing.

Introduction

In the previous chapter we saw how budgets can be used to assist managers in controlling activities. Standard costing systems provide more detailed control information by applying budgetary control principles to individual products. Budgets ('standards') are set for each product and actual costs and revenues compared with these in order to highlight deviations from plans. The precise way in which standard costing variances are calculated gives an indication of the reasons for these deviations and directs management to the issues requiring their attention. The technique is applicable in situations where repetitive operations are performed and although most commonly used in manufacturing organisations, can also be applied to service activities where tasks are repetitive.

In this chapter we will consider how standards are established and see how the calculation of variances can indicate the reasons for differences between planned and actual results in a period and provide a basis for further investigation and action.

Setting Standards

A standard cost is an estimate of how much costs should be under specified operating conditions. As we saw in Chapter 10, product costs comprise various elements and standards can be established for each as illustrated in Figure 16.1.

Standard Product Cost	
Product: **Bookcase**	**£**
Direct Materials	
Timber (15 m^2 @ £5 per m^2)	75
Direct Labour	
Joiners (5 hours @ £7 per hour)	35
Production overheads – Fixed (5 hours @ £6 per hour)	30
– Variable (5 hours @ £2 per hour)	10
Standard Cost of Production	150
Production overheads are absorbed on the basis of labour hours	

Figure 16.1 A Standard Product Cost

In each case the cost comprises a quantity (i.e. m^2 or hours) and a price (ie. a cost per m^2 or rate per hour) and these may be determined as follows:

Direct Materials

The quantity of materials required is usually obtained from a technical specification prepared for the product in question. The price of each type of material used should be available from prospective suppliers.

Direct Labour

The standard labour time required can be estimated by timing trial runs using work measurement techniques. The rate per hour for each category of labour can be obtained from wages records.

Overheads

Separate overhead absorption rates may be used for fixed and variable production overheads. Where overheads are absorbed on the basis of labour hours as in the above example, absorption rates are calculated using estimated overhead costs and labour hours for the period as follows:

$$\text{Fixed OAR} \quad = \quad \frac{Budgeted\ Fixed\ Overheads}{Budgeted\ No.\ of\ Labour Hours}$$

The variable OAR is calculated in the same manner using the budgeted variable overheads for the period.

Variance Analysis

As explained in the previous chapter, a variance represents a difference between planned and actual costs or revenues. The aim of variance analysis is to explain these differences in order that any necessary remedial action can be taken.

Variances may arise due to :

a) **The pricing aspect** (Eg. Paying more or less than £5 per m^2 for timber or £7 per hour to joiners).

b) **The quantity aspect** (Eg. Using more or less than 15 m^2 of timber or 5 hours per bookcase).

To determine the extent to which variances can be attributed to each of these, separate price and usage variances can be calculated as demonstrated in the following example:

Example 16.1

Business Systems (BS) Limited produces bookcases and has set the standard cost we saw earlier for each unit produced:

	£
Direct Materials	
Timber (15 m^2 @ £5 per m^2)	75
Direct Labour	
Joiners (5 hours @ £7 per hour)	35
Production overheads – Fixed (5 hours @ £6 per hour)	30
– Variable (5 hours @ £2 per hour)	10
Standard Cost of Production	$\underline{150}$

Budgeted output for February was 1,100 bookcases and fixed overhead costs were estimated at £33,000.

During the month 1,200 bookcases were actually produced and the following costs recorded:

Direct materials - 20,000 m^2 of timber were used at a cost of £4.80 per m^2.

Direct Labour   - 5,500 hours were worked for which a rate of £7.40 per hour was paid.

Fixed overhead costs incurred in the month amounted to £40,000 and variable overheads were £10,000.

From this information the actual costs incurred in the production of the 1,200 bookcases can be compared with the expected cost as shown below:

		£
Planned costs (1,200 bookcases x £150)		180,000
Actual costs		
Direct materials (20,000 m^2 x £4.80 per m^2)	96,000	
Direct labour (5,500 hrs. x £7.40 per hr.)	40,700	
Production overheads – Fixed	40,000	
– Variable	10,000	186,700
Total Cost Variance		6,700 Adverse

Note that as actual costs exceeded those planned, the variance is described as being adverse. To help managers to establish why this occurred, detailed variances can be calculated in respect of each cost element.

Direct Materials Variances

Direct Materials Total Variance

The total direct materials variance shows the difference between the expected material cost of the bookcases produced and the actual costs incurred. It is calculated as follows:

Direct Mats. Total Variance = Standard mat. cost for actual production – Actual mat. cost

For BS Limited	=	$(1,200 \text{ bookcases} \times £75) - (20,000 \text{ m}^2 \times £4.80 \text{ per m}^2)$
	=	£90,000 - £96,000
	=	£6,000 *Adverse*

To help determine the cause of this variance it can be subdivided into price and usage variances.

Direct Materials Price Variance

This variance indicates the effect of paying more or less than anticipated per unit of material and is calculated as follows:

Materials Price Variance = Actual quantity used x (Standard price - Actual price)

	=	$20,000 \text{ m}^2$	x (£5 - £4.80)
	=	$20,000 \text{ m}^2$	x £0.20
	=	£4,000 *Favourable*	

As the materials were obtained for 20p per m^2 less than expected the variance is favourable in this case.

Direct Materials Usage Variance

The usage variance shows the effect of using more or less materials than anticipated for the production achieved:

Mats. Usage Variance = (Std. quantity for actual production - Quantity used) x Std. price

	=	$(1,200 \text{ bookcases} \times 15 \text{ m}^2 - 20,000 \text{ m}^2) \times £5$
	=	$(18,000 \text{ m}^2 - 20,000 \text{ m}^2) \times £5$
	=	£10,000 *Adverse*

Note that as the aim of the usage variance is to show only the impact of using more materials and not the effect of paying more per square metre, the standard material price of £5 is used.

As the production of the 1,200 bookcases required 2,000 m^2 more wood than planned, at a standard cost of £5 per m^2, costs were £10,000 greater than expected.

We can now see why actual material costs exceeded those planned:

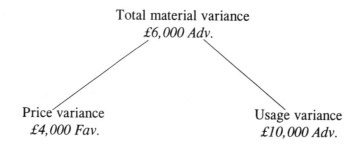

Total material variance
£6,000 Adv.

Price variance
£4,000 Fav.

Usage variance
£10,000 Adv.

Using more materials than expected resulted in additional costs of £10,000. However this was partially offset by savings of £4,000 due to paying less than expected for the materials and the total overspend was therefore £6,000.

Typical Reasons for Material Variances

Calculating variances is only the start of the control process. They must be investigated to ascertain their precise cause and any necessary remedial action taken. Possible causes of direct material variances are given below:

Price Variances

- Discounts offered by suppliers.

- Price rises.

- Using different suppliers.

- Using different materials (E.g. higher quality materials may cost more).

Usage Variances

- Using different materials (E.g. poor quality materials may incur more wastage).

- Using poorly trained employees (Again more wastage may result).

Note that in some cases there may be a relationship between variances. For example BS Limited's favourable price variance and adverse usage variance may both be due to buying poor quality materials at a lower price which resulted in high wastage levels.

Direct Labour Variances

Direct labour costs also have a price and a quantity aspect (i.e. the rate per hour and the number of hours used) and any variances can again be attributed to these factors. Consequently they are calculated in the same manner as direct materials with the price variance in this case being referred to as the 'rate variance' and the usage variance as the 'efficiency variance'.

Direct Labour Total Variance

The total direct labour variance shows the difference between the expected labour costs for the bookcases produced and the actual costs incurred. It is calculated as follows:

Direct Lab. Total Variance = Std. lab. cost for actual production - Actual labour cost

= (1,200 bookcases x £35) – (5,500 hours x £7.40 per hr)

= £42,000 – £40,700

= £1,300 *Favourable*

To help determine the reasons for this variance the rate and efficiency variances can now be calculated.

Direct Labour Rate Variance

This variance shows the effect of paying more or less per hour than expected and is calculated as follows:

Labour Rate Variance = *Hours paid for* x *(Standard rate - Actual rate)*

= 5,500 hours   x (£7 - £7.40)

= 5,500 hours   x   £0.40

= £2,200 *Adverse*

Each of the 5,500 hours worked cost 40p more than expected, causing an adverse rate variance of £2,200.

Direct Labour Efficiency Variance

The efficiency variance shows the effect of taking more or less hours than expected to produce the output achieved.

Lab. Efficiency Variance = *(Std. hours for actual production – Hours worked)* x *Std. rate*

= (1,200 bookcases x 5 hours - 5,500 hours) x £7 per hour

= (6,000 hours - 5,500 hours) x £7 per hour

= £3,500 *Favourable*

Note that as with the materials usage variance, the standard rate is used here to isolate the effect of using more hours.

As the 1,200 bookcases required 500 hours less than planned at a standard rate of £7 per hour, costs were £3,500 lower than anticipated.

The total labour variance can now be explained as follows:

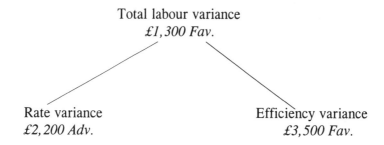

Total labour variance
£1,300 Fav.

Rate variance
£2,200 Adv.

Efficiency variance
£3,500 Fav.

Although greater efficiency resulted in savings of £3,500, the higher wage rate increased costs by £2,200 resulting in a total favourable variance of £1,300.

Typical Reasons for Labour Variances

Rate Variances

- A wage rise not reflected in the standard rate.

- Using higher/lower grades of labour.

- Paying bonuses/premiums which were not planned for.

Efficiency Variances

- Using unskilled employees.

- Using inefficient equipment.

- Using poor quality materials (which may be more difficult to work with).

Note that again there may be a relationship between variances. In this case BS Limited's adverse rate and favourable efficiency variances may be due to recruiting highly skilled employees at a higher hourly rate.

Overhead Variances

In Chapter 10 we saw how production overheads are assigned to products using pre-determined overhead absorption rates (OAR's) calculated as follows:

$$\text{OAR} \quad = \quad \frac{Estimated\ overheads}{Estimated\ labour\ hours}$$

BS Limited's fixed OAR of £6 per labour hour was therefore calculated as follows using the budget information supplied in Example 16.1:

$$\text{OAR} \quad = \quad \frac{£33,000}{1,100\ bookcases \times 5\ hours}$$

$$= \quad \frac{£33,000}{5,500\ labour\ hours}$$

$$= \quad £6 \text{ per labour hour}$$

As we saw in Chapter 10, because this rate is determined using estimated rather than actual figures, it will only result in charging all overheads to units produced if these estimates are correct. As this is unlikely overheads will probably be over or under absorbed. (It may be useful to revise 'Over/Under Absorption of Overheads' in Chapter 10 at this point).

Overhead variances help to explain this over or under absorption.

Overhead Absorption Using Standard Costing

Although overheads may be absorbed on the basis of hours worked, when using standard costing systems absorption is normally based on standard hours of production (SHP). SHP is a standard measurement of output used by businesses producing a variety of products and can be ascertained as follows:

SHP = Quantity produced x Standard time per unit

So for BS Limited:

SHP = 1,200 units x 5 hours per unit = 6,000 hours

(i.e. 6,000 hours worth of work was produced in the month).

This figure can be used in the calculation of fixed and variable overhead variances as demonstrated below:

Fixed Overhead Variances

Fixed Production Overhead Total Variance

The total overhead variance shows the extent to which fixed overheads have been under or over absorbed in the period and is calculated as follows:

$Fixed\ Overhead\ Total\ Variance$ = *Fixed overheads absorbed – Actual fixed overheads*

= (SHP x OAR) – Actual overheads

= (6,000 hours x £6 per hour) – £40,000

= £36,000 - £40,000

= £4,000 *Adverse*

As costs of £40,000 were incurred and only £36,000 charged to products, overheads have been under absorbed by £4,000. Costs have therefore been understated and as the £4,000 must be added to February's reported costs to compensate for this, the variance is adverse.

As explained earlier, over absorption of overhead is due to incorrectly estimating the overhead expenditure and/or the activity level for the period (i.e. the SHP). These can be investigated using two further variances.

Fixed Overhead Expenditure Variance

This shows the effect of variations in expenditure and is calculated as follows:

Fixed O'head Expenditure Variance = *Actual fixed o'heads – Budgeted fixed o'heads*

= £40,000 – £33,000

= £7,000 *Adverse*

Fixed Overhead Volume Variance

The volume variance assesses the effect of variations in output and is calculated as follows:

Fixed Overhead Volume Variance = *(Budgeted hours – SHP) x OAR*

= (1,100 units x 5hrs. – 6,000 hrs.) x £6

= (5,500 hrs. – 6,000 hrs.)   x £6

= £3,000 *Favourable*

(NB. As output was higher than expected the variance is favourable).

The fixed overhead variances we have examined are summarised in Figure 16.2 which should help you to understand their calculation and the relationship between them.

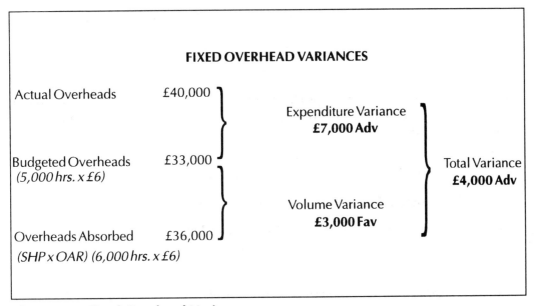

Figure 16.2 Fixed Overhead Variances

The under absorption of fixed overheads by £4,000 was therefore due to:

		£
a)	Spending more than expected	(7,000)
b)	Offset to an extent by producing more than expected	3,000
		(4,000)

Variable Overhead Variances

Variable Production Overhead Total Variance

The total variance, as in the case of fixed overheads, shows the extent to which overheads have been over or under absorbed. It is calculated as follows:

$$\textit{Variable O'head Total Variance} = \textit{Variable o'heads absorbed} - \textit{Actual variable o'heads}$$

$$= \text{(SHP x OAR)} - \text{Actual Overheads}$$

$$= \text{(6,000 hours x £2 per hour)} - £10,000$$

$$= £12,000 - £10,000$$

$$= £2,000 \textit{ Favourable}$$

As £12,000 has been charged to products when only £10,000 was incurred, overheads have been over absorbed. Costs have therefore been overstated and £2,000 must be added to the profit reported in February to compensate. Consequently the variance in this case is favourable.

This total variance can again be investigated further using two sub-variances.

Variable Overhead Expenditure Variance

This shows the difference between expected and actual expenditure and is ascertained as follows:

$$\textit{Variable O'head Expenditure Variance} = \textit{Actual variable o'heads} - \textit{Budgeted variable o'heads}$$

$$= £10,000 - \text{(Hours worked x OAR)}$$

$$= £10,0000 - \text{(5,500 hours x £2)}$$

$$= £10,000 - £11,000$$

$$= £1,000 \textit{ Favourable}$$

Note that as variable overheads are expected to fluctuate with the number of hours worked, a flexed budget is used here. The resulting variance shows that expenditure was £1,000 lower than expected given the number of hours actually worked.

Variable Overhead Efficiency Variance

This variance assesses the effect of efficiency on overhead absorption and is calculated as follows:

Variable Overhead Efficiency Variance = *(SHP– Hours worked) x OAR*

= (6,000 hours – 5,500 hours) x £2 per hour

= £1,000 *Favourable*

During February 6,000 hours worth of work was produced in only 5,500 hours. With an OAR of £2 per hour, the 500 hour efficiency gain has resulted in a favourable variance of £1,000.

The variances calculated in respect of variable overheads are summarised in Figure 16.3.

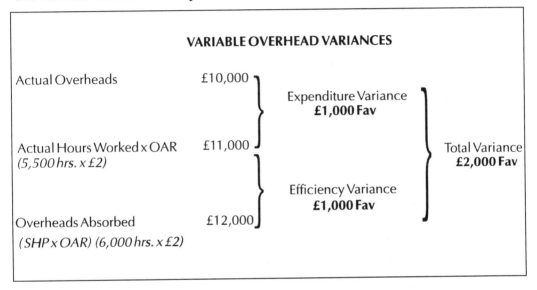

Figure 16.3 Variable Overhead Variances

The over absorption of variable overheads by £2,000 was therefore attributable to:

		£
(a)	Spending less than expected in relation to the hours worked	1,000
(b)	Producing more than expected in the hours worked	1,000
		2,000

Reconciliation of Planned and Actual Costs

Having calculated cost variances, the reasons for the £6,700 difference between the expected cost of producing 1,200 bookcases and the actual costs incurred become more apparent. Figure 16.4 shows a statement which should draw management attention to significant variances requiring further investigation.

Business Systems Limited

Reconciliation of Planned and Actual Costs - February

	Favourable £	Adverse £	£
Planned Costs *(1,200 bookcases* x *£150)*			*180,000*
COST VARIANCES			
Direct Materials			
Price	4,000		
Usage		10,000	
Direct Labour			
Rate		2,200	
Efficiency	3,500		
Production Overheads Fixed			
– Expenditure		7,000	
– Volume	3,000		
Variable			
– Expenditure	1,000		
– Efficiency	1,000		
Total Cost Variance	12,500	19,200	6,700
Actual Costs			186,700

Figure 16.4 Reconciliation of Planned and Actual Costs

Note that as the total cost variance is £6,700 adverse, it must be added to the planned costs to obtain the figure for actual costs.

Sales Variances

To achieve planned profits managers must control sales as well as costs. Although not as commonly used as cost variances, sales variances may be used to show the effect of sales activity on profits. They will be demonstrated using further information related to Business Systems Limited:

Example 16.2

Budgeted sales for February were 1,000 bookcases to be sold at £200 each. However actual sales in the month were 1,200 bookcases at £175 each.

Using this and the information supplied earlier, the expected profit (or 'sales margin') per bookcase can be calculated as shown below:

	£
Budgeted selling price	200
Standard cost of production	150
Standard margin	50

The planned margin for the month was therefore:

1,000 bookcases x £50 = £50,000

However actual profits would differ from this due to variations in both selling price and sales volume. The impact of each can be assessed separately by calculating sales margin variances as demonstrated below:

Sales Margin Total Variance

This shows the combined effect of variations in selling price and sales volume and is calculated as follows:

Sales Margin Total Variance = (Actual sales vol. x Actual margin) – (Std. sales vol. x Std. margin)

$$= \ 1{,}200 \text{ units x } (£175 - £150) \ -1{,}000 \text{ units x } (£200 - £150)$$

$$= (1{,}200 \text{ units x } £25) \qquad (1{,}000 \text{ units x } £50)$$

$$= £30{,}000 - £50{,}000$$

$$= £20{,}000 \ Adverse$$

Note that sales variances show only the impact of changes in selling price and volume and are not concerned with any cost differences. Consequently the bookcases are all valued at the standard cost of £150.

As with the materials and labour variances calculated earlier, the total variance has arisen due to variations in price and quantity and the effect of each can be shown separately by calculating two further variances as illustrated below:

Sales Margin Price Variance

This shows the effect of selling at above or below the standard selling price and is calculated as follows:

Sales Margin Price Variance = Actual sales volume x (Actual margin – Standard margin)

$$= \quad 1,200 \text{ units} \qquad x \text{ (£25 - £50)}$$

$$= \quad £30,000 \text{ } Adverse$$

Selling 1,200 bookcases at £25 below the standard selling price reduced profits by £30,000 and the variance is therefore adverse.

Sales Margin Quantity Variance

This shows the effect of selling more or less than the planned quantity as demonstrated below:

Sales margin quantity variance = (Actual sales vol. – Std. sales vol.) x Std. margin

$$= (1,200 \text{ units} – 1,000 \text{ units}) \quad x \quad £50$$

$$= £10,000 \text{ Favourable}$$

Selling more bookcases than planned will increase profits and the variance in this case is therefore favourable. The total sales margin variance can now be explained as follows:

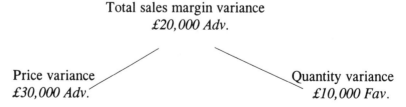

Total sales margin variance
£20,000 Adv.

Price variance
£30,000 Adv.

Quantity variance
£10,000 Fav.

Selling at a lower price resulted in a £30,000 reduction in planned profits which was partially compensated by the extra £10,000 generated from the higher sales volume at this price.

Operating Statements

Having now calculated cost and sales variances, Figure 16.5 shows an operating statement indicating the reasons for the difference between budgeted and actual profit. This should draw management attention to issues which should be investigated more fully in order to determine whether any remedial action is necessary.

Business Systems Limited
Operating Statement – February

			£
Budgeted Profit (1,000 bookcases x £200 – £150)			50,000
SALES VARIANCES			
Price variance		(30,000)	
Quantity variance		10,000	(20,000)
			30,000
COST VARIANCES	*Favourable* £	*Adverse* £	
Direct Materials			
Price	4,000		
Usage		10,000	
Direct Labour			
Rate		2,200	
Efficiency	3,500		
Production Overheads Fixed			
– Expenditure		7,000	
– Volume	3,000		
Variable			
– Expenditure	1,000		
– Efficiency	1,000		
	12,500	19,200	(6,700)
Actual Profit			23,300

Figure 16.5 Business Systems Limited – Operating Statement

Summary of Variances

The variances calculated in respect of BS Limited are summarised in Figure 16.6. This should provide a clear picture of the relationships between them and illustrate how they can assist in the control process by highlighting reasons for differences between planned and actual profits.

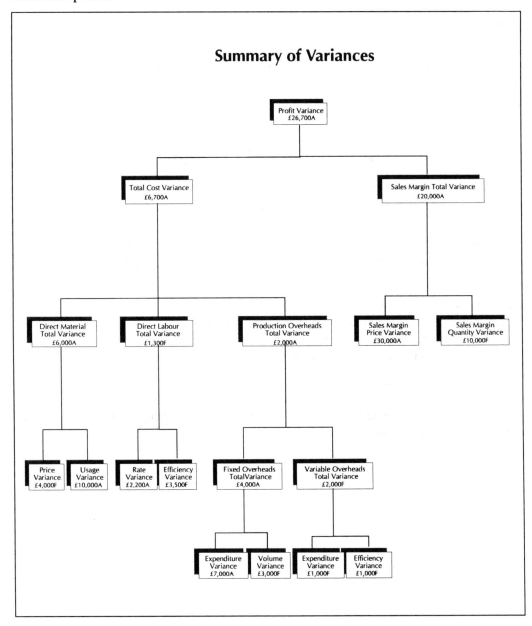

Figure 16.6 Summary of Variances

Advantages of Using Standard Costing

Using standard costing systems for short term planning and control may produce numerous benefits including the following:

Closer Control. Variances can help to explain the reasons for not achieving planned results and prompt remedial action.

Management by Exception. Variance reporting directs management towards the issues most urgently requiring their attention.

Motivation. Setting standards gives employees targets to aim for which, provided they are realistic, may increase motivation.

Appraisal of Current Methods. Setting standards draws attention to current operating procedures and may highlight the need for revised, more efficient methods.

Potential Problems in Standard Costing

Problems which may be encountered when using standard costing include:

Inappropriate Standards. To produce meaningful variances the standards on which they are based must be reasonable. Inappropriate standards will result in information of little value which may induce apathy or even resentment from employees. Standards should therefore be agreed with those expected to work to them and continually updated to reflect current operating conditions and methods.

Cost Effectiveness. Setting and updating standards, measuring actual results, calculating variances and circulating the resulting information can be a time consuming and expensive process. The associated cost should be compared with the benefits resulting from better control information to assess whether or not standard costing is a worthwhile exercise.

Misunderstood Variances. Standard costing systems will fail to achieve their potential if the information produced is not fully understood by those for whom it is intended. The aims of the system and significance of variances should be explained to operational managers to ensure that they are in a position to make full use of the information available.

Summary

- Standard costing is the application of budgetary control techniques to individual products or services and is applicable in situations where repetitive tasks are performed.

- A standard cost is an estimate of the cost expected under a specific set of working conditions.

- Standard costing variances show the effect of deviations from pre-determined standards and can be used to analyse costs and sales revenue.

- Formulae for the variances explained in this chapter are summarised in Figure 16.7.

- Significant variances should be investigated more fully to ascertain their cause and determine whether any remedial action is necessary.

- Standards should be agreed with operational staff and regularly updated.

VARIANCE FORMULAE

DIRECT MATERIALS

Total Variance

= Standard material cost for actual production – Actual material cost

Price Variance

= Actual quantity used x (Standard price – Actual price)

Usage Variance

= (Std. quantity for actual production – Quantity used) x Std. price

DIRECT LABOUR

Total Variance

= Std. labour cost for actual production – Actual labour cost

Rate Variance

= Hours paid for x (Standard rate – Actual rate)

Efficiency Variance

= (Std. hours for actual production – Hours worked) x Std. rate

PRODUCTION OVERHEADS

Fixed Overheads
Total Variance

= Fixed overheads absorbed – Actual fixed overheads

=   (SHP x OAR)   – Actual fixed overheads

Expenditure Variance

= Actual fixed overheads – Budgeted fixed overheads

Volume Variance

= (Budgeted hours – SHP) x OAR

Variable Overheads

Total Variance

= Variable overheads absorbed – Actual variable overheads

=   (SHP x OAR)   – Actual overheads

Expenditure Variance

= Actual variable overheads – Budgeted variable overheads (flexed)

Efficiency Variance

= (SHP – Hours worked) x OAR

SALES

Sales Margin Total Variance

= (Actual sales volume x Actual margin)
– (Standard sales volume x Standard margin)

Sales Margin Price Variance

= Actual sales volume x (Actual margin – Standard margin)

Sales Margin Quantity Variance

= (Actual sales volume – Standard sales volume) x Standard margin

Figure 16.7 Variance Formulae

Questions   (See Appendix C for Answers)

16.1

JB plc operates a standard marginal cost accounting system. Information relating to product J, which is made in one of the company's departments, is given below.

Product J	Standard marginal product cost	
		Unit £
Direct material	6 kilograms at 4 per kg	24
Direct labour	1 hour at £7 per hour	7
Variable production overhead*		3
Total variable production cost		34

* Variable production overhead varies with units produced.

Budgeted fixed production overhead per month: £100,000.

Budgeted production for product J: 20,000 units per month.

Actual production and costs for month 6 were as follows:

Units of J produced		18,500
		£
Direct materials purchased and used	113,500 kgs	442,650
Direct labour	17,800 hours	129,940
Variable production overhead incurred		58,800
Fixed production overhead incurred		104,000
		735,390

You are required

    (a)   To prepare a columnar statement showing, by element of cost, the

        (i)   original budget

        (ii)   flexed budget

        (iii) actual costs

        (iv) total variances

(b)   To subdivide the variances for direct material and direct labour shown in your answer to (a) (iv) above to be more informative for managerial purposes.

(CIMA)

16.2

Business Systems Limited manufactures office furniture and has set the following standards for one cabinet:

	£
Direct materials	
15 m^2 at £3.00 per m^2	45
Direct labour	
5 hours at £4.00 per hour	20
Standard prime cost per cabinet	65

Actual results for February were as follows:

Production	1,400 cabinets
Direct materials	22,000 m^2 used at £3.50 per m^2
Direct wages	6,800 hours worked at £5.00 per hour

Required

Calculate variances in respect of direct materials and labour and prepare a statement reconciling planned and actual prime costs for February.

16.3

GPR Limited, a manufacturing company operating a standard costing system, has the following information available in respect of its operations:

- For each 100 units produced, direct material requirements are 2,000 kg at 80p per kg.

- Ten direct workers are employed working a 40 hour week at a rate of 8.00 per hour and there are 48 working weeks in a year. It is expected that each unit will take 4 hours to produce.

- Budgeted production overhead for the year is £134,400 (of which £19,200 is variable and £115,200 Fixed) and planned output is 4,800 units.

- Overheads are absorbed on the basis of labour hours.

Actual results for week 11.

Output was 110 units.
Direct materials used were 2,100kg at 90p per kg.
Direct wages were paid at £8.10 per hour and 420 hours were worked.
Actual production overhead was £3,160 of which £410 was variable and £2,750 fixed.

Required

(a) Calculate all variances in respect of:

- Direct materials

- Direct labour

- Variable overheads

- Fixed overheads

(b) Produce a statement reconciling planned with actual costs.

Questions Without Answers

16.4

Saunders Limited manufactures a single product and operates a standard costing system. The standard cost per unit is as follows:

		£
Materials	(4 kg at £3.50 per kg)	14.00
Labour	(3 hours at £8.00 per hour)	24.00
		38.00

Planned production for May was 6,000 units.

Actual production during May was 6,500 units and costs incurred were:

Materials	(27,500 kg at £3.30 per kg)
Labour	(23,000 hours at £7.50 per hour)

Required

(a)   Calculate all appropriate material and labour variances.

(b)   Suggest a possible reason for each variance calculated and comment on any possible relationships between the variances.

(c)   Explain the objectives of operating a standard costing system.

16.5

The summary production budget of a factory with a single product for a four week period is as follows:

Production quantity   240,000 units

Production costs:
Material: 336,000kg at £4.10 per kg
Direct labour: 216,000 hours at £4.50 per hour
Variable overheads: £475,200
Fixed overheads: £1,521,600

Variable overheads are absorbed at a predetermined direct labour hour rate. Fixed overheads are absorbed at a predetermined rate per unit of output.

During the four week period the actual production was 220,000 units which incurred the following costs:

Material: 313,060kg costing £1,245,980
Direct labour: 194,920 hours costing £886,886
Variable overheads: £433,700
Fixed overheads: £1,501,240

Required

(a)   Calculate the cost variances for the period.

(b)   Give reasons in each case why the direct labour efficiency, variable overhead efficiency and fixed overhead volume variances may have arisen.

(ACCA)

16.6

A company manufactures two components in one of its factories. Material A is one of several materials used in the manufacture of both components.

The standard direct labour hours per unit of production, and budgeted production quantities, for a 13 week period were:

	Standard direct labour hours	Budgeted production quantities
Component X	0.40 hours	36,000 units
Component Y	0.56 hours	22,000 units

The standard wage rate for all direct workers was £5.00 per hour. Throughout the 13 week period 53 direct workers were employed, working a standard 40 hour week.

The following actual information for the 13 week period is available:

Production:
Component X, 35,000 units
Component Y, 25,000 units
Direct wages paid, £138,500
Material A purchases, 47,000 kilos costing £85,110
Material A price variance, £430F
Material A usage (component X) 33,426 kilos
Material A usage variance (component X), £320.32A

Required

(a) Calculate the direct labour variances for the period.

(b) Calculate the standard purchase price for Material A for the period and the standard usage of Material A per unit of production of Component X.

(c) Describe the steps, and information, required to establish the material purchase quantity budget for Material A for a period.

(ACCA)

16.7

A manufacturing business operates a standard costing system and has established standards for a product as follows:

Direct materials 6 Kg @ £4.80 per Kg

Direct labour 4.5 hours @£9.50 per hour

The full manufacturing capacity of the business is 12,000 units per month. In the month of May actual output was 9,600 units and the following information was recorded:

Direct materials used – 61,300 Kg @ £4.55 per Kg

Direct labour   – 48,500 hours worked and paid at £9.80 per hour

Required

(a) Calculate all direct materials and labour variances and present your results in a management report showing the difference between expected and actual costs for May.

(b) Suggest one possible reason for each of the variances you have calculated.

(c) Explain how the standards given above for the product nay have been determined.

Assignments
and Appendices

Assignment 1 -- Morley Computer Supplies

(Preparation and Interpretation of Financial Statements)

Chris Morley commenced business on 1st April 19X4 selling computer supplies. The following trial balance was extracted from her books of account at the end of the first year.

Trial Balance as at 31st March 19X5

	Debit £	Credit £
Capital		30,000
Loan		45,000
Premises at cost	40,000	
Fixtures at cost	10,000	
Motor vehicle at cost	12,000	
Wages	65,400	
Motor expenses	2,480	
Advertising	4,000	
Purchases	351,000	
Sales		462,000
Heat and light	870	
Telephone	1,040	
Repairs and maintenance	330	
Miscellaneous expenses	15,060	
Debtors	9,400	
Creditors		33,250
Interest paid	2,500	
Drawings	24,000	
Bad debts written off	800	
Cash in hand	450	
Cash at bank	30,920	
	570,250	570,250

Additional information relating to the first year:

1. Stock at 31st March 19X5 valued at cost price was £21,000.

2.   Heat and light accrued at 31st March 19X5 amounted to £130.

3.   Interest on the loan accrued at 31st March 19X5 was £500.

4.   Motor expenses include road tax and insurance amounting to £520 which has been paid in March 19X5 but refers to the year ended 31st March 19X6.

5.   Depreciation is to be provided on fixed assets as follows:
        Motor vehicles 25% per annum using the reducing balance method.
        Fixtures 15% per annum using the straight line method.

At the end of the second year of trading the following trial balance was prepared:

Trial Balance as at 31st March 19X6

	Debit £	Credit £
Capital		30,000
Loan		40,000
Premises at cost	55,000	
Fixtures at cost	14,000	
Motor vehicles at cost	25,000	
Provision for depreciation at 1st April 19X5:		
Motor vehicles		3,000
Fixtures		1,500
Stock at cost at 1st April 19X5	21,000	
Wages	71,200	
Motor expenses	5,150	
Advertising	3,400	
Heat and light	1,090	
Purchases	385,000	
Sales		532,000
Repairs and maintenance	640	
Telephone	1,170	
Interest paid	2,700	
Miscellaneous expenses	16,040	
Debtors	17,500	
Creditors		31,280
Bad debts written off	440	
Cash in hand	620	
Bank overdraft		1,260
Drawings	30,000	
Retained profit		10,910
	649,950	649,950

Additional information relating to 19X6:

1. Stock at 31st March 19X6 valued at cost price was £26,000.

2. Heat and light accrued at 31st March 19X6 was £230.

3. Motor expenses paid in advance at 31st March 19X6 amounted to £780.

4. During the year Chris had decided to seek the help of a professional accountant who advised him to:

    (i)   Continue depreciation of fixed assets at the rate of 25% per annum using the reducing balance method for motor vehicles, and 15% per annum using the straight line method for fixtures.

    (ii) Make a provision for doubtful debts equal to 4% of the debtors at 31st March 19X6.

    Chris agreed to both of these proposals.

5. Chris had not yet paid any fees to the accountant but had been told that the fee for the year ended 31st March 19X6 would be £1,200

During each year 30% of sales and 80% of purchases were on credit and the remainder for cash.

Required

1. For each year prepare a profit and loss account together with a balance sheet as at 31st March.

2. Chris cannot understand why the profit earned in year two has not resulted in a corresponding increase in the bank and cash balance. Write a short note to her explaining the reason for this and draft a statement which explains the movement in the balance over the year.

3. Using the information prepared in parts 1 and 2 above write a report for Chris explaining the results of the business over the first two years and assessing its financial position as at 31st March 19X6.

Assignment 2 -- Shops plc

(Interpretation of Published Financial Statements)

The following profit and loss account and balance sheet have been taken from as set of published financial statements for a UK company which operates a chain of retail shops.

Shops plc
Profit and Loss Account for the year ended 30th September 19X8

	19X8 £000	19X7 £000
Turnover	13,984	6,175
Cost of sales	7,190	3,318
Gross profit	6,794	2,857
Distribution and administrative expenses	5,079	2,079
Operating profit	1,715	778
Interest receivable	112	5
	1,827	783
Interest payable	2	10
Profit on ordinary activities before taxation	1,825	773
Taxation on ordinary activities	668	295
Profit on ordinary activities after taxation	1,157	478
Dividend	176	–
Retained profit	981	478

Shops plc
Balance Sheet at 30th September 19X8

	Note	19X8 £000	19X8 £000	19X7 £000	19X7 £000
Fixed assets:					
Intangible assets			2		–
Tangible assets	1		4,549		1,200
Investments			78		–
			4,629		1,200
Current assets:					
Stock		2,131		608	
Debtors	2	662		258	
Cash in hand		8		3	
		2,801		869	
Creditors: amounts falling due within one year	3	3,865		1,358	
Net current liabilities			(1,064)		(489)
Total assets less current liabilities			3,565		711
Provision for liabilities and charges	4		(122)		(68)
			3,443		643
Capital and reserves					
Called up share capital	5		1,100		50
Share premium account			1,719		–
Retained profits	6		624		593
			3,443		643

Notes to the accounts

1. Tangible fixed assets

	Leasehold Properties £000	Fixtures & Fittings £000	Motor Vehicles £000	Total £000
Cost:				
At beginning of year	590	816	56	1,462
Additions	2,520	1,179	32	3,731
Less: Disposals	–	–	(15)	(15)
At end of year	3,110	1,995	73	5,178
Depreciation and amortisation				
At beginning of year	38	210	14	262
Provision for year	117	242	13	372
Less: Disposals	–	–	(5)	(5)
At end of year	155	452	22	629
Net book value at end of year	2,955	1,543	51	4,549

In the year ended 30th September 19X8, sale proceeds on fixed asset disposals mounted to £10,000.

2. Debtors

	19X8 £000	19X7 £000
Trade debtors	–	4
Prepayments	525	208
Other debtors	137	46
	662	258

3.   Creditors

	19X8 £000	19X7 £000
Bank overdraft	1,492	345
Trade creditors	1,098	289
Corporation tax	616	*320
Accruals and other creditors	483	404
Dividend	176	–
	3,865	1,358

*In 19X7 £320,000 was provided for tax liabilities but the amount actually paid in 19X8 was £318,000.

4.   Provision for liabilities and charges.
This item relates to deferred taxation provided on timing differences.

5.   The share capital consists of fully paid shares of 5p each.

6.   Retained profits

	19X8 £000	19X7 £000
At beginning of year	593	115
Profit for year	981	478
	1,574	593
Less: Capitalisation of reserves at end of year	(950)	–
	624	593

Required

1.   (a)   Prepare a cash flow statement for Shops plc for the year ended 30th September 19X8.

(b)   Calculate the following financial statistics for both 19X8 and 19X7, using end of year figures where appropriate.

(i)   Return on shareholders' funds

(ii)   Net profit margin

(iii)   Gross profit margin

(iv)   Current ratio

(v)   Liquid ratio

(vi) Days creditors

(vii) Stock turnover

(viii) Fixed asset turnover

(ix) Earnings per share.

2. Comment on the performance and future prospects of Shops plc from the viewpoint of:

(a) an individual with a small shareholding in Shops plc;

(b) a financial institution considering making a substantial loan to Shops plc.

3. Describe, concisely, what is meant by each of the following terms used in the financial statements of Shops plc.

(a) Intangible assets

(b) Fixed asset – investments

(c) Share premium account

(d) Prepayments.

(ACCA)

Assignment 3 -- A Chosen Company Limited

(Analysis of Published Financial Statements)

Obtain a copy of the latest annual accounts of a company of your choice and use them to perform the following tasks.

1. Review the results of the business comparing performance in the year in question with the previous year using ratios and other indicators.

2. Assess the financial position of the Company as at the end of the year in question comparing it with the previous year and commenting on any significant changes.

3. Explain why the total expenditure shown in the Profit and Loss Account will not equal the cash payments made in the same period. You should refer to relevant accounting concepts in your answer.

4. Ascertain which methods of depreciation the Company uses and explain the purpose of depreciation (again referring to accounting concepts).

5. Identify the principal sources of finance used by the business.

6. Explain why the reserves shown on the balance sheet do not necessarily represent a cash surplus.

Assignment 4 -- Fashion Conscious Limited

(Cost Behaviour and Decision Making)

The following statement relates the activities of Fashion Conscious Limited, a company selling exclusive fashion accessories.

Fashion Conscious Limited

Operating Statement for 8 weeks to 5.6.X2 (£'000s)

	Hats	Handbags	Gloves	Scarves	Total
Sales	350		250	250	
Less Costs					
Variable Costs	(200)		(260)	(200)	
Fixed Costs	(70)		(50)	(90)	
Profit	80		(60)	(40)	

Due to staff shortages in the finance department the costs for Handbags have not been analysed between the fixed and variable elements. However, the following information has been collated in respect of Handbags.

Week	Sales Revenue £	Total Cost £
1	30,000	23,000
2	22,500	19,000
3	23,750	19,250
4	25,000	19,650
5	20,000	17,000
6	27,500	21,850
7	25,000	20,000
8	26,250	20,250
Total	200,000	160,000

Selling price = £250 per handbag

Required

    (a)   From the information given above, you are required to:

        (i)   Calculate how many handbags were sold in the eight week period.

(ii)   Estimate the variable cost per handbag and the fixed costs per week.

(iii) Describe an alternative method of arriving at the result obtained in (ii) and comment on any advantage/disadvantage it has compared with the method you used.

(iv)   Complete the operating statement for the eight week period.

(b)   The Marketing Director has proposed that the company ceases selling gloves and scarves in order to increase profits to a more acceptable level. As Management Accountant of Fashion Conscious, state whether or not you agree with this proposal giving reasons for your views.

(c)   A fashion magazine has shown interest in offering the handbags marketed by Fashion Conscious as competition prizes and has offered to buy 100 for £175 each.

(i)   State, giving your reasons, whether or not the offer should be accepted.

(ii)   What is the lowest price per handbag (to the nearest £) which should be accepted?

(iii) What other factors should be taken into account when considering selling below normal selling price?

(d)   Define fixed costs and variable costs and give three examples of each which may be incurred by Fashion Conscious Limited.

Assignment 5 -- Hairy Hadrian and his Roman Walls

(Cost Behaviour and CVP Analysis)

This year the town of Morpeth celebrates its 900th anniversary. As part of its festivities, the Borough Council resolves that it should hold a series of concerts reflecting the town's musical heritage. The Director of Leisure Services, Mr Chris Booth, is given the task of promoting these concerts and, although the Borough Council has allocated a substantial budget for these events, it is clear that some will make considerable losses while others will prove profitable.

The concerts will include early church music, medieval music, chamber music and rock and roll. One of the events it is hoped will prove profitable is a 'gig' to be given by 'Hairy' Hadrian and the Roman Walls. 'Hairy' Hadrian – real name Dave Spigot – is an ageing thrash rock star, a 'local boy made good' and should prove to be a crowd puller. However the Director is wary in case crowd trouble should break out and blemish the festival, so he insists that there must be a more than adequate number of bouncers to control fans. The event is to held in the Chantry, one of the Borough Council's public halls in the town centre. The hall is very old and not particularly safe, and so stringent conditions have to be laid down.

Under these conditions, there must be at least thirty bouncers if 3,000 or fewer tickets are sold; one extra bouncer for each 20 tickets sold, between 3,000 and 4,000; and one extra bouncer for each extra 10 tickets sold over 4,000. Each bouncer is to be paid £40 per night. The capacity of the hall is 5,000 and the price of tickets is set at £6 each. The cost of heating, lighting and administrative staff for the event is £2,500 and this must be paid, regardless of the number of tickets sold. 'Hairy' Hadrian's specially discounted fee for his performance is £2,000, and £850 must be spent on hiring a PA system for the evening.

It is clear that, in order to sell tickets for the concert, it must be advertised, and this can be done in three ways: on posters at a cost of £40 each; in the local papers at £80 per advert; and on the local radio at £200 per spot. The Director estimates that to attract 3,000 customers it is necessary to spend £400 on posters and £800 on newspaper ads. If local radio is used, however, more tickets can be sold, as follows:

> 1st radio advertisement sells 1,000 more tickets;
> 2nd radio advertisement sells an extra 500 tickets;
> 3rd radio advertisement sells an extra 250 tickets
> 4th radio advertisement sells an extra 50 tickets.

Required

As an officer in the Leisure Services Department of the Borough Council, advise the director on the following points:

    (a)   What the fixed costs of the concert are and what its variable costs are;

(b)   How many tickets will have to be sold in order to break even;

(c)   How many tickets should be sold to make the maximum profit;

(d)   How much advertising should be carried out.

Explain your advice in words and in the form of a break-even chart.

Assignment 6 -- The Housemartin Hotel

(Short Term Planning and Decision Making)

Dave and Jane have been given the opportunity to obtain a 20 year leasehold on a building in London which they plan to operate as a hotel for 365 days each year.

Income

The hotel has thirty rooms which they believe could be let at a rate of £60 per night (regardless of single or double occupancy). At this price it is expected that an average occupancy of 55% could be obtained throughout the year.

From their experience working in hotels of a similar size they expect that other income generated will bear a close relationship with the level of room sales. This income will fall into a number of categories and the following projections have been made:

	£'s per room per night
Room rate	60.00
Catering	18.00
Telephones	2.00
Souvenirs	6.00
Total estimated income	86.00

The anticipated costs for the venture are detailed below:

Catering/Telephones/Souvenirs

The mark-ups applied to these items in arriving at a selling price will be as follows:

Catering	50%
Telephones	100%
Souvenirs	100%

Toiletries

A complimentary bag of toiletries is to be provided in each room for each night occupied. These will be obtained locally at a cost of £1.50 per bag.

Room Cleaning

Cleaning services are to be provided by hiring casual labour at a rate of £6.00 per hour. Rooms will be cleaned only after being occupied and it is estimated that each room will take on average, twenty minutes to clean. (n.b. Cleaners will be hired only for the time required to clean rooms occupied).

Laundry

Linen is to be cleaned after occupancy of a room, by a local firm who have agreed to do so at a rate of £3.00 per room.

Premises

Annual premises costs are expected as follows:

Lease rental	£90,000
Maintenance	£28,000
Gas	£15,000
Electricity	£11,000
Water	£ 4,000

Staff

With the exception of the services already mentioned,the hotel is to be run by the following persons:

	Annual Salary
Manager(ess)	£22,000
Assistant Manager(ess)	£16,000
6 Hotel Operatives	£9,000 each

Advertising/Promotion

Advertising and promotion costs are expected to amount to £14,000 per annum.

Depreciation

Depreciation is to be provided on a straight line basis on the following equipment:

	Estimated Cost (£'s)	Useful Life (Yrs)
Furnishings	60,000	6
Catering Equipment	12,000	3
Administration Equipment	4,500	3
Cleaning Equipment	3,600	4
Other Equipment	8,000	5

Administration

Dave and Jane have estimated that administration costs will amount to £24,000.

Required

Dave and Jane would like some information which will help in appraising the viability of the venture and have enlisted your assistance. In order to help them in planning you are required to:

1.   Develop a spreadsheet model which will:

   (a)   Produce a statement projecting the estimated profit/loss in the first year.

   (b)   Estimate the break - even point of the hotel.

   (c)   Re-calculate the results in (a) and (b) above to show the effect of changes in any variables given.

2.   Write a short report to Dave and Jane to include:

   (a)   A general description of the nature of your model and the benefits arising from its use.

   (b)   Instructions on its use.

   (c)   Any limitations of the model and their impact on results produced.

3.   Using your model, estimate the revised profitability and break-even point of the hotel in the light of the following changes :

   (a)   Toiletries increase to £1.75 per bag.

   (b)   The hotel is shut for two weeks at Christmas.

   (c)   The room rate is increased to £65 per night and as a result, average occupancy falls to 50%.

   (d)   All the events in (a) to (c) above occur.

4.   Again using your model advise Dave and Jane on the viability of the following courses of action:

   (a)   It has been estimated that the occupancy rate could be increased to 60% by spending an additional £25,000 on advertising.

   (b)   Feelbrite Cleaning Services have offered to supply cleaners at a rate of £8.50 per hour on the basis that the agreed cleaning time per room will be 15 minutes. If the offer is accepted there will be no necessity to buy cleaning equipment and maintenance costs of £200 per annum could be avoided.

   (c)   Reducing the mark-up on catering to 20% (which would reduce catering income to £14.40 per room per night). It has been estimated that this would increase the number of repeat bookings and that average occupancy would rise to 58%.

Assignment 7 -- Dritech Limited

(Budgetary Control)

Dritech Limited is a member of the Trustpower group of companies which produces sports equipment. It has operated from premises in South Wales for many years and currently employs 450 people.

For the past four to five years, although sales have been maintained, profits have gradually reduced and are now giving some concern to Trustpower.

The Chief Accountant retired some months ago and Steve Donaldson, a recently qualified management accountant has been appointed to the position on an initial probationary period of one year.

Steve, knowing the importance of making an impression in this time and hearing through the grapevine about some dissatisfaction among a number of recently promoted young managers has decided to spend some time looking at the budgeting procedures operating within the business.

He invited a number of these managers to give their views in writing and received the replies shown below.

After reading the memos Steve checked records and found that expenditure in the last quarter (and the last month in particular) seemed to be unusually high in many years.

He also asked Jim Reed, the trainee accountant to summarise the expenditure in the racquets department from the past year's budget statements and to note the output in each quarterly period (see attached).

Steve talked with the accounts supervisor Ron Cooper about the preparation of budget statements and Ron's main concern was that he was overworked at the end of each quarter. Much time was spent speaking to suppliers or trying to trace purchase invoices internally to find out exactly what costs had been incurred.

The information Steve had now accumulated confirmed his earlier suspicion that changes were needed. He decided to compile a report for the consideration of the Board of Directors at their next meeting.

Memos Received:

DRITECH LIMITED

Internal Memorandum

To: S. Donaldson,
Chief Accountant.

From: H. Bell,
Manager,
Indoor Clothing.

Budgeting

In your response to our talk earlier this week I would like to give you a manager's perception of the budgeting system 'operating' in Dritech.

The system seems to be a device for producing reams of paper which we don't understand and I fail to see what purpose it serves to anyone.I believe they are sent to Group headquarters so presumably they have a use for them. I just hope they don't assume that they give any indication of what goes on in the factory here.

No-one seems to know where the budgets used come from, although I did hear recently that in the past few years a lot of it is based on the previous year's figure plus a bit for inflation (or if things are a bit tight, less a percentage to make us cut costs).

Harry Bell

DRITECH LIMITED

Internal Memorandum

To: S. Donaldson
Chief Accountant

From: P. Drummond,
Manager,
Racquets Dept.

Budget System

To help you with your enquiries into the budgeting system I've attached my most recent budget statement. Although it appears to show a very poor position I would draw your attention to the following:

1. The budget was produced last November on the basis of producing 8,000 units in the quarter it turned out business has picked up this year and we actually produced 9,800 units. Its no wonder I over spent!

2. Even where I've under spent I get no recognition. I was a supervisor short in August through sickness and instead of covering her absence by short term internal promotion I took on some of the work myself. This made for a long hard month but it doesn't even seem to be recognised by anyone let alone appreciated.

3. I'm told that materials are charged to the department at the rate Purchasing Department buys them in at but I know for a fact that when they're busy they don't shop around and their regular supplier isn't always the cheapest.

4. When Purchasing do shop around they often buy poor quality materials and we suffer through more wastage and production delays.

I've been told that my predecessor was 'moved on' because he couldn't control the costs. If the budget statement is supposed to be measuring this neither can I!

I'm not afraid of taking responsibility but I'd like to be given a fair chance.

Paul Drummond

Racquets Dept. Budget Statement
3 Months Ended 30/9/X3

Budget Controller: P. Drummond

	Expenditure	Budget	Variance
Materials	58,250	50,200	8,050
Direct labour	92,100	75,700	16,400
Consumables	1,430	1,000	430
Maintenance	14,450	12,500	1,950
Depreciation	12,600	9,200	3,400
Supervision	8,000	8,100	
Power	7,100	5,800	1,300
Heating	200	1,400	
Central O/heads	34,000	27,400	6,600
Total	228,130	191,300	

R. Cooper
Accounts Supervisor
12/11/X3

Racquets Dept. Expenditure (£'s)

	Dec X2	Mar X3	Jun X3	Sep X3	Total
Output (Units)	8,700	9,400	10,800	9,800	38,700
Materials	53, 940	57,120	66,960	58,250	236,270
Direct labour	84,390	90,080	104,760	92,100	371,330
Consumables	1,274	1,265	1,316	1,430	5,285
Maintenance	13,305	13,530	13,620	14,450	54,905
Depreciation	9,200	9,200	12,600	12,600	43,600
Supervision	8,100	8,200	8,100	8,000	32,400
Power	6,696	6,693	6,864	7,100	27,353
Heating	2,100	2,300	200	200	4,800
Central O/heads Allocated	27,400	27,400	34,000	34,000	122,800
Total	206,405	215,788	248,420	228,130	898,743

J. Reed

DRITECH LIMITED

Internal Memorandum

To: S. Donaldson,
Chief Accountant.

From: L. Hall,
Manager,
Winter Sports.

Following our telephone conversation yesterday I'd like to make the following points about the budgeting system:

- How can I find out where the figures actually come from? At times they just don't seem to bear out what has actually been happening in the department.

- If we are supposed to be controlling how the money is being spent, why is there lots of expenditure on unnecessary things at the end of each financial year (painting walls, buying new chairs etc.etc.)

- I under spent last year and my budget has been cut this time around. I'm painting the walls in December this year (as many coats as it takes!).

Len Hall

Required

Prepare Steve's report to the board of directors assessing the current situation within Dritech Limited and making recommendations as you see fit.

You should include in the report a re-drafted budget statement for the Racquets Department which you feel would be more appropriate than the current version.

Assignment 8 -- South Western Mining Supplies Limited

(Cost Control and Standard Costing)

South Western Mining Supplies Limited is a manufacturing company which has produced capital equipment for the mining industry from a factory in southern England for the past fifty years.

For much of that time the business was very successful, selling most of its output to the nationalised domestic coal industry and the remainder (approximately 10%) in the overseas market.

However, in recent years the domestic market has been shrinking rapidly and South Western's share of the market has been gradually falling. It has tried to expand its overseas sales but again has found life very difficult despite a reputation for a very high quality product with an excellent reliability record.

At a recent board meeting Jack McCall, the Managing Director, asked Terry Peters the sales director why the Company's sales performance was so poor.

"Look its not our fault. My team have been working day and night throughout Europe and North America as well as at home trying to shift this stuff but they're banging their heads against a brick wall. We just can't compete. The prices we're quoting are getting us nowhere."

"But I thought you said the some of the competition were taking losses to drive out the weaker suppliers. That was over two years ago and we're still not selling" replied Jack.

"Well that's what we thought at first but it looks like they're making money at those prices. They must be operating in a different league to us. We can't get near them and the sales force are becoming more cheesed off by the day. They're not magicians,they can't pull orders out of a hat. We've got to give them a fighting chance. Even with our reputation for quality the customers won't pay our prices. Times are hard!" Terry was feeling very much on the defensive.

"Well what about our costs" said Jack looking at Dave Johnson the recently appointed Financial Director, "If the rest can live with those prices why can't we? "

"There's no doubt that we're not producing the same product" said Dave. "Our product reliability costs more to produce and one question we need to address is, do they think its worth paying for.If not then we'd better look at designs again and give them what they really need, not what we happen to produce."

"We could certainly look at that" said Terry "but the feeling coming back from the sales team is that they want the products and that they would pay more for what we can offer. But not as much as we're asking."

"Okay" replied Dave "Another thing that has been bothering me since I've joined is our approach to cost control. I'm especially concerned with the cost of production. At the moment we produce equipment, record the cost through time sheets and material requisitions with a bit of overhead added, and either make a profit or a loss on the sale. Or in some cases don't make a sale at all. We just record what happened and that's it."

"That's what you're here for isn't it" interrupted Bill Butcher the Production Manager. "The last guy told us it was a legal obligation to record what happened and report it in our accounts."

"Yes it is" replied Dave. "But we should be looking in a lot more detail at what is happening to find out ways we might be able to improve. In the past, with a good relationship with the Coal Board, maybe there hasn't been such a critical need to look at what's going on so closely. The profits were there and presumably everyone was happy with them."

"Look, I know what's going on in the factory. I've got foremen to tell me that,although not much escapes my attention anyway. I walk through the factory every day. Problems aren't solved looking at accounts you know. I need to see what's happening for myself. And if your people are going to start poking around telling us what we should and shouldn't be doing I don't think that'll go down well. It's the last thing we need at the moment with the threat of redundancies in the air and morale being so low. What about us coming into your department and telling you what you're doing wrong."

"I think I know some of the things we're doing wrong Bill" said Dave. "I think we could help you more for a start. And if something isn't done quickly we'll all have a bigger morale problem. We'll be finished."

"Right let's leave it there" interrupted Jack McCall. "We've got the Canadian visitors arriving shortly and I want to talk to them with Terry and Bill about the Toronto order. We've certainly got problems and Dave's right, something has to be done quickly. Dave why don't you produce a report for the board meeting next Friday and we'll look at it then? I think we've got to look at things constructively and be open with each other. I'm sure if we were all honest we could all use any advice which helps to do the job better. If there are things which can be changed for the better we owe it to everyone to look closely at them. No matter how painful it may be."

"Well if it's less painful than not paying the mortgage next month its got to be worth a try" said Terry and the meeting was wound up on this sober note.

Dave returned to his office and called in Brian Kelly the wages clerk."You've worked here a long time Brian" he said. "You must know a lot of people working in production. What do you think the general feeling is."

"I think there are a lot of very worried people out there" Brian started. "They know they're producing good equipment but that it's not selling and that it can only go on for so long. I think most of them genuinely feel they would like to do something to improve the situation but they're not sure how they can help. I don't think they get many opportunities to have a say. Butcher tends to run the show his way and doesn't think he needs too much advice. They come in and do a day's work then go home. No-one tells them whether they've done enough, too much or too little and they know themselves that at times jobs take longer than they should and that materials are sometimes wasted. Underneath it all I think they take a pride in what they produce but at the moment morale is low and most of the production workers feel helpless and frustrated."

"Right thanks Brian. We'll certainly have to do something. We can't just throw our jobs away."

Dave then started working on his report for the board meeting the following week.

Required

Draft a report which Dave can present to the board meeting which addresses the following as well as any other issues you believe should be raised:

Cost control

The importance of cost control.

The features of an effective cost control system.

Advice as to how they might be implemented at South Western Mining.

The benefits which may arise.

Any problems which may result from such measures and advice to help overcome these.

Standard costing

An explanation of standard costing systems.

Advice as to how such a system could be implemented at SWM Limited.

The benefits/problems which may arise.

Appendix A
Present Value Factors

Rate of discount

Years	1%	2%	3%	4%	5%	6%	7%	8%	9%	10%	11%	12%	13%	14%	15%	16%
1	0.990	0.980	0.971	0.962	0.952	0.943	0.935	0.926	0.917	0.909	0.901	0.893	0.885	0.877	0.870	0.862
2	0.980	0.961	0.943	0.925	0.907	0.890	0.873	0.857	0.842	0.826	0.812	0.797	0.783	0.770	0.756	0.743
3	0.971	0.942	0.915	0.889	0.864	0.840	0.816	0.794	0.772	0.751	0.731	0.712	0.693	0.675	0.658	0.641
4	0.961	0.924	0.889	0.855	0.823	0.792	0.763	0.735	0.708	0.683	0.659	0.636	0.613	0.592	0.572	0.552
5	0.952	0.906	0.863	0.822	0.784	0.747	0.713	0.681	0.650	0.621	0.594	0.567	0.543	0.519	0.497	0.476
6	0.942	0.888	0.838	0.790	0.746	0.705	0.666	0.630	0.596	0.565	0.535	0.507	0.480	0.456	0.432	0.410
7	0.933	0.871	0.813	0.760	0.711	0.665	0.623	0.584	0.547	0.513	0.482	0.452	0.425	0.400	0.376	0.354
8	0.924	0.854	0.789	0.731	0.677	0.627	0.582	0.540	0.502	0.467	0.434	0.404	0.376	0.351	0.327	0.305
9	0.914	0.837	0.766	0.703	0.645	0.592	0.544	0.500	0.460	0.424	0.391	0.361	0.333	0.308	0.284	0.263
10	0.905	0.820	0.744	0.676	0.614	0.558	0.508	0.463	0.422	0.386	0.352	0.322	0.295	0.270	0.247	0.227
11	0.896	0.804	0.722	0.650	0.585	0.527	0.475	0.429	0.388	0.350	0.317	0.287	0.261	0.237	0.215	0.195
12	0.887	0.789	0.701	0.625	0.557	0.497	0.444	0.397	0.356	0.319	0.286	0.257	0.231	0.208	0.187	0.168
13	0.879	0.773	0.681	0.601	0.530	0.469	0.415	0.368	0.326	0.286	0.258	0.229	0.204	0.182	0.163	0.145
14	0.870	0.758	0.661	0.578	0.505	0.442	0.388	0.341	0.299	0.263	0.232	0.205	0.181	0.160	0.141	0.125
15	0.861	0.743	0.642	0.555	0.481	0.417	0.362	0.315	0.275	0.239	0.209	0.183	0.160	0.140	0.123	0.108
16	0.853	0.728	0.623	0.534	0.458	0.394	0.339	0.292	0.252	0.218	0.188	0.163	0.142	0.123	0.107	0.093
17	0.844	0.714	0.605	0.513	0.436	0.371	0.317	0.270	0.231	0.198	0.170	0.146	0.125	0.108	0.093	0.080
18	0.836	0.700	0.587	0.494	0.416	0.350	0.296	0.250	0.212	0.180	0.153	0.130	0.111	0.095	0.081	0.069
19	0.828	0.686	0.570	0.475	0.396	0.331	0.277	0.232	0.195	0.164	0.138	0.116	0.098	0.083	0.070	0.060
20	0.820	0.673	0.554	0.456	0.377	0.312	0.258	0.215	0.178	0.149	0.124	0.104	0.087	0.073	0.061	0.051

Rate of discount

Years	17%	18%	19%	20%	21%	22%	23%	24%	25%	26%	28%	30%	35%	40%	45%	50%
1	0.855	0.847	0.840	0.833	0.826	0.820	0.813	0.807	0.800	0.794	0.781	0.769	0.741	0.714	0.690	0.667
2	0.731	0.718	0.706	0.694	0.683	0.672	0.661	0.650	0.640	0.630	0.610	0.592	0.549	0.510	0.476	0.444
3	0.624	0.609	0.593	0.579	0.565	0.551	0.537	0.525	0.512	0.500	0.477	0.455	0.406	0.364	0.318	0.296
4	0.534	0.516	0.499	0.482	0.467	0.451	0.437	0.423	0.410	0.397	0.373	0.350	0.301	0.260	0.226	0.198
5	0.456	0.437	0.419	0.402	0.386	0.370	0.355	0.341	0.328	0.315	0.291	0.269	0.223	0.186	0.156	0.132
6	0.390	0.370	0.352	0.335	0.319	0.303	0.289	0.275	0.262	0.250	0.227	0.207	0.165	0.133	0.108	0.088
7	0.333	0.314	0.296	0.279	0.263	0.249	0.235	0.222	0.210	0.198	0.178	0.159	0.122	0.095	0.074	0.059
8	0.285	0.266	0.249	0.233	0.218	0.204	0.191	0.179	0.168	0.157	0.139	0.123	0.091	0.068	0.051	0.039
9	0.243	0.226	0.209	0.194	0.180	0.167	0.155	0.144	0.134	0.125	0.108	0.094	0.067	0.048	0.035	0.026
10	0.208	0.191	0.176	0.162	0.149	0.137	0.126	0.116	0.107	0.099	0.085	0.073	0.050	0.035	0.024	0.017
11	0.178	0.162	0.148	0.135	0.123	0.112	0.103	0.094	0.086	0.079	0.066	0.056	0.037	0.025	0.017	0.012
12	0.152	0.137	0.124	0.112	0.102	0.092	0.083	0.076	0.069	0.063	0.052	0.043	0.027	0.018	0.012	0.008
13	0.130	0.116	0.104	0.094	0.084	0.075	0.068	0.061	0.055	0.050	0.040	0.033	0.020	0.013	0.008	0.005
14	0.111	0.099	0.088	0.078	0.069	0.062	0.055	0.049	0.044	0.039	0.032	0.025	0.015	0.009	0.006	0.003
15	0.095	0.084	0.074	0.065	0.057	0.051	0.045	0.040	0.035	0.031	0.025	0.020	0.011	0.006	0.004	0.002
16	0.081	0.071	0.062	0.054	0.047	0.042	0.036	0.032	0.028	0.025	0.019	0.015	0.008	0.005	0.003	0.002
17	0.069	0.060	0.052	0.045	0.039	0.034	0.030	0.026	0.023	0.020	0.015	0.012	0.006	0.003	0.002	0.001
18	0.059	0.051	0.044	0.038	0.032	0.028	0.024	0.021	0.018	0.016	0.012	0.009	0.005	0.002	0.001	0.001
19	0.051	0.043	0.037	0.031	0.027	0.023	0.020	0.017	0.014	0.012	0.009	0.007	0.003	0.002	0.001	0.000
20	0.043	0.037	0.031	0.026	0.022	0.019	0.016	0.014	0.012	0.010	0.007	0.005	0.002	0.001	0.001	0.000

Appendix B

Annuity Factors
(For equal cashflows arising over a number of successive years)

Rate of discount

Years	1%	2%	4%	6%	8%	10%	12%	14%	15%	16%	18%	20%	22%	24%	25%	26%	28%	30%
1	0.990	0.980	0.962	0.943	0.926	0.909	0.893	0.877	0.870	0.862	0.847	0.833	0.820	0.806	0.800	0.794	0.781	0.769
2	1.970	1.942	1.886	1.833	1.783	1.736	1.690	1.647	1.626	1.605	1.566	1.528	1.492	1.457	1.440	1.424	1.392	1.361
3	2.941	2.884	2.775	2.675	2.577	2.487	2.402	2.322	2.283	2.246	2.174	2.106	2.042	1.981	1.952	1.923	1.888	1.816
4	3.902	3.808	3.610	3.466	3.312	3.169	3.037	2.914	2.855	2.798	2.690	2.589	2.494	2.404	2.362	2.320	2.241	2.166
5	4.853	4.713	4.452	4.212	3.996	3.791	3.605	3.433	3.352	3.274	3.127	2.991	2.864	2.745	2.689	2.635	2.532	2.436
6	5.795	5.601	5.242	4.917	4.623	4.355	4.111	3.889	3.784	3.685	3.498	3.326	3.187	3.020	2.951	2.885	2.759	2.643
7	6.728	6.472	6.002	5.582	5.206	4.868	4.564	4.288	4.160	4.039	3.812	3.605	3.416	3.242	3.161	3.083	2.937	2.802
8	7.652	7.325	6.733	6.210	5.747	5.335	4.968	4.639	4.487	4.344	4.078	3.837	3.619	3.421	3.329	3.241	3.076	2.925
9	8.668	8.162	7.435	6.802	6.247	5.759	5.328	4.946	4.772	4.607	4.303	4.031	3.786	3.586	3.463	3.366	3.184	3.019
10	9.471	8.983	8.111	7.360	6.710	6.145	5.650	5.216	5.019	4.833	4.494	4.192	3.923	3.682	3.571	3.465	3.269	3.092
11	10.368	9.787	8.760	7.887	7.139	6.495	5.988	5.453	5.234	5.029	4.636	4.327	4.035	3.776	3.656	3.544	3.336	3.147
12	11.255	10.575	9.385	8.384	7.636	6.814	6.194	5.660	5.421	5.197	4.793	4.439	4.127	3.851	3.726	3.606	3.387	3.190
13	12.114	11.343	9.986	8.853	7.904	7.103	6.424	5.842	5.583	5.342	4.910	4.533	4.203	3.912	3.780	3.656	3.427	3.223
14	13.004	12.106	10.583	9.295	8.244	7.367	6.628	6.002	5.724	5.468	5.008	4.611	4.265	3.961	3.824	3.695	3.459	3.249
15	13.865	12.849	11.118	9.712	8.559	7.606	6.811	6.142	5.847	5.575	5.092	4.675	4.315	4.001	3.859	3.726	3.483	3.268
16	14.718	13.578	11.652	10.106	8.851	7.824	6.974	6.265	5.954	5.669	5.162	4.730	4.357	4.033	3.887	3.751	3.503	3.283
17	15.662	14.292	12.166	10.477	9.122	8.022	7.120	6.373	6.047	5.749	5.222	4.775	4.391	4.059	3.910	3.771	3.518	3.295
18	16.328	14.992	12.659	10.828	9.372	8.201	7.250	6.467	6.128	5.818	5.273	4.812	4.419	4.080	3.928	3.788	3.529	3.304
19	17.226	15.678	13.134	11.158	9.604	8.365	7.366	6.550	6.198	5.877	5.316	4.844	4.442	4.097	3.942	3.799	3.539	3.311
20	18.046	16.351	13.590	11.470	9.818	8.514	7.469	6.623	6.259	5.929	5.353	4.870	4.480	4.110	3.954	3.808	3.546	3.316
21	18.857	17.011	14.029	11.764	10.017	8.649	7.562	6.687	6.312	5.973	5.384	4.891	4.476	4.121	3.963	3.818	3.551	3.320
22	19.660	17.658	14.451	12.042	10.201	8.772	7.645	6.743	6.359	6.011	5.410	4.909	4.488	4.130	3.970	3.822	3.556	3.323
23	20.458	18.292	14.857	12.303	10.371	8.883	7.718	6.792	6.399	6.044	5.432	4.925	4.499	4.137	3.976	3.827	3.559	3.325
24	21.243	18.914	15.247	12.550	10.529	8.985	7.784	6.815	6.434	6.073	5.451	4.937	4.507	4.143	3.981	3.831	3.562	3.327
25	22.023	19.523	15.622	12.783	10.675	9.077	7.843	6.873	6.464	6.097	5.467	4.948	4.514	4.147	3.985	3.834	3.564	3.329

Appendix C

Answers to questions at end of chapters

1.1

(a) | **Financial Accounting** | **Management Accounting** |
|---|---|
| Used by external parties | Used internally by management |
| Focuses on the past | Focuses on the future |
| Legal and professional reguations | Discretionary |
| Aggregate information | Detailed information |
| Reports results | Aims to influence results |

(b) | **Characteristics** | **Possible Consequences of Information not Complying** |
|---|---|
| Relevant | Information not used by management |
| Easily understood | Information not used or used misguidedly |
| Accurate | Poor decisions. Lack of confidence in the |
| Timely | information system |
| Cost effective | Remedial action not taken promptly |
| | Ineffective use of resources |

1.2

A spreadsheet is not a complicated concept. In essence it is simply a two-dimensional grid consisting of a number of cells, each uniquely described by reference to a position on each of the two dimensions; in other words, a matrix of rows and columns.

It is convenient for a wide range of accounting activities. The effects of varying one or several of a complicated data set can be instantly presented through a suitable computer programme.

None of this in any way makes accounting out of date. Accounting is far more than a technical process, manual or otherwise, and even the technical elements have to be designed with accounting expertise in order to meet accounting objectives. Accounting is in the end a process of communication and a new medium of recording does not alter this. Remember that accounting preceded the invention of paper by thousands of years!

(ACCA)

1.3

Answers to this question may have some differing emphasis depending upon the particular business environments under consideration. The management accountant will operate in profit-seeking and non-profit sectors, the manufacturing and service sectors. It is inevitable that the information needs of decision makers will differ in these different contexts.

There are no hard and fast rules but the following have been suggested to be involved in the management accountant's duties.

(i)   Provision of information to assist planning and control, involvement in budget preparation and division of budgets into operating periods and responsibility centres. The collection and reporting of timely actual results which can be compared with plans to permit the agreement to corrective action.

(ii)   The organising of information for decision making which may be of a short run tactical nature involving, perhaps, product rationalisation or the pricing of product or service. The establishment of a longer run pricing policy.

(iii) The provision of data for periodic, perhaps monthly, income statements which may include stock values.

The above three sections tend to answer the questions which managers pose such as:

(i)   Which activities should I look into?

(ii)   Which course of action shall I take?

(iii) How well am I doing?

The management accountant must never feel constrained and only look within his own organisation. It is most important that he provides information on features outside the firm. For example, competitors' prices, market size and share, new developments and new opportunities.

The use of the computer offers considerable opportunities and challenges to the 'information manager', opportunities in the quantity, speed and range of data he can deal with and challenges in terms of sifting out relevant data.

The computer takes over the routine repetitive calculations such as product costing, debtor control and stock control and so eliminates some of the drudgery from accounting work whether on the factory floor, the supermarket check-out or the hotel reception desk.

Its capacity for rapid calculation permits change to the components of a particular model with the revised implications of such a change to be almost immediately available. One can envisage such a situation in relation to final accounts and cash flow projections. This also offers greater flexibility in the control situation where standards can be changed to a current level.

A wider opportunity to evaluate alternative courses of action is also permitted in decision making. Perhaps various scenarios of the price-demand relationship can be tried. It facilitates sensitivity analysis and the posing of a variety of 'what if' questions of any particular model. Uncertainty can be incorporated into projections. If management will give a range of possible outcomes and costs, a distribution of profits rather than a certainty equivalent is available.

If he is to retain his position as 'information manager', it is vital that he comes to terms with the computer and makes maximum use of its undoubted potential. If he fails to do this the accountant's position may be challenged by the systems analyst or the operational researcher.

(ACCA)

2.1

(a)   The four fundamental accounting concepts are defined in SSAP 2 and have been incorporated in the Companies Act 1985.

The going concern concept states that in the preparation of financial statements it is assumed that the enterprise will continue in operational existence for the foreseeable future. This results in assets usually being valued on the basis of cost (less depreciation where necessary) and not on a realisation or liquidation basis.

The accruals or matching concept states that revenue is recognised when it is earned and costs are recognised as they are incurred; this is in contrast to recognising items when there is a movement of money. The resulted this is that income is matched against the costs which were incurred to earn the income and that the resulting profit or loss is matched to the appropriate accounting period. This concept is the basis of many accounting practices, particularly depreciating fixed assets rather than charging their full cost at the time they were bought.

The consistency concept requires that the same accounting treatment is given to similar items within each accounting period to the next. This is important as comparison between companies at one point in time and through time is one of the basic uses for financial statements.

The prudence concept is an overriding concept which may take precedence over the others, particularly the accruals concept. This concept requires that revenue and profits are not anticipated. They are only to be included in the financial statement when realised in the form of cash (or an asset for which there is reasonable certainty that it will ultimately become cash). Further, provision is to be made for all known liabilities and losses; where the amount is not known with certainty, the best estimate of the liability or loss is to be used. Thus it is clear that this concept is not symmetric and treats profits and losses in a different manner.

(b)   SSAP 2 also defines these two terms.

Accounting bases are the methods developed for applying the fundamental accounting concepts to financial transactions and items in the financial statements. In particular, this will involve determining (a) the accounting periods in which costs and revenues should be recognised and (b) the amounts at which material items should be included in the balance sheet. Accounting bases will be more diverse than the fundamental concepts as they will be developed in response to a variety of business situations and transactions.

'*Accounting policies* are the specific accounting bases selected and consistently followed by a business enterprise as being, in the opinion of the management, appropriate to its circumstances and best suited to present its results and financial position' – SSAP 2. Accounting policies are thus specific to each enterprise and must be disclosed in in a note to the accounts so that the user of the accounts can see which of the many possible bases have been selected.

(c)   A number of accounting bases and policies are given below, though only two were required in the question.

Accounting bases	Accounting policies
Different methods of depreciating fixed assets	Plant and machinery is depreciated by the straight-line method over five years.
Methods of valuing stock	Stocks and work in progress are valued on the last in first out basis.
Methods of dealing with deferred taxation	Deferred taxation is calculated using the liability method.
Methods for calculating turnover	Turnover comprises the value of sales (excluding VAT) in the normal course of business.

(d)   The audit report in its usual form makes no reference to the fundamental accounting concepts but there is an important implicit relationship between the two. As mentioned above, the financial statements are drawn up on the basis of these four concepts and if no mention is made in the audit report this implies that the concepts have not been breached in any way. If the fundamental concepts have not been complied with, for example if the company is in partial liquidation or there has been a material change in the accounting policies, the accounts should make this clear. If this is not the case, then the auditor will state in his report where the fundamental concepts have not been followed and quantify the effects if possible.

(ACCA)

2.2

(a)   *Separate Entity.* The cost of the goods should be shown as a withdrawal of funds by the owner and not a business expense.

(b)   *Money Measurement.* The state of employee morale cannot be measured in monetary terms and should therefore be excluded from the accounts.

(c)   *Matching.* As the goods have been received, they should be reflected in the accounts as stocks of goods for re-sale.

(d) *Prudence*. It should be assumed that the cash will not be received and the £1,000 should be included in the costs shown in the accounts.

(e) *Separate Entity*. The owner's personal transactions are kept separate from those of the business.

(f) *Realisation*. Sales revenue should not be recorded until the orders are fulfilled.

(g) *Materiality*. Although the stationery has a future value to the business and will be used in the following year the sum is so small that the cost may be included in the current year.

2.3

This question tests an understanding of important concepts, and the ability to give simple but clear explanations.

(i) Accounting is concerned with the provision of useful information to people about business. Financial accounting restricts itself to providing information to those outside the business management – i.e. to potentially everybody except managers. The term is taken to include the operations necessary to provide the information - collecting data, recording it, etc., and is usually considered to be restricted to financial information.

(ii) Realisation is concerned with the recognition of revenue. This may be stated as follows. Revenue is recognised as soon as and is allocated to the period in which it is capable of objective measurement, and the asset value receivable in exchange is reasonably certain. This is not really very helpful- how certain is reasonably certain? What we can say perhaps is that an external transaction and evidence of a transfer of ownership are necessary. This is not to imply that completion of the transaction is necessary before realisation takes place, and this is where the uncertainty lies.

(iii) The matching convention states that profit determination is a process of matching against revenue the expenses incurred in earning that revenue. Thus a resource becomes an expense when it is used to derive revenue. The determination of expense is not related to the timing of the payment for the resource.

(iv) The key idea here is that of significance, or usefulness. Items need not be disclosed, or complicated treatments can be simplified or ignored, if their size is not sufficient to make any difference to the decisions which the reader of the information wishes to make. This is clearly rather a subjective concept. In some circumstances it is overridden by specific legal requirements.

(v)   Inflation is concerned with the general rise in the cost of living or with the general fall in the value of money. It is an average concept, and says nothing at all about the change in price of any particular item. Traditionally accountants have prepared their statements on the assumption their measuring unit (the pound, or whatever) is a fixed and constant unit. Inflation makes this assumption invalid and comparisons, the addition of cumulative figures over several years, and so on, become increasingly distorted. Inflation must be distinguished from the notion of particular (specific) price changes.

(ACCA)

3.1

A balance sheet may be viewed as a statement, static rather than dynamic, of sources and applications. Assets show how available resources have been applied and liabilities show where those resources came from – the sources of those resources. Profits and liabilities are both sources of resources, and both represent causes of an increase in resources within the control of the business. Equally, both represent claims on those resources and, following from the business entity convention, liabilities of the business.

(ACCA)

3.2

Date	Bank	Cash	Van	Stock	Debtors	Capital	Creditors	Profit
Mar. 1	10,000					10,000		
Mar. 2	–400	400						
Mar 3	–6,000		6,000					
Mar 4				6,000			6,000	
Mar 7	1,600							1,600
				–800				–800
Mar 12	–250							–250
Mar 13		–30						–30
Mar 14		–120						–120
Mar 16	280				2,520			2,800
				–1,800				–1,800
Mar 18	–200							–200
Mar 20	–350							–350
Mar 24	–2,000			2,000				
Mar 26	2,700							2,700
				–1,400				–1,400
Mar 28					–250			–250
				200				200
Mar 31	–1,300							–1,300
	4,080	250	6,000	4,200	2,270	10,000	6,000	800

3.3

(a)

Transaction	Bank	Fittings	Stock	Debtors	Capital	Profit	Creditors
1	5,000				5,000		
2	−1,200	1,200					
3	−500		500				
4(a)	500					500	
(b)			−250			−250	
5	−150					−150	
6			150				150
7	−50						−50
8(a)				360		360	
(b)			−200			−200	
9	−100					−100	
	3,500	1,200	200	360	5,000	160	100

(b)

Bank

Capital	5,000	Shopfittings	1,200
Sales	500	Purchases	500
		Wages	150
		Creditors (Bloggs)	50
		Premises costs	100
		Bal c/f	3,500
	5,500		5,500
Bal b/f	3,500		

Purchases

Bank	500		
Creditors (Bloggs)	150		
		Bal c/f	650
	650		650
Bal b/f	650		

Capital

		Bank	5,000

Shop Fittings

Bank	1,200		

Sales

		Bank	500
Bal c/f	860	Debtors	360
	860		860
		Bal b/f	860

Creditors (J. Bloggs)

Bank	50	Purchases	150
Bal c/f	100		
	150		150
		Bal b/f	100

Wages

Bank	150		

Rent

Bank	100		

Debtors

Sales	360		

(c)

Trial Balance

	Debit	Credit
	£	£
Bank	3,500	
Capital		5,000
Shop Fittings	1,200	
Purchases	650	
Sales		860
Wages	150	
Creditors		100
Debtors	360	
Rent	100	
	5,960	5,960

3.4

(a) (i) Excess debit balance of £4,600 (Sales understated and expenses overstated by £2,300 each).

(ii) Excess debit balance £900. (Bank account overstated by this amount).

(iii) No effect. (However the bank balance would be overstated by £350 and electricity charges understated by the same sum).

(iv) Excess credit balance £1,640. (Debtors understated and creditors overstated by £820 each).

(v) Excess credit balance of £840. (As rent expenses would be understated by this sum).

(vi) No effect. (However cash would be overstated and debtors under-stated by £4,000).

(b)

	Excess Debit	Excess Credit
	£	£
(i)	4,600	
(ii)	900	
(iv)		1,640
(v)		840
	5,500	2,480

Total imbalance = excess debit £3,020 (£5,500 - £2,480).

4.1

    (a)   Current liabilities (Trade creditors)

    (b)   Fixed assets

    (c)   Capital

    (d)   Current liabilities

    (e)   Current assets (Stock)

    (f)   Owner's funds

    (g)   Current assets (Trade debtors)

    (h)   Long term liabilities

4.2

    (a)   Capital

    (b)   Revenue

    (c)   Revenue

    (d)   Revenue

    (e)   Capital

    (f)   Revenue

    (g)   Capital

    (h)   Revenue

    (i)   Capital

    (j)   Strictly speaking capital. However, as the cost would be negligible it would usually be treated as revenue expenditure.

4.3

Ashleigh's Fashions
Profit and Loss Account for the Year Ended 31.12.X7

	£	£
Sales		104,800
Less Cost of Goods Sold		
Opening Stock	–	
Purchases	66,200	
	66,200	
Less Closing Stock	(10,800)	(55,400)
Gross Profit		49,400
Less Expenses		
General Expenses	8,400	
Rent	6,800	
Salaries	26,700	(41,900)
Net Profit		7,500

Ashleigh's Fashions
Balance Sheet as at 31.12 19X7

			£
Fixed Assets			11,000
Shop Fittings			
Current Assets			
Stock		10,800	
Trade Debtors		4,500	
		15,300	
Less Current Liabilities			
Trade Creditors	6,700		
Bank Overdraft	2,100	(8,800)	6,500
			17,500
Capital			10,000
Retained Profit			7,500
			17,500

4.4

Samantha Balance Sheet as at 30.6 19X8

	£	£
Fixed Assets		
Shop fittings		10,600
Motor Vehicle		6,000
		16,600
Current Assets		
Stock	9,400	
Debtors	2,100	
Bank	8,450	
Cash	1,450	
	21,400	
Less Current Liabilities		
Creditors	(7,700)	
Net Current Assets		13,700
Less Long Term Liabilities		
Bank Loan		(4,000)
		26,300
Capital		7,500
Retained Profit (14,500 + 6,500 – 2,200)		18,800
		26,300

4.5

(a) (i) An asset is a resource possessed or controlled by a business and which has economic value, i.e. which will give valuable benefits in the future. In addition accountants usually only recognise assets when they have been acquired through a recognisable transaction i.e. they have a purchase cost.

(ii) Fixed assets are assets which the business intends to keep and use within its operations over an extended period.

(iii) A current asset is an asset which is expected to change its state in the short term (usually regarded as 12 months).

(iv) Depreciation is the process of allocating the net cost of a fixed asset (cost or value) less estimated disposal value over the expected useful life in proportion to the expected benefit, i.e. matching in a systematic and rational manner.

(b) (i) In strict logic yes: within the above definitions it is a fixed asset, but materiality would usually lead to it being treated as an expense on purchase.

(ii) No, the machine cannot be an asset: it has not been acquired and is not fully controlled, certainly not owned, by the business. It could be argued that the right to use the machine for the hire period, however, is an asset.

(iii) In logical economic terms this is an asset, but accountants would usually ignore it, assuming it is created rather than acquired, even though it may be the most valuable thing a business possesses!

(c) The £4.5m consists of £3m relating to land, £1m relating to buildings, and £0.5m relating to plant and equipment. These are all fixed assets, i.e. resources being retained and used by the business, not purchased for resale. The land is stated to be at valuation, i.e. at a (presumably current) market value, usually interpreted as market selling price. The buildings are said to be at cost, i.e. the figure is the amount that was paid for the buildings when they were purchased – which of course could have been many years ago when price levels were vastly different from current figures.

The plant and machinery figure of £0.5m is harder to explain. Briefly it is arrived at by taking the cost of the plant when purchased, and spreading that cost on some agreed basis over the number of years of the asset's expected useful life to the business. The £0.5m is the unspread bit still left to be taken account of in future years.

The obvious point from all this is that the total figure of £4.5m consists of three different numbers added together which have been calculated on entirely different bases. This figure is fundamentally illogical and inconsistent within itself, and of little use to a shareholder either for estimating asset values of for predicting profit trends

(ACCA)

5.1

(a)   Depreciation may be defined as a measure of the wearing out, consumption or other loss in value of a fixed asset arising from use, time or obsolescence through technical and market changes.

(b)   It is charged in most profit and loss accounts because most business entities use fixed assets which depreciate. It would not be appropriate to charge the whole cost as an expense at the time of purchase. The depreciation charge is an attempt to charge each accounting period for the use of the asset which has, presumably, helped to produce the income for the period, i.e. an example of the matching concept. Over the useful life of the asset the expectation is that the whole cost will have been charged.

(c)   As the value of the asset will, in the normal conditions envisaged by the use of the historical cost basis of accounting, diminish over time it would be misleading to include it 'at cost' on the balance sheet. The convention of deducting the depreciation provided or or charged for its use means that the unexpired cost appears as an asset. In some circumstances it may be more appropriate to to show assets at a valuation. The unexpired cost (NBV) does not represent a valuation but if in the opinion of the directors the value of the assets has permanently fallen below NBV then a value must be substituted for NBV.

(d)   The usual methods of calculation for published financial statements are straight line, whereby the total depreciation over the life of the fixed asset (cost minus estimated scrap value) is divided into equal annual amounts; or reducing balance, whereby the net book amount at the beginning of the year is written down by a fixed percentage over the life.

(ACCA)

5.2

(a)   (i)   An expense is a resource which has been used up. Normally this will imply an asset of service which has been used, wholly or partly, in the operations of the business. Sometimes however it will arise because an asset has ceased to be useful or usable, so an alternative explanation would be that an expense arises from the acquisition of resources which have to no remaining potential usefulness.

(ii)   Matching is the process by which expenses are charged against revenues to give a net profit figure. Profit is what remains after matching against revenue those items (expenses) used up in earning that revenue in that accounting period.

(iii) Prudence is the tendency that accountants have, when in doubt, to seek to understate profits rather than risk any overstatement, and to understate assets rather than risk any overstatement.

(iv) Objectivity implies in effect that any individual accountant faced with a given accounting problem or situation would arrive at the same conclusion or treatment as any other accountant. There is freedom from bias, and no element of opinion coloured by the role or personality of either the producer or the user of the information. It is perhaps worth noting that prudence represents a deliberate bias, and the two ideas are therefore in conflict.

(b) To: Client
    From   Accountant
    Invoice from Marketing Services plc.

The first item, £3,000 for agreed general advice for October, November and December 19X2, is clearly an expense of the year to 19X2. The services (if there were any) were received at the time and must be matched against the results of the same period. If in fact no services were received for one or more of those months then they obviously now never will be, so either way this £3,000 is an immediate expense.

The photocopier supplied on 1 October 19X2 is going to be used in your marketing department over a number of years. It is, in other words, a fixed asset. We need to make an estimate of the number of years we expect that you will be using it. This should be done on a prudent basis i.e. taking the shortest of the range of likely estimates. Since the machine is guaranteed for five years this is the period most likely to be chosen. However, if you think it likely that in fact the photocopier will be sold or exchanged before then then we should use the shorter period. We then need an estimate of the scrap value of the photocopier at the end of that period. Prudence, and the degree of uncertainty involved, and the lack of significance (i.e. of materiality), would probably suggest taking a scrap value of nil. The net figure of £10,000 less the scrap value if any then needs to be spread as an expense, i.e. to be matched, over the useful life in proportion to the usefulness or benefit. If the photocopier is expected to be equally useful throughout the period, which is probably a reasonable assumption, then the expense should be charged equally on a time basis, starting from 1 October 19X2. A five year life with zero scrap value would give, on this basis, an expense for 19X2 of one fifth of one quarter of £10,000, i.e. of £500. You may feel that this process is rather uncertain and not very objective.

Moving on to the deposit paid for the advertisements in February 19X3, the matching principle referred to earlier gives a very clear answer, namely that the £5,000 will not be an expense of 19X2 as there has not yet been any usage. The £5,000 would represent an asset in your balance sheet. You own the right to receive £5,000 worth of advertising time. It might be argued on the other hand that advertising is such an uncertain activity that the figure should in fact be written off immediately as an expense on the grounds of prudence. However in our view, and recognising you may possibly even receive the money back if the advertisements do not take place, this would be excessively prudent, and the £5,000 should appear as an asset in your 31 December 19X2 balance sheet.

To consider finally the £50,000 for the advertising campaign in November 19X2. The arguments of the previous paragraph when applied to this situation would suggest that the whole of the cost should be treated as an expense of 19X2, i.e. when the advertisements took place. It could of course be argued that, under the matching convention, the cost should be spread over the period during which the advertising campaign can be shown to have led to increased sales and revenues. We would be happy to consider any views you may have on this point, but in the absence of some strong argument to the contrary prudence would suggest to us that the whole figure should be regarded as an expense of 19X2.

We hope you find our comments clear and helpful.

(ACCA)

5.3

(a)   The straight line method of calculating depreciation spreads the loss in value of the assets equally over the useful life of the asset:

$$\frac{Original\ cost - salvage\ value}{Number\ of\ years\ useful\ life} = \text{depreciation charge per annum}$$

The reducing balance method spreads the charge over the years of useful life so that a higher charge is made in the earlier years. This may be achieved by applying a fixed percentage to the net book amount after charging the calculated depreciation for earlier years. An output based method may be used for plant which deteriorates through use rather than time. This will produce a rate of depreciation per unit of output rather than a fixed amount per annum.

(b) Charge for 19X5 Office plant and equipment

19X0 £70,000 cost – £10,000 salvage value = £60,000 total depreciation.

Straight line over 10 years = £6,000 p.a.

Reducing balance to £10,000 in 10 years = 18% p.a.*

In 19X5, the 6th year of life, depreciation will be 18% of WDV at end of 19X4, i.e. of £25,952. 18% thereof = £4,671 (approx.)

$$*R, \text{ the } \% \text{ rate; } 1 - 10\sqrt{\frac{10,000}{70,000}} = 18\% \text{ approx}$$

(c) The purpose of the depreciation charge is two-fold.

   (i) To charge the profit and loss account with an appropriate amount for the use of the capital asset during each period of its life. This is an example of the matching concept whereby each period would be charged with the costs that have enabled revenue to be earned. SSAP 12 on Depreciation defines the purpose of deprecation in the following terms:'Depreciation is a measure of the wearing out, consumption or other loss of value of a fixed asset whether arising from use, effluxion of time or obsolescence through technical or market changes. Depreciation should be allocated to accounting periods so as to charge a fair proportion to each accounting period during the expected useful life of the asset'.

   (ii) To withhold from 'profits available for distribution' the amount by which it is estimated that the assets have lost value during the period. To the extent that distributions to shareholders are less that they otherwise would be, more resources are retained for use within the business.

(ACCA)

5.4

Provision for Doubtful Debts

		As at 30.4.X5		As at 30.4.X6
		£		£
Opening debtors		330,000		337,000
Add credit sales	375,000		347,200	
Less returns	(7,500)	367,500	(5,800)	341,400
		697,500		678,400
Less: receipts		(347,500)		(348,700)
discounts allowed		(8,000)		(6,400)
bad debts written off		(5,000)		(6,300)
Closing debts		337,000		317,000
		x 5%*		x 4%
Provision		= £16,850		= £12,680

$$*Provision \ for \ doubtful \ debts \ at \ 30.4.X4 = \frac{£16,500}{£330,000} \quad x \quad 100 = 5\%$$

5.5

Vincent
Profit and Loss Account for the Year Ended 31.12.X1

		£000
Sales		400
Less Cost of Sales		
Opening Stock	23	
Purchases	280	
	303	
Less Closing Stock	(20)	(283)
Gross Profit		117
Expenses		
Wages (38 + 2)	40	
Admin. (32 -3)	29	
Distribution	4	
Depreciation (2 + 2)	4	
Bad Debt Provision	1	(78)
Net Profit		39

Vincent
Balance Sheet as at 31.12X1 (£000's)

Fixed Assets	Cost	Accumulated Dep'n.	NBV
Office Equipment	20	6	14
Vehicles	10	4	6
	30	10	20
Current Assets			
Stock		20	
Trade Debtors	40		
Less Provision for BadDebts	(1)	39	
Prepayments		3	
Bank		16	
		78	
Less: Current Liabilities			
Trade Creditors	19		
Accruals	2	(21)	
Net Current Assets			57
Net Assets			77
Financed by:			
Capital			20
Profit and Loss Account (18 + 39)			57
Owner's Funds			77

5.6

Mr Bends (all figures £000)

Trading Account for New Cars

	£000	£000	£000
Sales (27 at £12,000)			324
Purchases (37 at £10,000)		370	
Less: Destroyed by fire	(10)		
Transferred to fixed assets	(20)	(30)	
Available for sale		340	
Closing stock		(70)	
Cost of sales			270
Gross Profit			54

Trading Account for Second Hand Cars

	£000	£000
Sales*		93
Purchases (given)	93	
Closing stock	(27)	
Cost of sales		66
Gross Profit		27

Note: Sales of second hand cars

Total cash received from customers	400
Of which (324–12) is for new cars	(312)
Therefore balance is for second hand cars	88
Plus car sold but never paid for	5
Sales	93

Profit and Loss Account for Year

	£000	£000
Gross Profit (27 + 54)		81
Expenses:		
Wages	36	
Rent	12	
Depreciation furniture and equipment	2	
Depreciation cars	4	
Insurance, electricity and stationery	7	
Loss by fire	10	
Bad debt	5	
Bank charges	1	
Loan interest	5	
		82
Net Loss		(1)

Balance sheet at 31st December

	£000	£000	£000
Fixed assets:	Cost	Dep.	Net
Cars	20	4	16
Furniture	5	1	4
Equipment	5	1	4
	30	6	24
Current assets:			
Stock(70 + 27)		97	
Debtors		12	
Prepayments −rent		3	
Bank		42	
		154	
Current liabilities:			
Creditors for new cars	(50)		
Loan interest	(5)	(55)	
Working capital			99
Net assets			123
Represented by:			
Capital			100
Less loss			(1)
			99
Less drawings			(26)
			73
Loan			50
			123

(ACCA)

6.1

(a)

Stores Ledger Account (Component X)

		Receipts					Issues		
		Units	Price £	Value £			Units	Price £	Value £
1/1	Balance	200	50	10,000	16/1	Issues	400	56	22,400
8/1	Purchases	600	58	34,800	31/1	Balance c/f	400	56	22,400
		800	56	44,800			800	56	44,800
1/2	Balance b/f	400	56	22,400	12/1	Issues	600	60	36,000
3/2	Purchases	400	64	25,600	28/2	Balance c/f	200	60	12,000
		800	60	48,000			800	60	
									48,000
1/3	Balance b/f	200	60	12,000	23/3	Issues	200	69	13,800
11/3	Purchases	600	72	43,200	31/3	Balance c/f	600	69	41,400
		800	69	55,200			800	69	55,200
1/4	Balance b/f	600	69	41,400					
3/4	Purchases	200	73	14,600					
		800	70	56,000					

(b) *First in First Out (FIFO)*

Assumes that issues to production are made in the order in which they are received. Hence the first items received are the first used.

Last in First Out (LIFO)

Makes the opposite assumption to FIFO (i.e. the most recent purchases are issued to production first).

Effect of Profit

FIFO – When costs are rising as in part (a) using the FIFO method, which deems issues to be at older and lower prices, will result in lower costs and therefore higher profits than those reported using the weighted average price method.

LIFO would value issues at the most up to date prices and therefore result in higher costs and lower reported profits.

6.2

(a)

LIFO

Year 1	Purchases	Cost of sales	Stock	Sales
buy 10 at 300	3,000		3,000	
buy 12 at 250	3,000		6,000	
sell 8 at 400		2,000[1]	4,000	3,200
buy 6 at 200	1,200		5,200	
sell 12 at 400		2,800[2]	2,400	4,800
	7,200	4,800	2,400	8,000

Year2			Stock	
Opening stock			2,400	
buy 10 at 200	2,000		4,400	
sell 5 at 400		1,000[3]	3,400	2,000
buy 12 at 150	1,800		5,200	
sell 25 at 400		5,200[4]	0	10,000
	3,800	6,200	0	12,000

[1] 8 at 250

[2] 6 at 200 + 4 at 250 + 2 at 300

[3] 5 at 200

[4] 12 at 150 + 5 at 200 + 8 at 300

FIFO

Year 1	Purchases	Cost of sales	Stock	Sales
buy 10 at 300	3,000		3,000	
buy 12 at 250	3,000		6,000	
sell 8 at 400		2,400[5]	3,600	3,200
buy 6 at 200	1,200		4,800	
sell 12 at 400		3,100[6]	1,700	4,800
	7,200	5,500	1,700	8,000

Year2

Opening stock			1,700		
buy 10 at 200	2,000		3,700		
sell 5 at 400		1,100[7]	2,600	2,000	
buy 12 at 150	1,800		4,400		
sell 25 at 400		4,400[8]	0	10,000	
	3,800	5,500	0	12,000	

[5] 8 at 300

[6] 2 at 300 + 10 at 250

[7] 2 at 250 + 3 at 200

[8] 3 at 200 + 10 at 200 + 12 at 150

Trading Accounts	LIFO		FIFO	
	£	£	£	£
Year 1				
Sales		8,000		8,000
Opening stock	0		0	
Purchases	7,200		7,200	
	7,200		7,200	
Closing stock	2,400		1,700	
Cost of sales		4,800		5,500
Gross profit		3,200		2,500
Year 2				
Sales		12,000		12,000
Opening stock	2,400		1,700	
Purchases	3,800		3,800	
	6,200		5,500	
Closing stock	0		0	
Cost of sales		6,200		5,500
Gross profit		5,800		6,500

(b)   We are asked to consider the effects of the LIFO method on the stock figure at the end of year 1, and on both the gross profit figures. Since the closing stock at the end of year 2 is nil, the situation is presented with unusual clarity. Note however that purchase costs are falling, not rising which is more common.

Relevant points to mention might include the following:

- at the end of year 1 the closing stock is higher under LIFO than under FIFO, the cost of sales is lower, and therefore the gross profit is higher, than under FIFO. With these particular figures it could be argued that LIFO lacks prudence, but this would mean that in the normal situation where costs are rising rather than falling, FIFO would lack prudence as compared with LIFO.

- because the closing stock in year 1 is obviously the opening stock of year 2, the effect reverses in year 2. The choice of method affects the annual gross profit, and will affect the trend of annual gross profits, but does not affect the long-run amount of the gross profit. This is demonstrated by the figures, as total gross profit for the two years is £9,000 under both methods.

- the cost of sales figure under LIFO is more up-to-date than under the alternative historical cost methods. This means that expense and revenue figures are more internally consistent in terms of dates, and therefore it can be argued that the matching principle is better followed by LIFO than by FIFO. SSAP 9 seems to take the opposite view.

- the balance sheet figure will often be based on very out-of-date costs under LIFO

- LIFO can be regarded as having some similarity to replacement cost accounting as regards profit calculation (though not as regards the balance sheet stock figure).

(ACCA)

6.3

Laurel Manufacturing

Manufacturing, Trading and Profit and Loss Account for the Year Ended 31/12/X8

	£	£	£
Sales			415,600
Less Cost of Sales			
Opening stock of finished goods		41,500	
Cost of finished goods produced			
Opening work in progress	37,400		
*Direct materials consumed	113,500		
Direct labour	71,300		
Indirect production expenses	63,200		
	285,400		
Less closing work in progress	(36,000)	249,400	
		290,900	
Less closing stock of finished goods		(40,600)	250,300
Gross profit			165,300
Less Expenses			
Administrative		(79,100)	
Selling and distribution		(38,000)	(117,100)
Net Profit			48,200

*Working

Direct Materials Consumed	£
Opening stock	27,500
+ Purchases	116,300
	143,800
– Closing stock	(30,300)
	113,500

6.4

Amos Manufacturing

Manufacturing, Trading and Profit and Loss Account for the Year Ended 30/9/X7

	£	£	£
Sales (250,400–5,000)			245,400
Less Cost of Sales			
Opening stock of finished goods		30,800	
Cost of finished Goods Produced			
Opening work in progress	23,500		
Raw materials consumed	102,000		
Direct Wages	64,200		
Production overheads (18,500–300 + 900)	19,100		
	208,800		
Less closing work in progress	(21,300)	187,500	
		218,300	
*Less closing stock of finished goods		(33,900)	184,400
Gross profit			61,000
Less Expenses			
Administrative (21,600 + 2,900)		(24,500)	
Selling and distribution (12,300–600 + 1,500)		(13,200)	(37,700)
Net Profit			23,300

	£
*Closing stock of finished goods	
As shown in accounting records	29,900
Add cost of goods returned (5,000 x 100/125)	4,000
	33,900

7.1

(a) Ordinary Shares

- Owners of the company.

- Take highest risk (re. profit distribution and repayment of capital in the event of the company being wound up).

- Can potentially take highest rewards (limitless profit if the company performs well).

- Entitled to vote at Annual General Meeting.

- Can be sold.

(b) Preference Shares

- Also co-owners.

- Take less risk (get first slice of profits/repayment of capital).

- Take less reward (share of profits is limited).

- May have restricted voting rights at AGM.

- Cumulative preference shares give entitlement to 'back-dated' dividends in future years if dividend is not paid in current year.

(c) Debentures

- A loan to the company (therefore debenture holders are creditors and not owners).

- Holders are entitled to interest on the loan and repayment of the capital on the 'redemption date'.

- Are not usually allowed to vote at AGM.

- Take less risk than shareholders as they must be paid even if no profits are made.

- May be re-sold.

7.2

(a) *Relevant* means giving the user the information needed for the particular decision being considered.

Understandable means comprehensible to the particular users concerned – i.e. the complexity of the reports must reflect the abilities of the reader.

Reliable means that the user can have confidence in it. The information should preferably have been 'confirmed' or verified in some way. This does not necessarily mean it has to be factual.

Complete means that the report should give a total picture – a rounded picture of the reporting entity. It should cover all relevant aspects.

Objective means that the information presented is unbiased and 'neutral'. It should not favour one user at the expense of another and should not reflect the views of the preparer.

Timely means that the information must reach the user in time for him to actually make use of it. It must be available in time to be used in the decision-making process.

Comparable means that information presented can be easily compared with earlier periods, and with different businesses.

(b)   It is not difficult to juxtapose these characteristics in incompatible ways. Timely v Complete; Complete v Understandable; Relevant v Reliable are obvious examples. With such conflicts, the user needs should prevail.

(ACCA)

7.3

(a)   A balance sheet is a summary of the financial position of a business at an instant in time. It shows the resources of the business (assets) and the sources (claims) from which the business obtained them.

(b)   An asset is something owned by a business which will be of future benefit. In traditional accounting, it must have been acquired through a transaction i.e. it must have a measurable cost.

(c)   A liability is an amount owed. In balance sheet terms it does not include the ownership claim on the business.

(d)   Share capital is the nominal value of new shares issued by a company. It is the minimum amount which owners contribute permanently to the business.

(e)   Reserves are ownership claims on the business resources over and above the share capital. They include retained profits, revaluation surpluses and share-related items other than the share capital itself.

(f)   The balance sheet balances because it shows assets, outside claims thereon (liabilities), and ownership interest. The owners are entitled to the residual resources of the business. so their claim is the balancing figure.

(g) The value of shares is a function of supply and demand on the stock market and the balance sheet certainly gives no direct indication of their value. Nor does the balance sheet show the value either of the business as an entity, or of the assets considered individually. All it really shows is the cost of some of the assets, less an allowance where some proportion of them has been used, plus money and debtors (i.e. money soon to be received). On the other side it shows the creditors and outside liabilities, and the claim of you and your fellow owners collectively on what is 'left-over'. Since the assets are mainly expressed on a historic cost basis, it follows that your claim is similarly expressed. If you find this confusing, and feel it suggests that a traditional balance sheet is perhaps not quite as immediately useful as you hoped, you may be right!

(ACCA)

7.4

Nibble Pie Limited

Profit and Loss Account for Year Ended 30/4/X2

	£000's
Turnover	15,150
Cost of Sales (WI)	11,100
Gross Profit	4,050
Distribution Costs (410 + 120)	(530)
Admin. Expenses (W2)	(3,010)
Operating Profit	510
Interest Payable	(14)
Profit on ordinary activities before taxation	496
Tax on profit on ordinary activities	(160)
Profit on ordinary activities after taxation	336
Dividends – Final (proposed)	(100)
Retained profit for the year	236

Workings

(W1) Cost of Sales

Opening Stock	820
Add Purchases	10,800
Less closing stock	(520)
	11,100

(W2) Admin. Expenses

Admin. Expenses	2,100
Admin. Salaries	750
Accruals	10
Prepayments	(30)
Depreciation:	
Fixtures & fittings (1,720 x 5%)	86
Office equipment (940 x 10%)	94
	3,010

Balance Sheet as at 30/4/X2

			£000's
Fixed Assets			
Tangible Assets (W3)			1,760
Current Assets			
Stocks		520	
Debtors:			
Trade Debtors	1,900		
Prepayments	30	1,930	
		2,450	
Creditors: Due Within 1 Yr.			
Bank Overdraft	80		
Trade Creditors	1,060		
Accruals	10		
Corporation Tax	160		
Dividends	100	(1,410)	
Net Current Assets			1,040
			2,800
Financed By			
Called up Share Capital (500,000 shares @ £1)			500
Profit and Loss Account			
-- Balance at 1st May X1		2,064	
-- Profit retained this yr.		236	2,300
			2,800

Workings

(W3)   Fixed Assets

	Cost	Accum. Dep'n.	NBV
Fixtures and Fittings	1,720	486	1,234
Office Equipment	940	414	526
	2,660	900	1,760

7.5

Rigoletto Limited

Profit and Loss Account for the Year Ended 31/10/X5

Note		£000's
	Turnover	4,200
1.	Cost of Sales	(3,055)
	Gross Profit	1,145
	Distribution Costs (310 + 15)	(325)
2.	Administrative Expenses	(332)
	Operating Profit Before Interest	488
	Interest Payable (15 + 15)	(30)
	Profit Before Tax	458
	Taxation	(110)
	Profit After Tax	348
3.	Dividends Paid and Proposed	(162)
	Retained Profit	186

Balance Sheet as at 31/10/X5

Note		£000's
	Fixed Assets	
4.	Tangible Assets	1,083
	Current Assets	
	Stocks	795
	Debtors:	
	Trade debtors	780
	Prepayments	13
		1,588
	Creditors: Amounts falling due within 1 year	
	Bank loans and overdrafts	116
	Trade creditors	430
	Taxation	110
	Dividends (21 + 120)	141
	Accruals (15 + 18 + 15)	48
		845	743
			1,826
	Creditors: Amounts falling due after more than 1 year	(200)
		1,626
	Capital and Reserves	
	Called up share capital (600 + 300)	900
	Share premium account	100
	General reserve (400 + 180)	580
	Profit and loss account (40 + 186–180)	46
		1,626

Notes

1.	Cost of Sales		£000's
	Opening stock		850
	Purchases		3,000
			3,850
	Closing stock		(795)
			3,055

2.	Administrative Expenses		
	Admin expenses		240
	Prepayments		(13)
	Audit fee		18
	Depreciation:		
	Office equipment (360–160) x 25%		50
	Motor vehicle (200–100) x 30%		30
	Fixtures and fittings (120–50) x 10%		7
			332

3.	Dividends		
	Preference dividend (21 + 21)		42
	Dividend (1,200,000 x £0.10)		120
			162

4.	Fixed Assets	Cost	Accum. Depn.	NBV
	Land and buildings	800	–	800
	Office equipment	360	210	150
	Motor vehicles	200	130	70
	Fixtures and fittings	120	57	63
		1,480	397	1,083

7.6

(a)

Capital Accounts

	Al £	Bert £	Hall £
30/6 Opening balance	12,000	15,000	
Cash			20,000
Goodwill	9,000	9,000	
1/7 Opening balance	21,000	24,000	20,000

(b)

Elimination of goodwill	(9,000)	(9,000)	
*Adjustment	3,000	3,000	(6,000)
	15,000	18,000	14,000

*i.e. because Hall is now entitled to one third of goodwill, Al and Bert are compensated. The goodwill was built up during the time in which only they ran the business and the adjustment made effectively deprives Hall of a share of this. His entitlement as at 1st July is therefore restricted to the £20,000 he has invested (£14,000 capital and £6,000 share of the £18,000 goodwill).

(c) Goodwill is the sum by which the value of a business as a going concern exceeds the value of its assets. Adjustments must be made when a new partner is admitted to ensure that the accounts do not credit him with any goodwill arising before his admission.

7.7

(a)

			£
	Original Profit*		8,780
	Adjustments		
(i)	Goods charged to Guy (100–65)		(35)
(iii)	Stock re-valuation (550–200)		(350)
(iv)	Excess depreciation charges		
	-- Amount charged (4,000 x 10%)	400	
	-- Correct charge (2,000 x 15%)	300	100
(vi)	Provision for doubtful debts (1,100 x 3%)		(33)
(vii)	Electricity accrued	(82)	(400)
	Revised net trading profit		8,380

* Original Net Trading Profit

	£
Share of profit (4,500 + 1,500)	6,000
Interest on capital (480 + 300)	780
Salary	2,000
	8,780

(b)

Amended Current Accounts

	Webb £	Guy £		Webb £	Guy £
Drawings	4,280	3,950	Balance at 1/1/X8	900	100
Goods		65	Salary		2,350
			Interest on capital	400	250
Balance at 31/12/X8	1,055	30	Share of profit	4,035	1,345
	5,335	4,045		5,335	4,045

(c)

Balance Sheet as at 31/12/X8

	Cost £	Accum. Dep'n £	NBV £
Fixed Assets			
Premises	10,400	–	10,400
Equipment	4,000	2,300	1,700
	14,400	2,300	12,100
Current Assets			
Stock (2,800–350)		2,450	
Debtors (1,100–33)		1,067	
Cash		200	
		3,717	
Less Current Liabilities			
Creditors and accruals (1,650 + 82)		(1,732)	1,985
			14,085
Capital Accounts – Webb		8,000	
– Guy		5,000	13,000
Current Accounts – Webb		1,055	
– Guy		30	1,085
			14,085

8.1

(a)

Robson Limited

Cash Flow Statement for the Year Ended 31/12/X6

		£000's
W1	Net Cash Inflow from Operating Activities	41
	Returns on Investments and Servicing of Finance	
	Interest paid	(1)
	Taxation	
W2	Tax paid	(21)
	Capial Expenditure and Financial Investment	
W3	Payments to acquire tangible fixed assets	(15)
	Acquisitions and Disposals	–
W4	Equity Dividend Paid	(12)
	Net cash outflow before use of liquid resources and financing	(8)
	Management of liquid resources	–
	Financing	
	Issue of ordinary share capital	10
	Redemption of debentures	(10)
	Net cash inflow from financing	–
	Decrease in Cash (13–21)	(8)

Notes/Workings

W1   **Net Cash Inflow from Operating Activities**   £000's

Net profit before interest and tax (46 + 1)	47
Depreciation	8
Decrease in stock	4
Increase in debtors	(10)
Decrease in creditors	(8)
	41

Analysis of Changes in Net Debt

	As at 1.1.X6	Cash flows	As at 31.12.X6
	£000	£000	£000
Cash in hand and at bank	21	(8)	13
Due after one year (debentures)	–	(10)	(10)
Total	21	(18)	3

Reconciliation of Net Cash flow Movement in Net debt	£000
Decrease in cash in the year	(8)
Cash inflow from increase in debt	(10)
Movement in net debt	(18)
Net debt at 1.1.X6	21
Net debt at 31.12 X6	3

W2   **Tax Paid**

Outstanding at 31/12/X5	13
Tax due for 19X6	18
	31
Less outstanding at 31/12/X6	(10)
Paid	21

W3   **Purchase of Fixed Assets**

Land and buildings (95–85)	10
Plant and machinery 62–(65–8)	5
	15

W4   **Dividends Paid**   **£000's**

Outstanding at 31/12/X5	5
Dividend due for 19X6	14
	19
Less outstanding at 31/12/X6	(7)
Paid	12

(b)   A Profit and Loss Account measures performance by comparing revenue with costs incurred in generating that revenue.

A Cash Flow Statement shows the cash flowing in and out of a business and explains why profits do not necessarily result in cash surpluses.

8.2

Hartleyburn Limited

Cash Flow Statement for the Year Ended 31/12/X8

		£000's
W1	Net Cash Inflow from Operating Activities	100
	Returns on Investments and Servicing of Finance	(12)
	Interest paid	
	Taxation	
W2	Tax paid	(19)
	Capital Expenditure and Financial Investment	
W3	Payments to acquire tangible fixed assets	(130)
	Acquisitions and Disposals	–
W4	Equity Dividend Paid	(30)
	Net cash outflow before use of liquid resources and financing	(91)
	Management of liquid resources	–
	Financing	
	Issue of share capital (340–240)	100
	Repayment of loans	(20)
	Net cash inflow from financing	80
	Decrease in Cash (14–25)	(11)

Notes/Workings

		£000's
W1	Net profit before interest and tax	84
	Add depreciation (190–150)	40
	Increase in stocks (105–82)	(23)
	Increase in debtors (74–58)	(16)
	Increase in creditors (50–35)	15
		100

Analysis of Changes in Net Debt

	As at 1.1.X8	Cash flows	As at 31.12.X8
	£000	£000	£000
Cash in hand and at bank	25	20	45
Due after one year	(30)	(20)	(50)
Total	(5)	(–)	(5)

Reconciliation of Net Cash flow Movement in Net debt	£000
Increase in cash in the year	20
Cash inflow from increase in debt (loan)	(20)
Movement in net debt	–
Net debt at 1.1.X7	(5)
Net debt at 31.12 X7	(5)

		£000's
W2	Tax outstanding at 31/12/X7	23
	Due for 19X8	16
		39
	Less amount outstanding at 31/12/X8	(20)
	Tax Paid	19

		£000's
W3	Purchase of fixed assets	
	Land and Buildings (240–170)	70
	Equipment (340–280)	60
		130

		£000's
W4	Dividend outstanding at 31/12/X7	10
	Dividend due for 19X8	25
		35
	Less dividend at 31/12/X8	(5)
	Dividends Paid	30

8.3

Brioche plc

Cash Flow Statement for the Year Ended 31/3/X5

			£000's
W1	Net Cash Inflow from Operating Activities		4,820
	Returns on Investments and Servicing of Finance		
	Interest paid		(84)
	Taxation		
W2	Tax paid		(1,050)
	Capital Expenditure and Financial Investment		
W3	Payments to acquire tangible fixed assets		(3,450)
	Acquisitions and Disposals		--
W4	Equity Dividend Paid		(810)
	Net cash ouflow before use of liquid resources and financing		(574)
	Management of Liquid Resources		--
	Financing		
	Issue of share capital (11,000–9,000)	2,000	
	Redemption of debentures	(600)	
	Net cash inflow from financing		1,400
	Increase in Cash (1,350–524)		826

Notes/Workings

W1	Net Cash Inflow from Operating Activities	£000's
	Net profit before interest and tax (4,510+84)	4,594
	Depreciation (1,360–900) + (1,450–1,000)	910
	Increase in stock	(400)
	Increase in debtors	(580)
	Increase in creditors	296
		4,820

Analysis of Changes in Net Debt

	As at 1.4.X4	Cash flows	As at 31.3.X5
	£000	£000	£000
Cash in hand and at bank	524	826	1,350
Due after one year (debentures)	(1,000)	600	(400)
Total	(476)	1,426	950

Reconciliation of Net Cash flow Movement in Net debt	£000
Increase in cash in the year	826
Cash outflow from decrease in debt (loan)	(600)
Movement in net debt	1,426
Net debt at 1.4.X4	(476)
Net debt at 31.3 X5	950

W2	Tax Paid	£000's
	Outstanding at 31/12/X4	1,050
	Due for 19X5	1,344
		2,394
	Less outstanding at 31/12/X5	(1,344)
	Paid	1,050

W3	**Purchase of Fixed Assets**	£000's
	Land and buildings (15,200–12,600)	2,600
	Motor vehicles (2,750–2,400)	350
	Other equipment (4,000-3,500)	500
		3,450

W4	**Dividends Paid**	£000's
	Outstanding at 31/12/X4	810
	Due for 19X5	1,000
		1,810
	Less outstanding at 31/12/X5	(1,000)
	Paid	810

9.1

(a)   Algernon Ltd. ratios

	19X6			19X7		
ROCE	$\frac{40+10}{177}$	=	28%	$\frac{20+15}{259}$	=	14%
ROOE	$\frac{40}{77}$	=	52%	$\frac{20}{109}$	=	18%
Debtors turnover	$\frac{200}{40}$	=	5 times	$\frac{200}{50}$	=	4 times
Creditors turnover	$\frac{100}{40}$	=	2.5 times	$\frac{120}{60}$	=	2 times
Current ratio	$\frac{98}{60}$	=	1.6:1	$\frac{115}{84}$	=	1.4:1
Quick assets	$\frac{43}{60}$	=	0.7:1	$\frac{50}{84}$	=	0.6:1
Gross profit percentage	$\frac{100}{200}$	=	50%	$\frac{80}{200}$	=	40%
Net profit percentage	$\frac{40}{200}$	=	20%	$\frac{20}{200}$	=	10%
Dividend cover	$\frac{40}{20}$	=	2 times	$\frac{20}{20}$	=	1 times
Gearing ratio	$\frac{100}{177}$	=	56%	$\frac{150}{259}$	=	58%

(b)   Algernon Ltd. appears to be trying to expand unsuccessfully. Generally, ratios of all types are changing adversely. Sales are static, profits are falling and the assets being used have sharply increased (though not quite as sharply as the ratios imply: the revaluation of land causes some distortion of the figures). All this leads to a sharp fall in the efficiency of the business as a whole (ROCE) and as it affects the shareholders (ROOE). The dividend policy seems extremely dangerous in the circumstances. The sharp increase in the assets base may of course have occurred near the end of the year, and its benefits therefore may not have yet appeared. Even allowing for this possibility, however, the adverse movement in profitability is deeply worrying.

(ACCA)

9.2

(a)   Nine ratios are readily available.

	A			B		
Gearing	$\dfrac{100}{200}$	=	50%	$\dfrac{130}{650}$	=	20%
Working capital	$\dfrac{180}{160}$	=	9:8	$\dfrac{200}{120}$	=	5:3
Quick assets	$\dfrac{100}{160}$	=	62%	$\dfrac{100}{120}$	=	83%
ROOE	$\dfrac{30}{100}$	=	30%	$\dfrac{100}{520}$	=	19%
ROCE	$\dfrac{30+10}{200}$	=	20%	$\dfrac{100+13}{650}$	=	17%
$\dfrac{\text{Gross profit}}{\text{sales}}$	$\dfrac{600}{1,000}$	=	60%	$\dfrac{1,000}{3,000}$	=	33%
$\dfrac{\text{Net profit}}{\text{sales}}$	$\dfrac{30}{1,000}$	=	3%	$\dfrac{100}{3,000}$	=	3%
$\dfrac{\text{Debtors x 365}}{\text{sales}}$	$\dfrac{100 \times 365}{1,000}$	=	36 days	$\dfrac{90 \times 365}{3,000}$	=	11 days
$\dfrac{\text{Creditors x 365}}{\text{Cost of sales}}$	$\dfrac{110 \times 365}{400}$	=	100 days	$\dfrac{120 \times 365}{2,000}$	=	22 days

(b)   Whilst A and B have very similar net profit to sales percentages, they reach this point in different ways. A has a high gross profit percentage (lower turnover, higher margin) and a higher ROCE. Its materially higher gearing ratio turns this slightly higher ROCE into a considerably higher ROOE. From a shareholder viewpoint most of this makes A sound preferable to B. But it should be remembered that B has more 'slack' in its structure. A lender might well feel happier granting further loans to B – lower gearing ratio: better liquidity ratios. A's debtors' payback and, particularly and worryingly, creditors' payback periods are much higher.

It must be noted that B's balance sheet includes a large revaluation of its land. This is a major inconsistency, and distorts the figures considerably. In terms of return on original investments ROOE and ROCE for B are considerably understated. Perhaps more usefully to you, in terms of return on current value invested, ROOE and ROCE for A are overstated.

(ACCA)

9.3

(a)

	19X1		19X0	
Current ratio	$\frac{30,500}{24,000}$	= 1.27	$\frac{28,500}{20,000}$	= 1.43
Quick assets ratio	$\frac{16,500}{24,000}$	= 0.69	$\frac{15,500}{20,000}$	= 0.78
Stock (number of days held)	$\frac{14,000}{42,000}$ x 365	= 122 days	$\frac{13,000}{34,000}$ x 365	= 140 days
Debtors (no. of days outstanding)	$\frac{16,000}{60,000}$ x 365	= 97 days	$\frac{15,000}{50,000}$ x 365	= 109 days
Creditors (no. of days outstanding)	$\frac{24,000}{42,000}$ x 365	= 209 days	$\frac{20,000}{34,000}$ x 365	= 215 days
Gross profit %	$\frac{18,000}{60,000}$	= 30%	$\frac{16,000}{50,000}$	= 32%
Net profit % (before taxation)	$\frac{300}{60,000}$	= 0.5%	$\frac{1,700}{50,000}$	= 3.4%
Interest cover	$\frac{2,500}{2,200}$	= 1.14	$\frac{3,000}{1,300}$	= 2.31
Dividend cover	$\frac{-50}{600}$	= -0.08	$\frac{1,100}{600}$	= 1.83
ROOE (before taxation)	$\frac{300}{13,000}$	= 2.3%	$\frac{1,700}{14,000}$	= 12%
ROCE	$\frac{2,500}{19,000}$	= 13%	$\frac{3,000}{19,500}$	= 15%
Gearing	$\frac{6,000}{19,000}$	= 32%	$\frac{5,500}{19,500}$	= 28%

(b) The general position in 19X0 might be characterised as dull. All the turnover ratios are high, especially creditors' turnover, although this may partly be a question of the industry involved. Current and quick ratios are probably safe enough, provided of course that the going-concern convention can assumed, i.e. that we can assume the operating cycle will continue in the normal way. Profits and returns are distinctly unexciting, gearing is not excessive.

In 19X1 the position has clearly worsened. Turnover ratios are all slightly lower, the net effect being a fall in the current and quick assets ratios. Turnover has increased substantially, at least in money terms, but cost of sales has increased more than in proportion. Perhaps the most significant events relate to gearing and interest. Borrowing has increased somewhat, but interest expense has increased very substantially indeed; the interest cover ratio shows a very shaky position. The other important point which must surely be emphasised is that the dividend payment is being fully maintained in spite of the complete absence of available profits from this year's trading.

Management has probably been caught by a year of difficult trading conditions and rapidly rising interest rates. They are perhaps trying to spend their way out of trouble – note the increase in fixed assets – with an eye to the future. The maintained dividend is certainly an attempt to persuade the shareholders of management confidence in the future. Such a policy is usually either successful or completely catastrophic.

(ACCA)

10.1

(i)   A blanket overhead absorption rate is where a single overhead absorption rate is applied to a whole plant. Departmental overhead absorption rates are where a separate rate is calculated for each department/cost centre, depending upon the expenditure and level of activity for the appropriate activity base in each department. As a result departmental rates are likely to lead to a fairer apportionment of indirect costs, because the expenditure in each department can be related as closely as possible to the nature of the particular work going on within it. A blanket rate should only be used in the unlikely event of each job requiring similar work.

(ii)   Overhead rates calculated from actual expenditure and activity have the advantage that all costs incurred are apportioned to product costs. Against this, product costs may alter significantly from period to period as the result of changes in activity which makes cost plus pricing (if used) and the assessment of product profitability difficult. Further problems are that the calculation has to be repeated frequently, and after the event.

The calculation of a predetermined rate enables product costs to be estimated reasonably accurately in advance and avoids the distortions caused by short-term fluctuations in activity in intermediate periods. Against this, large over or under absorbed balances, and thus wrongly costed products, can occur in the longer term if expenditure or activity are wrongly estimated.

(ACCA)

10.2

(a)   As a noun 'cost' relates to the expenditure incurred in producing a product or rendering a service.

Used as a verb, to cost a product or service is to ascertain the expenditure incurred in producing or rendering it.

(b)   The speaker's comments are true. It is not possible to ascertain with complete accuracy the true cost of a product or service for a number of reasons including the following:

(i)   Direct material costs can be assigned using various pricing methods (FIFO, LIFO etc.) each of which is likely to produce a different result.

(ii)   Determining the costs incurred in a period (to be attributed to individual products/services) is a subjective exercise requiring estimation of accruals, useful lives of assets etc.

(iii) It is difficult to determine the overhead cost attributable to individual products/services. (See 'Limitations of Absorption Costing' in Chapter 10).

(c)   Costs may be used by businesses for:

- Planning

- Control

- Decision making

- Determining profit

10.3

(a)

Allocation/Apportionment of Overheads (£000's)

	Basis	Total	A	B	Stores	Mtce	Tool Room
Indirect labour	Allocate	1,837	620	846	149	115	107
Supervision	No. Employees	140	30	50	10	20	30
Power	Kw. Hrs	160	80	40	4	20	16
Rent	Area	280	50	125	55	30	20
Rates	Area	112	20	50	22	12	8
Plant insurance	Plant value	40	20	16	–	2	2
Plant depreciation	Plant value	20	10	8	–	1	1
		2,589	830	1,135	240	200	184
Apportion stores	No. Req'ns.		75	90	(240)	30	45
		2,589	905	1,225	–	230	229
Apportion mtce	Hours		80	90		(230)	60
		2,589	985	1,315		–	289
Apportion tool room	Hours		119	170			(289)
		2,589	1,104	1,485			

Machine hour rates

$$A = \frac{£1,104,000}{55,200 \; hours} = £20 \text{ per machine hour}$$

$$B = \frac{£1,485,000}{99,000 \; hours} = £15 \text{ per machine hour}$$

10.4

(a)

	Basis	Total £	A £	B £	C £	X £	Y £
Allocated overheads	Allocated	7,100	2,800	1,700	1,200	800	600
Rent and rates	Area	12,800	6,000	3,600	1,200	1,200	800
Machine insurance	Machine value	6,000	3,000	1,250	1,000	500	250
Telephone charges	Area*	3,200	1,500	900	300	300	200
Depreciation	Machine value	18,000	9,000	3,750	3,000	1,500	750
Prodn Svisor's salaries	Labour hrs.	24,000	12,800	7,200	4,000	–	–
Heating and lighting	Area	6,400	3,000	1,800	600	600	400
		77,500	38,100	20,200	11,300	4,900	3,000
Apportion Dept. X	%'s given		2,450	1,225	1,225	(4,900)	
Apportion Dept. Y	Hours		600	900	1,500		(3,000)
		77,500	41,150	22,325	14,025	–	–

*Telephones would be better apportioned on usage. As this information is not available area has been used.

Overhead absorption rates

$$\text{Dept. A} = \frac{£41,150}{3,200 \; labour \, hrs} = £12.86 \text{ per labour hr.}$$

$$\text{Dept. B} = \frac{£22,325}{1,800 \; labour \, hrs} = £12.40 \text{ per labour hr.}$$

$$\text{Dept. C} \quad = \quad \frac{£14,025}{1,000 \; labour \, hrs} \quad = \quad £14.03 \text{ per labour hr.}$$

(b)

	Job 123 £	Job 124 £
Direct materials	154.00	108.00
Direct labour:		
– Dept. A	76.00	60.80
– Dept. B	42.00	35.00
– Dept. C	34.00	47.60
Prime cost	306.00	251.40
Overheads:		
– Dept. A	257.20	205.76
– Dept. B	148.80	124.00
– Dept. C	140.30	196.42
Total Cost	852.30	777.58

(c)

	Job 123 £	Job 124 £
Total cost	852.30	777.58
Add mark up (33.33%*)	284.10	259.19
Selling price	1,136.40	1,036.77

*25% on selling price $= {}^{25}/_{75}$ on cost (i.e. 33.33%)

10.5

(a)

Overhead	Basis of Apportionment	Annual Cost	Process A	Process B	Stores	Canteen
		£	£	£	£	£
Indirect wages	Direct	95,000	25,000	40,000	20,000	10,000
Indirect materials	Direct	119,750	51,510	58,505	1,310	8,425
Rent and rates	Area	450,000	150,000	75,000	150,000	75,000
Plant depreciation	Book value of plant	140,000	100,000	20,000	15,000	5,000
Power	HP of plant	50,000	40,000	10,000	–	–
Fire insurance	Area	3,750	1,250	625	1,250	625
W.C. insurance	2% of total wages	12,000	6,100	5,300	400	200
Heat and light	Area	4,500	1,500	750	1,500	750
		875,000	375,360	210,180	189,460	100,000
Canteen	No. of employees		50,000	37,500	12,500	(100,000)
Stores	No. of stores issues		134,640	67,320	(201,960)	
		875,000	560,000	315,000	–	–

(b)

	Process A	Process B
Overhead cost	£560,000	£315,000
Labour hours	70,000	45,000
Overhead rate per hour	£8	£7

(c)

Product Costs

	X £		Y £	
Direct materials-- P	37		93	
– Q	2		48	
– R	4	43	15	156
Direct wages – A	8		16	
– B	5	13	15	31
Production overhead – Process A	16		32	
-- Process B	7	23	21	53
		79		240
Royalty		1		–
Commission		5		15
Packing materials		1		4
Transport		2		5
Advertising*		2		6
Total cost		90		270

*Advertising absorption rate

$$= \frac{Advertising\ cost}{total\ sales\ revenue} \quad x\ 100$$

$$= \frac{£90,000}{(15,000X\ x\ £100) + (10,000Y\ x\ £300)} \quad x\ 100$$

$$= \frac{£90,000}{£4,500,000} \quad x\ 100 \quad = 2\%$$

$$\therefore \quad X \ = \ £100\ x\ 2\% \ = \ £2$$

$$Y \ = \ £300\ x\ 2\% \ = \ £6$$

(d)

	X £ per unit	Y £ per unit
Selling price	100	300
Total cost	(90)	(270)
Profit	10	30

10.6

(a)

	Production Department		
	A	B	C
Budgeted allocated expenses (£)	143,220	125,180	213,700
Budgeted service department apportionment (£)	39,780 (i)	26,520 (ii)	66,300
Normal machine capacity (hours)	15,000	18,500 (iii)	20,000 (v)
Predetermined absorption rate (£ per machine hour)	12.20 (vi)	8.20	14.00 (iv)
Actual machine utilisation (hours)	14,700 (vii)	19,050	19,520
Over/(under) absorption of overhead (£)	(3,660)	4,510 (viii)	(6,720)

Solution Notes

(i)   Service department apportionment ratio = 3:2:5

$$\text{Dept A apportionment} = \frac{£66,300}{5} \times 3 = £39,780$$

(ii)
$$\text{Dept B apportionment} = \frac{£66,300}{5} \times 2 = £26,520$$

(iii) Dept B total costs = £125,180 + £26,520 = £151,700

$$\text{OAR} = \frac{Total\ costs}{Machine\ hrs}$$

$$£8.20 = \frac{£151,700}{Machine\ hrs}$$

$$\therefore \text{Machine hrs} = \frac{£151,700}{£8.20} = 18,500$$

£

(iv) Dept C total costs = £213,700 + £66,300 =   280,000

Under absorption of overheads   (6,720)

∴ Overheads absorbed   273,280

Machine hrs utilised x OAR = Overheads absorbed

19,520 x OAR = £273,280

$$OAR = \frac{£273,280}{19,520} = £14.00 \text{ per machine hr.}$$

(v) $$OAR = \frac{Total\ costs}{Normal\ machine\ capacity}$$

$$£14.00 = \frac{£280,000}{Normal\ machine\ capacity}$$

$$Normal\ machine\ capacity = \frac{£280,000}{£14.00} = 20,000 \text{ hrs.}$$

(vi) $$OAR = \frac{Total\ costs}{Normal\ machine\ capacity}$$

$$= \frac{£143,220 + £39,780}{15,000 hrs} = £12.20 \text{ per machine hr.}$$

(vii) Overheads absorbed   = Machine utilisation x OAR

(£143,220 + £39,780) − £3,660 = Machine utilisation x £12.20

Machine utilisation $$= \frac{£179,340}{£12.20} = £14,700 \text{ hrs.}$$

(viii) Over/underabsorptionofoverheads

= overheadsabsorbed − actualoverheads

= (19,050 hrs x £8.20) − (£125,180 + £26,520)

= £156,210 − £151,700

= £4,510 over absorbed

(b)   At the end of the period over/under absorbed overheads are reported
      in the profit and loss account. In this case the total under absorption
      of £5,870 means products have been undercosted and to compensate
      this figure should be reported as a cost in the profit and loss account.

11.1

(a) Descriptions of each type of cost and graphs can be found in the text.

(b) Business: Mail order book club.

Stepped	–	Rental of premises
Curvilinear	–	Books purchased with quantity discounts.
Variable	–	Packaging.
Fixed	–	Salary of finance manager.
Semi-variable	–	Postage.

11.2

(a) (i) The type of cost can be determined by looking at the relationship between the costs recorded for the two months. Those which increased directly in proportion with output (i.e. by 50%) are variable costs, those which remained constant are fixed costs and those which did neither are likely to be semi-variable costs (or perhaps, it could be argued, curvilinear variable costs).

(ii) The fixed and variable elements for the semi-variable costs can be separated using the range method.

(iii) The total cost for any item can be estimated as follows:

Total Cost = Fixed Cost Per Month + (Variable Cost Per TV x No. Of TV's Sold)

	(i)	(ii)	(iii)	(iii)
	Type of Cost	Fixed Cost Per Month £'s	Var. Cost Per TV £'s	Cost @ 1,050 TV's £'s
Delivery costs	Variable			5,250
Postage	Semi-Var	150	1.00	1,200
Admin.salaries	Fixed			1,900
Insurance	Semi-Var	3,000	6.00	9,300
Cost of TV's	Variable			325,500
Telephones	Semi-Var	1,200	4.50	5,925

(b)   Having ascertained the way in which costs are likely to behave, costs (and profits) can be estimated at any activity level. It is also possible to use marginal costing techniques to assist in decision making (e.g. dropping products, special order pricing etc.)

11.3

(a)   Catering   Semi-variable
Maintenance   Fixed
Management   Semi-variable
Staff   Stepped
Laundry   Variable (curvilinear)

(b)

	(i)	(ii)
	£	£
Catering	1,950	2,750
Maintenance	150	150
Management	500	600
Staff	1,200	1,600
Laundry	275	425

12.1

Setting selling prices above marginal cost ensures that contribution is earned. However in the long term income must be sufficient to cover *all* costs in order to generate profits. Thus selling prices must be set at a level which ensures that total contribution is sufficient to at least cover fixed costs. Having achieved this, for any additional output, selling prices set at any level above marginal cost will increase profits.

12.2

(a)   (i)

	Spanish £000's	Greek £000's	Total £000's
Sales Income	77	180	257
Less variable Costs	(63)	(91)	(154)
Contribution	14	89	103
Less Fixed Costs			(66)
Profit			37

As they generate contribution of £14,000 Spanish cruises are worth retaining.

    (ii)   Other Factors

- Would fixed costs change if Spanish cruises were discontinued?

- Would another cruise generate higher contribution than the £14,000 from the Spanish Islands?

(b)   (i)

	£
Sales income per cruise	700
Less variable cost per cruise*	455
Contribution per cruise	245

Accept as sales income exceeds variable costs. Profit will increase by £9,800 (40 cruises x £245).

Variable cost per Greek cruise

$$= \frac{Variable\ costs\ last\ month}{No.\ cruises\ sold} = \frac{£130,000 \times 70\%}{£180,000 \div £900} = \frac{£91,000}{200\ cruises}$$

(ii) - Reaction of existing customers paying £900 per cruise.

    - Reaction of competitors.

    - The possibility that the cruises could be sold for more than £700.

12.3

(a) Contribution per Constructor Hour

	Country Manor	De-Luxe	Continental
Contribution per unit (SP – Mats–Labour)	£494	£513	£224
Hours per unit (Labour costs ÷ £8.40per unit)	13	19	8
Contribution per hour	£38	£27	£28
RANK	1	3	2

Product Mix

	Units	Hrs. per Unit	Hrs. Required	Contribution per Unit (£)	Total Contribution (£)
Country Manor	750	13	9,750	494	370,500
Continental	800	8	6,400	224	179,200
De-Luxe	110	19	2,090	513	56,430
			18,240		606,130
Less fixed costs					(400,000)
Profit					206,130

(b) (i) In each case contribution per constructor hr. would reduce by £2.

Revised Profit Statement

	Prodn.	Const. Hrs.	Contb'n Per Hr. (£)	Total Contribution (£)
Country Manor	750	9,750	36	351,000
De-luxe	350	6,650	25	166,250
Continental	800	6,400	26	166,400
				683,650
Less Fixed Costs				400,000
Profit				283,650

i.e. rise in profit of (£283,650 – £206,130)   =   £77,520

(ii)   Consider:

Will increase in production affect other costs e.g.:

(a)   Materials (are there enough supplies at current price/will discounts reduce the price).

(b)   Labour (would installers also demand a rise).

(c)   Machinery (could existing machinery cope/would maintenance costs rise).

(d)   Efficiency (how quickly would new workers learn/will material wastage increase in learning period).

(e)   Fixed costs (are they stepped).

12.4

(a)   Sunk costs are those which have already been incurred and which will therefore be unaffected by future decisions. They are irrelevant for the purpose of decision making.

An opportunity cost is the benefit sacrificed by pursuing an alternative course of action. As they represent benefits foregone, such costs should be included when assessing the financial consequences of decisions.

(b)   Depreciation costs are the consequence of past decisions to acquire fixed assets. They are therefore irrelevant when considering the effect of future decisions.

(c)   Treating fixed costs as irrelevant assumes that they will remain unchanged as a result of a decision. As by definition they tend not to change with changes in activity, marginal costing ignores fixed costs and considers only those which are variable. However in certain circumstances fixed costs may change with a variation in activity and will therefore be relevant. Examples include (a) situations where certain fixed costs are specific to a product line and could therefore be avoided if the product was discontinued (b) stepped costs changing when certain activity levels are reached.

Note also that not all decisions affect activity levels (e.g. acquiring new premises) and in these cases fixed costs may well change.

12.5

(a)

HGC Limited

		£
Estimating Costs		
Materials – Timber 30m x £7.50	225	
– Other mats. £11,600 –(30m @ £8)	11,360	11,585
Labour		
– Craftsmen (4 x 15 x £75)	4,500	
– Labourers (1 x 15 x £45)	675	5,175
Supervision		
Overheads 6 x 15 x (£55 x 20%)		990
		17,750
Income		20,000
Net benefit		2,250

The above figures suggest that as the contract is expected to produce a net benefit, HGC should proceed. However as this benefit is relatively small, it may be worth reviewing the figures as an error in estimation could result in the project being unacceptable.

(b)   Sunk costs result from previous decisions and are unavoidable and therefore irrelevant for decision making. Estimating costs and the £8 paid for timber are examples in this case.

Incremental costs are additional costs incurred as a result of taking a particular decision and are therefore relevant. All those itemised in the answer above are examples of such costs.

An opportunity cost is the value of a benefit sacrificed as a result of pursing a particular course of action. An example in this case is the £45 per day which would be received from the small building business for the use of one of the labourers.

12.6

(a) Cost of one-off job:

Raw materials:	£
Material X: 960 kgs at £3.10/kg	2,976
Material Y: 570 kgs at £2.30/kg	1,311
Other materials	3,360
	7,647
Direct labour:	
2,000 hours at £4.00/hr	8,000
200 hours at £5.20/hr	1,040
	16,687
Variable overhead:	
2,200 hours at £2.40/hr	5,280
	21,967
Plus: overtime premium saving forgone by not bringing forward production of future order 2,000 hours at £1.20/hr	2,400
	24,367

Thus, the minimum quote in order to increase Company A profits is £24,368

Note: Material X valuation is based on replacement cost as this is the cost that would be incurred if existing stock is used and thus require replacement.

Material Y valuation is based on disposal value as the material would not be re-placed and disposal is the only foreseeable use of the material (other than using it in the one-off job).

(b) (i) Sunk costs are costs which have already been incurred. As such they are always irrelevant in decision-making as they have already taken place and thus cannot be changed. The cost incurred for raw materials in stock is an illustration of a sunk cost, for example the average cost of £3.02 per kg for the purchase of Material X.

(ii) Opportunity costs are benefits foregone by not accepting another opportunity. They are relevant in decision making as it is essential to ensure that the benefits of taking a course of action are greater than the opportunity cost (benefit foregone) by not accepting another alternative. Ultimately, the opportunity cost is the benefit that would have been derived from the next best alternative. If the one-off quote (in excess of £24,367) is accepted, the saving of overtime premiums, that could have been made by bringing forward production of another order, is the opportunity cost.

(iii)   Incremental costs are costs that are incurred as a result of taking a course of action. They are relevant in decision making as they are avoidable costs i.e. costs incurred as a result of taking action that would not be incurred if it was not taken. Purchasing replacement Material X if existing material is used in the one-off job is an example of an incremental cost.

(ACCA)

13.1

(a)   Break even point $= \dfrac{Fixed\ Costs}{Contribution\ per\ telephone}$

$$= \dfrac{£240,000}{£15} \qquad = 16,000\ \text{telephones}$$

Margin of safety = Expected activity – Break even activity

$$= 24,000 - 16,000$$

$$= 8,000\ \text{telephones}$$

As a % $= \dfrac{8,000}{24,000} \quad \text{x} \quad 100 = 33.3\%$

(b)

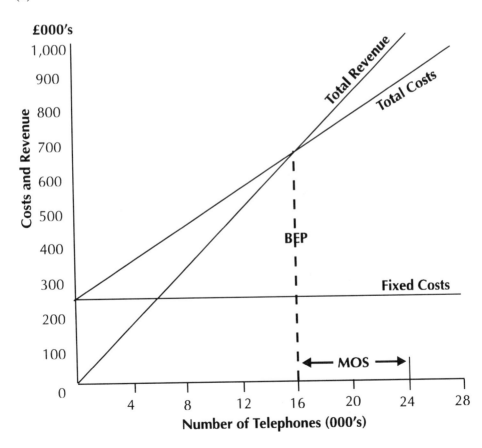

(c)
$$\text{No. of telephones} = \frac{\pounds240,000 + \pounds30,000}{\pounds15}$$

$$= 18,000 \text{ telephones}$$

(d)   Advantages

- Can give quick indication of financial consequences of short term plans.

- Can easily re-calculate results with different assumptions on selling price, variable costs etc.

- Graphs give clear indication of results at different activity levels and can be easily amended to show the effect of changes in figures.

Limitations

- Can only be used for a single product or a constant product mix.

- Depends on accurate estimation of fixed and variable elements of cost.

- Assumes output is the only factor influencing costs and revenues.

- Assumes linearity in respect of costs and revenues

13.2

(a)   (i)

Fixed Costs	£
Tents (120 x £300 x 20 wks.)	720,000
Representatives (2 x £250 x 20 wks.)	10,000
Coach Hire (£2,400 x 20 wks.)	48,000
Office Admin. (£12,000 x 20 wks.)	240,000
	1,018,000

Variable Cost per Person	£
Flights	75
Welcome Pack	5
Refreshments	10
	90

$$\text{Break even point} = \frac{\pounds1,018,000}{\pounds200-\pounds90} = 9,255 \text{ customers}$$

(ii)   Expected activity level
  =   120 tents x 80% x 8 people x 20 wks.
  =   15,360 persons

Margin of safety   =   15,360 – 9,255
  =   6,105 persons

As a % $= \dfrac{6,105}{15,360} \times 100 = 40\%$

(b)   (i)   **Family Tours Limited Break Even Chart**

£000's

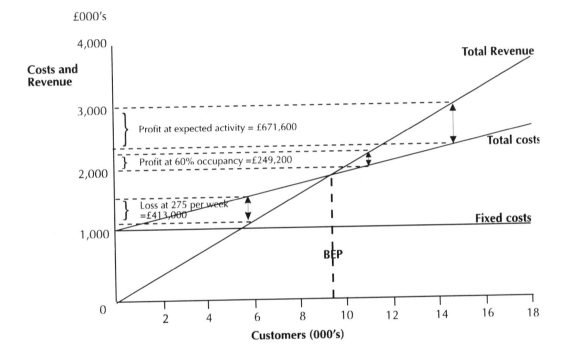

(ii) Expected activity level (15,360 persons) = £671,600 profit
      275 customers per wk.   (5,500 persons) = £413,000 loss
      60% of available tents (11,520 persons) = £249,200 profit

13.3

(a) **Armoury Limited Contribution Break Even Chart**

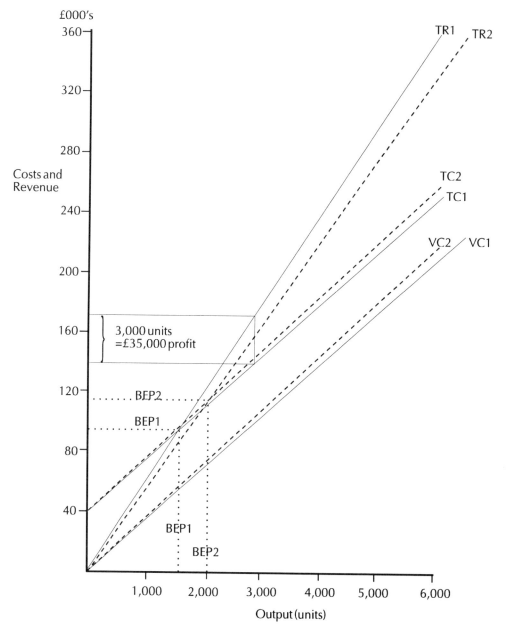

(i) BEP = 1,600 units (£96,000)

(ii) Profit at 3,000 units = £35,000

(b) (i) See Chart

(ii) Revised BEP = 2,000 units (£114,000)

(c) Existing Profit

= total contribution – fixed costs
= (4,000 units x (£60–£35) – (4,000 units x £10)
= £100,000 – £40,000
= £60,000

Units Required to Maintain Profit

$$= \frac{Fixed\ costs + Target\ profit}{Contribution\ per\ unit}$$

$$= \frac{£40,000 + £60,000}{£57 - (£22 + £8 + £7)}$$

= 5,000 units

i.e. an additional 1,000 units.

14.1

(a) **Project A**

$$\text{ARR} \quad = \quad \frac{£100,000 \div 4 \text{ yrs.}}{£200,000} \quad \text{x} \quad 100 \quad = \quad 12.5\%$$

$$\text{Payback period} \quad = \quad 2 + \frac{£20,000}{£60,000} \quad = \quad 2 \text{ years 4 months}$$

NPV

Year	Net Cash Flow	10% D.F.	NPV(£)
0	(200,000)	1.000	(200,000)
1	100,000	0.909	90,900
2	80,000	0.826	66,080
3	60,000	0.751	45,060
4	60,000	0.683	40,980
			43,020

Project B

$$\text{ARR} \quad = \quad \frac{£100,0000 \div 4 \text{ yrs}}{£200,000} \quad \text{x} \quad 100 \quad = \quad 12.5\%$$

$$\text{Payback period} \quad = \quad 3 + \frac{£40,000}{£120,000} \quad = \quad 3 \text{ years 4 months}$$

NPV

Year	Net Cash Flow	10% D.F.	NPV(£)
0	(200,000)	1.000	(200,000)
1	30,000	0.909	27,270
2	50,000	0.826	41,300
3	80,000	0.751	60,080
4	140,000	0.683	95,620
			24,270

(b) Choose Project A with a quicker payback and higher NPV.

14.2

(a)   (i)   Net Cash Flows (£000's)

Note	Year	1	2	3	4	5
1	Contribution	320	360	440	280	280
	Sale of equipment					100
	Promotion	(108)				
2	Other costs	(208)	(208)	(208)	(208)	(208)
		4	152	232	72	172

Workings

1.   Demand   x   (£20–£12)

2.
$$\text{Annual depreciation} \quad = \quad \frac{£460,000-£100,000}{5 \text{ years}}$$

$$= \quad £72,000 \text{ p.a.}$$

Incremental other costs $= \quad £280,000 - £72,000$

$$= \quad £208,000 \text{ p.a.}$$

NPV

Year	Net Cash Flow	12% D.F.	NPV(£)
0	(460,000)	1.000	(460,000)
1	4,000	0.893	3,572
2	152,000	0.797	121,144
3	232,000	0.712	165,184
4	72,000	0.636	45,792
5	172,000	0.567	97,524
			(26,784)

(ii)   Payback period   =   4 years

(b)   The project with its negative NPV, should be rejected on the basis of the estimates provided unless there are sound non-financial reasons for proceeding.

14.3

(a)   NPV

Year	Net Cash Flow	12% D.F.	NPV(£)
0	(14,000)	1.000	(14,000)
1	4,000	0.893	3,572
2	4,000	0.797	3,188
3	4,000	0.712	2,848
4	10,000	0.636	6,360
			1,968

Payback Period

$$= \ 3 + \frac{£2,000}{£4,000} \ = \ 3.5 \ \text{years}$$

Internal Rate of Return

NPV @ 20% D.F.:

Year	Net Cash Flow	20% D.F.	NPV(£)
0	(14,000)	1.000	(14,000)
1	4,000	0.833	3,332
2	4,000	0.694	2,776
3	4,000	0.579	2,316
4	10,000	0.482	4,820
			(756)

$$\text{IRR} \quad = \ 12 + \left\{ \frac{1,968}{1,968 + 756} \right\} \times (20 - 12)$$

$$= \quad 17.8\%$$

(b) Payback Period

Compare with pre-determined target.

NPV

A positive figure (as in this case) indicates that the investment is financially worthwhile as discounted cash inflows exceed outflows.

IRR

A rate of return which exceeds the cost of capital indicates a financially accept-able investment. This suggests that the vending machine is worth obtaining.

14.4

(a) Option 1

Year	Net Cash Flow*	15% D.F.	NPV(£)
0	(8,000)	1.000	(8,000)
1	5,000	0.870	4,350
2	10,000	0.756	7,560
3	3,000	0.658	1,974
4	4,000	0.572	2,288
			8,172

Net cash flows
$$Yrs\ 1\text{–}3 \ = \ Contribution\ from\ sales - running\ costs$$
$$= \ (Sales\ x\ 25\%) \qquad - (£3,000 + £12,000)$$
$$NB\ 33.33\%\ of\ cost \ = \ 25\%\ of\ sales$$

$$Yr\ 4 \quad = \ as\ above\ plus\ selling\ price\ of\ van$$

$$\text{Payback Period} \ = \ 1 + \frac{£3,000}{£10,000} \ = \ 1.3\ \text{years}$$

Option 2

Year	Net Cash Flow*	15% D.F.	NPV(£)
0	(5,000)	1.000	(5,000)
1	7,500	0.870	6,525
2	5,500	0.756	4,158
3	5,500	0.658	3,619
4	1,500	0.572	858
			10,160

Net cash flows
Yrs 1–4 = *(Sales x 33.33%) – (£2,500 + £10,000)*
NB 50% of cost = *33.33% of sales*

$$\text{Payback Period} = \frac{£5,000}{£7,500} = 2/3 \text{ of a year (i.e. 8 months)}$$

(b)   Option 2 with a shorter payback period and higher NPV should be chosen.

15.1

Budgets can be used for a whole variety of purposes in a small business. Most particularly they could be of benefit in the following areas.

(i) Use of resources: small businesses are often short of resources, particularly finance and cash. Budgets would identify what and when additional resources might be required. They might also identify some periods when excess resources were available e.g. a slack production period, which could then be filled with extra orders. Although budgets need quantitative information this does not imply they are absolutely accurate. In fact budgets help reduce risk because the times when problems might arise can be identified in advance, in time to find some way around them.

(ii) Budgets provide a basis for a comparison with actual out-turns. This might then enable the business to measure its progress economically as its moves towards a target, for example a particular amount of profit. As this process of comparison saves time on a 'management by exception' basis, scarce management time can be devoted to creating new business.

(iii) The use of a micro-computer could be of substantial benefit in various areas; specifically it could assist in the following areas:

preparation of a budget: there is normally substantial numerical work in budget preparation which could be conveniently handled by a computer;

review of budget: budget preparation is often an iterative process with need to examine alternative combinations of plans. Computers can assist in handling 'what if' type questions;

reporting: the comparison of actual out-turn against budget is of vital importance; a computerised accounting system should accommodate some budget comparison facility;

statistical data: a data-base of statistical information on costs and sales can be of value in budgeting to ensure that data are reliable; it can also provide another source of comparison for actual out-turn.

(ACCA)

15.2

(a) A limiting factor restricts a business's activity level in the short term. Examples include space, finance and availability of skilled staff but sales demands tends to be the most common limiting factor.

(b) Budgetary Control

- Monitor activities

- Compare with plan
- Analyse variances
- Take action.

(c) Benefits of Budgeting

- Planning
- Communication
- Co-ordination
- Control
- Management by exception
- Motivation
- Performance appraisal.

15.3

(a)

Summer Camping Budget – July

No. of tents utilised *(120 x 4wks) x 80%*	384
No. of guests *(384 tents x8)*	3,072

Income	£	£
Bookings *(3,072 x £200)*	614,400	
Excursions *(3,072 x 25%) x £20*	15,360	629,760

Costs		
Tent Hire *(120 x 4 wks x£300)*	144,000	
Flights *(3,500 x £75)*	262,500	
Welcome Pack *(3,072 x £5)*	15,360	
Resort Reps.*(4 reps. x £220 x 4 wks.)*	3,520	
Excursions – Coaches *(4 Coaches* x £120 x 4 wks.)*	1,920	
– Refreshments *(3,072 x 25%) x £6*	4,608	
Admin. *(£32,000 x 4wks)*	128,000	559,908
Profit		69,852

(b)

Summer Camping Budget – July

No. of tents utilised *(120 x 4wks) x 95%*	456
No. of guests *(456 tents x 8)*	3,648

	£	£
Income		
Bookings *(3,648 x £200)*	729,600	
Excursions *(3,648 x 25%) x £20*	18,240	747,840
Costs		
Tent Hire *(120 x 4 wks x£300)*	144,000	
Flights *(3,648 x £75)*	273,600	
Welcome Pack *(3,648 x £5)*	18,240	
Resort Reps. *(6 reps. x £220 x 4 wks.)*	5,280	
Excursions – Coaches *(4 Coaches* x £120 x 4 wks.)*	1,920	
– Refreshments*(3,648 x 25%) x £6*	5,472	
Admin. *(£32,000 x 4wks)*	128,000	
Advertising	90,000	666,512
Profit		81,328

* Excursion Coaches Required per Week

	(a)		(b)	
Excursion guests per wk.	$\dfrac{3,072 \times 25\%}{4 \text{ wks}}$	= 192	$\dfrac{3,648 \times 25\%}{4 \text{ wks}}$	=228
Coaches required	$192 \div 60 = 3.2 = 4$ coaches		$228 \div 60 = 3.8 = 4$ coaches	

The higher profit with the advertising campaign suggests that it may be worth considering. However, there is no guarantee that the average occupancy will rise to the extent predicted and it would be worth reviewing this estimate before committing the company to the advertising.

15.4

Working

Unit Production Costs and Selling Prices

	Aye £		Bee £	
Direct materials				
X	48		60	
Y	50		40	
Z	30	128	60	160
Direct wages				
Unskilled	30		15	
Skilled	30	60	25	40
Production overheads*				
16 hrs @ £12		192		
10 hrs @ £12				120
		——		——
Production cost		380		320
Other overheads (20% of production cost)		76		64
Total cost		456		384
Mark up (20/80 x total cost)		114		96
Selling price		570		480

$$\text{*Overhead absorption rate} = \frac{£900{,}000}{75{,}000 \, labour \, hours} = £12 \text{ per labour hour}$$

(a) Production Budget

		Aye (Units)		Bee (Units)
Sales	(£1,368,000 ÷ £570)	2,400	(£1,536,000 ÷ £480)	3,200
Add closing stock	(£190,000 ÷ £380)	500	(£352,000 ÷ £320)	1,100
		2,900		4,300
Less opening stock	(£152,000 ÷ £380)	(400)	(£256,000 ÷ £320)	(800)
Production		2,500		3,500

(b) Purchases Budget

	Material X Kg	Material Y Kg	Material Z Kg
Production requirement			
Aye (2,500 units)	60,000	25,000	12,500
Bee (3,500 units)	105,000	28,000	35,000
	165,000	53,000	47,500
Add closing stock*	35,000	27,000	12,500
	200,000	80,000	60,000
Less opening stock*	(30,000)	(25,000)	(12,000)
	170,000	55,000	48,000
Cost per Kg.	£2	£5	£6
Cost of purchases	£340,000	£275,000	£288,000

*Value ÷ standard cost per kg.

(c)   Production Cost Budget

	Aye	Bee	Total
Units	2,500	3,500	
Cost per unit	£380	£320	
Production cost	£950,000	£1,120,000	£2,070,000

15.5

(a)

Cash Budget (£'s)

	Jan	Feb	Mar
Opening balance	30,000	25,500	-3,500
Receipts from sales	81,000	75,000	78,000
Insurance claim			30,000
Cash available	111,000	100,500	104,500
Payments			
Purchases	55,500	46,000	54,000
Wages	15,000	15,000	15,000
Overheads	15,000	15,000	15,000
Taxation		28,000	
Total payments	85,500	104,000	84,000
Closing balance	25,500	-3,500	20,500

(b)   The business needs to address the anticipated deficit at the end of February. The following measures should be considered:

- Negotiating earlier settlement of insurance claim.

- Asking credit customers to pay earlier (an inducement such as a discount may help).

- Requesting credit from more suppliers (most are currently paid cash).

- Negotiating later payment of tax.

- Obtaining a temporary overdraft.

15.6

(a) - Cash budgets are an essential part of the planning process.

- Many organisations (even profitable ones) go out of business due to cash shortages.

- Projected cash shortages are highlighted – management can investigate steps to remedy this (policies to improve cash flow/obtain additional funds).

- Projected cash surpluses are highlighted – management can consider possible future investments.

- Once in place, cash budget can be used as a basis for control (like any other budget).

- Providers of finance are likely to ask about projected cash flows.

(b)

Cash Budget (£000's)

	May	June	July
Opening Balance	−2.0	1.4	−23.6
Receipts			
Cash sales	2.0	0.5	3.0
Debtors	18.9	18.0	18.0
Available	18.9	19.9	−2.6
Payments			
Purchases	15.5	37.5	4.0
Wages	2.0	1.0	2.0
Rent	0.0	0.0	6.0
Tax	0.0	5.0	0.0
Total Payments	17.5	43.5	12.0
Closing Balance	1.4	−23.6	−14.6

(c) - Even without purchase of new equipment a cash shortage is anticipated (overdraft limit will be exceeded).

- Main problem is high level of purchases for stock planned for June (is this necessary – any discounts obtained may not be worth taking given cash problem it creates).

- A large proportion of purchases are on cash terms. Can credit be obtained? It is worth investigating (although any lost discount would have to be considered).

- It may be worth encouraging more customers to buy on cash terms rather than credit. It may be necessary to offer discounts to induce immediate payment, otherwise sales may be lost. Again the cost to the business would have to be compared with the benefit of improved cash flow.

- If the above measures fail to satisfactorily resolve the projected cash shortage it will be necessary to obtain further finance.

15.7

(a) The statement is unsuitable for control and performance appraisal in its current format as the budget does not reflect the actual activity level. Variable costs will change with activity and as room occupancy is higher than anticipated, additional costs for catering, staffing and laundry should be expected. Also the depreciation costs appear to be outside the control of the manager who has no authority to purchase equipment. When appraising the manager's performance a distinction should be made between controllable and uncontrollable costs.

(b)

Revised Budget Statement - May

	FLEXED Budget	Actual	Variance
Rooms Occupied	800	800	
Costs	£	£	£
Catering	10,000	10,400	(400)
Staffing	12,000	11,700	300
Premises	5,000	4,300	700
Laundry	2,400	2,300	100
Controllable Costs	29,400	28,700	700
Depreciation	4,000	4,800	(800)
Total	33,400	33,500	(100)

(Adverse variances are shown in brackets)

15.8

(a) Issues for discussion

- Ensure communication of objectives.
- Seek participation of those involved.
- Ensure targets are demanding but attainable.
- Aim for goal congruence (attempt to match business and individual objectives).

- Adopt a flexible approach. Use budgets as a positive aid to achieve objectives.

(b) Decentralisation

Benefits

- Better decisions from individuals closer to activity.

- Development of junior managers.

- Increased motivation.

Drawbacks

- Cost of information system.

- Possibility of individuals not acting in best interests of business.

16.1

(a)

	Original Budget	Flexed Budget	Actual Costs	Total Variance
Units	20,000	18,500	18,500	
	£'s	£'s	£'s	£'s
Direct materials	480,000	444,000	442,650	1,350
Direct labour	140,000	129,500	129,940	(440)
Variable overhead	60,000	55,500	58,800	(3,300)
Fixed overhead	100,000	100,000	104,000	(4,000)
	780,000	729,000	735,390	(6,390)

(Adverse variances are shown in brackets)

(b) **Direct Materials**

	£
Price Variance	
= (113,500 kg x £4) -- £442,650 =	11,350 Fav.
Usage Variance	
= (18,500 units x 6 kg) – 113,500 kg x £4 =	(10,000) Adv.
Total Variance	1,350 Fav.

Direct Labour

	£
Rate Variance	
= (17,800 hrs x £7) – £129,940 =	(5,340) Adv.
Efficiency Variance	
= (18,500 units x 1 hr) – 17,800 hrs x £7 =	4,900 Fav.
Total Variance	(440) Adv.

16.2

Direct Materials

Price variance	$= 22{,}000m^2 \times (£3 - £3.50)$
	$= £11{,}000$ Adverse
Usage variance	$= (1{,}400 \text{ cabinets} \times 15m^2) - 22{,}000m^2 \times £3 \text{ per } m^2$
	$= £3{,}000$ Adverse

Direct Labour

Rate variance	$= 6{,}800 \text{ hrs.} \times (£4-£5)$
	$= £6{,}800$ Adverse
Efficiency variance	$= (1{,}400 \text{ cabinets} \times 5 \text{ hrs}) - 6{,}800 \text{ hrs} \times £4 \text{ per hr}$
	$= £800$ Favourable

Planned v's Actual Costs

			£
Planned Costs			91,000
Variances	**Favourable**	**Adverse**	
Direct Materials			
Price		11,000	
Usage		3,000	
Direct Labour			
Rate		6,800	
Efficiency	800		
Total variance	800	20,800	20,000
Actual Costs			111,000

Workings

Planned Costs	£
Direct Materials (1,400 cabinets @ £45)	63,000
Direct Labour (1,400 cabinets @ £20)	28,000
	91,000

Actual Costs	£
Direct Materials (22,000 sq. m. @ £3.50)	77,000
Direct Labour (6,800 hrs. @ £5)	34,000
	111,000

16.3

Workings

Standard Cost Per Unit

		£
Materials	(20 kg @ £0.80)	16
Labour	(4 hrs. @ £8)	32
Variable Overheads	(4 hrs. @ £1*)	4
Fixed Overheads	(4 hrs. @ £6*)	24
		76

Overhead Absorption Rates

$$Planned\ hours\ =\ 10\ workers\ x\ 40\ hrs.\ x\ 48\ weeks$$
$$=\ 19,200\ hours$$

$$Variable\ OAR\ =\ \frac{£19,200}{19,200\ hrs}\ =\ £1\ per\ hr.$$

$$Fixed\ OAR\ =\ \frac{£115,200}{19,200\ hrs.}\ =\ £6\ per\ hr.$$

(a)

Direct Materials

Total Variance
= Standard material cost for actual production – Actual material cost
= (20 kg. x 110 units x £0.80)   – (2,100 kg. x £0.90)
= £1,760   – £1,890
= £130 Adverse

Price Variance
= Actual quantity used x (Standard price – Actual price)
= 2,100 kg.   x (£0.80 – £0.90)
= £210 Adverse

Usage variance	=	(Standard quantity for actual production – Actual quantity) x Standard price		
	=	(20 kg. x 110 units	– 2,100 Kg.)	x £0.80
	=	(2,200 kg.	– 2,100 kg.)	x £0.80
	=	£80 Favourable		

Direct Labour

Total Variance	=	Standard labour cost for actual production – Actual labour cost	
	=	(4 hrs x 110 units x £8)	– (420 hrs. x £8.10)
	=	£3,520	– £3,402
	=	£118 Favourable	

Rate Variance	=	No. hours paid for x (Standard rate – Actual rate)	
	=	420 hrs. x (£8.00 – £8.10)	
	=	£42 Adverse	
Efficiency variance	=	(Standard hours for actual production – Actual hrs. worked) x Standard rate	
	=	(4 hrs x 110 units	– 420 hrs.) x £8.00
	=	£160 Favourable	

Variable Overheads

Total Variance	=	Variable overhead absorbed – Actual variable overheads	
	=	(110 units x £4)	– £410
	=	£30 Favourable	

Expenditure Variance	=	Standard variable overheads for hrs. worked – Actual variable overheads	
	=	(420 hrs. x £1 per hr.)	– £410
	=	£10 Favourable	

Efficiency Variance	=	(SHP – Actual hrs. worked) x V.O.A.R.	
	=	(440 hrs. – 420 hrs.)	x £1
	=	£20 Favourable	

Fixed Overheads

Total variance	=	Fixed overhead absorbed – Actual fixed overheads	
	=	(110 units x £24)	– £2,750
	=	£110 Adverse	

Expenditure Variance = Budgeted fixed overheads – Actual fixed overheads

   = (100 units x £24)   – £2,750

   = £350 Adverse

Volume Variance = Fixed overhead absorbed – Budgeted fixed overheads

   = (110 units x £24)   – (100 units x £24)

   = £240 Favourable

(b)

Reconciliation
Planned v's Actual Costs

			£'s
Planned Costs (110 units @ £76)			8,360

Variances		Fav.	Adverse
Materials	– Price		210
	– Usage	80	
Labour	– Rate		42
	– Efficiency	160	
Var O/h's	– Expenditure	10	
	– Efficiency	20	
Fixed O/h's	– Expenditure		350
	– Volume	240	
		510	602

			92
Actual Costs			*8,452

*Actual Costs	£
Direct materials (2,100 kg. x £0.90)	1,890
Direct labour (420 hrs. x £8.10)	3,402
Production overheads	3,160
	8,452

Index

A

Account
  manufacturing 142, 143
  trading 144
Accountancy profession 17
  examinations 11
  membership of 11
  practical experience 11
  professional accounting firms 11
Accounting 44
  date 66
  equation 31, 42, 50
  for income and expenditure 42
  management 277
  nature and purpose of 4
  period 66, 73, 75, 88
  policies 176,181
Accounting information
  Aim 10
  external users 5
  level of detail 10
  limitations of 10
  regulations 10
  time focus 10
  users 10
Accounting principles 17
  consistency 21
  disclosure 21
  going concern 19
  historical cost 18, 70
  matching 21, 22, 75, 110, 113
  materiality 21
  money measurement 18, 73
  objectivity 22
  prudence 22
  prudency 113
  realisation 19, 112
  separate entity 19, 32
Accounting Rate of Return (ARR) 404

Accounting statements 56
  comparison of 21
  interpretation of 32, 48
  interpretation of 201-229, 231
  published 284
  users of 22
Accruals 109, 110, 119, 125
Activity Based Costing (ABC) 308
Analysis
  horizontal 234
  of trends 235
  ratio 207-227, 237
  vertical 205-206, 235
Assets
  current 70, 71, 143, 250
  definition of 32
  fixed 70, 71, 77, 87, 205
  liquid 68
  long term 18
  residual value 205
  revaluation 70, 180
  sale of 215
  turnover ratio 243
  valuation of 18, 19
Audit
  exemptions 182
  external 428
  internal 428
Auditing 11
Auditor's
  report 176, 181
Average cost (AVCO) 149, 150, 284

B

Bad debts 20
Balance sheet 66, 67, 68, 69, 70, 72,
  74, 76, 77
  consolidated 183
  forecast 437